The Law of Regulated Gambling

A Practical Guide for Business Lawyers

Keith Miller
Editor

Cover design by Catherine Zaccarine.

The materials contained herein represent the opinions of the authors and/or the editors, and should not be construed to be the views or opinions of the law firms or companies with whom such persons are in partnership with, associated with, or employed by, nor of the American Bar Association or the Business Law Section unless adopted pursuant to the bylaws of the Association.

Nothing contained in this book is to be considered as the rendering of legal advice for specific cases, and readers are responsible for obtaining such advice from their own legal counsel. This book is intended for educational and informational purposes only.

© 2020 American Bar Association. All rights reserved.

No part of this publication may be reproduced, stored in a retrieval system, or transmitted in any form or by any means, electronic, mechanical, photocopying, recording, or otherwise, without the prior written permission of the publisher. For permission contact the ABA Copyrights & Contracts Department, copyright@americanbar.org, or complete the online form at http://www.americanbar.org/utility/reprint.html.

Printed in the United States of America.

23 22 21 20 19   5 4 3 2 1

ISBN: 978-1-64105-589–5 (Paperback)

Library of Congress Control Number: 2019917919

Discounts are available for books ordered in bulk. Special consideration is given to state bars, CLE programs, and other bar-related organizations. Inquire at Book Publishing, ABA Publishing, American Bar Association, 321 N. Clark Street, Chicago, Illinois 60654-7598.

www.shopABA.org

Table of Contents

Acknowledgments v

Preface vii

PART 1: AN INTRODUCTION TO GAMBLING IN THE UNITED STATES

Chapter 1: Regulated Gambling in the United States   3
Kate Lowenhar-Fisher, Greg Gemignani, Jennifer Gaynor, and Jeff Silver

Chapter 2: What Is Gambling?   23
Karl Rutledge and Glenn Light

PART 2: COMMERCIAL GAMBLING IN THE UNITED STATES

Chapter 3: The Basics of Gaming Regulation   47
Anthony Cabot

Chapter 4: Currency Reporting and Anti–Money Laundering Requirements for Gaming Properties   81
Peter J. Kulick

Chapter 5: Corporate Reorganizations, Bankruptcy, and Restructuring   99
Sean McGuinness and Adam M. Langley

Chapter 6: Gaming Contracts   111
Keith C. Miller

Chapter 7: Problem Gambling and the Business Lawyer   137
Stacey A. Tovino

PART 3: OTHER FORMS OF GAMBLING

Chapter 8: Tribal Gaming 167
Kathryn R. L. Rand and Steven Andrew Light

Chapter 9: Internet Gambling 193
Karl Rutledge, Glenn Light, Mary Tran, and Jason Bacigalupi

Chapter 10: State Lotteries 215
David M. Ranscht

Chapter 11: Sports Betting in the United States 243
Tamara S. Malvin

Chapter 12: Data Privacy Issues and GDPR 265
Sean McGuinness and Katie Fillmore

About the Authors 275

About the Editor 279

Index 281

Acknowledgments

Many people contributed to this project of the Gaming Law Committee. The authors are lawyers and academics who have a passion for gaming law. Their enthusiasm for expanding the field of attorneys with an understanding of the area was the impetus for the book. I thank all of them for their efforts, and for their patience when I importuned them about deadlines, edits, and important matters such as the proper use of italics for case names in footnotes.

Karl Rutledge is the chair of the Gaming Law Committee, and his leadership is a reason why the committee undertook the challenge of writing this book. Karl has worked hard to raise the profile of the committee in the Business Law Section, and he viewed this book as an important way of doing that. I appreciate the commitment he has given to the book and to the committee.

Thanks as well to Karl's predecessor Chris Hinckley, with whom I had conversations a few years ago about a book like this. Chris offered valuable guidance and advice.

Rick Paszkiet, content development manager of the ABA's Business Law Section, has at all times been a helpful and supportive resource as the book took shape and progressed. I could always count on prompt, professional counsel from him and that was much appreciated.

The dean of Drake Law School, Jerry Anderson, has been characteristically supportive and encouraging of my work on this book. It is indicative of his commitment to scholarship for the profession. The law school, and the legal academy, are fortunate to have his service.

Last but certainly not least, I want to thank my research assistant Billy Daniel for his substantial contributions to the book. He was indefatigable and steady, patient with my often unreasonable appeals for work to be done on weekends, and at all times a source of mature professional judgment. Billy is a pleasure to work with and will be a credit to the legal profession.

Keith Miller
July 2019

Preface

The practice of an attorney in the field of regulated gambling is remarkably cross–doctrinal. The range of issues presented spans contract law, administrative practice, state constitutional law, securities regulation, and business entity issues such as reorganizations and currency reporting requirements, to name just a few.

This book emerged from conversations Gaming Law Committee members have had with business attorneys whose practice does not predominantly involve gaming clients. Nevertheless, these attorneys reported numerous instances where client matters they handled touched up against gaming law. The examples included the following:

- A client was a lighting contractor who did a substantial amount of business with an Indian tribe. The tribe failed to pay the contractor's invoice for equipment for the tribe's casino property, and claimed the person who entered the contract on behalf of the tribe didn't have authority to do so. What were the contractor's remedies?
- A valued employee of a firm represented by the business attorney disclosed that he had a serious gambling problem and sought treatment. The firm's health insurer resisted extending coverage to the individual even though employees with alcohol and substance disorders were being covered. What are the rights of this employee whom the firm wants to retain?
- A high school booster club contacted the attorney to ask about sponsoring a fund-raising "sweepstakes" for the high school athletic teams. The "sweepstakes" event was a trivia contest with five-person teams paying $100 to enter. The winning team would receive 60 percent of the money collected and the remainder would go to paying for a new weight room at the high school. Does this type of activity constitute illegal gambling?
- The creditor of a casino that had filed for reorganization wanted the casino to continue to operate during the pendency of the proceeding. The creditor also wanted to purchase assets of the casino. Is this a matter of

interest only to the debtor, the creditors, and the court? What is the role of gaming regulators in the state where the casino is located?
- An elderly grandmother apparently won a $10 million slot machine jackpot at a local casino and several neutral witnesses observed the machine display a win of $10,000,000. The casino refused to pay, however, claiming that the machine had malfunctioned and that they had no liability whatsoever. Isn't this just a simple contracts case?

These are just a few illustrations of situations where business lawyers were contacted by clients or prospective clients on matters directly or indirectly involving gaming law. All the lawyers involved commented that an awareness of regulated gambling law would have been helpful in evaluating these situations.

The committee decided that a book that would familiarize the business attorney with some of the basics of gaming law would be a worthy undertaking. Lawyers and academics with specialties in gaming law have written this book with a goal of helping the practicing business lawyer better understand this challenging area of practice. Authors have worked to keep their audience in mind. This book is for the lawyer who may be described as the "inadvertent" or "accidental" gaming law attorney, or one who does not have gaming clients as the core of a business practice.

Our goal with this book is to impart to a business attorney a heightened awareness of regulated gambling law. If and when a client issue arises in the gaming field, we hope this book helps to give that attorney the confidence of knowing how to handle the matter, or the wisdom to recognize when to consult a gaming law specialist.

The following descriptions provide a brief summary of the chapters. The book is divided into three sections.

Part One offers an introduction to gambling in the United States.

Chapter 1, *Regulated Gambling in the United States,* written by **Kate Lowenhar-Fisher, Greg Gemignani, Jennifer Gaynor, and Jeff Silver**, introduces the reader to the various gaming markets that operate in the United States. The expansion of regulated gambling in the United States has been dramatic, and technological advances promise future business opportunities. The chapter also provides a helpful history of the development of gambling in the United States, including a guide to landmark events in the world of regulated gaming.

Chapter 2, *What Is Gambling?*, written by **Karl Rutledge and Glenn Light,** examines the fascinating question of what activities actually constitute gambling and which do not. States have developed a variety of tests to decide this question, and the chapter guides the reader through this maze. What does it mean to say a contest is a "game of skill"? Why does it matter? The answers to these questions implicate a variety of games and contests.

Part Two presents legal issues in the world of commercial gambling in the United States.

Chapter 3, *The Basics of Gaming Regulation*, written by **Anthony Cabot**, offers a comprehensive outline of how gaming is regulated in the United States, including the process of seeking a gaming license. While states differ in some of the details, common elements are present and the chapter explores these features. States regulate gambling to further several interests, and the material makes it clear that gaming regulation takes a backseat to no area of law in its detail and breadth.

Chapter 4, *Currency Reporting and Anti–Money Laundering Requirements for Gaming Properties*, is written by **Peter Kulick**. Currency reporting and anti–money laundering requirements are not unique to the gaming world, and many business lawyers are familiar with the Bank Secrecy Act. However, because gambling is primarily a cash business, gaming entities are saddled with special requirements that the chapter details. Failure to comply, as the discussion illustrates, can produce very expensive consequences for casinos.

Chapter 5, *Corporate Reorganizations, Bankruptcy, and Restructuring*, written by **Sean McGuinness and Adam Langley**, discusses the issues of corporate reorganizations and bankruptcies in the context of a gaming entity. The peculiar nature of gaming operations has implications for how the Bankruptcy Code applies and how creditors protect their interests. In some instances, gaming law intersects with bankruptcy proceedings, adding an additional layer of issues for the attorney.

Chapter 6, *Gaming Contracts*, written by **Keith Miller**, looks at several settings where contract law is entangled with the statutory and regulatory framework for gaming. Casino credit is a controversial issue, as is the process of a casino collecting on outstanding debts. Contract principles are also at play when patrons have conflicts with casinos over matters such as disputes about machine jackpots.

Chapter 7, *Problem Gambling and the Business Lawyer*, is written by **Stacey Tovino**, who explores issues relating to disordered gambling. The material digs into the nuanced insurance and employment issues that can arise when a person is diagnosed with gambling disorder. When the *Diagnostic and Statistical Manual of Mental Disorders*, fifth edition (*DSM-5*) reclassified gambling disorder from an "impulse-control disorder" to a "substance-related and addictive disorder," there were many implications. The chapter also offers case studies of disbarred attorneys with gambling disorders seeking to regain their license.

Part Three covers other forms of gambling.

Chapter 8, *Tribal Gaming*, written by **Kathryn Rand and Steven Light**, considers the subtle issues associated with tribal gaming. Many tribes have gained economic self-sufficiency from casinos on their tribal lands, though the majority of tribal gaming operations are modest and supply jobs if not riches to the tribe. The sovereignty of tribes, even when acting in a commercial environment, can present challenges to businesses, and their lawyers, to protect their economic interests. The chapter navigates the reader through the mix of federal, state, and tribal law.

Chapter 9, *Internet Gambling*, is written by **Karl Rutledge, Glenn Light, Mary Tran, and Jason Bacigalupi.** This chapter mines down into the controversial world of Internet gambling. Few issues are as fraught with political intrigue as online or mobile gambling. The chapter assesses the range of federal laws that govern Internet gambling, including how the Department of Justice has created confusion with various interpretations of a 1961 law that was directed at organized crime but is now being applied to states.

Chapter 10, *State Lotteries*, written by **David Ranscht**, is a comprehensive treatment of issues involving state lotteries. Disputes involving lottery jackpots are numerous and state law can vary on important details. Sometimes the clashes are between the lottery and a player, but the chapter also discusses the litigation between lotteries and vendors and between players.

Chapter 11, *Sports Betting in the United States*, authored by **Tamara Malvin**, immerses the reader in one of the most topical of gaming issues—sports wagering. A Supreme Court decision in 2018 opened the door to states to authorize and regulate sports betting, and several states have already jumped in. However, it isn't simply a matter of adding betting windows. The chapter delves into the many issues that policymakers have to consider in legislating to permit this venerable form of gambling.

Chapter 12, *Data Privacy Issues and GDPR*, written by **Sean McGuinness and Katie Fillmore**, evaluates the emerging issues of data privacy law in a casino context. The authors alert the reader to the broad application to U.S. companies and casinos of the General Data Protection Regulation (GDPR) of the European Union. This regulation, in addition to the regulation of data privacy by state law, creates compliance problems for casinos, which value the information they can obtain from their gambling patrons.

PART I

An Introduction to Gambling in the United States

Chapter 1

Regulated Gambling in the United States

Kate Lowenhar-Fisher, Greg Gemignani,
Jennifer Gaynor, and Jeff Silver

I. INTRODUCTION

Gambling is a pastime that is as old as time and can be found, in varied iterations, all across the globe. In the United States, gambling has become big business, with multi-billion-dollar casino resorts to be found in all corners of the nation today—from the expected locations, such as Las Vegas and Atlantic City, to some less expected, like Thackerville, Oklahoma (WinStar World Casino and Resort), and Mashantucket, Connecticut (Foxwoods Resort Casino). In addition to casino resorts, gambling opportunities also include horse racing, racinos, riverboat casinos, high-stakes bingo halls, off-track betting, sports wagering, slot routes offering video poker in taverns and other locations, card rooms, state lotteries, and online gambling.

It is an understatement to say that the gambling industry has come a long way from its less-than-desirable beginnings in America. Today it is a vibrant and growing industry. Industry experts estimate that regulated gaming contributes $261 billion to the U.S. economy; generates $40.28 billion in tax revenues to federal, state, and local governments; and supports nearly 1.8 million jobs across the country.[1]

This chapter begins by offering a brief history of the regulated gambling industry in the United States and how it came to be the multi-billion-dollar industry it is today. It then provides an overview of the U.S. regulated gambling market, including the basics of how it is regulated, a discussion of some of the market segments (commercial gaming, sports wagering, lotteries, etc.), how they've developed, and what they look like today.

---

1. *See Economic Impact of the U.S. Gaming Industry*, AM. GAMING ASS'N (June 1, 2018). Note that the commercial gambling market numbers do not include revenue from the nation's tribal casino resorts.

II. HISTORY OF AMERICAN GAMING REGULATION

A. The 1800s and Early 1900s—Gambling First Legalized in Nevada

In the late nineteenth century and early twentieth century, gambling, with the exception of on-track betting, was illegal in most U.S. states and local jurisdictions. This was due to a combination of state constitutional prohibitions, state laws, and local ordinances.[2] Despite being illegal, gambling proliferated in areas of the country considered frontier land. As Samuel Clemens, a young newspaper reporter who later knew fame as the author Mark Twain, stated in his book *Roughing It*, gamblers were considered prominent members of the community. "In Nevada," he wrote, "for a time, the lawyer, the editor, the chief desperado, the chief gambler, and the saloon-keeper occupied the same level in society, and it was the highest."[3]

In 1869, however, Nevada legalized gambling. Under the 1869 law, county sheriffs issued gaming licenses to anyone who paid a fee ranging from $250 to $400 per quarter. The state made no effort to control gamblers or gambling operations except to make cheating a misdemeanor. In 1877, it also banned gambling on Sundays and raised the legal gaming age to twenty-one. From 1869 to 1907, the Nevada legislature passed several laws changing the amount and method of collecting gaming taxes. In 1905, the Nevada legislature authorized a separate license for slot machines. In 1907, the state ordered that all gaming tax revenues, except slot machine taxes, go to the local governments.[4]

By 1909, however, the mining boom in Nevada had run its course. Reno, the primary city in Nevada, was shedding its rough-and-tumble frontier image, and antigambling forces became a significant voice in the state. Following efforts in neighboring states, in 1909 the Nevada legislature banned all casino gaming, to take effect on October 1, 1910. Despite the ban on gambling, a Reno newspaper reported: "There is a place in town where the roulette wheel spins nightly and where the faro bank is dealt of old."[5]

In 1915, Nevada legislators approved a bill permitting slot machines that awarded prizes not exceeding $2 in value, as well as poker and similar games that alternated the deal. But these legal games were largely ignored, as illegal casinos proliferated and attracted the public's business. From 1915 until 1931, Nevada's

---

    2. For example, in the late 1600s and early 1700s, both Pennsylvania and New Jersey passed acts outlawing gambling, condemning it as "an idle activity." A good overview of state and local laws that outlawed gambling in the early years of the United States can be found in George G. Fenich, *Chronology of (Legal) Gaming in the U.S.*, 3 Gaming Res. & Rev. J. (1996), https://digitalscholarship.unlv.edu/cgi/viewcontent.cgi?article=1223&context=grrj.

    3. *See* Lionel Sawyer & Collins, Nevada Gaming Law 4 (3d ed. 2000) (hereinafter Nevada Gaming Law Third).

    4. *Id.* at 6.

    5. *Id.* at 10.

legislature tinkered with making certain games legal and others illegal, but wide-open gambling and casino gambling remained prohibited.[6]

B. The Great Depression and the Introduction of Wide-Open Gambling in Nevada

It was an event outside the control of the Nevada legislature that had the greatest impact on gambling in Nevada—the Great Depression. A combination of a declining economy, loss of state revenues, and the diminishing popularity of the temperance movement of the early twentieth century created strong popular sentiment to legalize all forms of gaming. Casino gambling presented a vehicle for increasing business and providing much-needed tax revenue.[7]

Despite public support for gambling as an economic tool, the bill to permit wide-open gambling was not universally supported. There was a hard-fought battle in the legislative session of 1931 regarding the measure. Antigaming forces in Nevada were strong, but a freshman lawmaker from Humboldt County by the name of Phil M. Tobin introduced Assembly Bill 98, popularly known as the Wide Open Gambling Bill of 1931, because he believed that antigambling laws were unenforceable and the local governments in the state needed tax revenue.[8] The bill faced formidable opposition. The Public Morals Committee hearing on the proposed legislation attracted quite a crowd, and Washoe County assemblyman Howard Malone protested that "such legislation undermined, rather than aided society" and that "poor old Nevada has some honor left, I hope, and will not pass such a law."[9]

Despite the opposition, the bill passed the Nevada Assembly on a 24 to 11 vote and the Nevada Senate on a 13 to 3 vote. Governor Balzar signed the bill into law, and Nevada became the first state to permit wide-open gambling in the United States.[10]

Under the 1931 law, a person did not have to obtain a state license to conduct gambling. Instead, the potential casino owner only had to obtain a local license from the county sheriff and, where mandated by local ordinance, from any incorporated city or county. License fees were $25 per month for each table game and $10 per month for each slot machine. The fees were divided between the state (25 percent) and the county where the casino was located (75 percent), with the caveat that if the casino is located within the boundaries of any incorporated city or town, the county shall retain 25 percent, and the incorporated city or town shall receive 50 percent.[11]

---

6. *Id.* at 10.
7. *Id.*
8. Assemblyman Tobin was quoted as declaring that the bill's purpose "was not to make a Monte Carlo of Nevada, but merely to provide police regulation for an existing situation, and through taxation, to force a profitable business to bear its share of the state's expenses." *See* Brett McGinness, *From the Archives: Here's How Nevada Banned Gambling, Reintroduced It on March 19, 1931*, Reno Gazette Journal, March 18, 2016.
9. *Id.*
10. *Id.*
11. Statutes of Nevada 1931, Nev. Stat. 165, Assembly Bill No. 98 (1931).

The 1931 act provided for no state regulation of gambling, only *taxation* of gambling. Local governments were the sole regulators of gambling under the 1931 act, and even then, their powers were somewhat limited, with the focus being on issuing licenses and collecting license fees, although cheating and "thieving" at games was prohibited and licenses were able to be revoked for violations of the 1931 act.[12]

The first challenge to local regulation of gambling occurred within months of the enactment of the 1931 act. Applicants for a casino license sued the City of Las Vegas for denying their gambling license, claiming the City acted beyond the scope of its authority under the 1931 act.[13] The City defended the suit by claiming that there were already six licenses issued and that the public interest did not favor additional licenses. Ultimately, the Nevada Supreme Court upheld the City's action, holding that the City had the right to limit acts with a "deleterious tendency," including gambling, as part of its power to police the government of the municipality. The Nevada Supreme Court's decision was the first decision confirming the authority of government to regulate gambling.[14]

In the 1940s, spending on World War II and public works revitalized the economy across the United States. The robust national economy helped to invigorate the Nevada economy and the gambling industry as well. Prior to World War II, casino gambling was generally restricted to the backrooms of saloons, out of the public eye. But a number of factors contributed to an environment that fueled investment in Nevada's new gambling industry. These included the rejuvenated national economy, the proliferation of personal automobiles, the lack of state taxation of gambling, air-conditioning, and affordable air travel.[15] Tax revenue for the state and local governments was not increasing, however, because local authorities were lax in enforcing the state's requirement of a license for each game. In response, the Nevada legislature created the first casino gambling tax in 1945. The tax rate was 1 percent of gross casino revenues in excess of $3,000, calculated as the amounts wagered by patrons less winnings paid to patrons.[16] The 1945 legislation also made the Nevada Tax Commission the primary state regulatory authority for the gambling industry.[17]

The low tax rate, lack of significant regulation, and easy access to population centers in California attracted many developers to the Nevada gambling industry. This included some people with ties to organized crime. Scandals such as the shooting death of Benjamin "Bugsy" Seigel in 1947, which was related to his involvement

---

12. *See id.*
13. *See* State *ex rel.* Grimes v. Board of Commissioners of City of Las Vegas, 53 Nev. 364, 1 P.2d 570 (1931).
14. *Id.*
15. *See* Nevada Gaming Law Third, *supra* note 3, at 13.
16. *See* Robert D. Faiss & Gregory R. Gemignani, *Nevada Gaming Statutes: Their Evolution and History*, University of Nevada, Las Vegas: Center for Gaming Research, Occasional Paper Series 2 (Number 10, September 2011) (Hereinafter Faiss & Gemignani).
17. *Id.*

in the development of the Flamingo casino, brought unwanted attention to the Nevada gambling industry.[18]

Additional problems arose as illegal operators in Northern California moved into the Reno/Tahoe area to avoid increased law enforcement efforts in California. In 1947, one of these new operators in northern Nevada, Harry Sherwood, was shot dead in the Tahoe Village Casino, a business in which Sherwood was a part owner.[19] In addition, there were many complaints regarding cheating and swindling by casino operators in Nevada, and Governor Vail Pittman, angry with the growing number of criminal problems associated with gambling, demanded action.[20]

Following the well-publicized death of Seigel, the Nevada Attorney General, Alan Bible, issued an opinion that the Nevada Tax Commission had the right to issue regulations to regulate gambling. In his 1947 opinion, Attorney General Bible stated that current statutes allowed the commission to adopt regulations requiring "inquiry into the antecedents, habits, and character of applicants in order to satisfy the Commission that they will not violate the gambling law . . . prohibiting thieving and cheating games. . . ."[21] He told the commission that if it "finds reasonable ground to apprehend that the grant of a license would be against the public interest, you would be within the powers delegated to you to refuse the license."[22]

In 1949, the Nevada legislature amended the state's gambling statutes to clearly state that a state license was required to operate any gambling game and that the Tax Commission was to administer the laws to protect the public interest and could enact regulations to carry out this goal.[23] The 1949 amendments also allowed the Tax Commission to require fingerprinting of casino employees and to deny gaming licenses to protect the public interest. This was the first statute that permitted regulation of gambling and regulation of those applying for a gambling license.[24]

C. The 1950s and 1960s—Legal Gambling Faces Federal Challenges

The postwar growth of gambling was accompanied by a postwar political climate that regarded communism and organized crime as the two primary threats to the American way of life. In 1950, Republican senator Joseph McCarthy from Wisconsin began his focus on the infiltration of communism into the U.S. government and society. In the same year, Democratic senator Estes Kefauver of Tennessee began televised committee hearings on the influence of organized crime in the United States.[25]

---

18. Nevada Gaming Law Third, *supra* note 3, at 17.
19. *See* Faiss & Gemignani, *supra* note 16, at 2.
20. *See* Nevada Gaming Law Third, *supra* note 3, at 17.
21. *Id.*
22. *Id.*
23. *Id.* at 18.
24. *Id.*
25. *Id.* at 19.

Senator Kefauver was an aspiring presidential candidate, and the Kefauver committee investigation of organized crime propelled Kefauver and his televised hearings into the national spotlight. The Kefauver committee soon focused on organized crime's involvement in gambling and in the Nevada gambling industry. The hearings, televised in prime time and held in Las Vegas, featured Nevada's lieutenant governor and its tax commissioner. Both testified that the state made little or no effort before 1949 to screen gambling license applicants.[26]

The Kefauver committee report was critical of the Nevada regulatory apparatus. "The licensing system which is in effect in the state has not resulted in excluding the undesirables from the state," the committee wrote, "but has merely served to give their activities a seeming cloak of respectability."[27] The committee concluded that many casino owners were members of organized crime or "had histories of close associations with underworld characters who operate those syndicates." The message was clear that unless Nevada could clean up the industry, the federal government would close it down.[28]

Congress took up the issue in 1951 and sought to tax the industry out of existence with a proposed federal law to assess a 10 percent tax on the gross receipts of all gaming transactions.[29] However, Nevada had a powerful champion in its senator, Pat McCarran. McCarran was chairman of the Senate Judiciary Committee and a senior member of the Appropriations Committee. McCarran led the fight against the proposed federal law, which would have forced the closure of virtually every Nevada casino and sports book and devastated Nevada's economy. "If . . . the proposed tax is intended to suppress all gaming, whether legal or illegal, throughout the United States, it goes far beyond the recommendations of the Kefauver Committee," McCarran said.[30]

McCarran successfully convinced his colleagues to pass a modified wagering excise tax bill that exempted card games, roulette, slot machines, and dice. He felt it would be a bureaucratic nightmare for the federal government to attempt to regulate the games for tax purposes.[31] McCarran's efforts staved off the federal effort to legislate gambling out of existence.

In 1955, the Nevada legislature responded to federal pressure by creating a full-time agency to serve as the investigative and enforcement arm of the Nevada Tax Commission. The 1955 legislation gave the commission, and the newly created Gaming Control Board, authority to investigate applicants' business probity and their ability to finance projects and generate working capital.[32] Investment in Nevada's gaming industry soon soared, and concerns were raised by northern Nevada

---

26. *Id.*
27. *Id.*
28. *Id.*
29. *Id.* at 20.
30. *Id.*
31. *Id.*
32. *See* Faiss & Gemignani, *supra* note 16, at 3.

lawmakers that oversaturation of the Las Vegas market would doom the industry and state. Despite these concerns and the division it created within the state, investment continued to flow into Las Vegas, and even the bankruptcy of a few casinos did not slow the growth of new developments.[33]

Even with the 1955 enhancements, however, many loopholes remained in Nevada's gambling laws and regulatory structure. Undesirable developers were still able to play a role in Nevada's gambling industry. Nevada's need to completely restructure its regulatory system and the industry did not go unnoticed. In 1958, Grant Sawyer, a young, progressive Democrat from Elko County, ran a tireless gubernatorial campaign to reform the gambling industry with the slogan "Nevada is not for sale." In a surprise, Sawyer won the election in 1958.[34]

Sawyer's first initiative as governor was to champion and sign a bill that removed control of gambling from the Tax Commission. A new, independent agency, the Nevada Gaming Commission, was created and would be the entity that regulated gambling in the state.[35]

The commission was composed of five members. Sawyer had a strong mandate for the new commission. "Exhaustive investigations [must] be made as to present licensees in order to be as certain as humanly possible that criminal elements, mobs, or syndicates have neither interests nor control of existing businesses," he said.[36]

Although the Gaming Control Board continued to conduct investigations and administer gambling regulations, it was given more autonomy than it had under the Tax Commission. Previously, the board chairman served as secretary to the commission. Under the proposal championed by Sawyer, the Tax Commission and Gaming Control Board were independent agencies. Sawyer appointed a former assistant to FBI director J. Edgar Hoover as the new board chairman and doubled the agency's budget. His revisions launched the modern era of gambling control in Nevada.[37] Sawyer's bill established the two-agency model for gambling regulation, established the implementation of a comprehensive regulatory system, and declared gambling to be a privilege not a right. Governor Sawyer knew it would take some time to reshape the industry, and he was hopeful that the federal government would afford Nevada the time it needed to do this.

Approximately one year later, John F. Kennedy was elected President. Governor Sawyer was an early supporter of Kennedy for the presidential nomination of the Democratic Party and had a strong relationship with the President. Upon becoming President, John F. Kennedy appointed his brother Robert Kennedy as the U.S. Attorney General. Robert Kennedy had long been a champion against organized crime, and his new position as U.S. Attorney General provided him with the power

---

33. *See* Nevada Gaming Law Third, *supra* note 3, at 22–25.
34. *See* Faiss & Gemignani, *supra* note 16, at 3.
35. *Id.* at 4.
36. *Id.*
37. *Id.*

to aggressively pursue his goal to eliminate the influence of organized crime in the United States.[38]

In May 1961, Robert Kennedy asked the Nevada attorney general to deputize fifty federal agents and raid a number of casinos. Sawyer believed the raids would generate immense negative publicity that would be devastating to the state's economy. He flew to Washington, D.C., where he met with both Attorney General Kennedy and his brother, President John Kennedy.[39]

The raids never took place. Instead, a cooperative agreement was worked out to allow federal agents to work with the Gaming Control Board to conduct investigations of Nevada casinos. The FBI staff in Las Vegas was tripled. The U.S. Internal Revenue Service was staffed with forty experts to investigate alleged skimming operations.[40]

In 1961, Nevada was the only state with legal and regulated casino-style gambling. At this time in the United States, there were no state lotteries, no tribal casinos, and no racinos. On-track horse race wagering was the only form of wagering outside of Nevada.[41]

It was in this climate that the Federal Wire Act of 1961, promoted by Robert Kennedy, was enacted.[42] The Federal Wire Act was part of a package of laws aimed at the interstate revenue-generating operations of organized crime. The Wire Act was directly aimed at gambling operations (previous laws addressed the interstate transportation of lottery tickets, lottery information, and gaming devices). The Federal Wire Act prohibited those in the business of betting or wagering from transmitting the following in interstate or foreign commerce: (1) bets or wagers and information assisting in the placement of bets or wagers on any sporting event or contest, (2) a communication entitling the recipient to money or credit based on a bet or wager, and (3) the transmission of information assisting in the placement of bets or wagers. The Wire Act exempted two activities: legitimate news reporting and the transmission of information assisting in the placement of bets or wagers on any sporting event or contest between jurisdictions where wagering is legal.[43]

D. The 1960s through 1990s—The Nationwide Growth of Regulated Gambling

Nevada's gaming industry continued to flourish under the new gambling regulatory regime implemented by Governor Sawyer and as refined by successive governors

---

38. *See* Nevada Gaming Law Third, *supra* note 3, at 26–28.
39. *Id.*
40. *Id.*
41. *See* Faiss & Gemignani, *supra* note 16, at 5.
42. The Interstate Wire Act of 1961, 18 U.S.C. § 1084 (2012).
43. The U.S. Department of Justice has recently published a new interpretation of the application of the Wire Act. For more information, see *Reconsidering Whether the Wire Act Applies to Non-Sports Gambling*, Opinion of the Office of Legal Counsel, January 14, 2019. See detailed discussion of this issue in Chapter 10.

and legislative sessions. But Nevada stood alone in having legal forms of wagering outside of on-track horse race wagering.

This changed in 1964 when New Hampshire authorized the first modern state lottery. The success of the New Hampshire state lottery was not lost on other states, and state lotteries began to expand. As will be noted later, state lotteries can now be found in all but five states.[44]

In the 1970s, the federal government sought to strengthen its statutory tools against organized crime, and the Illegal Gambling Business Act, among other laws, was enacted. The Illegal Gambling Business Act makes it a federal crime to own, manage, finance, supervise, or conduct any business that violates state gambling prohibitions so long as the business has five or more people involved and is either in continuous operations for thirty days or earns more than $2,000 in revenue in a single day. The net effect is that the Illegal Gambling Business Act aids states in enforcing state gambling prohibitions for activities that impact interstate commerce.[45]

Despite the proliferation of state lotteries, Nevada remained alone in offering legal and regulated casino wagering. That changed in 1978, when New Jersey used casino gaming as an economic tool to revitalize Atlantic City. Though New Jersey incorporated elements of Nevada's regulatory system, the state designed its regulatory structure so as to address the particular issues it would face in offering regulated casino gambling. Notably absent from New Jersey's regulation of gambling in 1978 was the regulation of sports wagering.[46]

In the 1980s, Indian tribes began to become involved in high-stakes bingo and card room gambling on tribal land. Early ventures were often leased operations, in which a developer would fund the building of a bingo hall or card room facility, and would then operate that facility in exchange for payments to the tribe on whose land the facility was located. The proliferation of gaming on Indian land was caused by steep cuts in federal funding for tribes and a federal policy that encouraged tribes to take control of their own economic development. Tribal gaming was not without controversy, and many states took issue with gaming activity occurring on Indian land that was within state borders. The U.S. Supreme Court settled the issue in 1987, holding that tribes could conduct gaming free of state regulation if the state regulated the same forms of gaming.[47] Congress acted swiftly after the Supreme Court opinion and enacted the Indian Gaming Regulatory Act,[48] which is addressed in detail in Chapter 9.

In response to the rapid proliferation of tribal gaming, several states in the late 1980s and early 1990s authorized riverboat gambling. Many of these states studied

---

44. *See* Todd Eilers & Phil Bernard, *Eilers: U.S. Lottery Tracker—3Q18*, EILERS & KREJCIK GAMING (July 30, 2018).
45. 18 U.S.C. § 1955 (2012).
46. *Casino Gaming in New Jersey*, NEW JERSEY CASINO CONTROL COMMISSION, https://www.nj.gov/casinos/home/gamingnj/ (last accessed June 3, 2019).
47. *See* California v. Cabazon Band of Mission Indians, 480 U.S. 202 (1987).
48. Indian Gaming Regulatory Act, 25 U.S.C. § 2701 et. seq. (2012); *see infra* Chapter 9.

the regulation of gaming in Nevada and New Jersey and crafted laws and regulations that were consistent with the regulatory policies of Nevada and New Jersey. As riverboat gambling became more popular, the creativity of the gaming industry transformed riverboat gambling from an activity occurring on boats, to dry docked vessels, to constructions over water. Soon it was clear that riverboats were becoming full-fledged casinos, and many states began to do away with boat requirements for regulated casino gambling.

In 1992, in response to state lotteries planning to expand offerings to include sports wagering products, Congress enacted the Professional and Amateur Sports Protection Act (PASPA). PASPA prohibited states and tribes from authorizing or conducting sports wagering, and it prevented anyone from conducting, advertising, or promoting sports wagering based on a state law that authorized that action.[49]

PASPA did have three exemptions. The first exemption applied to state lotteries that had sports wagering products in the past, and it essentially allowed them to continue to offer or reintroduce offering such products. Only Delaware and Oregon qualified for this exemption. The second exemption was for states that had statutes and regulations permitting sports wagering prior to the enactment of PASPA to the extent that these wagers were actually conducted in the state. Only Nevada and Montana qualified for this exemption, and Nevada was the only state with broad-based sports wagering offerings. The final exemption was for any state that regulated casino gaming for at least ten years, provided that sports wagering legislation was enacted by the state within one year of the enactment of PASPA and that the wagering occurred within regulated casinos. The only state other than Nevada with ten years of regulated casino gambling in 1992 was New Jersey. New Jersey, however, did not take advantage of this exemption before it expired.[50]

E. Recent U.S. Gambling History

In 2014, New Jersey challenged the constitutionality of PASPA, and in 2018, the U.S. Supreme Court deemed PASPA to be unconstitutional.[51] (A more detailed analysis of this case and sports wagering generally are in Chapter 11.) Another notable recent development in U.S. gambling law was the opinion published by the U.S. Department of Justice (DOJ), providing an updated interpretation on how the Wire Act shall be applied.[52]

The days when Nevada was viewed by others as the outlier fostering the growth of a pariah industry in a forsaken wasteland are long gone. The threat of federal closure of the gaming industry is also long gone. The Modern Gaming Control Act of

---

49. 28 U.S.C. § 3701 et. seq. (2012) *declared unconstitutional by* Murphy v. NCAA, 138 S. Ct. 1461 (2018).
50. *See infra* Chapter 11.
51. *See* Murphy v. NCAA, 138 S. Ct. 1461 (2018).
52. *See Reconsidering Whether the Wire Act Applies to Non-Sports Gambling*, Opinion of the Office of Legal Counsel, January 14, 2019. This is discussed in detail in Chapter 10.

1959 in Nevada and the concepts it embodied became the blueprint for successful gaming regulation in other states and countries. Today, some form of legal and regulated gambling can be found within the borders of forty-eight states and the District of Columbia.[53]

III. GAMBLING REGULATION IN THE UNITED STATES

A. Generally

With this history of gaming as a backdrop, the focus turns to how the gambling industry is regulated in the United States. First, it is helpful to have a basic understanding of what "gambling" includes.[54] Generally, in the United States, gambling involves any activity in which a person places a bet or wager. A bet or wager usually occurs when (1) a person risks something of value (consideration) on (2) the outcome of an uncertain event in which the bettor does not exercise primary control or which is determined predominantly by chance (chance) with (3) the opportunity to win something of value (prize).[55] In most, but not all, states, when any one of the three elements is missing, the activity is not considered gambling.[56]

There are many forms of gambling, including lotteries, pari-mutuel wagering, house-banked games, player-banked games, and bookmaking. Gambling crimes in most jurisdictions also include bookmaking, an activity in which someone accepts wagers, records wagers, or holds stakes for wagers of others when the wagers are placed on the outcome of other events such as athletic contests, races, or other contests.[57]

States, tribes, and the federal government share concurrent jurisdiction with regard to gambling prohibitions. Gambling prohibitions and regulation in the United States are primarily the domain of state law. Federal laws typically act as an overlay to provide assistance to the states in enforcing state gambling prohibitions across state and national borders.[58] Gaming offered by Indian nations on tribal lands is regulated through a complex patchwork of federal and state laws.[59]

---

53. Hawaii and Utah are the two states that do not allow regulated gambling in any of its various forms.
54. *See infra* Chapter 2, *What Is Gambling?*, for more information.
55. *See* KATE LOWENHAR-FISHER, ET AL, GAMING LAW & PRACTICE § 2.02 (2018).
56. *See, e.g.,* Stepnes v. Ritschel, 663 F.3d 952, 958 (8th Cir. 2011) (Minnesota Gambling Control Board statement that illegal gambling consists of three elements: consideration, chance, and a prize, and a contest involving analytical skill would remove the element of chance and would not be in violation of Minnesota's gambling laws).
57. *See, e.g.,* CAL. PENAL CODE § 337a (2018).
58. There are at least four federal acts that assist states in enforcement of their gambling laws: the Illegal Gambling Business Act (18 U.S.C. § 1955 [2012]), the Wagering Paraphernalia Act (18 U.S.C. § 1953 [2012]), the Travel Act (18 U.S.C. 1952 [2012]), and the Unlawful Internet Gambling Enforcement Act (31 U.S.C. §§ 5361–5367 [2012]).
59. *See infra* Chapter 9 on Indian gaming.

For interstate and international wagering, U.S. courts have determined that wagers occur both where the bettor resides and at the location from which the betting service provider offers its services.[60] Therefore, U.S. federal and state gambling laws will apply to any operation that takes payments from U.S. players for a chance to win a prize, regardless of whether the operation may be located outside of the United States.

B. U.S. Gambling Industry Segments—An Overview

1. Commercial Casino Gambling

As noted above, in 2017 the U.S. commercial casino industry reported gross gambling revenue[61] of $40.28 billion.[62] This produced an estimated $9.23 billion in direct gaming tax revenue in 2017 for the jurisdictions that have regulated gambling.[63]

As of 2019, there are 460 commercial casino locations in twenty-four states, with approximately 215 of these in Nevada.[64]

2. Tribal Gaming

The legal foundation of tribal gambling in the United States has its origin in the sovereignty of Indian nations on Indian land. Congress's authority over Indian tribes is grounded in the U.S. Constitution and in decisions of the Supreme Court.

First, Article I, Section 8 of the Constitution states, "Congress shall have the power to regulate Commerce with foreign nations and among the several states, and with the Indian tribes."[65] This provision has been the basis for laws such as the Indian Gaming Regulatory Act, noted below.

Second, in the cases known as the "Marshall Trilogy,"[66] the Supreme Court pronounced that Congress, and not the states, had authority over the Indian tribes, which were considered "dependent domestic sovereigns." These cases, and the

---

60. *See* United States v. $734,578.82 in United States Currency, 286 F.3d 641 (3d Cir. 2002); *see also* United States v. Cohen, 260 F.3d 68 (2d Cir. 2001).

61. "Gross gambling revenue" refers to the amount earned by commercial casinos after winnings have been paid out to patrons. *See State of the States 2018*, AM. GAMING ASS'N, https://www.americangaming.org/wp-content/uploads/2018/08/AGA-2018-State-of-the-States-Report_FINAL.pdf.

62. *See id.*

63. *Id.* Note that this figure does not represent tax revenue generated by activities other than direct gaming, including income, payroll, sales, or various other corporate taxes.

64. *See id.* For the sake of its report, the American Gaming Association (AGA) defines "commercial casino" as "licensed, individual land-based casinos, riverboat casinos, racetrack casinos (racinos) and jai alai frontons, and casino locations in states such as Delaware, Maryland, New York and Ohio that offer gaming devices classified as video lottery terminals or video gaming terminals." The AGA's report and numbers do not include other forms of commercial gaming locations, such as bars, taverns, or truck stops with video lottery terminals, animal racetracks without gaming machines, slot-route operation locations, off-track betting operations, lottery/retail locations, tribal casinos, card rooms, standalone sportsbooks, or other locations in which gaming is "incidental" to the location's primary purpose.

65. U.S. Const. art. I, § 8.

66. *See* Johnson v. M'Intosh, 21 U.S. 543 (1823); Cherokee Nation v. Georgia, 30 U.S. 1 (1831); Worcester v. Georgia, 31 U.S. 515 (1832).

grant of power in Article I, Section 8, were the basis for the Supreme Court in 1987 giving Indian tribes the right to conduct gambling on Indian lands within states that offered some form of gambling.[67] The effect of this case, *California v. Cabazon Band of Mission Indians*, was to marginalize states in their desire to regulate gambling on Indian lands. In response to the concerns of states, the very next year Congress enacted the Indian Gaming Regulatory Act of 1988 (IGRA).[68] Among other things, IGRA defines three classes of gaming on Indian land that divides regulatory responsibility between state and federal authorities. This put states back into the mix for regulating some forms of Indian gambling. Chapter 9 addresses the many details of tribal gaming that are implicated by IGRA.

Today, thirty years after the landmark *Cabazon* case, the tribal gaming market in the United States includes more than 500 tribal gaming facilities in at least twenty-eight states across America. Tribal casinos produced revenues of $32.4 billion in 2017.[69]

3. Sports Wagering

The United States' relationship with sports betting has long been a controversial one. As will be further addressed in Chapter 11, the regulated sports betting market in the United States was transformed by the May 14, 2018, Supreme Court decision in *Murphy v. National Collegiate Athletic Association*.[70] This ruling struck down PASPA,[71] which had limited sports betting to Nevada, and opened the door for states outside of Nevada to authorize and regulate sports betting within their respective borders.

Prior to the *Murphy* decision, the illegal sports betting market in the United States was estimated to be anywhere from $50 billion to $400 billion.[72] Today, as various states grapple with whether and how to bring regulated sports betting to their citizens, estimates of the potential size of the regulated market vary widely. The American Gaming Association predicts that $4.2 billion in annual revenue will be realized by the professional leagues alone through increased fan engagement and sponsorship and promotion opportunities.[73]

---

67. California v. Cabazon Band of Mission Indians, 480 U.S. 202 (1987).
68. 25 U.S.C. § 2701 et. seq. (2012).
69. *See State of the States 2018*, AMERICAN GAMING ASSOCIATION, https://www.americangaming.org/wp-content/uploads/2018/08/AGA-2018-State-of-the-States-Report_FINAL.pdf.
70. 138 S. Ct. 1461 (2018).
71. 28 U.S.C. §§ 3701–3704 (2012).
72. One of the high estimates of $400 billion was cited by National Basketball Association Commissioner, Adam Silver, in a *New York Times* op-ed, *Legalize and Regulate Sports Betting* (Nov. 13, 2014), https://www.nytimes.com/2014/11/14/opinion/nba-commissioner-adam-silver-legalize-sports-betting.html?_r=0. The American Gaming Association was widely cited as estimating the market to be at $150 billion, *see, e.g.*, Lawrence Hurley, *U.S. High Court Paves Way for States to Legalize Sports Betting*, REUTERS (May 14, 2018), https://www.reuters.com/article/us-usa-court-gambling/u-s-top-court-backs-new-jerseys-bid-to-legalize-sports-betting-idUSKCN1IF1WN.
73. *How Much Do Leagues Stand to Gain from Legal Sports Betting?*, AMERICAN GAMING ASSOCIATION, https://www.americangaming.org/wp-content/uploads/2018/10/Nielsen-Research-All-4-Leagues-FINAL.pdf.

Adding a twist to the sports betting story in the United States is the federal government's changing interpretation of the Federal Wire Act of 1961.[74] The impact of the federal government's role in state regulation of sports betting will be further addressed in Chapter 11.

4. Horse Racing

According to a study commissioned in 2017 by the American Horse Industry Council Foundation, the horseracing sector of the U.S. equine industry adds approximately $36.6 billion in total economic impact to the U.S. economy, and is responsible for the employment of 472,000 persons.[75] The same study reported that almost $12.5 billion was wagered on various types of horse races in the United States.[76]

There are many types of horse races that attract the interest of the wagering public, each category of which is intended to make the racing competitive and fair. Horses of the same age and capabilities race against one another. Claiming races are events in which every horse contestant is up for sale, with the claiming price established by the race track promoter (the higher the claiming price, the better the quality of competition). Allowance races are those in which only horses that have similar past performances compete against one another, and stakes races require the horse owners to pay an entry fee that is commensurate with the prize offered (owners have a "stake" in the race). The most prominent of these stakes races are the Thoroughbred races in the Triple Crown (the Kentucky Derby, the Preakness, and the Belmont Stakes), as well as the Breeders' Cup and international events such as the Dubai World Cup, which has a $10,000,000 top prize.

There is also wagering on events held with horses with different ancestral breeding. While the most publicized breed is the Thoroughbred, there is also Standardbred racing, often referred to as harness racing, where the driver is in a cart pulled by the horse. Quarter Horse racing has the horse sprinting short distances—one-quarter mile or less.

Wagering on horses is legal in thirty-eight states.[77] However, horse racing didn't become an economic factor in the United States until 1908, when the concept of pari-mutuel wagering was adopted for the Kentucky Derby, bringing greater safety and security for wagers placed at the race tracks and ostensibly removing bookmakers from the wagering process. While the original idea for pari-mutuel wagering was first introduced in 1867 at French tracks, it was popularized with the invention of the totalizator machine in 1913, which automated the real-time posting of odds on the tote board at the track.[78]

---

74. 18 U.S.C. § 1081 et. seq. (2012).
75. *Economic Impact of the United States Horse Industry*, AM. HORSE COUNCIL, https://www.horsecouncil.org/resources/economics/.
76. *Id.*
77. Steve Beauregard, *States Where It Is Legal to Bet on Horse Racing Online*, GAMBOOOL! (Apr. 26, 2019), https://gamboool.com/states-where-it-is-legal-to-bet-on-horse-racing-online.
78. Ed DeRosa, *What Does Pari-Mutuel Betting Mean in Horse Racing*, TWINSPIRES, https://www.twinspires.com/betting-guides/what-is-pari-mutuel-betting.

Under a pari-mutuel system, odds on wagers are a function of the amounts wagered on particular horses in a race, including combination wagers or more exotic bets. Consequently, the bettors determine the favorites and the payouts for winning bets. The money paid out, however, reflects reductions for the track and for state taxes. When the total amount wagered ("handle" or "turnover") is large, it becomes more difficult for an individual bettor to manipulate the final payout odds.[79]

Off-track betting (OTB) sites and simulcasting of races allow for betting on races conducted at other tracks. This increases the total handle and allows patrons who are at a racetrack to fill in the gaps in time between races by wagering on races being held elsewhere. By reviewing the data of wagering patterns from multiple OTB locations, racing officials are continuously looking for unusual betting patterns that may indicate illicit activity, as well as monitoring computer systems to prevent wagers from being placed after the event has begun (past-posting) or other manipulations of the system.

Many states have allowed racetracks to become racinos. In addition to a racetrack, a racino features other forms of traditional casino gaming. Recently, this has included sports wagering. Revenue generated by the casino-gaming elements at a racino are used to subsidize purses paid to owners and trainers of horses. These additions have increased the value of racetracks as a business model and have helped to maintain the quality of live-racing cards at many locations.

Although each state that permits horse racing has its own laws affecting how the track is operated, the payout system, and internal controls for online wagering, all states are subject to the Interstate Horseracing Act (IHRA), which was enacted in 1978[80] specifically to regulate interstate off-track wagers.

The law provides:

1. the states should have the primary responsibility for determining what forms of gambling may legally take place within their borders.
2. the federal government should prevent interference by one state with the gambling policies of another and should act to protect identifiable national interests.
3. in the limited area of interstate off-track wagering on horse races, there is a need for federal action to ensure states will continue to cooperate with one another in the acceptance of legal interstate wagers.
4. an interstate off-track wager may be accepted by an OTB system only if consent is obtained from the host racing association that has an agreement with the horsemen's group, the host racing commission, and the off-track racing commission.[81]

The authority to conduct online race wagering under IHRA should be read in conjunction with the Wire Act, which was designed to combat organized crime as

---

79. *See id.*
80. 15 U.S.C. § 3001 et seq. (2012).
81. *Id.*

part of a series of antiracketeering laws. It affected the transmission of wagering information assisting in the placement of bets or wagers for sporting events and other contests.[82]

Since the Wire Act predated the IHRA, the common assumption was that transmission of horse racing wagers or information assisting in the placement of wagers is lawful. However, Congress never specifically said as much and given the turmoil surrounding new interpretations of the scope of the Wire Act by the DOJ, Office of Legal Counsel, the legal status of OTB wagering may still have some degree of uncertainty.[83]

5. Online Gambling

In response to the global growth of online gambling, in 2001 Nevada enacted the Interactive Gaming Act, the first enabling legislation in the U.S. for online gambling.[84] As part of this enabling legislation, the Nevada Gaming Commission was required to determine if the activity could be licensed in compliance with federal law.

In 2002, however, the DOJ issued a letter to Nevada regulators stating its opinion that conducting online gaming would violate the federal Wire Act.[85] This letter put a damper on plans to allow for online gambling in Nevada and elsewhere, so growth in this area was limited. Nevertheless, in 2005 the Nevada legislature approved a form of online gaming called mobile gaming, which was limited to taking wagers on a mobile device within the footprint of a casino premises.[86] And in 2011, the Nevada legislature enacted a revision to the 2001 Interactive Gaming Act that required the Nevada Gaming Control Board to draft and the Nevada Gaming Commission to adopt regulations regarding the licensing of online poker before February of 2012.[87]

In 2009, the lotteries of Illinois and New York began to offer online, intrastate lottery subscription sales. The states sought an opinion from the Office of Legal Counsel (OLC) of the DOJ as to whether aspects of their operation might be viewed as violating the Wire Act.[88] On December 23, 2011, the online gambling market gained new life when the OLC of the DOJ issued an opinion that the federal Wire Act applied only to sports wagering and that intrastate wagering (where the bettor and the betting service provider are in the same state) was not subject to that law.[89] The result of the 2011 Opinion was to limit application and enforcement of the federal Wire Act

---

82. Discussed in Chapter 9 on Internet gambling.
83. *See Reconsidering Whether the Wire Act Applies to Non-Sports Gambling*, Opinion of the Office of Legal Counsel, January 14, 2019.
84. *See* Nevada Assembly Bill 466 (2001).
85. *See* Letter from Assistant Attorney General Michael Chertoff to Chairman Peter C. Bernhard, August 23, 2002.
86. *See* Assembly Bill 471 (2005).
87. *See* Assembly Bill 258 (2011).
88. *See Whether Proposals by Illinois and New York to Use the Internet and Out-of-State Transaction Processors to Sell Lottery Tickets to In-State Adults Violates the Wire Act*, Opinion of the Office of Legal Counsel in Volume 35, December 23, 2011.
89. *Id.*

to interstate or international sports wagering. The Opinion also led other states, including Delaware and New Jersey, to offer intrastate, online, casino-style games.

On January 14, 2019, however, all these plans were turned on their head. Reversing course, the OLC of the DOJ issued a new opinion that concluded the Wire Act applies to *all* forms of wagering, not just sports wagering. The Opinion also called into question the foundation for the 2011 Opinion's conclusion that the Wire Act does not apply to intrastate wagering.[90] Although the 2019 DOJ Opinion regarding the Wire Act takes an expansive view of the prohibitions in that law, it remains to be seen if the DOJ will undertake enforcement actions based on the new interpretation, or whether state regulators will require adherence to the expressed and implied conclusions of the 2019 DOJ Opinion.

6. Lotteries

The first modern state lottery in the United States was New Hampshire's state lottery, which was launched in 1964. That lottery was introduced following a successful sweepstakes bill sponsored by State Representative Larry Pickett of Keene and a special ballot vote that received approval from 198 of the state's 211 communities.[91] Today, state lotteries can be found in all but five states,[92] with total U.S. lottery sales in the third quarter of 2018 totaling an estimated $18.9 billion.[93]

The initial New Hampshire lottery was introduced with the goal of additional state funding for education. That goal of additional state revenues for education remains a large driver of state lotteries today.

Lottery games have evolved over the years, and today there is a wide range of lottery products on the market in the United States, including multi-state jackpots, instant tickets, and even a growing market of online, or iLottery, products. Currently, there are ten states that offer iLottery services: Georgia, Illinois, Kentucky, Michigan, New Hampshire, New York, North Carolina, North Dakota, Pennsylvania, and Virginia.[94]

7. eSports

Edward Pitoniak, CEO of VICI Properties, Inc., (a real estate investment trust [REIT] that invests in casino properties), was interviewed in late 2018 and stated that the mission of his company was to invest in the experience.[95] What that meant was

---

90. *See Reconsidering Whether the Wire Act Applies to Non-Sports Gambling*, Opinion of the Office of Legal Counsel, January 14, 2019.
91. *See History*, N.H. STATE LOTTERY, https://www.nhlottery.com/About-Us/History.aspx.
92. States with no lotteries include Alaska, Hawaii, Mississippi, Nevada, and Utah. Lotteries are also offered in the District of Columbia, Puerto Rico, and the U.S. Virgin Islands.
93. *See* Todd Eilers & Phil Bernard, *Eilers: U.S. Lottery Tracker—3Q18*, EILERS & KREJCIK GAMING (July 30, 2018).
94. *See id.*
95. *VICI Properties Says Experiential Real Estate Can Disrupt Amazon*, NAREIT (Jan. 15, 2019), https://www.reit.com/news/videos/vici-properties-says-experiential-real-estate-can-disrupt-amazon.

that the eSports customer experience was vital in maintaining the durability of cash flows and preserving or increasing property values. The company recently raised $2.4 billion in equity, evidencing their investors' belief in that premise.

The growing eSports phenomenon seems to fit these prerequisites. eSports is the name given to competitive contests of traditional video games that might be accessed on a computer, a PlayStation, or an Xbox. They are skill-based games that can be multiparty and feature head-to-head play by individual contestants or teams, either in a tournament setting or online. This type of social entertainment has become increasingly popular as a test of strategy, reflexes, and coordination of team members. Some of the titles of such games that have been played competitively in this milieu are *League of Legends*, *Fortnite*, *Counter-Strike*, and *Dota 2*. With the competitive play of professional video gamers has come fan adoration and sanctioned tournaments, and with sanctioned tournaments have come the potential of wagering.

According to Newzoo, a leading eSports data site, "the global eSports economy will grow to $905.6 million, a year-on-year growth of 38%," and "consumer spending on tickets and merchandise will total $96 million."[96] More importantly, "the global eSports audience will reach 380 million this year, made up of 165 million eSports enthusiasts and 215 million occasional viewers."[97] There are tournaments with substantial prize pools on the pro circuits[98] to enhance the excitement and arena attendance at some of these contests has exceeded 40,000.

eSports wagering on the outcome of a pro contest is currently permitted at sports books in Nevada on a case-by-case basis because the 2017 legislature added the words "or other event" to authorized forms of wagering in its pari-mutuel wagering statutes and regulations.[99] Currently, bets have been allowed only on game outcomes, but as the statistical information about past performances of the eSports professional contestants becomes more accessible and reliable, other betting propositions may be approved.

Additionally, for security purposes, an information-sharing memorandum has been entered into between Nevada regulators and the game manufacturer's watchdog, ESIC (eSports Integrity Coalition). Other jurisdictions, such as Isle of Man and Malta, have also approved some form of eSports or skill-based wagering. Contrarily, the State of Maryland is considering a bill for eSports that would remove it from their gaming statutes.[100] It would require video game contests to eliminate random events in the game, making these head-to-head contests skill-based only.

---

96. *Global 2018 Esports Market Report*, Newzoo, https://newzoo.com/insights/trend-reports/global-esports-market-report-2018-light/.

97. *Id.*

98. Epic Games' *Fortnite* announced a $100 million prize pool for its pro circuit, *Dota 2* offered a $24 million prize for its 2017 championship, *League of Legends* paid $5 million for its 2017 championship (some of which was raised by crowdfunding), and Blizzard Games' *Overwatch* received a pledge of $3.5 million for its championship.

99. Nevada Senate Bill 240 (2017) and Regulation 22.010, 22.120.

100. David Jahng, *Bill Proposed to Define and Allow eSports in Maryland*, AP News (Jan. 31, 2019), https://www.apnews.com/c604ecc67cdb480eb4aec01e388cdc72.

Although there are still issues for the gambling component of eSports, such as competitive integrity, underage wagering, and gambling addiction, casinos—anxious to tap into a market of younger millennials of gambling age—are looking to stage events at their properties that will enhance the customers' social experience and take gaming to the next level.

Chapter 2

What Is Gambling?

Karl Rutledge and Glenn Light

I. INTRODUCTION

The United States operates under a dual-sovereign system with both federal and state governance. Under this framework, the U.S. Constitution and federal law are the supreme law of the land and thus generally circumscribe the laws in the fifty states. The federal government, however, has not traditionally played a major role in the regulation of gaming. Instead, gaming regulation has been viewed as being the province of state and local jurisdictions with enforcement responsibilities primarily left to the individual states. With the notable exception of laws governing sports wagering,[1] federal criminal law serves to assist individual states in enforcing their gambling laws by giving concurrent jurisdiction to federal law enforcement to police and prosecute multistate and international gambling operations. Most federal restrictions, therefore, merely prohibit gambling activities in states where such activities are already illegal under state law. State law is therefore key in assessing gambling activities.

There is general agreement among states as to a common law definition of gambling, one that prohibited only those activities in which a person pays consideration—usually cash—for the opportunity to win a prize in a game of chance.[2] That is, gambling involves any activity in which the following elements are present: (1) the award of a prize, (2) determined on the basis of chance or a future contingent event outside the user's control, and (3) where consideration must be paid.

If an activity is structured so as to remove one of these three elements, it will not be considered gambling. Also, in some instances, states can authorize and regulate chance-based gambling activities (e.g., poker, slots, and other casino games) that

---

1. Interstate Wire Act of 1961, 18 U.S.C. § 1084 (2018); Professional and Amateur Sports Protection Act, 28 U.S.C. §§ 3701-3704 (2018) *declared unconstitutional by* Murphy v. NCAA, 138 S. Ct. 1461 (2018).
2. *See, e.g.*, F.C.C. v. Am. Broad. Co., 347 U.S. 284, 289–91 (1954) (subsequently distinguished on different grounds); *see also* Commonwealth v. Plissner, 4 N.E.2d 241, 244–45 (Mass. 1936) (holding similarly).

would otherwise be prohibited. The offering of such gambling games is highly regulated with numerous restrictions on the types of activities that can be conducted as well as who can conduct them. Offering gambling games without scrupulous adherence to these restrictions, not having proper licensure, or offering unapproved gambling games is unlawful and subjects the operator to criminal penalties.

In contrast to activities that constitute gambling, sweepstakes, skill-based contests, and prizeless casino games are generally lawful. Specifically, if any of these three elements—prize, chance, or consideration—of gambling are missing, then the activity is generally allowed under state law. Moreover, such offerings generally do not require licensure to operate.[3]

Nevertheless, states differ in their analysis of these three elements. This chapter examines the elements that comprise gambling and how states analyze them. The discussion includes determining whether a promotion constitutes illegal gambling or whether it is a legal sweepstakes, and how contests of skill generally avoid prohibition because they do not constitute gambling. This latter situation will be our initial focus.

II. SKILL VS. CHANCE

Games of skill have long been differentiated from games of chance.[4] From carnival midways at local fairs to trivia contests, the opportunity to win prizes has long drawn the interest of both young and old. Local arcades extended these opportunities to the young with prize-redemption games where tickets were exchanged for trinkets. In the last two decades, the Internet has given rise to a new style of skill game, most notably with the boom in eSports contests. The basic issues surrounding the legality of eSports contests are no different than those of the simple games of the past, but the emergence of eSports rekindles antiquated, misunderstood, or clumsily applied laws.

True skill games generally avoid prohibition simply because they are not considered gambling.[5] Historically, contests of skill were considered to have social merit through their teaching of valuable talents.[6] Simply put, skill contests provide

---

3. A caveat to the general rule of an absence of licensure does exist for daily fantasy sports. Despite the argument that they are contests of skill, daily fantasy sports have been the recent focus of legislation in some states. As a result, in order to lawfully offer such contests in those states, operators now need to obtain licensure or register (depending on the state).

4. *See, e.g.*, State v. Am. Holiday Ass'n, 727 P.2d 807, 809–11 (Ariz. 1986) (describing how different jurisdictions have distinguished between games of chance and games of skill).

5. *See, e.g.*, COLO. REV. STAT. § 18-10-102(2)(a) (2016) (defining gambling as "risking any money, credit, deposit, or other thing of value for gain contingent in whole or in part upon lot, chance, the operation of a gambling device, or the happening or outcome of an event, including a sporting event, over which the person taking a risk has no control, but does not include bona fide contests of skill . . . in which awards are made only to entrants or the owners of entries").

6. Anthony N. Cabot, Glenn J. Light, & Karl F. Rutledge, *Alex Rodriguez, a Monkey and the Game of Scrabble: The Hazard of Using Illogic to Define the Legality of Games of Mixed Skill and Chance*, 57 DRAKE L. REV. 383, 389 (2009) (citing *Am. Holiday Ass'n*, 727 P.2d at 812).

motivation to excel at a particular activity or sport. Trivia contests and history competitions stress academics, while photograph competitions encourage development of photography skills. These tests, whether of physical abilities, academics, or traits of skill, have become historically intertwined with U.S. culture.[7] As noted by the Arizona Supreme Court in 1986:

> Paying an entrance fee in order to participate in a game of skill . . . in the hope of winning prize money guaranteed by some sponsor to successful participants, is a traditional part of American social life. . . . [W]e are reluctant to adopt a statutory interpretation which would turn sponsors of golf, tennis or bridge tournaments, rodeos, livestock, poultry, and produce exhibitions, track meets, spelling bees, beauty contests, and the like into class 6 felons. . . .[8]

To accommodate this variety of socially acceptable, skill-based contests, a common law definition of gambling arose in the United States that prohibited only those activities in which a person pays consideration for the opportunity to win a prize in a game of chance. The challenge for states, however, is that most games have *some* element of chance. For instance, even chess—a game widely considered to be one purely of skill—nevertheless has an element of chance in selecting who moves first.[9] Accordingly, states have developed different tests for distinguishing skill and chance games.

A. Tests for Distinguishing Skill and Chance Games

1. Predominance Test

Most states use the predominance test,[10] also known as the *dominant factor test*, which focuses on whether the element of skill in a particular game predominates over chance. If it does, the game is permitted. That is, the presence of skill becomes significant only when skill predominates over chance.

To understand this test, one must "envision a continuum with pure skill on one end and pure chance on the other."[11] Games of pure skill, like chess (notwithstanding the luck of the initial draw), are legal, while games of pure chance such as roulette are illegal. However, between these ends of the spectrum lie many activities containing both elements of skill and chance. In this area, a legal risk is present because a question exists as to where a game of mixed skill and chance lies on the continuum.

---

7. *Id.*
8. *Am. Holiday Ass'n*, 727 P.2d at 812 (citations omitted).
9. *See* Rob Weir, *First Move Advantage in Chess* (Jan. 24, 2014), https://www.robweir.com/blog/2014/01/first-move-advantage-in-chess.html (stating that it has "long been known that players moving first have a slight advantage 'due to their ability to develop their pieces faster and their greater ability to coax the opening phase of the game toward a system that they prefer'").
10. *See, e.g.*, Wis. Stat. § 945.01(1) (2018) ("A bet is a bargain in which the parties agree that, dependent upon chance even though accompanied by some skill, one stands to win or lose something of value specified in the agreement. . . .").
11. Cabot et al., *supra* note 6, at 390.

In applying the predominance test, courts ask whether "player skill" or "uncontrollable chance" is the more likely factor influencing the outcome of a contest.[12] Stated another way:

> If the result of the distribution is to be determined solely by skill or judgment, the scheme is not a lottery, even though the result is uncertain or may be affected by things unforeseen and accidental. Where elements both of skill and of chance enter into a contest, the determination of its character as a lottery or not is generally held to depend on which is the dominating element.[13]

By way of an illustration, if skill determines 51 percent of the results and chance determines 49 percent, then one would expect a skilled player to win over a non-skilled player 51 percent plus one half of 49 percent, or 75.5 percent of the time. Contrast this with a game where the outcome is determined 1 percent of the time by skill and 99 percent of the time by chance. In a single trial, a skilled player is expected to win 1 percent plus one half of 99 percent, or 50.5 percent of the time. Because the predominance test requires skill to have the dominant influence in determining a result, a skilled player winning an average of just more than 50 percent of the games would arguably be insufficient. Rather, the expected average win percentage should be much higher (the aforementioned 75.5 percent) if the game itself is greater than 50 percent skill. If an operator can demonstrate such a win rate by skilled competitors, a strong defense that the contests are ones of skill could be made.

2. The Material Element Test

The predominance test is not the only test states use in determining the skill vs. chance issue. In a few states, either by statute or common law, courts will find a particular game to be unlawful if it contains chance as a material element impacting the outcome of the game.[14] For example, an Alabama statute defines a contest of chance as "[a]ny contest, game, gaming scheme or gaming device in which the outcome depends in a material degree upon an element of chance, notwithstanding that skill of the contestants may also be a factor therein."[15]

The material element test recognizes that although skill may *primarily* influence the outcome, if chance has more than an incidental impact on the game, the chance element of gambling is satisfied.[16] This test is not as easily quantifiable as the predominance test. Specifically, the material element standard lacks the mathematical bright line of the dominant factor test and replaces it with a test that depends upon a court's, or jury's, judgment of when the outcome of a contest is "materially

---

12. *Id.* at 391.
13. *Id.*
14. *Id.* at 392.
15. Ala. Code § 13A-12-20(3) (2018); *see also* N.Y. Penal Law § 225.00(1) and (2) (2018) (providing that a person "engages in gambling" when "he stakes or risks something of value upon the outcome of a contest of chance," with "contest of chance" defined as a contest or game "in which the outcome depends on a material degree upon an element of chance").
16. Cabot et al., *supra* note 6, at 393.

affected" by chance. Consequently, this is inherently a subjective test that offers little predictability for those wanting to offer contests.

3. Any Chance Test

In a small number of states, courts determine the element of chance by asking whether a particular game or contest contains *any* chance affecting the outcome.[17] As virtually every activity has some element of chance, few skill games can survive scrutiny in states applying this test. For instance, even a trivia contest when offered in a multiple-choice format (e.g., five possible answers) has a chance element. Here, even a completely unskilled person has a 20 percent chance of selecting the correct answer.

4. Gambling Instinct Test

Finally, in a small number of states, the role of skill or chance is irrelevant and wagering on a game or contest is unlawful if the nature of the activity appeals to one's "gambling instinct."[18] Thus, the focus of this test is to ignore skill and chance and to somehow determine whether the activity appeals to a person's gambling instinct.[19]

For example, in *City of Milwaukee v. Burns*, the court, in condemning pinball machines as gambling devices, held:

> The machine makes an appeal to the gambling instinct, because the player has constantly before him the chance that the next play will assure him of the right on the next succeeding play to secure from 2 to 20 checks. Were it not for this appeal to the gambling instinct, these machines, which attempt to adhere to the letter of the law while violating its spirit, would never have been placed upon the market.[20]

B. Defining Skill and Chance

The meaning of the words *skill* and *chance* is not always obvious and may require definition. The Alabama Supreme Court, for example, defined *skill* as "merely the exercise, upon known rules and fixed probabilities, of 'sagacity,' which is in turn defined as 'quickness or acuteness of sense perceptions; keenness of discernment or penetration with soundness of judgment; shrewdness; [the] ability to see what is relevant and significant.'"[21]

---

17. Anthony N. Cabot & Louis V. Csoka, *Fantasy Sports: One Form of Mainstream Wagering in the United States*, 40 J. Marshall L. Rev. 1195, 1205 (2007) ("Under the Any Chance Test, if the contest contains any element of chance, however small, wagering on such contest is always prohibited as gambling."); *see, e.g.*, Tenn. Code. Ann. § 39-17-501 (2018) ("Gambling is contrary to the public policy of this state and means risking anything of value for a profit whose return is to any degree contingent on chance. . . .").
18. Cabot et al., *supra* note 6, at 393.
19. *Id.*
20. City of Milwaukee v. Burns, 274 N.W. 273, 275 (Wis. 1937).
21. *See* Opinion of the Justices No. 358, 692 So. 2d 107, 111 (Ala. 1997) (quoting Webster's New International Dictionary 2198 [2d ed. 1953]).

In contrast, "'chance' eludes precise definition."[22] The term *chance* was analyzed in *State v. Lindsay* in the context of a lottery.[23] That case involved the operator of a popularity contest under which merchants issued ballots to customers, entitling customers to vote for any person.[24] The court found the operator was not guilty of operating a lottery prohibited by statute, since the element of chance was lacking. Specifically, the court, using *Webster's New International Dictionary*, concluded that chance should be understood as "an unforeseen or inexplicable cause or its operation; accident; as to happen by chance."[25] In other words, chance is the opposite of something that is planned or designed.[26]

Chance is not, however, a concept that can be expressed simply. Rather, there are various types of chance, and courts have struggled to differentiate and determine the relevance of these variations.

C. Types of Chance

The most common type of chance is systemic. Systemic chance exists where the game itself has random elements created either by a random number generator in a computer program or some other random event, such as a dice throw, ball draw, or card shuffle. In Scrabble, for example, systemic chance is the random selection of tiles. In poker, it is the shuffle and deal of the cards.

A second type of chance involves imperfect knowledge or information. This occurs where the outcome of a game is not solely determined by skill but is also influenced by information that can impact game results that is not known by the contestants. This type of chance can occur even where the players have identical "draws" but otherwise have imperfect knowledge—particularly where they need to make decisions based on unexposed icons, symbols, or an absence of information.

A straightforward illustration of the imperfect information type of chance is the game of rock, paper, and scissors. While the game does not have systemic chance, imperfect information is present since players need to make decisions based on the absence of information. Each player must act simultaneously and thus acts without knowledge as to the other player's choice of rock, paper, or scissors. This is in contrast to chess, where players move sequentially and have complete information regarding the factors that can impact the outcome. After a player moves in chess, the game board is instantaneously updated, there are no undisclosed facts regarding the status of the match, and the opposing player can make a skilled and knowledgeable response.

---

22. *FCC Attacks Radio Give-Away Programs*, 1 Stan. L. Rev. 475, 482 (1949).
23. State v. Lindsay, 2 A.2d 201, 203–04 (Vt. 1938).
24. *Id.*
25. *Id.* at 203 (quoting Webster's New International Dictionary 2198 [2d ed. 1953]).
26. *Id.*

Other forms of chance may exist. One example is a game designed to negate skill by making the skill levels beyond the participants' capabilities. For example, if a multiple-choice test on quantum physics was administered to ordinary eight-year-olds, the test results would be based on pure guesswork rather than the skill of the participants.

D. Question of Fact

Ultimately, in any jurisdiction that distinguishes games of chance from skill contests, the determination as to whether a game is one of skill or chance is not a question of law but one of fact.[27] The operator would need to convince a fact-finder, such as a jury, that the game's skill levels meet the applicable standard used in the state.

Because the skill vs. chance issue will be decided on a case-by-case basis by a fact-finder, different states applying the same test can often come to opposite decisions in evaluating games of mixed skill and chance. For example, compare *Commonwealth v. Plissner*,[28] a Massachusetts case that upheld jury instructions that allowed jurors to conclude that the "crane game" was a game of chance under the dominant factor test, with a Kansas attorney general opinion concluding that "crane games" are games of skill under the dominant factor test.[29]

Therefore, the decision on the skill vs. chance issue can be significantly affected by the quality of evidence presented, the experience and qualifications of counsel, and the experience, qualifications, and biases of the triers of fact. Indeed, the variances in decisions involving the same game or contest is often attributable to these factors.[30]

III. CONSIDERATION ELEMENT

The second key element to determining whether an activity constitutes gambling is consideration. Consideration, a well-known concept in contract law, has been defined as that which is given to induce a promise or performance in return.[31] Determining what constitutes consideration in gambling settings has presented some subtle issues for courts. Over time they have developed three major theories of consideration in addressing gambling cases: the simple contract consideration test, the promoter benefit test, and the economic value test.[32]

---

27. People v. Mason, 68 Cal. Rptr. 17, 21 (Dist. Ct. App. 1968) ("Whether a pinball machine is a game of skill or chance is largely a question of fact.").
28. Commonwealth v. Plissner, 4 N.E.2d 241, 245 (Mass. 1936).
29. Kan. Op. Att'y Gen. No. 87-140 (Sept. 18, 1987), 1987 WL 290378.
30. *See* Mason, 68 Cal. Rptr. at 21.
31. Affiliated Enter. v. Waller, 5 A.2d 257, 259 (Del. Super. Ct. 1939). *See* Restatement (Second) of Contracts §§ 71(1), 71(2) (Am. Law. Inst. 1981). Consideration can consist of either a benefit to the promisor or a detriment to the promisee. First Mortgage Co. v. Fed. Leasing Corp., 456 A.2d 794, 795–96 (Del. 1982).
32. Anthony N. Cabot et al., *Economic Value, Equal Dignity and the Future of Sweepstakes*, 1 UNLV Gaming L.J. 1, 6 (2010).

A. Tests for Analyzing Consideration

1. Simple Contract Consideration Test

Historically, the simple contract consideration test has served as the standard for evaluating consideration in gambling settings.[33] Under this test, courts found sufficient consideration in a gambling context if the consideration could support a simple contract.[34] That is, either a detriment to the patron or a benefit to the promoter acts as sufficient consideration. Consequently, consideration "need not consist of money or something of actual pecuniary value, but could consist of an act done at the request of the holder of the lottery if that act is one bargained for by the holder of the lottery."[35]

A well-known case that illustrates how a benefit can constitute consideration is *Beck v. Fox Kansas Theatre*.[36] This case involved a promotion in which a theater gave raffle tickets to both paying customers and anyone else who asked.[37] The court held that even though free raffle tickets were provided to anyone who asked, the mere design of the promotion to stimulate demand for a product was sufficient to be consideration.[38] Consequently, the court determined the promotion constituted an illegal lottery.[39]

A series of older cases in Washington further demonstrate the operation of the simple contract consideration approach. In *Seattle Times Co. v. Tielsch*, the Supreme Court of Washington examined a newspaper contest based on football forecasting where contestants filled out forms printed in the newspaper. The contestant who submitted twenty correct predictions received $10,000, and the week's high scorer was paid $100. The court ruled that this contest constituted an illegal lottery.[40] The court explained that while the contestants did not purchase chances, they were nonetheless required to "do something" for the chance to win.[41] The fact that the "something" that contestants were required to do was pleasurable was not important to the court. In fact, the court ruled that the opinion of the participant regarding whether he has given up anything of value was not determinative.[42] The court stated, "[I]f the participant is required to do something which he might not otherwise do, and if there is in fact a benefit flowing to the promoter . . . consideration is met."[43]

---

33. *Id. See also* State v. Eckerd's Suburban, Inc., 164 A.2d 873, 875 (Del. 1960); State *ex rel.* Beck v. Fox Kansas Theatre Co., 62 P.2d 929, 934 (Kan. 1936); Lucky Calendar Co. v. Cohen, 117 A.2d 487, 495 (N.J. 1955) (citing Maine v. Bussiere, 154 A.2d 702, 705 [Me. 1959]); Dorman v. Publix-Saenger-Sparks Theatres, 184 So. 886 (Fla. 1938).
34. Cabot et al., *supra* note 32, at 6 (citing Mark B. Wessman, *Is "Contract" the Name of the Game? Promotional Games as Test Cases for Contract Theory*, 34 ARIZ. L. REV. 635, 652 (1992); *see also, e.g.*, Blackburn v. Ippolito, 156 So. 2d 550, 552–53 (Fla. Dist. Ct. App. 1963).
35. *State v. Eckerd's Suburban, Inc., supra* note 33.
36. State *ex rel.* Beck v. Fox Kansas Theatre Co., 62 P.2d 929 (Kan. 1936).
37. *Id.* at 932.
38. *Id.* at 937.
39. *Id.*
40. Seattle Times Co. v. Tielsch, 495 P.2d 1366, 1370 (Wash. 1972).
41. *Id.* at 1369.
42. *Id.*
43. *Id.*

Similarly, in *State v. Readers' Digest Assoc., Inc.*, the Supreme Court of Washington considered whether a mail-in sweepstakes promoted by *Reader's Digest* (a scheme that had significantly increased Reader's Digest's sales) was an illegal lottery.[44] The court concluded that the sweepstakes did constitute a lottery and that the consumer's effort in reviewing the literature and selecting the free method for entering the contest constituted consideration.[45] The court stated:

> [T]he Sweepstakes does not require a trip to the store to secure an entry form. That difference, however, is not sufficient to distinguish the cases. The store visit, standing alone, was not the detriment to the participant that produced the benefit to Safeway. More critical was the participant's expenditure of time, thought, attention and energy in pursuing Safeway's advertisements.[46]

Opinions from the Washington attorney general provide further insight on the simple contract consideration issue. For example, in one opinion, the attorney general was asked whether, at an opening for a bank branch, the bank could conduct a drawing for a free TV if no purchase was necessary, anyone could register, and the winner did not need to be present for the drawing.[47] The attorney general stated that an analysis would need to be made of the benefit, if any, the bank would receive to determine if the element of consideration had been met.[48]

In short, courts following the simple contract consideration test consider virtually any inconvenience to the patron entering a promotion as a sufficient detriment to constitute consideration. Not only does this capture a requirement that you must be present to win, but it also could capture compliance with the rules of the promotion. It is common for jurisdictions that use this test to have antigambling laws that "are designed to prevent other evils incident to the operation of schemes of chance, such as the general excitement of the gambling instinct and the purchase of luxuries that might not otherwise be bought."[49]

2. Promoter Benefit Test

Another test used to determine the consideration element for gambling is known as the "promoter benefit" test. This approach, frequently used by courts in the 1960s

---

44. State v. Reader's Digest Assn., 501 P.2d 290, 294 (Wash. 1970).
45. *Id*. at 297.
46. *Id*.
47. Wash. Atty. Gen. Op. No. 51, 1971 WL 122969 (Mar. 24, 1971).
48. *Id*. at 3 (citing *Schillberg v. Safeway Store, Inc.,* 450 P.2d 949 [Wash. 1969]).
49. Cabot et al., *supra* note 32, at 7 (citing Note, *Bank Night and Similar Devices as Illegal Lotteries*, 50 Yale L.J. 941, 946 [1940–1941]); *See also* State *ex inf*. McKittrick v. Globe-Democrat Pub. Co., 110 S.W.2d 705, 713 (Mo. 1937); State *ex rel*. Home Planners Depository v. Hughes, 253 S.W. 229, 231 (Mo. 1923); State v. Becker, 154 S.W. 769, 771 (Mo. 1913); State *ex rel*. Hunter v. Fox Beatrice Theatre Corp., 275 N.W. 605, 606 (Neb. 1937); State v. Schwemler, 60 P.2d 938, 939 (Or. 1936); Charles Pickett, *Contests and the Lottery Laws*, 45 Harv. L. Rev. 1196, 1205 (1932) ("The theory behind lottery laws is that people should be protected from dissipating their money by gambling against odds which usually are not fully appreciated.").

and early 1970s, focuses on the economic benefit received by the promoter.[50] As one court stated, the element of consideration is satisfied when "a class of persons who, in addition to receiving or being entitled to chances on prizes, supply consideration for all the chances in bulk by purchasing whatever the promoter is selling, whether the purchasers were required to do so or not under the wording of the promoter's rules."[51] In other words, whether the valuable consideration comes from one or all participants is irrelevant. Instead, the focus is on whether the promoter has derived a direct economic benefit from any of the participants.

In *State v. Schubert Theatre Players Co.*, the court held that a "free" ticket for a chance at a prize given with the purchase of each theater show ticket was not in fact free because the purchase price was for both the admission and the chance.[52] While the court noted "a person may distribute or give away his property or money by lot or chance provided he does so without a consideration," evidence that anyone could get the tickets for free was immaterial because "the moment some pay for the chance of participating in the drawing of the prize it is a lottery under the law, no matter how many receive a chance to also participate free and without any consideration."[53] To determine if the promotion was a lottery, the court focused on whether any economic benefit had flowed to the promoter through the operation of the drawing.[54] The *Schubert Theatre* case's emphasis on the fact that a promotion game may increase the patronage of a business, even though a vast majority of the participants in the game did not make purchases, further dilutes the consideration requirement.

In short, under the promoter benefit test, a game does not cease to be a lottery because some of the players were allowed to play for free, so long as others continued to pay for their chances.[55] If it is a lottery as to those who pay, it is necessarily a lottery as to those who do not pay for their chances.[56]

3. Economic Value Test

The last several decades have seen the simple contract consideration and promoter benefit tests diminish in importance. The approach that has gained favor is called the "economic value" test. An important reason for this shift is the Supreme Court's 1954 decision in *FCC v. American Broadcasting Co.*, where the Court differentiated

---

50. Cabot et al., *supra* note 32, at 6 (citing Boyd v. Piggly Wiggly S., Inc., 155 S.E.2d 630, 637 (Ga. Ct. App. 1967) (quoting Whitley v. McConnell, 66 S.E. 933 (Ga. 1910))); Winn-Dixie Stores, Inc. v. Boatright, 155 S.E.2d 642 (Ga. Ct. App. 1967); Idea Research & Dev. Corp. v. Hultman & Cent. Broad. Co., 131 N.W.2d 496, 510 (Iowa 1964); Smith v. State, 127 S.W.2d 297, 299 (Tex. Crim. App. 1939); Featherstone v. Indep. Serv. Station Ass'n of Texas et al., 10 S.W.2d 124, 127 (Tex. App. 1928); State *ex rel.* Schillberg v. Safeway Stores, Inc., 450 P.2d 949, 955–56 (Wash. 1969); 61 Wis. Op. Att'y Gen. 405 (1972).
51. *Boyd*, 155 S.E.2d at 632.
52. State v. Schubert Theatre Players Co., 281 N.W. 369, 370–71 (Minn. 1938).
53. *Id.* at 370.
54. *Id.*
55. State v. Razorback Room, Inc., No. 91-7596 (Pulaski Co. Ch., 6th Div., Sept. 29, 1992).
56. *Id.* (internal citations omitted); *see also* F.A.C.E. Trading, Inc. v. Dep't of Consumer & Indus. Serv., 717 N.W.2d 377, 386 (Mich. Ct. App. 2006).

consideration for contract purposes from consideration related to gambling situations.[57] In the *FCC* case, the court considered whether sufficient consideration existed for a promotional activity to become an illegal lottery when the activity required only that listeners accept a phone call from the radio station.[58] While listening to the radio may be sufficient consideration to support a contract, Chief Justice Earl Warren explained that the lottery laws' consideration element in a criminal context should be more rigorously interpreted in a defendant's favor.[59] Warren cautioned "that it would be stretching the statute to the breaking point to give it an interpretation that would make such programs a crime."[60] The *FCC* case thus became the basis for departing from contract law's definition of consideration for gaming law purposes.

The rationale of the economic value test is that consideration requires some measurable economic value flowing from the participant to the promoter. In other words, consideration "means something of value and not merely the formal or technical consideration, such as registering one's name or attending a certain place, which might be sufficient consideration to support a contract."[61] Rather, the consideration requirement is met only when the participant must provide something of economic value. The benefit an operator receives generally from a promotional scheme is insufficient.

The provision of consideration does not, however, have to be a direct payment for entry into the sweepstakes (i.e., buying a drawing ticket). A promotion that requires participants to buy a product or service to enter also constitutes consideration, since the only way to enter the promotion is to buy a product or service.

In *State v. Cox*, a 1960 Montana Supreme Court case, the court held that the requirement to purchase an item to gain entry into the contest resulted in the patron necessarily suffering a pecuniary loss.[62] In *Cox*, a grocery store hosted a "Chinese lottery," where people received numbered cards for a drawing whenever they made a purchase at a grocery store.[63] The court found the lottery unlawful because participants suffered a pecuniary detriment—purchasing goods—as a condition to being eligible for the drawing.[64] It did not matter to the court that participants received value for the payment for the groceries purchased and that customers did not have to pay an additional charge to participate.

A limitation to this standard is that the economic value given by the participant must be more than an incidental amount paid to a third party to facilitate the entry into the promotion. A participant does not provide consideration where

---

57. FCC v. American Broadcasting Co., 347 U.S. 284 (1954).
58. *Id.* at 285.
59. *Id.* at 294.
60. *Id.*
61. Mobil Oil Corp. v. Att'y Gen., 280 N.E.2d 406, 411 (Mass. 1972) (quoting Commonwealth v. Heffner, 24 N.E.2d 508, 508–09 [Mass. 1939]).
62. State v. Cox, 349 P.2d 104, 106–07 (Mont. 1960).
63. *Id.* at 105.
64. *Id.* at 106.

some nominal amount is paid to a third party, such as the cost of postage or fees for Internet service, to enter a sweepstakes.[65] But disguising entry fees as telephone or text message charges that accrue to the benefit of the sweepstakes promoter may be problematic. An example of this could be a rate arrangement in which a cellular carrier shares the fees received from the customer with the sweepstakes promoter. Regardless of whether the actual fee charged to the customer is less than the cost of postage, this arrangement creates potential legal risk because both aspects of the economic value test are met: the customer is paying something of value, money, and that money is at least partially accruing to the promoter's benefit.

Legal ambiguity may exist under the economic value test when a promotion requires participants to expend some degree of effort that ultimately benefits the promoter. For example, in more traditional sweepstakes, efforts by participants can include mailing in an entry form, calling a toll-free number, visiting a store, or completing a product questionnaire. The advent of the Internet has brought new twists to older concepts of promotions.

The interactive nature of the Internet allows promoters to run sweepstakes that are supported by third-party advertisers. The promoters can derive revenues from the sale of information received from participants in the sweepstakes through questionnaires and data mining. In these instances, participants provide information to the promoter that can be sold to others who hope to market their products to a certain demographic identified during the information-gathering stage of the sweepstakes.

In addition, sweepstakes and contests requiring user-generated content are becoming more common. For example, a participant in a contest may need to provide some content as a condition of entry, such as a drawing or a song. While some portion of the contest may be judged on skill, winners can be picked randomly among finalists.

Neither federal nor state law specifies how much effort the consumer must expend before the activity crosses the consideration line. Generally, the more effort required, the greater the likelihood it will be deemed consideration. This is an issue that needs to be closely monitored, as some courts may hold certain information valuable enough to amount to consideration. When there is a considerable amount of data that could be mined with current technology and subsequently sold, an entrant's authorization for a company to access personal data could possibly be deemed sufficient consideration.

---

65. Haskell v. Time, Inc., 857 F. Supp. 1392, 1404 (E.D. Cal. 1994) provides:

Plaintiff concedes that no purchase is required to enter defendants' sweepstakes, but instead asserts that the payment of twenty-nine cents postage is "valuable consideration." This assertion is untenable. The California Supreme Court has held that a requirement that a sweepstakes entrant deposit the entry form at the sponsor's place of business is not "valuable consideration" sufficient to state a cause of action under California law (citing California Gas Retailers v. Regal Petroleum Corp., 50 Cal.2d 844, 861–62, 330 P.2d 778 [1958]).

B. Removing Consideration

Removing the element of consideration from a prohibited gambling activity generally converts the activity to a sweepstakes. A sweepstakes always contains the elements of chance and the award of a prize, but the element of consideration is absent. Consequently, an essential ingredient of gambling is not present. Two methods of removing consideration are common: making participation completely free, and providing a free alternative method of entry.

1. Completely Free to Participate

Under the first method, the operator does not charge any participants to enter the sweepstakes. Promoters have a myriad of reasons to hold such a sweepstakes. In many instances, the promoter hopes that the sweepstakes will assist in branding itself or creating customer traffic. The increased sales of goods created by the advertising value of the sweepstakes drives an operator's revenues up.

In other circumstances, the promoter may use the sweepstakes to benefit the branding of third parties who in turn pay the promoter. For example, there are many permanent sweepstakes websites where the prizes for the chance-based games are provided by sponsors who advertise on the sites. The games are typically a traditional raffle or instant-win promotion but also can extend to any game of chance, including casino-style gaming.

The underlying idea behind these sites is that the sweepstakes will help build a sponsor's brand while letting users play completely for free. Regardless of whether the promoter is using the sweepstakes for its own products or services or to promote third-party products or services, where no participants pay to enter, consideration does not exist under the economic value test.

2. Free Alternative Method of Entry

A second sweepstakes model allows participants to enter either by paying indirect consideration through the purchase of a good or service, or by using a free alternative method of entry (AMOE) by which they can enter the promotion. Common examples of popular AMOEs are distribution at point-of-purchase, mail-in entries, or entries through a toll-free telephone number. One of the more recognizable illustrations of a promotion using the AMOE model is that used by fast-food restaurants. Participants receive game pieces in exchange for purchasing hamburgers or soft drinks. These game pieces, either by themselves or in combination, provide an opportunity for the purchaser to win valuable prizes in lottery-type games.

The key feature of this promotion that distinguishes it from illegal gambling is the alternative opportunity to participate without having to purchase anything. As explained by a Kentucky attorney general opinion discussing a "no purchase necessary" beverage promotion:

> [T]he mere fact that some of the participants in a promotional scheme in fact make purchases of the sponsor's products does not, in and of itself, constitute consideration

supporting a lottery, where chances to participate in the scheme are also freely given away on a reasonably equal basis without respect to the purchase of merchandise. These schemes, known as "flexible participation" schemes, are not to be confused with "closed participation" gift enterprise schemes, which are open only to patrons purchasing goods, services or whatever the promoter is trying to push by the scheme.[66]

Since a participant in a sweepstakes with an AMOE does not have to give up valuable consideration to play, games that offer a free method of entry do not meet the requirements of the economic value test.[67] Thus, courts in jurisdictions that apply the economic value test have ruled that a free method of entry negates consideration. For example, in *California Gasoline Retailers v. Regal Petroleum Corp.*, the California Supreme Court held that a promotional scheme lacked consideration because it included a free method of entry that allowed participants to play without purchasing the sponsor's products.[68] The court commented that because anyone could have the ability to participate for free, "it would seem that the relative numbers of tickets distributed with purchases or without purchases should not be determinative of the issue involved which is whether the holder, or holders, of the tickets paid, or promised to pay a valuable consideration for the chance of winning a prize."[69] The court reasoned that the participants who made a purchase "could not be said to have paid a consideration for the prize tickets since they could have received them free."[70]

3. Equal Dignity

Most state sweepstakes laws require operators to disclose the no-purchase method of entry in a clear and conspicuous manner. Often the phrases *no purchase necessary* and *purchase will not increase your chances of winning* are displayed prominently on the offering and on all accompanying sweepstakes materials.

The concept of "equal dignity" has been frequently addressed by courts. This principle requires equal treatment of paying and nonpaying participants. As the Kentucky attorney general noted above, a sweepstakes must treat nonpaying entries on an equal basis as paying participants in order to negate consideration.[71] Several aspects of the equal dignity concept have been identified, including method of entry, opportunity to win, claiming prizes, and prizes awarded.[72]

At a fundamental level, these principles taken together require that nonpaying participants have an equal opportunity to enter and win the sweepstakes, just as the paying participants do. Any obstacles that would prevent them having an equal

---

66. Ky. Att'y Gen. Op., 81-259, 2-799, 2-801 (1981).
67. *See* Cudd v. Aschenbrenner, 377 P.2d 150, 155 (Or. 1962).
68. Cal. Gasoline Retailers v. Regal Petroleum Corp. of Fresno, 330 P.2d 778, 782, 789 (Cal. 1958).
69. *Id.* at 786.
70. *Id.* (quoting People v. Carpenter, 297 P.2d 498, 500-01 [Cal. Ct. App. 1956]).
71. Ky. Att'y Gen. Op., 81-259, 2-799, 2-801 (1981).
72. *See generally* Cabot & Csoka, *supra* note 17, at 238–39.

chance to win any of the prizes offered would violate the equal dignity rule. Ultimately, whether a method of free entry is unreasonably burdensome is a question of fact.[73]

For example, the court in *Commonwealth v. Frate* upheld the conviction of an individual who set up a device whereby a person could insert a coin and win a prize but also could receive a chance to win a prize without making a purchase by mailing in a stamped, self-addressed envelope, and a 3 x 5 card with his name and address printed on it.[74] The court found the "cumbersome requirement to request free play by mail, rather than immediately on the site of the game machine itself . . . [to] pose a significant practical disadvantage to a player wishing to play for free as compared to a paying player."[75] This precluded a finding of equal dignity.

Similarly, a person who enters a contest by paying consideration cannot get a disproportionate number of entries compared to a nonpaying participant. This issue was addressed in *Animal Protection Soc. v. State*.[76] In that case, a charity offered a "free bingo" game by which persons buying items such as combs and candy received bingo cards.[77] Individuals who did not want to purchase such items also were given cards, but those buying items could receive more free cards than those who did not.[78] Ruling that the scheme violated state lottery laws, the court found the bingo game did not satisfy the equal dignity requirement, despite the fact players could obtain bingo cards without paying:

> This alone did not transform the bingo games offered by plaintiffs into "free bingo" since patrons who obtained the cards without making a purchase received fewer cards than patrons who did buy the items; thus, it follows that the other patrons had to pay to obtain a greater number of bingo cards.[79]

Also, customers cannot have the opportunity to win different or more expensive prizes. For example, separate prize pools may invalidate a sweepstakes because the nonpaying participants do not have the opportunity to win the same prizes as paying participants.

The problems of having separate prize pools is illustrated by *Classic Oldsmobile-Cadillac-GMC Truck, Inc. v. State*. Here, the court examined a promotion whereby new vehicle lessees of a specified four-week period could automatically receive

---

73. In *G.A. Carney, Ltd.*, the court suggested that consideration is absent where the chance to win is free, even if some participants win by making a purchase, if Illinois's interpretation of the Equal Dignity Rule is honored. G.A. Carney, Ltd. v. Brzeczek, 453 N.E.2d 756, 761 (Ill. App. Ct. 1983). This case, however, concluded that the existence of a free entry form is not dispositive and that a free entry should not be illusory. The court concluded "the obstacles to obtaining a free entry blank are so formidable, the publisher's offer of a free entry blank must be regarded as chimerical." The *G.A. Carney, Ltd.* court went on to indicate that "we do not inquire into the theoretical possibilities of the scheme, but . . . examine it in actual practical operation."
74. Commonwealth v. Frate, 537 N.E.2d 1235, 1235–36 n.1 (Mass. 1989).
75. Commonwealth v. Webb, 860 N.E.2d 967, 971 n.11 (Mass. App. Ct. 2007) (citing *Frate*, 537 N.E.2d at 1235–36).
76. Animal Prot. Soc'y of Durham, Inc. v. State, 382 S.E.2d 801, 802–3 (N.C. Ct. App. 1989).
77. *Id.*
78. *Id.* at 807.
79. *Id.*

twelve paid monthly lease payments from the dealership if the temperature at the Portland International Jetport reached or exceeded 96 degrees Fahrenheit on a later date.[80] The AMOE option of the promotion allowed persons who did not buy or lease vehicles to submit their name into a drawing during the same four-week period, and only one winner could receive $5,000 if the Portland International Jetport reached or exceeded 96°F on a later date.[81] In analyzing the promotion, the court "found that the plan involved two promotions—one for those who enter[ed] into a lease agreement and one for those who d[id] not."[82] That is, "[e]very lessee [would] win the lease payments if the temperature [was] reached. . . . [T]he other entrants [would have to] participate in a drawing in which only one [would] win."[83] In light of the preceding, the court concluded that the promotion constituted an unlawful game of chance.[84]

The most important points to remember about equal dignity are these: the no-purchase method of entry must be disclosed in a clear and conspicuous manner and any material disparity (actual or perceived) between paying and nonpaying entrants can invalidate the AMOE and render the sweepstakes illegal.

4. Thinly Veiled Lottery

Even when the requirements discussed above are satisfied, the legality of a contest may not be assured. Over the years, promoters have attempted to use the AMOE exception to devise schemes that prosecutors often describe as "a thinly veiled lottery."[85] This phrase is used when promoters attempt to make money not from the sale of a product unrelated to the sweepstakes but from paying customers desiring to win prizes in the sweepstakes.

One example of this is the "Lucky Shamrock" sweepstakes. The Lucky Shamrock emergency phone card was a one-minute or two-minute long-distance phone card, usually sold at market value, that also had a sweepstakes entry attached to it. The Lucky Shamrock emergency phone card dispensers came in two varieties: one that dispensed the cards with a pull tab sweepstakes entry and one that displayed the sweepstakes results in a display as the card was dispensed. Regardless of delivery and sales method, the Lucky Shamrock sweepstakes offered an alternative free method of entry (participants received one game piece each by sending postage-paid postcards or making written requests to the address on the side of the machine).[86]

Despite the existence of a free AMOE, legal challenges were brought asserting that operators were attempting to make money from paying customers desiring to

---

80. *Classic Oldsmobile-Cadillac-GMC Truck, Inc. v. State*, 704 A.2d 333, 333 (Me. 1997).
81. *Id.* at 334.
82. *Id.* (alteration in original).
83. *Id.* (alteration in original).
84. *Id.* at 335.
85. *Bohrer v. City of Milwaukee*, 635 N.W.2d 816, 819 (Wis. Ct. App. 2001).
86. *Midwestern Enterprises, Inc. v. Stenehjem*, 625 N.W.2d 234, 239 (N.D. 2001).

win prizes, as opposed to promoting a product unrelated to the sweepstakes. For example, the Illinois attorney general concluded that "although the [Lucky Shamrock sweepstakes] scheme has been carefully designed to appear to meet the criteria generally prescribed by the courts in approving giveaway schemes, a review of the underlying purpose of the scheme leads inexorably to the conclusion that the Lucky Shamrock sweepstakes is but a thinly veiled lottery."[87] In other words, even though the Lucky Shamrock sweepstakes was designed to avoid the consideration element by using an AMOE in a manner consistent with court opinions in Illinois, the Illinois attorney general found that it was an illegal gambling game.[88]

In similar situations, courts have focused on whether the products promoted had an independent and real value—that is, value that was not inflated for purposes of the activity. For example, in *F.A.C.E. Trading, Inc. v. Todd*, the court held that the winning coupons, Ad-Tabs, could not be used to buy products because they were retained by the retail establishment. As the court stated, "there is no evidence that the product discount parts of the Ad-Tab™ coupon cards were ever offered for sale independently of the instant win games."[89] In contrast, in *Mid-Atlantic Coca-Cola v. Chen*, the court found it significant that the soft drinks had a clear independent market value apart from the promotion and that value was not raised during the promotion.[90]

Accordingly, in addition to offering a free AMOE for promotions involving the purchase of a product or service, operators must also understand the importance of the product or service having a viable and independent market value. The more the promoted product (e.g., a McDonald's cheeseburger) has value independent of the sweepstakes entry, the less likely a court will take issue with the promotion.

IV. PRIZE ELEMENT

The final element of gambling is the awarding of a prize. As discussed earlier, if the elements of chance and prize are present but consideration is absent, a lawful sweepstakes exists. If the elements of consideration and prize are present but chance is eliminated, it is a lawful contest of skill. Finally, if the elements of consideration and chance are present but prize is eliminated, the thought was that the game may be legal but no one would want to play. However, in recent years, nontraditional prizes have become increasingly popular. These include offering extended play, avatars, the accumulation of points or poker chips for bragging rights, and similar items.

Which of these nontraditional items constitutes a prize for purposes of gambling? Typically, a prize requires the awarding of something of value. State gambling statutes, for example, may define gambling as risking "something of value upon the

---

87. Ill. Op. Att'y Gen. No. 98-010 (July 13, 1998).
88. *Id.*
89. F.A.C.E. Trading, Inc. v. Todd, 903 A.2d 348, 359 (Md. 2006).
90. Mid-Atlantic Coca-Cola v. Chen, 460 A.2d 44, 47 (Md. 1983).

outcome of a contest of chance or a future contingent event not under the [person's] control," with the goal of winning *something of value*.[91] The phrase *something of value* has been read to mean:

> Any money or property, any token, object or article exchangeable for money or property or any form of credit or promise directly or indirectly contemplating transfer of money or property or of any interest therein, or involving extension of a service entertainment or a privilege of playing at a game or scheme without charge.[92]

A Missouri statute has an almost identical definition of the phrase *something of value*.[93] Such provisions can have broad application.

This issue is rarely problematic in the physical realm. For instance, the awarding of cash, cars, or merchandise are all clearly items that have value. However, in the online world, what constitutes something of value is far murkier. For instance, does the awarding of virtual chips or other virtual items to the winners of a game constitute a prize?

In practice, the concept of whether virtual items have value is one that is subject to the vagaries of state law. Because of the novelty of the issue, certainty in the law is often lacking. Nevertheless, in cases involving the delivery of entertainment, there is support for the position that virtual items do not constitute something of value.

For example, in one Arkansas case, the court considered whether the visual reward from seeing a virtual person take off his or her clothes qualifies as a reward for gambling. The Supreme Court of Arkansas noted:

> [T]his court has never held that an *intangible reward*, such as viewing nudity, qualifies as a reward for gambling purposes. These countertop machines are more akin to video arcade machines intended for amusement, because a player inserts money and can play gambling-like games but never receives anything in return except amusement. We agree with the circuit court that these machines are not actually used for gaming due to the absence of any payoff mechanism or reward.[94]

Two fundamental questions exist when determining whether an item has value. The first is whether the item awarded has a market value. While noncash prizes such as cars or vacations are common, courts generally require prizes to have a reasonably determined value. Therefore, a difference exists between an honor, where one is crowned as a champion or receives an acknowledgment in the form of a virtual item, and a prize, where one receives goods or services that have a defined market value. The same distinction could apply to a virtual item that has functional

---

91. ALA. CODE § 13A-12-20(4) (2018) (emphasis added).
92. ALA. CODE § 13A-12-20(11) (2018).
93. MO. ANN. STAT. § 572.010 (2018) ("Any money or property, any token, object or article exchangeable for money or property, or any form of credit or promise directly or indirectly contemplating transfer of money or property or of any interest therein or involving extension of a service, entertainment or a privilege of playing at a game or scheme without charge.").
94. State v. 26 Gaming Machines, 145 S.W.3d 368, 374–75 (Ark. 2004) (emphasis added). This issue was not preserved for appeal.

utility only in the game in which it is awarded, such as the award of a virtual race car that can only be used in a racing game. The more the virtual item is comparable to a bragging right, the lower the risk that a prize exists. However, the more the virtual item can be shown to have a demonstrable market value, the greater the risk.

The second question relating to whether an item has value is whether the item, despite having no market value, can be exchanged for cash or an item of value. If one wins tickets that can be exchanged for merchandise, ranging from candy to gaming consoles, those are items with value for purposes of determining whether a gambling prize exists.

Online operators using the prizeless gaming model must take precautions that the virtual objects awarded cannot be purchased, sold, or transferred in the game or via secondary markets outside the game. Secondary markets, even if operated by independent third parties, can create a reasonably determinable value for the items. Even in the absence of an operator's authorization or support, a prosecutor could argue that the company knowingly profits from the secondary market.

A key factor in the analysis of potential liability is an operator's efforts to stop the secondary markets. Operators need to be diligent and aggressive in eradicating such markets.[95] An effective method to limit these secondary markets is to bind the virtual items to a player. If the virtual items are bound to the player, the ability to transfer or exchange the items is eliminated and so is the secondary market. Eliminating a secondary market for these virtual items supports the argument that they are merely bragging rights with no market value.[96]

Finally, operators need to understand the risks of awarding extended play without offering free play to potential participants. Some state laws provide that an extension of a service is something of value and, therefore, conforms to or satisfies the definition of a prize.[97] The reason for prohibiting extended play is traceable to crafty entrepreneurs placing poker machines in bars that only accumulated additional credits, which ostensibly could be used only for additional plays. Ordinarily this would not pose a problem. Bar owners, however, told players to notify the bartender when they were ready to leave the bar. The bartender would then verify the credits left on the machine, pay the player the remaining credits in equivalent cash, and remove the credits by a reset button or simply unplugging and replugging the

---

95. Kater v. Churchill Downs Inc., 886 F.3d 784, 788 n.2 (9th Cir. 2018) (citing Mason v. Mach. Zone, Inc., 851 F.3d 315, 320 n.3 [4th Cir. 2017] (holding that virtual items were not a "thing of value" as the sale of chips on secondary markets violate the company's terms of use).

96. Mason v. Mach. Zone, Inc., 851 F.3d 315, 320 (4th Cir. 2017) (holding that virtual items were not equivalent to money, as items were not sold on secondary markets; instead entire accounts that included level advancements were sold in violation of the company's terms of use).

97. A "thing of value" is defined in Wash. Rev. Code § 946.0285 as the following: "[a]ny money or property, any token, object or article exchangeable for money or property, or any form of credit or promise, directly or indirectly, contemplating transfer of money or property or of any interest therein, or involving extension of a service, entertainment or a privilege of playing at a game or scheme without charge."

machine. Thus, the machine was made ready for the next customer. In essence, this is gambling using hand pays.

Legislatures have thwarted these schemes by passing laws specifying that extended play constitutes a prize. Consequently, in states that forbid extended play, even a lawful social game would likely be considered unlawful if players risk something of value (consideration) on the outcome of a game of chance with the understanding that they will receive extended play (prize). A recent case illustrates how this can be a problem.

In *Kater v. Churchill Downs, Inc.*,[98] a social gaming application provided "freemium" online casino games. Users are awarded free chips when they create their account and may obtain additional chips by winning games, via free chip replenishment, or by purchasing additional chips. This is a widely used format.

In 2015, Cheryl Kater brought a class action alleging that she (and others similarly situated) should recover monies they spent on the site Big Fish Casino. Kater relied on Washington's Recovery of Money Lost at Gambling Act (RMLGA) and Consumer Protection Act and asserted a theory of unjust enrichment.[99] The crux of the argument was that Big Fish conducted illegal gambling under Washington state law; therefore, Ms. Kater should recover any monies she spent with Big Fish.[100]

The U.S. District Court for the Western District of Washington dismissed Kater's complaint in November 2015.[101] Kater filed an appeal, and the Ninth Circuit overturned the lower court's decision.[102] The court held that the virtual chips constituted a "thing of value," and therefore, Big Fish had conducted illegal gambling under Washington law.[103] The decision was based on Washington's unusual statutory definition of *thing of value*, which reads:

> [A]ny money or property, any token, object or article exchangeable for money or property, or any form of credit or promise, directly or indirectly, contemplating transfer of money or property or of any interest therein, or involving extension of a service, entertainment or a privilege of playing at a game or scheme without charge.[104]

Notably, this decision contradicted the Washington State Gambling Commission's (WSGC) prior publications regarding the legality of such social gaming in Washington. One week after the opinion was issued, the WSGC issued a neutral news release noting that some online social gaming sites had made business decisions to block Washington residents.[105] The WSGC advised concerned customers to contact

---

98. Kater v. Churchill Downs, Inc., *supra* note 95.
99. *Id.* at 785–86.
100. *Id.* at 787.
101. Kater v. Churchill Downs Inc., 2015 WL 9839755 (W.D. Wash. Nov. 19, 2015), *rev'd*, 886 F.3d 784 (9th Cir. 2018).
102. *Kater*, 886 F.3d at 789.
103. *Id.* at 787.
104. Wash. Rev. Code § 9.46.0285 (2018) (emphasis added).
105. Washington State Gambling Commission, *Statement Regarding Access to Free Online Poker Sites* (Apr. 4, 2018), https://www.wsgc.wa.gov/news/press-releases/statement-regarding-access-free-online-poker-sites.

the operators directly and expressed no opinion on the legality of such games in light of the recent opinion.[106] Additionally, the WSGC stated, "We are not a party to the civil court case, we did not testify in the case, and we did not order these sites to discontinue free online play for Washington residents."[107]

The Ninth Circuit's decision was based on a dismissal, which requires that the reviewing court accept all allegations in the complaint as true.[108] Consequently, the Ninth Circuit opinion qualifies many of their statements with the phrase as *alleged in the complaint*. The opinion also displays several confusing statements—such as Ms. Kater "must buy more chips to have 'the privilege of playing the game'" (chips were awarded every thirty minutes for free and if the patron was successful in the game).[109]

At the time of writing, this case remains ongoing. Several other potential class action lawsuits have been filed to date in U.S. District Court in Seattle and Tacoma against social gaming operators—each of which offer freemium online casino games. The ultimate ruling in these cases could significantly alter the legal landscape in Washington as well as other states.

V. GOALS: ADEQUATE PREPARATION TO AVOID LEGAL PROBLEMS

Current U.S. gambling laws afford many opportunities for operators and their counsel to develop businesses and build their brands with games and sweepstakes, but careful attention must be given to the legal complexities of doing so. Counsel unfamiliar with this area of the law are entering an intricate and specialized industry.

Operators must comply not only with federal gambling laws but also with the laws of all states where they accept participants. That is, merely complying with the laws where the operator has its offices or houses its servers is insufficient. As gambling laws vary from state to state, you would be wise to conduct thorough research on each before initiating contests, sweepstakes, or games in any given location.

To avoid legal problems, a fifty-state review should be conducted to individually analyze the case law, statutes, attorney general opinions, and other available legal materials for each state in order to categorize the states by level of risk. Doing this will help an operator determine the states from which the company will accept participants and those from which it will not. Failure to do so could result in a state regulator posing questions to your client as to why they are offering a service that violates state gambling prohibitions.

---

106. *Id.*
107. *Id.*
108. *Kater*, 886 F.3d at 786.
109. *Id.* at 787.

PART II

Commercial Gambling in the United States

Chapter 3

The Basics of Gaming Regulation

Anthony Cabot

I. INTRODUCTION: PUBLIC POLICY DRIVES GAMING REGULATION

Gaming regulation is the primary tool that the government uses to accomplish its goals in permitting casinos. Determining the government's policy goals toward casinos starts with a question of why a government permits and then regulates gambling. In other words, what is it about an otherwise consensual agreement between a casino and a player that justifies government intervention? Only valid policies should propel governments to treat casino gambling unlike other commercial relationships, such as retail sales, movie sales, or landscaping services. States often have different goals. For example, Nevada has a low tax environment intended to maximize investment and create jobs, while Pennsylvania has a limited number of casinos and imposes a high tax rate intended to maximize state revenues.

The six common groups of policy goals justifying regulation of permitted gambling are: (1) preserving free market competition, (2) protecting players from unethical practices, (3) protecting vulnerable players from problem gambling, (4) maximizing taxes, (5) stimulating job growth or other economic development, and (6) leveraging the gambling contract as a vehicle for redistribution of wealth. Because states that allow casino gambling do not always share the same goals, the regulations designed to achieve those goals necessarily differ between states. For example, states that emphasize protecting vulnerable players from problem gambling may have regulations that, for example, prohibit gambling on credit, allow players to self-exclude themselves from casinos, or have loss limits. Despite these differences among states, many policy goals—such as ensuring the honesty of games and that winning patrons are paid—will be found in all states. Consequently, state regulatory systems typically have similar characteristics and functions.

II. GAMING REGULATION PRIMARILY GOVERNS THE GAMING CONTRACT

Gambling regulation primarily involves the regulation of a contract between the person placing a wager and a person accepting it. Gambling, at its heart, is a consensual agreement between parties where money exchanges hands based at least partially on a chance outcome. The casino player makes an offer by agreeing to place a wager, typically money or equivalents like chips. In casino play, if the casino accepts the offer, it promises to pay the player a predetermined sum if certain conditions occur. Take electronic gaming machines. A player deposits the correct number of coins or tokens or selects the requisite number of credits and pushes the play button or pulls the handle (the offer), and the machine registers the wager and activates the spinning of the reels (the acceptance). Symbols will appear on the pay line after the reels stop. The casino promises to pay the player if a predetermined (winning) combination of symbols (such as four 7s if the player is lucky) align on the pay line. If the electronic gaming machine produces no winning combination, the casino retains the wager. In either case, the contract is concluded.

What makes gambling contracts different from most contracts is that the primary condition to the contractual obligations of the casino and the player is that chance, typically a "random" event, determines the outcome, in whole or part. Again, using the modern electronic gaming machine example, what determines the alignment of the symbols on the pay line is a random number generator within the computer program that runs the electronic gaming machine.[1] Each number generated corresponds to a combination of symbols on a reel-type machine. Some random combinations result in the player winning, and others result in the player losing.

The economic outcome of the gambling contract in a casino, determined by the random event, will almost without exception favor the casino over time. Every wager is designed to exact a certain percentage of the player's money. This is how the casino makes money. The positive expectation the casino holds over the player in any given gambling contract is the house advantage. Casinos can modify the house advantage by making rule variations that are more or less favorable to the player or by altering the payoffs on wagers.

---

1. A random number generator is an algorithm within the computer program with a well-defined set of instructions, finite in number, which produces numbers that appear to be random. Brendan Koerner, *Russians Engineer A Brilliant Slot Machine Cheat—And Casinos Have No Fix*, Wired Magazine (Feb. 6, 2017), https://www.wired.com/2017/02/russians-engineer-brilliant-slot-machine-cheat-casinos-no-fix/.

The government interferes in gambling contracts through regulation in one of four broad categories:

- Determining who, if anyone, can offer the contract (e.g., licensing)
- Determining who, if anyone, may accept the contract (e.g., age restrictions)
- Regulating the time, place, manner, or terms of the contract
- Conditioning the right to provide the contract on paying a tax or undertaking some other burden

A. Government Uses Its Police Powers to Govern the Gambling Contract

A state's police power allows it to interfere with otherwise consensual gambling contracts between persons who are physically located within the state's borders. Where the government bans gambling contracts, offering casino gaming is a crime that could lead to arrest and detention. Even where casino gaming is permitted, it is an exception to the general prohibition and subject to strict regulation. Almost all regulation of permitted casino gaming is command-type regulation, which uses the force of the state to achieve policy goals by establishing legal proscriptions. These provisions allow the regulator to either arrest or bring civil disciplinary actions against violators, as well as provide a basis for regulatory or judicial sanctions to be imposed. For example, if a casino licensee offers a game that has not been previously approved by the regulators, the casino could face criminal or civil penalties. The same result could occur if the casino failed to pay taxes on the gaming contract. Likewise, if the casino player (the offeror) is under the permissible age for entering gambling contracts, both the casino and the player could be subject to criminal or civil sanctions.

B. Governments Put into Place Structures to Carry Out These Police Powers

Six critical gaming regulatory functions are (1) investigating and enforcing the laws and regulations, (2) resolving patron disputes, (3) investigating and licensing applicants, (4) reviewing and approving gaming equipment, (5) establishing internal control standards to account for revenues, and (6) auditing of casinos.[2]

As important as these regulatory functions are, they are useless unless a process is established for adopting rules that govern the conduct of the regulated and define the powers of the regulators. This is a legislative function that can be performed by the legislative body or, more commonly, be delegated in part or whole to a regulatory agency. Where this delegation occurs, the agency must establish rulemaking procedures for the promulgation of regulations that govern the conduct

---

2. *See e.g.*, National Indian Gaming Commission, *Functions of a Tribal Gaming Commission*, https://www.nigc.gov/compliance/detail/functions-of-a-tribal-gaming-commission.

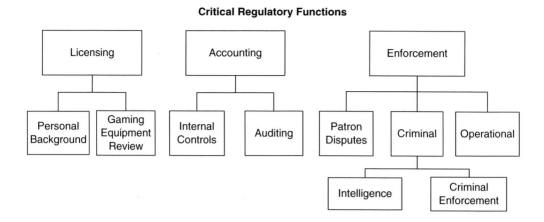

Critical Regulatory Functions

of the casino industry. Regulators have two methods to create these rules. The first is through rulemaking, a process by which the regulators consider and adopt rules that define the expected conduct of licensees or set out the criteria for approval of applicants or others things, such as gaming equipment. The second method is through the adjudication of cases.[3] This occurs when regulators consider applications or disciplinary actions and make decisions that stand as precedent for similar situations.[4]

Rulemaking can take many forms. A regulatory agency might set rules through very informal methods, such as letters to the industry or setting internal guidelines. Regulators do this in many places with surprising frequency.[5] All states, however, have some system of formal rulemaking for gaming regulations that typically involves adopting regulations in a setting like a court trial, with the swearing in and examination of witnesses, formal submission of documents, application of rules of evidence, public deliberation, and written findings.[6]

Regulations that lack accompanying enforcement power, however, are meaningless. If regulators determine through an audit or observation of casino operations that the licensee is violating established regulations, the ability to punish the violator is essential. Disciplinary action, typically a judicial function, can be undertaken by the courts or delegated in part or whole to the regulators who can pursue administrative sanctions against the offending licensee. Regulators have several tools they can use to ensure regulatory compliance. This can include directives, fines, suspension, attachment of conditions to retain a license, or even revocation

---

3. 5 U.S.C. § 551(6) (1989).
4. Ralph F. Fuchs, *Agency Development of Policy Through Rule-Making* 59 NW. Univ. L. Rev. 781 (1964).
5. In Nevada, as an example, the regulators often send out industry notices that address how the agency interprets either the law or regulations. This industry notice concerned foreign gaming reporting. *Foreign Gaming Reporting Requirements Policy Statement*, Nev. Gaming Control Board, https://gaming.nv.gov/modules/showdocument.aspx?documentid=13385.
6. *See e.g.*, Nev. Rev. Stat. § 463.145 (2019).

of the license. All these measures are used to control the behavior of the offending licensee or, in the most serious cases, to remove the offender from the regulated industry. On the other hand, isolated and unintentional violations that do not undermine gaming integrity may be dealt with by working with the licensee to improve training or control.

A pattern of unintentional violations by a casino licensee may demonstrate a lack of commitment to hiring or training competent personnel. In such cases, regulators may impose a fine on the licensee. In a regulatory environment, a fine should not be used as punishment but as a motivational tool to deter behavior and ensure future compliance. If regulators ultimately decide that the licensee cannot, through lesser sanctions, conform its behavior to meet regulatory goals, then the solution is license revocation. In the regulatory scheme, revocation of a gaming license is tantamount to the death penalty.

Besides disciplinary proceedings, the regulatory structure must provide for functions like granting licenses, resolving disputes between patrons and licensees, and settling tax disputes. Regulatory structures also must include administrative and auxiliary functions to operate efficiently. Administrative functions include hiring, training, promoting and firing staff, and planning and budgeting. Auxiliary services refer to those matters that assist the regulators, such as computer information services, facility and equipment supply, and maintenance.

C. States Use Some Form of Administrative Agencies to Regulate Casino Gaming

If the government hopes to achieve the goals underlying its regulation of gaming, those controls need to be effectively enforced. Most states use a single administrative agency that has the rule (or regulation) making authority and the decision-making authority on matters such as licensing, disciplinary actions, patron disputes, and tax disputes. A separate division of the state police, the state attorney general's office, or other division will have investigative, audit, and enforcement authority. This is the case in mature gaming jurisdictions like New Jersey, California, and Mississippi.

Nevada is an exception in that it uses two separate agencies, the state Gaming Control Board, which has investigative, enforcement, and auditing and accounting authority, and its Gaming Commission, which adopts regulations, grants licenses, and resolves disciplinary actions, tax disputes, and patron disputes.

D. Typical Regulatory Powers

1. Investigative

Investigations involve trained personnel that collect and document critical information on persons or entities. The most common investigation involves a review

52 • The Law of Regulated Gambling: A Practical Guide for Business Lawyers

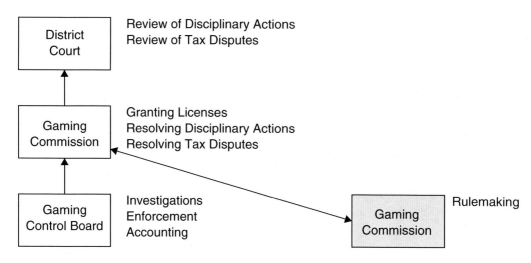

of applicants for gaming licenses, described later in this chapter. More difficult is the investigation of nonapplicants who have tangential relationships with the casino industry, such as suspected casino cheats or associates of casino licensees. These inquiries require agents with the skill to obtain information that is not readily available.

2. Enforcement

Enforcement involves both the detection and prosecution of violations. Many methods of detection are available, including self reporting and audits. Field observation is the equivalent of a casino patrol officer and usually involves both open investigations in response to reported problems and covert or undercover observations. Field observation is useful in detecting cheating scams, underage gambling, and casino floor regulatory violations. These rule breaches often involve casino employees not properly executing mandated procedures, such as preventing underage gambling or complying with internal controls in counting all gaming revenues. Undercover operations can allow regulatory agents to pose as patrons or criminals to uncover cheating scams, skimming, improper granting of casino credit, and currency violations.

3. Audit and Accounting

Government auditing and accounting controls help maintain the integrity of a tax system. Auditing in the casino industry concerns the accounting for cash and count transactions that occur in the casino. Accounting controls are procedures that a casino must implement to prevent or detect errors or irregularities. Casino accounting controls and auditing help prevent casino employees from stealing and prevent unscrupulous casino operators from "skimming" money (i.e., to remove casino revenue before it is counted for tax purposes). Without accounting controls, patron and employee theft can deprive governments of taxes.

III. LICENSING FUNDAMENTALS

Licensing is a tool to exclude persons from an industry, occupation, or profession before their actions compromise public goals. This is not unique to casino gaming. Governments often impose licensing requirements on various professions to protect the public. Lawyers, doctors, contractors, and even beauticians go through licensing scrutiny before they can offer their services. Gaming licensing is a form of occupational licensing.

States determining whether to license individuals or entities consider six major factors:

1. Criteria: matters that the government considers relevant in granting licenses. These can include moral character, honesty, connection to criminal elements, financial ability, and business experience.
2. Burden of proof: whether the applicant must prove its suitablity to hold a license or the government must prove its unsuitability.
3. Standard of proof: relates to how rigidly the regulators will apply the criteria set out for licensing. Under the same set of facts, an applicant may obtain a license in one state but not in another because of differing standards applied by the two states.
4. Level of review: the intensity of the investigative process. A low-level review might include simple criminal background checks.
5. Breadth: the extent to which a government requires persons or entities, such as owners and others having a connection with the gaming industry, to obtain a license.
6. Depth of licensing: the extent to which a government requires persons within a licensable entity, such as an officer, directors, shareholders, and employees, to undergo an investigation. A high-level review may entail that the regulatory agency train special agents to conduct a complete and independent review similar to a high government security review.

A. Criteria

Gaming regulators can consider many criteria in assessing an application for a gaming license. Criteria can be of a fixed or discretionary nature. Fixed criteria are quantifiable ones that an applicant either meets or does not, such as whether a person has not been convicted of a felony (South Dakota)[7] or whether

---

7. S.D. CODIFIED LAWS § 42-7B-33(3) (through 2011).

an applicant has been convicted of any crime involving gambling, prostitution, or sale of alcohol to a minor (Mississippi).[8] As indicated below, fixed criteria can vary widely in emphasis:

Examples of Fixed Criteria

State	Type of Fixed Criteria
Mississippi	A person who has not been convicted of any crime involving gambling, prostitution, or sale of alcohol to a minor
Nevada	Hotel with more than two hundred rooms, a bar for thirty people, and a twenty-four-hour restaurant

Discretionary criteria are minimum qualifications not subject to quantification but within the discretion of the gaming regulators.

Examples of Discretionary Criteria

State	Type of Discretionary Criteria
Nevada	The person must be of good character, honest, and have integrity.
Puerto Rico	The person must have organizational and financial ability to conduct casino operations.

1. Good Character or Good Moral Character

Gaming statutes and regulations often require regulators to consider character as a factor in screening applicants for professional and other vocational licenses involving a high degree of public trust. In Indiana, for example, gaming commissioners will examine the applicant's "good moral character."[9]

2. Integrity, Honesty, and Truthfulness

Integrity, honesty, and truthfulness are three concepts that licensing statutes use as criteria to assess an applicant's suitability. In New Jersey, the commission will grant a license only if the company is under the control of persons of integrity.[10]

While related, these concepts of integrity, honesty, and truthfulness have different meanings. Truthfulness means to tell the truth and is only one component of honesty. One can be truthful but dishonest. It is dishonest to express certain truths

---

8. Miss. Code Ann. § 75-76-67(3) (West 2013).
9. *Occupational Licenses*, Ind. Gaming Commission, http://www.in.gov/igc/2344.htm. Besides privileged licenses such as gaming, it is a common criterion in considering whether to grant a professional license, such as accounting, law, or medicine. Despite its frequent use, the term has limited practical utility because it is difficult to define and apply.
10. N. J. Stat. Ann. § 5:12-85 (West 2011).

and not disclose other truths in a way as to create a false impression.[11] Regulators want full disclosure by applicants and licensees; this requires that they both tell the truth and convey accurate impressions. Therefore, "honesty" as a criterion is preferable to truthfulness. When applying the honesty criterion, regulators usually apply a particular type of materiality standard.[12] Two general rules emerge. First, the honesty criterion is usually considered in a business rather than a personal context. This is justified because the purpose of licensing is to predict the conduct of an applicant in a business relationship as a gaming licensee. Second, honesty in business conduct is a function of the importance of the transaction. It may be of minor materiality that an applicant, to cut short a telemarketing call, lied by telling the salesman he recently bought the product being offered.

While conceptually a person with "integrity" generally exhibits "honest" behavior, honesty is simply a component of integrity. "The word integrity 'means soundness of moral principle and character, as shown by one's dealing with others in the making and performance of contracts.'"[13] Moral principles can extend beyond economic matters. Gaming regulators frequently look at broader societal issues such as sexual harassment and racial discrimination. For example, allegations of sexual harassment against Steve Wynn were the core of a $20 million fine imposed by the Nevada Casino Commission and a $35 million fine by the Massachusetts Gaming Commission against Wynn Resorts. These issues led to Wynn's exit from the industry.

a. Compliance with Law

An applicant's compliance with all laws pertaining to his or her role with the casino is material in granting a gaming license. One function of the licensing process is to predict whether, if granted a license, the applicant will comply with all gaming laws and regulations. Strict compliance with these laws and regulations is necessary for achieving the policy goals underlying them. Nothing is more predictive of future compliance with business laws and regulations than a review of past compliance in the same context.

Some states' laws and regulations have fixed criteria for determining suitability based on compliance. A felony conviction or an offense involving gambling may be a disqualifying factor and pose an insurmountable hurdle for convicted applicants.[14] Other states follow flexible standards where regulators must make a qualitative decision on suitability based on a totality of factors. As is the case with the honesty criterion, some instances of noncompliance may be less material than others.

---

11. Wiggins v. Texas, 778 S.W.2d 877, 889 (Tex. App. 1989).
12. In U.S. jurisprudence, the concept of materiality in relation to lying is well founded. Alan Heinrich, *Clinton's Little White Lies: The Materiality Requirement for Perjury in Civil Discovery*, 32 Loy. L.A. L. Rev. 1303 (1998).
13. *In re* Bauquier's Estate, 26 P. 178, *aff'd,* 26 P. 532 (Cal. 1891).
14. *See e.g.*, Miss. Revised Statutes, § 313.810 (2010).

Materiality of Noncompliance

Less Material	More Material
Does not involve dishonesty	Involves dishonesty
Civil violation	Criminal violation
Misdemeanor	Felony
Negligence	Intentional
Many years ago	Recent
Isolated	Repetitive
Accepted responsibility	Denied responsibility
Took corrective action	Took no affirmative action
Minor compared to the size of business	Major compared to the size of business

A material violation of laws is a useful licensing criterion because past compliance is a reliable indicator of future compliance. Compliance implicates more than whether the company has violated the law. It is connected to whether the company has institutional controls for ensuring compliance with all laws, domestic and foreign. Especially critical are situations where the company has business involvement with other casinos.

b. The Manner of Doing Business

Different people have distinct methods of doing business. Some people are conciliatory and resolve their disputes without litigation; others are more adversarial and regularly litigate disputes. The adversarial type may create disputes to delay payment and seek favorable settlement by threatening litigation. Regulators may have an easier time dealing with the conciliatory type who is cooperative and agrees on appropriate behavior. An adversarial person may challenge the authority of the regulators and tie up regulatory resources in court challenges.

c. Associations with Unsuitable Persons

If gaming licensees have associations with notorious persons, the public may believe that the unsuitable persons have an interest in, or influence over, gaming operations. A person's willingness to associate with disreputable people may also call into question one's judgment or propensities toward crime. The New Jersey Supreme Court has held that *unknowing* associations are not a basis for a finding of unsuitability by gaming regulators.[15] On the other hand, after an applicant knows of the unsuitability of an association, failing to dissociate becomes a knowing association. In that case, the New Jersey Casino Control Commission decided that the founder of a casino company was unsuitable because of, among other reasons, a recurring and enduring relationship with an individual who allegedly had ties to organized crime. In upholding the regulator's decision, the court noted it was "not

---

15. *In re* Boardwalk Regency Casino License Application, 180 N.J. Super. 324, 434 A.2d 1111 (N.J. 1982).

critical of a proposition denouncing guilt adjudication predicated solely on 'unknowing or otherwise innocent association' and [was] sensitive to the difficulties defending against such a premise."[16]

While the concept of unsuitable "associations" may be difficult to define, regulators typically focus on the following:

- Nature and intensity of the relationship. Factors considered include (1) type of relationship (i.e., business or friendship), (2) knowledge of the second person's unsuitability, (3) whether the relationship was voluntary, (4) frequency or involvement of the relationship, and (5) the applicant's attitude after becoming aware of the gaming authorities' concern with the relationship.
- The influence or control over the applicant by the other person.
- The nature of the concern about the second person and how that concern poses a threat to the public interest.
- The number of questionable relationships.

An inquiry based on these factors is more likely to avoid the injustices of a "guilt by association" approach while preserving regulators' ability to exclude persons truly unsuitable due to their associations.[17]

d. Conduct during the Investigation

Gaming laws require applicants to make a full and accurate disclosure of all information requested on the forms or by the regulatory agents.[18] The applicant's conduct during the investigation may become relevant to his suitability. If the applicant attempts to hide or mischaracterize a past transgression, the regulators may question the applicant's current credibility. If the applicant is not cooperative, the regulators may question whether the applicant will adopt a similar attitude toward compliance after licensing. If the applicant keeps disorganized and incomplete financial and personal records, the regulators may question the applicant's ability to account properly for taxes.

3. Competency/Management Abilities

Regulators may scrutinize managerial competency in determining the suitability of a person for a gaming license. Operating a casino takes specialized knowledge and skills. Regulators may have concerns that otherwise honest persons might undermine state goals if they lack the capacity to manage casino operations properly.

---

16. *Id.* at 340.
17. For example, that a restaurant is identified as a favorite of organized crime figures should not, in itself, make the restaurant owner unsuitable for a gaming license. If the only relationship was that the organized crime members were paying customers of a public restaurant and they were accorded no special treatment, it might be unfair to deny the restaurant owner a gaming license.
18. *See, e.g.*, Nev. Rev. Stat. Ann. § 463.339 (West 2011).

Incompetence can be just as destructive to a state's policy goals as malfeasance. Poor managers may not recognize when dishonest dealers cheat or steal from the player. This may frustrate a primary governmental goal by failing to ensure that games are honest. Similarly, professional cheaters and dishonest employees can more easily steal from gaming operations with poor management. This may thwart state goals of collecting taxes on all revenues derived from gaming operations.

The consideration given to management abilities is often a function of the complexity of the organization and gaming operation. For lower levels of employees, states can use occupational certification to address competence and reduce skill deficiencies. This could be beneficial where the skills required to perform a job are easily identifiable, can be quantified and framed in a license requirement, and can be tested.[19]

4. Financial Capabilities

Regulators consider the applicant's financial capabilities in licensing decisions. They may have legitimate concerns that, even after committing its monetary and other resources, the casino will never open or will close shortly after opening because its owners did not have sufficient financial resources. Concerns with an applicant's financial capability may vary depending upon the gaming environment in the jurisdiction. In a monopoly or small oligopoly situation, the government may be especially interested in ensuring the prospective casino operator is adequately financed. This is particularly the case where the government is committing its resources to the project through infrastructure, community development funds, hiring additional city personnel, or buying new city equipment. When the government has borrowed money to make the infrastructure improvements and is relying on gaming taxes to pay it back, the concerns are elevated further.

B. Burden of Proof

In licensing matters, the burden of proof is usually on the applicant. This requires the applicant to provide affirmative evidence of its suitability that exceeds the minimum licensing standards.[20] However, to say that the applicant "proves" his suitability is somewhat misleading. In practice, the applicant merely provides the requested information and documentation. In determining the applicant's suitability, regulators consider all the evidence whether offered by the applicant or otherwise discovered by regulators. The burden of proof is important because there is no presumption of suitability—if questions of suitability arise, the applicant must

---

19. Frontier Economics, Dept. for Educ. & Skills, An Economic Review and Analysis of the Implications of Occupational Licensing (2003), http://webarchive.nationalarchives.gov.uk/20130401151715/https://www.education.gov.uk/publications/eOrderingDownload/RR467.pdf.

20. "The burden of proving an applicant's qualification to receive any license, be found suitable or receive any approval required by this chapter is on the applicant." Nev. Rev. Stat. § 463.170 (2019).

address them by offering evidence that casts bad acts or information in the best light possible.

C. Standard of Proof

When regulators assess the information in a license application, their discretionary decision to grant or deny a license must be made by application of some standard of proof. However, unlike a court proceeding, the standard is rarely set out in statutes or cases, and standards such as "beyond a reasonable doubt" or "a preponderance of the evidence" are not commonly used. Instead, the standard is often that the applicant must prove its suitability to the satisfaction of the regulators.[21]

D. Levels of Review

Levels of licensing review consist of tiers that categorize groups of individuals or entities associated with the gaming industry. Each tier is then subject to a different level of licensing scrutiny. For example, regulators may extend the breadth of licensing to both owners and gaming employees. The level of review, however, will likely be very different. Owners will undergo a thorough investigation that requires the regulators to spend months vetting virtually all aspects of the owner's life. The review of the gaming employees merely seeking to obtain a work card may be little more than a cursory review of the police database and other nominal inquires.

1. Full Licensing

The most expensive and intrusive investigation is a full licensing investigation. It is a comprehensive independent review of the applicant's financial history and personal background. Depending upon the complexity of the investigation, an investigative team typically has varying numbers of agents. Two types of agents are generally used—financial agents and background agents. Financial agents have accounting backgrounds, while background agents have law enforcement training and often are former law enforcement agents.

As a prelude to the investigation, the prospective license holder first completes an application. The forms elicit basic information about the applicant's character, criminal record, business activities, financial affairs, and business associates. Almost all states offering regulated gambling use a universal application that is more than sixty pages long.[22] This application asks for complete financial statements, residences, and employment for the past twenty years, police and litigation records, and names, addresses, and birth dates of the applicant's extended family.

---

21. *Id.*
22. A copy of the multijurisdictional application form is available on the Pennsylvania Gaming Control Board website. https://gamingcontrolboard.pa.gov/files/licensure/applications/initial/Multi_Jurisdictional_Personal_History_Form.pdf.

Compiling and verifying such information is an arduous and time-consuming process for the applicant.

Background agents, who are often former law enforcement or are state police, conduct extensive interviews to evaluate the applicant's character. Their investigation goes beyond checking the applicant's police record for any criminal history. The applicant's business and personal associates and methods of doing business also interest the agents. For example, these agents review civil court records to find the types and nature of all civil litigation involving the applicant.

Financial agents undertake an exhaustive review of the applicant's finances. This includes a cash flow analysis, typically for a minimum of five years. The production of financial documentation is a significant part of the investigation. Typically, the applicant must provide copies of income tax returns, savings passbooks, bank statements, canceled checks, deposit slips, check registers, escrow documents for the purchase or sale of all real estate, loan documents, telephone records, and stock certificates or account statements. Investigating agents use these documents for many reasons. First, if the applicant provides part or all the financing for the casino, these records show the adequacy of the applicant's resources and the suitability of the sources. Second, financial records frequently reveal the identities of the applicant's associates and any financial arrangements with those persons. The agents also scrutinize the applicant's sources of income and records of payments. The applicant often must identify the source of bank deposits or the nature of payments reflected on canceled checks.

The agents typically have expansive powers. They can inspect premises; demand access to, inspect, and audit books or records; and interview witnesses. As part of this process, applicants typically must sign a variety of "hold harmless" releases to indemnify the agents and allow the government agencies, banks, and other private corporations to release information about the applicant directly to the agents. Furthermore, the agents may interview a wide range of persons, including references, business associations, adverse parties in litigation, friends, and others, to assess the applicant's character, activities, and associations. They also screen unsolicited information submitted by third parties who view the investigative process as an opportunity to harm the applicant's interests. After their investigation is complete, the agents prepare a written summary for the regulators.

2. Partial Licensing

A partial investigation involves reviewing only limited areas on each application. Instead of a field background investigation, the regulators may conduct only a computer review of federal, state, and local police data banks. If the review reveals no arrests, convictions, or investigations of the applicant, the regulators may issue a license. Partial investigations provide less protection to the government than a full investigation. A partial investigation usually consists of a criminal history check, reviewing responses from the applicant's references, and sometimes a personal interview. Partial investigations may not provide enough information or personal contact with the applicant to establish a basis for an accurate prediction of future conduct, and a cursory investigation with limited information verification often yields questionable information.

Nevertheless, a partial investigation provides some benefits. Most notably, it may inhibit persons with extensive criminal histories from obtaining employment in the casino. Regulators also may obtain useful negative information about applicants from third parties that may lead to denial of the application despite the absence of a negative criminal record. The partial investigation can also include a review of necessary certification, such as training, or even some level of proficiency testing.

Limited licenses are commonly issued to lower-level gaming employees. Such licenses can place specific restrictions on the applicant's employment activities or employment category. For example, New Jersey issues different licenses to key gaming employees, regular gaming employees, and nongaming employees.[23] States may use different terminologies, such as a work "permit" or "card" for licensing gaming and nongaming employees to differentiate types of licenses.

E. Breadth of Licensing

The casino gaming ecosphere has many participants besides the owner and operator. Employees, contractors, and suppliers of many types of gaming and nongaming equipment, goods, and services all have integral roles in creating and operating a casino. In licensing, the concept of *breadth* means the extent to which a government requires different categories of persons or entities to obtain a license.

The breadth of licensing prevents unsuitable persons from attempting to influence or profit from a casino's operations through control of labor, goods, or services critical to the casino.[24] Licensing may prevent third parties from sharing in the casino's net profits. Efforts to participate in the casino's finances include selling goods or services to the casino at prices far above market price, charging exorbitant "finder's fees" for arranging to finance the casino, and skimming.

The breadth of licensing can also relate to how the government achieves other goals, such as preventing persons from being cheated. An honest operator may be unaware that individual gaming devices are cheating patrons. Because this may potentially be detrimental to public policy, some level of licensing beyond the operator—here, the machine supplier—must be carried out.

The following is a description of the various groups involved in the gaming industry and their regulatory sensitivity.

---

23. *See generally,* Nicholas Casiello, Jr., International Casino Law 121 (Anthony Cabot, et al. eds., 3d ed. 1999).

24. Lester B. Snyder, *Regulation of Legalized Gambling: An Inside View*, 12 Conn. L. Rev. 665, 714 (1980).

1. Owners

Because owners hold the rights to conduct the casino business, they are subject to full licensing. Even owners who hire operators to run the casino on their behalf, and therefore do not have direct contact with customers or gaming operations, are subject to full licensing because they retain the rights to gaming profits and the ability to hire and fire the manager. The owner can exert direct influence over the honesty and fairness of the gaming operations and control over player funds. The owner has financial responsibility and can implement all the systems and procedures to ensure that players are protected from third-party cheating, privacy violations, and data theft. Owners also have primary responsibility for implementing compliance systems and programs designed to address problem gambling and other regulatory requirements. Because of their power, owners also can pose a high risk to achieving government goals. A government must consider not only the potential influence that an owner has over an operation but also public perception of unsuitable owners, as the owner is typically the most visible person to the public.

2. Operators

Operators typically have to undergo full licensing because they have the right to conduct gaming at a casino.

3. Landlords

Most states, but not all, require landlords to obtain full licensing. Nevada is an exception and mandates licensing only if the landlord receives a percentage of the gross or net revenues generated by the casino.[25]

4. Persons Entitled to Profits

Vendors (or others) may bargain for their goods or services to be paid for as a percentage of the other party's profits. This can include providing equipment, patent or other intellectual property rights, or by providing financing, management, or marketing services. Persons can obtain profits either narrowly from a game, more broadly from the casino revenues, or even more broadly from the general resort operating revenue that includes gaming, hotel, restaurants, and other revenue centers. Gaming regulators are particularly attentive to this arrangement because ownership interests can be disguised as a vendor's participatory interest in the gaming operation. The potential for abuse has led some states to require anyone sharing in a percentage of gaming revenues to obtain a license.[26]

---

25. Nev. Rev. Stat. §§ 463.160(1)(c), 463.162(1)(c) (2019). "Fixed" rental payments are not in conflict with this prohibition because they contain lease clauses providing for adjustments in rent due to changes in taxes, assessments, cost-of-living index escalations, or expansion or improvement of facilities.

26. *See e.g.*, Miss. Code Ann. § 75-76-57(1)(a).

5. Lenders/Creditors

Lenders/creditors are common parties to most casinos. A casino may have many types of creditors. Lenders of money usually are the largest. Other creditors can include suppliers of gaming and nongaming equipment, financial institutions, vendors that sell on credit, and others who provide furniture, fixtures, and equipment leases. The government may be a creditor if it is owed taxes. Another type of "lender" is a person who buys debt security, such as a debenture. A debenture is a bond issued by the casino company to evidence the debt owed. Debentures entitle the holder to certain rights, including the payment of interest. Some debentures or bonds are convertible into stock. In other words, a debenture holder can change his status from a debt holder to an equity investor. Requiring all creditors to obtain a license, however, raises costs and creates barriers that will deter many legitimate lenders. Therefore, most states exempt commercial and noncommercial creditors from licensing scrutiny. Three major types of regulated commercial creditors are (1) banks or savings and loan associations, (2) insurance companies, and (3) pension or retirement funds.

6. Suppliers and Vendors

a. Gaming Device Manufacturers

Gaming devices are equipment used in a casino that determines win or loss, such as a slot machine or roulette table. Most states require gaming device manufacturers to undergo full licensing.[27] This is, however, an increasingly complicated area because there may be multiple suppliers of both hardware and software that contribute to the gaming equipment ultimately reaching the casino floor. Many nonlicensed independent contractors may have touched the code before it is installed in a gaming device. A licensed manufacturer may use independent contractors based around the world to write portions of the software code that is integrated into a slot machine or gaming system. A common approach in states is not to require contractors to obtain a license but to place the responsibility for the final product on the manufacturer to ensure that an honest product reaches the casino floor.[28] This requires the manufacturer to undertake due diligence before contracting with suppliers. The manufacturer also must possess the technical capacity and security protocols to review and integrate all the hardware and software to ensure the final product meets all standards, including honesty. Thus, the manufacturer has final responsibility for design, assembly, and operation of the overall gaming device.

---

27. *Licensing by Jurisdiction*, Regulatory Management Counselors, P.C., www.gamingregulation.com/regulations/.
28. *See* Nev. Rev. Stat. § 463.01715 (2019); Nev. Gaming Comm'n Regulation 14.

b. Manufacturers of Associated Equipment

Casinos also use what is commonly called "associated equipment." This is any equipment used in connection with gaming.

Common Forms of Electronic Associated Equipment[29]

Automatic shufflers (mechanical and with a random number generator [RNG])	Ball drawing devices—automated reader
Ball drawing devices—manual	Bill validator (used in a gaming device or associated equipment)
Bingo systems	Bingo systems with electronic bingo cards
Electronic shoes	Bingo inter-casino linked systems
Cage and credit systems	Soft count systems
Coin counters (interfaced with a gaming system or associated equipment)	Computerized keno systems
Cashless wagering systems	Online slot metering systems
Currency counters (interfaced with a gaming system or associated equipment)	Keno display board
Cashless wagering systems and table games	Progressive sign controllers
Progressive controllers	Slot player tracking systems
Slot monitoring systems	

Nevada implemented a licensing requirement for manufacturers of cashless wagering systems in 1996. These systems allow players to wager without using chips, tokens, or legal tender of the United States. A standard methodology is a proprietary method called ticket in, ticket out (TITO), where players insert currency into a bill acceptor on a gaming device and establish credits on the device. The credits increase or decrease depending on the play. At the conclusion of the play, a player with credits receives a ticket printed at the device indicating the credits. The ticket can then be redeemed for cash at a redemption kiosk or cashier station or inserted into another gaming device for continued play. Other cashless wagering systems where a central computer administers, monitors, accounts, and retains the wagers between the casino and players are available. Some states, such as Ohio, mandate that the casino use cashless wagering.[30]

c. Suppliers of Gaming Devices or Associated Equipment

Unlike a manufacturer, suppliers do not build gaming devices or equipment, but they act as middlemen, buying the devices or equipment from manufacturers or others and selling them to casinos. The devices they buy can be new or old. Regulators typically require suppliers of gaming devices and equipment to undergo some level of licensing scrutiny.

---

29. Associated Equipment Matrix, Nev. Gaming Control Bd. (2010), http://gaming.nv.gov/modules/showdocument.aspx?documentid=2772.

30. Ohio Rev. Code Ann. § 3772.22 (West 2010).

d. Suppliers of Noncasino Goods and Services

Casinos, like other businesses, purchase a variety of noncasino goods and services. This can include mundane things such as uniforms, beds, televisions, cleaning supplies, and food products. They also can include significant goods, such as liquor, food, or services, such as constructing a new casino or running the hotel, restaurants, or other nongaming portions of a complex.

Regulatory concerns regarding the suppliers of noncasino goods or services have two major origins. The first concern is when a person or defined group controls the entire source of the supply and can therefore use its influence to charge the casinos extraordinary fees, acquire a hidden percentage of the revenues, or exert influence over operations. A second regulatory concern is that the supplying of noncasino goods or services can be used as a front for ownership by unsuitable persons. A person might use a "clean" applicant as a front to apply for, and obtain, the casino license but operate the casino under the guise of being the hotel operator. Practically speaking, it is impossible to license all suppliers. Only suppliers who receive a significant amount of revenue from the casinos would consider undergoing licensing scrutiny, not because of unsuitability, but because of the cost. If all suppliers had to obtain a license, casinos could not buy small amounts of supplies or replacement parts, or hire technicians to repair things such as copy machines. Consequently, most states either retain discretionary ability to license suppliers, require licensing only in certain areas,[31] or require it above certain amounts.

e. Persons Doing Business on the Casino Premises

Casinos often have many persons who are not employees working on the casino premises. These can include persons who rent space, such as shopkeepers, travel agents, and hairstylists, or those who pay the casino owner for the right to sell goods or services directly to patrons, such as roaming cigarette salespeople, photographers, florists, or valet parkers.

Most states give the regulators the discretion to require these persons to obtain a license. This allows the regulators to maintain control when needed without disrupting the competitive markets for these concessions.

f. Labor Organizations

Some states, such as New Jersey, give their regulators the ability to require licensing of labor unions because of the strength of the labor unions in the casino industry and the historical involvement of criminals in some unions.[32]

---

31. Supplying equipment or systems that directly tie to casino revenues, game honesty, or player data protections often falls into this area. Besides surveillance systems, other systems commonly found in casino resorts include back office casino accounting that provides information such as audit trails, slot and live-game summary reports, main-cage consolidation, staff planning, and security access/video surveillance.

32. N.J. Stat. Ann. § 5:12 et seq (2019). Under it, regulators can require key labor union officials to meet certain qualifications. Its law allows regulation of labor unions that represent employees working in both gambling activities and related service industries. The law also includes enforcement procedures.

F. Depth of Licensing

When a state requires a license to engage in an activity related to gaming, the entity that must apply and obtain the license often is not an individual. For example, the owners of most Nevada casinos are publicly traded corporations. *Depth of licensing* refers to those persons associated with the applicant–entity who must file an application for and obtain a license.

1. Individuals

To license an individual, the authorities need to investigate that person only, not an entire business entity. Because a sole proprietorship is usually the least desirable business form, very few operators choose it as a business structure. Most operators or other business entities associated with the gaming industry, such as manufacturers and suppliers, are corporations or partnerships.

2. Corporations

Depth of licensing for corporations concerns which officers, directors, and shareholders must undergo licensing scrutiny. Similar considerations are needed for other business formations, such as general and limited partnerships, trusts, joint ventures, limited liability companies, and joint stock associations.

3. Publicly Traded Corporations

A publicly traded company is a listed corporation[33] whose stock is traded on a public market and is typically regulated by a government entity such as a securities commission.[34] An attractive feature of being a publicly traded corporation is the ability to raise capital through a public offering.[35] Most often, a public offering occurs when the company, after registration with the securities commission,[36] sells either stock or debt instruments to the public through brokers. Public company stock is attractive to investors because it is usually liquid. If people buy the stock, they can usually sell it immediately in the public market.[37]

---

33. Before a company's stock can be traded on an exchange, through NASDAQ (National Association of Securities Dealers Automated Quotations), or over-the-counter, the corporation must register its stock with the Securities and Exchange Commission and meet the criteria of the Exchange or NASDAQ to list its stock.

34. The three major U.S. markets are local and national stock exchanges, an authorized quotation system (such as NASDAQ), or between broker-dealers (called over-the-counter). In the United States, the major national exchanges are the New York and American Stock Exchanges. An example of a local exchange is the Pacific Stock Exchange. The NASDAQ system is authorized by federal law but is an association regulated by private industry. NASDAQ has a board of directors that sets rules and policies. Shares in private companies are exchanged among persons or through private placements that meet federal or state securities laws.

35. In the United States, a "public offering" encompasses the sale of securities subject to the registration requirements of § 5 of the Securities Act of 1933.

36. In the United States, the role of the SEC is to evaluate the adequacy and accuracy of information in the registration statement and prospectus distributed to prospective investors. Securities brokers can offer only the stock for sale to their clients if the company receives SEC approval of their registration statement and prospectus.

37. In the United States, a public offering encompasses the sale of securities subject to the registration requirements of § 5 of the Securities Act of 1933.

Almost all securities offered to the public by a company in the United States require registration. The role of the Securities Exchange Commission (SEC) is to evaluate the adequacy and accuracy of the information in the registration statement and prospectus distributed to prospective investors. In effect, securities brokers can only offer the stock for sale to their clients if the company receives SEC approval of their registration statement and prospectus.

States that want publicly traded corporations to operate casinos in their state must balance these regulatory concerns with market realities. They do this by setting thresholds at which shareholders in publicly traded corporations must apply for and obtain a gaming license. In the United States, these levels are commonly set at either 5 percent, 10 percent, or 15 percent. The 5 percent level is tied to federal requirements on the reporting of stock ownership.[38] The purpose of this filing is to inform the company and the public of the person's ownership and his or her intentions, such as an attempt to acquire control or to merely be a passive investor.[39]

Different States and Level of Licensing Review

State	Level of Licensing Exemption
Colorado[40]	Shareholders in public or private companies owning less than 5 percent.
Louisiana[41]	Shareholders in public or private companies owning 5 percent or less (land-based and riverboat casinos).
Mississippi[42]	Shareholders owning 10 percent or less of public companies or qualified limited partnerships.
Nevada[43]	Regular shareholders owning less than 10 percent of public companies, qualified limited partnerships, or limited liability companies. Institutional investors owning less than 15 percent of public companies.
New Jersey[44]	Shareholders owning less than 5 percent of public corporation, shareholders owning more than 5 percent but who prove no ability to control company or elect directors, institutional investors owning less than 20 percent.
South Dakota[45]	Shareholders of public or private corporations owning less than 5 percent.
Puerto Rico[46]	Shareholders of public or private corporations owning less than 5 percent.

---

38. Under SEC requirements, a person acquiring more than 5 percent of the beneficial ownership of any class of voting securities in a publicly traded corporation must report this to the SEC (usually an SEC Schedule 13D or 13G). *Fast Answers: Schedule 13D*, SEC, https://www.sec.gov/fast-answers/answers sched13htm.html.

39. Jonathan R. Macey & Jeffry M. Netter, *Regulation 13D and the Regulatory Process*, 65 WASH. U. L. Q. 131 (1987).

40. ROBERT DUNCAN & DONALD OSTRANDER, *Colorado*, in INTERNATIONAL CASINO LAW 9 (2d ed. 1993).

41. HAROLD BUCHLER, JR., ET AL., *Louisiana*, in INTERNATIONAL CASINO LAW 37 (2d ed. 1993).

42. THOMAS SHEPARD & CHERYN NETZ, *Mississippi*, in INTERNATIONAL CASINO LAW 65 (2d ed. 1993).

43. ANTHONY N. CABOT & MARC RUBINSTEIN, *Nevada*, in INTERNATIONAL CASINO LAW 93 (2d ed. 1993).

44. NICHOLAS CASIELLO, JR., *New Jersey*, in INTERNATIONAL CASINO LAW 113 (2d ed. 1993).

45. DON GROMER & ANTHONY N. CABOT, *South Dakota*, in INTERNATIONAL CASINO LAW 133 (2d ed. 1993).

46. MARIA MILAGROS SOTO & DAN SCHIFFMAN, *Puerto Rico*, in INTERNATIONAL CASINO LAW 223 (2d ed. 1993).

Besides shareholders, most states require all C-level officers to obtain a license, including the CEO, CFO, COO, and increasingly the CTO. Some states require all directors to obtain a license while others distinguish between inside and outside directors and only require outside directors to obtain a license. The distinction between inside and outside directors is often based on the directors' shareholding or their responsibilities with the corporation. This could include directors who are also officers or employees, directors who head certain committees, and the chairman of the board.

4. Partnerships and Private Corporations

Some states treat limited partnerships and private corporations (and other business forms) like publicly traded corporations by exempting limited partners and shareholders holding less than a threshold amount. Others have no exemption. Still others grant limited waivers after requiring the limited partners or shareholders to apply and undergo a lower-level review.[47]

5. Casino Personnel

Some casino positions are of higher regulatory sensitivity than others. For example, a casino manager usually has more opportunity to steal from the casino, be involved in a skim, or participate in cheating the patrons than a chip runner. Thus, in general terms, a casino manager is subject to more regulatory review than a chip runner.

Beyond generalizations, however, no universal rules can exist as to which positions have greater regulatory sensitivity and what the regulatory requirements should be for each position. A state's regulatory system and technological advances help shape the regulatory sensitivity of casino positions. Where the government mandates an online monitoring system for all gaming devices, for example, the regulatory sensitivity of hard-count room personnel may decrease.

An Example of Employee Licensing

Independent agents	Must undergo a full investigation and obtain a license before beginning work.
Casino manager Controller (vice president—financial operations) Vice president—casino operations	Must obtain a work card or undergo other check that is less than full licensure before beginning work and must file an application for licensure. The investigation has high priority.
Assistant controller (operations controller) Director of surveillance Cage manager Poker manager Shift manager Slot manager Table games manager	Same as the controller mentioned above, but investigation priority is medium unless facts dictate otherwise.

---

47. *Licensing by Jurisdiction*, REGULATORY MANAGEMENT COUNSELORS, P.C., www.gamingregulation.com/regulations/.

Credit and collection manager casino hosts Keno manager Pit bosses	Same as the casino manager mentioned above, but licensing priority is low unless facts dictate otherwise.
Boxpersons and brushpersons Cashiers Dealers Floor persons Internal audit Keno supervisor/shift manager Keno second/third person and writers Pit clerks Poker assistant supervisors Security guards Poker shift supervisor Slot attendants and hosts Slot mechanics and supervisors Surveillance operator and shift manager	Is only required to obtain a work permit, but regulators have the discretion to require the person to undergo full licensing.
Change persons Chip runners Desk clerks Keno runners Shills Slot booth cashiers	Does not have to obtain a work card, but regulators should have the discretion to order the casino to terminate the person's employment or relationship.
Marketing director	Is not subject to regulatory scrutiny.

IV. AUDITING AND ACCOUNTING

After a company has obtained a license, regulators need to have controls over the operations to ensure that the licensee is operating according to the highest standards of wagering integrity. A primary tool to accomplish this is by the imposition of accounting controls. Governments may impose any of the following requirements: (1) minimum internal controls, (2) recordkeeping requirements, (3) reporting requirements, and (4) governmental and independent audits.

The government has three principal objectives in setting regulations governing the accounting of casinos. First, accounting regulations can prevent nonlicensed persons from sharing in casino revenues. The regulations can assist gaming regulators in learning the cash flow of casinos. If an unsuitable person is profiting from the casino, regulators may be able to detect it through audits facilitated by revenue trails created by internal controls. This ensures that unsuitable persons are not evading the licensing process through "hidden interests." Second, internal controls establish procedures that protect wagering integrity. Third, to some extent, depending on the tax rate, the government has an interest in ensuring that all revenues are properly accounted for so that it can receive all taxes. This prevents skimming, where the owners receive revenues but do not pay taxes on them. It can also deter employee theft and embezzlement.

A. Minimum Internal Controls

Internal controls are policies and procedures that are designed to prevent and detect errors or irregularities that may occur in the operation of a business. They are also intended to assist a business to operate effectively and cost-efficiently. In a gaming setting, internal controls operate as a method of checks and balances that help to maintain the integrity of wagering. States can require casinos to adopt and adhere to a comprehensive set of internal procedural operating controls, known as the *internal controls system*. Regulators typically set out minimum internal controls standards. Nevada, for example, has about 200 pages of mandated minimum internal controls that contain over 1,000 individual requirements covering all aspects of the casino including slots, table games, keno, bingo, race and sports, and cage and credit.[48]

These procedures governing the conduct of wagering, movement, and handling of cash and cash equivalents, and the accounting and record trail of all transactions, promote integrity in gaming and ensures the government receives the tax revenue it is due.[49] Internal control systems typically have several components.

1. Access Controls

Access controls are physical safeguards. They segregate the responsibilities of employees and allow employees to have physical access only to places or systems relevant to their assigned responsibilities. For example, only cage or certain accounting employees are permitted in the casino cage, and only table game employees and certain casino executives are permitted in the pit area.

2. Documentation Controls

Documentation controls require casino employees to make physical records of all transactions. This provides a full audit trail of every transaction. For example, Nevada gaming regulations applicable to larger casinos require certain operators to adopt controls that are "designed to reasonably ensure that . . . transactions are recorded adequately to permit proper reporting of gaming revenue and of fees and taxes, and to maintain accountability for assets."[50] These controls are quite broad, and virtually every transaction in the casino, except for the wager itself, is documented. For example, patrons wishing to draw against their credit line must sign the proper documentation.

3. Personnel Controls

Personnel controls are procedures that establish an organizational structure for the approval of transactions. Typically, personnel controls rely on the division of duties

---

48. Nevada has various checklists for their minimum internal controls. *Minimum Internal Control Standards*, NEV. GAMING COMM'N, https://gaming.nv.gov/index.aspx?page=182.

49. *Legislating and Regulating Casino Gaming: A View from State Regulators* (Mar. 1, 1999), https://govinfo.library.unt.edu/ngisc/reports/belletire.pdf [hereinafter *State Regulators*].

50. NEV. GAMING COMM'N Reg. 6.090.

and responsibilities. They also include the use of checks and balances to ensure that no single department or person within a casino gaming operator organization has unfettered control.

Internal control procedures established in a casino environment incorporate combinations of access controls, documentation controls, and personnel controls. For example, internal controls are critical in a table game environment since gaming activity is conducted by individuals (as opposed to mechanical devices). Table games typically have a "drop box" that is used to store currency received from patrons until it is counted and recorded in the casino's financial records. The casino secures the drop box with several locks, each of which requires a different key to avoid theft. All these procedures are access controls. Surveillance cameras and security officers also monitor all table game activity.

During table game play, if a particular table game has paid out more in winnings than it has collected in losing wagers, the inventory of chips at that table may become low. Conversely, if losing wagers exceed winning payouts, the table inventory may contain an excess of chips. Those employees in the gaming pit will either request additional chips from the cage (a fill) or send excess chips back to the cage (a credit) to bring the table's chip inventory back to normal. Activities such as chip fills and credits are monitored using documentation controls. To prevent a person from creating a fictitious transaction, unique forms designed to record the event are prepared, verified, and signed by the individuals who participate in the transaction (e.g., cage cashier and dealer). The accounting department subsequently audits the forms.

Personnel controls also are used extensively to monitor table game activity. Dealers put the currency received from players in exchange for chips directly into the locked drop box under the gaming table through a slot on the top. Table supervisory personnel carefully observe these transactions and others, such as patron wagers, chip purchases, and winning wager payouts, to ensure that improper activities do not occur. Table game supervisors, however, cannot handle chips or currency. Moreover, persons who count the cash stored in the drop boxes at each gaming table (called the soft count team) are independent of the table games department. The soft count team counts the currency in a separate room that has special access controls. The locked drop boxes are transported to this room by security. These soft count rooms are locked and monitored by surveillance. Soft count team members must wear uniforms that have been designed to prevent concealment of currency. Ultimately, the accounting department verifies the information recorded by the soft count team as additional documentation and personnel controls.

B. Recordkeeping

Documentation control is of little value unless the operator maintains the records. Recordkeeping facilitates the audit process by the government and independent auditors and allows for governmental investigations into the casinos' activities. Casinos may be required to retain all records for a fixed number of years.

C. Audits

Government audits are a method of ensuring proper cash controls. Regulators retain a trained staff to conduct the audits with sufficient regularity to be a deterrent to illegal or poor accounting practices. Government audits often are unannounced and conducted at irregular intervals to prevent licensees from following proper accounting principles only when they expect to be audited. These audits may involve detailed reviews or amount to spot compliance checks relating to specific regulations or procedures. Audit objectives should ensure that the casino (1) is not paying or allowing unlicensed persons to receive gaming revenues, (2) has adequate internal control procedures, (3) follows internal control procedures for the handling of cash and other transactions, (4) is properly reporting its revenues, and (5) is paying all taxes and fees. An essential function of audits is to ensure that the casinos are complying with internal controls and regulations. Because the casino industry is primarily a cash business, controls and regulations dealing with cash and cash equivalent accounting predominate over other regulations. Audits can often detect violations of these controls and regulations better than other forms of enforcement.

The failure of a licensee to allow agents to examine records on demand can be deemed an unsuitable method of operation and can subject the licensee to disciplinary action, including restrictions, fines, or potential revocation of the license.

D. Operating Requirements

Governments also can impose operating requirements on casinos. Failure to comply with these requirements can result in fines or loss of licenses. Frequently, the operating requirements consist of prohibited activities. Below are examples of operational requirements/prohibitions compiled from many states.

> **Over a Hundred Ways a Casino Can Lose Their License, or an Executive Can Get Fired**
>
> **General Failures**
> 1. Failure to comply with all laws—industrial espionage, antitrust, ADA, environmental laws, health, OSHA, tobacco use and sales, selling alcohol except from a licensed distributor, privacy laws
> 2. Failure to notify the regulators within 10 days if a licensee is convicted of a felony
> 3. Failure to file foreign gaming reports
> 4. Failure to adhere to requirements of an approved gaming compliance program
>
> **Operating Failures**
> 5. Unapproved gaming or gaming device on the casino floor
> 6. Approved but modified gaming device on the casino floor

7. Unapproved side bet on a game or unapproved modification to a permitted game on the casino floor
8. Unapproved promotional device at the casino (i.e., free play device)
9. Unsealed CPU (central processing unit)
10. Allowing players to use slot keys to put machines into "stand by mode"
11. Allowing a cheating device to remain on the premises
12. Failure to report a gaming dispute of $500 or more
13. Permitting persons who are visibly intoxicated to participate in gaming activity
14. Complimentary service of intoxicating beverages in the casino area to persons who are visibly intoxicated
15. Allowing minors to loiter on the casino floor
16. Allowing minors to play a game
17. Unapproved theme on a slot machine
18. Catering to someone of unsavory character, bad reputation, or criminal background
19. Failure to keep the gaming floor open to the public
20. Charging an admission to enter an area where gambling is conducted unless specifically approved by the regulators
21. Accepting a bet that you are not licensed to take
22. Changing the amount of or shutting down a progressive jackpot without transitioning the jackpot amount to other machines or approved method
23. Changing the rate of payoff progression of a progressive slot machine without recording it
24. Failure to conduct operations in accordance with good taste, custom, or decorum—strippers, publicity stunts that involve the gambling games, etc.
25. Failure to comply with the regulators' conditions to your gaming license
26. Failure to surrender your license upon stopping your operations
27. Failure to notify the regulators that you are closing
28. Failure to display or in some cases have access to payoff schedules on game or slot machines
29. Failure to have payoff schedules that accurately reflect the actual payouts
30. Allowing an officer, director, or key employee to gamble at the casino
31. Allowing race/sports employees betting at their own location (except pari-mutuel horseracing)
32. Failure to immediately notify the enforcement division of any suspected violation of a gaming crime
33. Cheating players or knowingly allowing employees to cheat players
34. Fixing the prize winners of a promotion
35. Using unapproved chips
36. Using unapproved tokens

37. Buying gaming equipment from an unlicensed manufacturer or distributor
38. Using unapproved gaming equipment
39. Using unapproved associated equipment or installing associated equipment without regulators' approval
40. Failure to pay winnings to a patron after being directed to by regulators' order (after all appropriate appeals)
41. Changing the number or types of games without permission
42. Failure to conspicuously post problem gambling information
43. Failure to maintain approved surveillance over all games
44. Failure to adequately supervise the games
45. Failing to follow the published/posted rules of a game
46. Failure to conduct training as required by the regulations
47. Failure to properly document uncollected baccarat commission

Ownership Failures
48. Transferring ownership to someone that is not licensed
49. Failure to escrow the purchase price for an interest in a casino until licensure
50. Transferring ownership between licensed owners without approval
51. Failure to notify the Board if the licensed owner dies
52. Failure to notify the Board if the licensed owner files bankruptcy
53. Failure to keep copies of all ownership records on premise
54. Failure to obtain approval for a pledge of securities of the licensee
55. Paying a percentage of profits of any gambling game without being licensed
56. Issuing an option to purchase stock in a gaming company without prior approval

Regulators' Relationship
57. Failure to truthfully answer direct questions asked by the Gaming Control Board
58. Failure to provide access to any portion of the casino to a gaming agent
59. Failure to provide any information or document to an agent upon request

Business Relationship Failures
60. Failure to exclude persons on the blacklist from your casino
61. Paying an unlicensed junket representative
62. Allowing an unregistered poker tournament conductor to host a poker tournament
63. Doing business with or employing someone on the gray list (denied applicants)
64. Doing business with persons of bad reputation or criminal background
65. Failure to control activities that occur at third party locations like nightclubs for drugs and prostitution

Accounting Failures

66. Failure to file CTR (Currency Transaction Report)
67. Failure to file SAR (Suspicious Activity Report)
68. Failure to properly complete CTR-Cs or SARCs
69. Failure to keep multiple transaction logs
70. Instructing a player on how to structure wagers to avoid reporting or otherwise assisting in money laundering
71. Failure to complete form W-2G (IRS tax form for gambling winnings) or doing so improperly
72. Failure to withhold income tax where required
73. Failure to follow your own property's internal controls
74. Modifying your internal controls without regulators' approval
75. Failure to keep your casino's minimum bankroll requirement (reserves for payouts)
76. Failure to collect a live entertainment tax
77. Failure to timely pay all gaming taxes
78. Failure to notify the regulators' that you fail under the minimum bankroll requirement
79. Failure to log out of a computer requiring a PIN to be accessed
80. Failure to separate restricted funds
81. Failure to report loans within 30 days of the close of the quarter
82. Failure to retain all accounting records for 5 years
83. Failure to prepare annual financial statement (if $1 million in revenue)
84. Failure to produce accurate reports that must be filed

Marketing/Advertising Failures

85. Failure to do advertising that is decent, within good taste, etc.
86. Doing advertising that is false or misleading
87. Conducting marketing or other activities that could embarrass the state if made public

Employee Failure

88. Paying out gaming revenues to someone who is not licensed that is supposed to be
89. Allowing employees that are not designated as casino or liquor employees to have involvement in those areas without adhering to the proper protocol including permitting someone to assume a key employee role but structuring his or her position to avoid registration
90. Failure to file a list of key employees
91. Failure to list all key employees on the required list of key employees
92. Failure to register all gaming employees
93. Failure to assure that all gaming employees have their work card while working

94. Failure to assure that all work cards are current
95. Employing registered employees at wrong locations
96. Employing someone who refuses to apply for a gaming license
97. Employing anyone ever found guilty of cheating by the commission or any court

Credit/Collection Failures

98. Selling or assigning markers to a third party
99. Allowing someone other than an employee, licensed collection agent, registered junket representative, or licensed attorney to collect markers
100. Allowing a denied applicant to collect markers
101. Failure to maintain records that describe all credit collection arrangements and to maintain all written contracts
102. Issuing credit to a player to satisfy a debt to another casino or person
103. Issuing credit to a key employee

V. SURVEILLANCE

Another tool that governments can use to control casino operations is surveillance. Casino surveillance involves covert observations of the casino operations, usually with video cameras. Casino surveillance should be an integral part of the casino plan of internal controls. The purpose of surveillance is to (1) safeguard the licensee's assets; (2) deter, detect, and prosecute criminal acts; and (3) maintain the public trust that licensed gaming is honest and free of criminal elements.[51] Regulations can dictate the number of cameras, their placement, recording capacities, and retention requirements.[52] Surveillance coverage in the casino typically covers, at a minimum, count rooms, casino cages, table games, bingo and keno, gaming devices, and security office detention rooms.

Surveillance can provide an independent check on casino operations and a video recording of persons making otherwise anonymous wagers. The surveillance operators can be either government regulators, casino employees, or both. Larger casinos can assign supervision over surveillance independent of an operation's personnel and management.[53] These casinos may have surveillance rooms that resemble a control center. In front of a sweeping desk are video monitors tied to computer hard drives that store the surveillance videos of the casino.

A. Enforcement

While regulatory enforcement is often associated with detecting and responding to regulatory and statutory violations, this is only one of five main functions that

---

51. *See* Nev. Gaming Comm. Reg. 5.160.
52. *State Regulators, supra* note 49.
53. *Id.*

enforcement agencies may perform. The other functions are (1) maintaining a visible regulatory presence, (2) information gathering and intelligence, (3) order maintenance, and (4) service-related duties and prevention programs.

B. Maintaining a Visible Regulatory Presence

A visible presence in the casino environment can be achieved by having regulatory agents stationed in the casino to observe operations, slot fills, and the count rooms. For example, in New Jersey, regulators station agents on the premises of casinos.[54] This visible presence allows the agents to observe, either in person or through surveillance, the most critical aspects of casino operations. Agents can observe sensitive functions such as the count. They also can personally and expeditiously respond to incidents on the casino floor that require them to settle disputes, conduct investigations, and preserve evidence. Another method of achieving a visible presence in the casino environment is through independent or concurrent government surveillance. This would involve the regulators having their own surveillance cameras or being able to tap into the casino's surveillance cameras to observe critical casino functions.

C. Investigations

Regulatory violations are often detected through three primary sources: overt investigations, undercover investigations, or information gathering.

1. Overt Investigations

Most enforcement procedures involve overt investigations. They range from investigating patron disputes to performing periodic checks of gaming equipment.

2. Investigating Complaints

An important enforcement function involves receiving and investigating complaints or allegations from the public. If, for example, a patron believes he or she was cheated, enforcement agents may conduct an overt investigation by interviewing witnesses and collecting evidence.

Regulators also conduct overt investigations on matters that are not initiated by patrons. For example, casinos may request help in investigating cheating or theft by patrons or employees. Another example is where the legislature or another regulatory agency that is responsible for adopting laws or regulations requests enforcement agents investigate a matter to help them decide whether a new or revised law is warranted. At other times, enforcement agents may work with other branches of

---

54. *About the Division of Gaming Enforcement*, N.J. Office of the Attorney General, https://www.nj.gov/oag/ge/mission&duties.htm.

government, such as the prosecutor's office or similar agency, to develop evidence to prosecute criminal offenses.

3. Routine Inspections

Another common overt investigation that enforcement agents undertake is the routine inspection of the casino. This may include inspecting cards, dice, gaming devices, surveillance cameras, and other areas of, and items in, the casino to ensure that they conform to regulations. For example, enforcement agents may measure dice to ensure that they are not loaded, count the cards in a deck to ensure they are a standard deck, and check the computer chip in gaming devices to ensure they contain the same program as the government-approved chip. Other overt routine inspections may include determining that no unauthorized or unlicensed persons are working in the casino, that no minors are participating in the casino games, or that no untaxed games are being offered for play.

4. Undercover Investigations

Besides overt operations, enforcement functions may include undercover operations. These operations may be directed at detecting criminal activities by casino owners, employees, or patrons. Such activities can be as simple as posing as patrons and observing whether patrons or dealers are stealing the chips of other patrons. This could include sending minors into the casino to learn if the casino will allow them to play casino games. "Deep" undercover work may involve penetrating slot cheating teams or posing as dealers to detect employee theft.

Another common use of undercover operations is to test the casino's internal control systems. An example might include posing as patrons in an attempt to induce casino employees to violate cash transaction rules or to exceed maximum loss restrictions.

D. Information Gathering and Intelligence

Regulatory agencies may gather considerable amounts of information through means other than investigations. The three principal methods include casino reporting, monitoring, and intelligence. By regulation, casinos may have to report various information to the regulators. This could include, for example, all discharges of employees and the reasons for those discharges. This information would allow regulators to track employees and initiate an investigation of an employee if theft or dishonesty is a basis for discharge or there is a pattern of unexplained discharges. Casinos also may have to provide information on table or gaming device holds. If the regulators detect a continuing deviation between the actual and theoretical hold, they could investigate the reasons for the deviation.

Regulators also may detect various criminal and regulatory violations by "intelligence gathering." Intelligence information may come from other police agencies, internal agency records, or through informants. For example, an informant may tell the agency that a gaming device team from another city intends to ply its trade in the state. The agency may obtain photographs and criminal information on the team from other police agencies. Regulatory agents may then run the names through their own records to determine if any of the team members ever worked in any casinos in the state or have internal files that may give clues to where or how the team intends to cheat. From that point, the matter may be referred for overt or undercover investigation.

Intelligence information could cover a broad range of subjects. Tracking the activities of known criminals or criminal organizations is often a high priority. For example, regulators may want to know if these persons or groups are profiting from the casinos through hidden ownership, skimming, extortion, or illegal activities such as prostitution. Other intelligence information can include information that may suggest skimming or cheating by owners or employees or the conduct of illegal activity on the casino premises by third parties, casino employees, or casino operators.

Chapter 4

Currency Reporting and Anti-Money Laundering Requirements for Gaming Properties

Peter J. Kulick

I. INTRODUCTION

The luster of bright flashing lights and the echoes of bells and whistles beckon you to a Shangri-la in the middle of a desert. The scene is punctuated with the trailing sound of laughter and boisterous exclamations of victory. As you look around, you watch a man toss wads of cash and chips onto a craps table, while an enraptured retiree overworks a one-armed bandit in the middle of the room. You think you have just strolled onto a casino floor! But you, my wise friend, are astonished when I lean toward you and say, "Welcome to a financial institution!" You can only shrug and utter a faint "Huh?!?"

The gaming industry is an economic engine. Large amounts of money flow into and out of casino properties and gambling sites literally every second of the day. While gambling dates back to the dawn of mankind, the modern gaming industry has evolved into a popular and exciting twenty-first-century form of entertainment. It should not come as much of a surprise that the legalized gambling industry is heavily regulated and subject to a plethora of legal obligations. Government has long had an interest in curtailing organized crime from participating in the gaming industry.[1] While organized crime has largely been—if not entirely—eradicated from

---

1. *See* PETER J. KULICK, *Accounting, Audits, and Recordkeeping in* REGULATING INTERNET GAMING 55 (Anthony Cabot & Ngai Pindell, eds. 2013). Historically, gaming regulations were designed to prevent unlicensed persons from participating in the profits of a licensed gaming operation. Over time, gaming regulations also focused on protecting the government's interest in receiving its proper tax revenue. *See id.*

sharing in the profits of a gambling operation (whether as an owner or financier), the sheer volume of money flowing through casinos and gambling sites on a daily basis make the gaming industry susceptible to money laundering. Consequently, U.S. laws impose anti-money laundering (AML) obligations on gambling operators.

We live in an era of increasing government investigations, which are often criminal investigations, of business entities.[2] The stakes are sufficiently high that corporations are often willing to agree to "expansive cooperation, monitoring, and institutional reform" to avoid criminal prosecution.[3] The gaming industry is not immune to governmental criminal investigations, particularly with respect to compliance with AML laws. Noncompliance can result in significant monetary penalties and expose gaming operators to criminal and state regulatory enforcement actions.[4] In 2013, the Las Vegas Sands Co. paid $47,400,300 to the U.S. government as part of a nonprosecution agreement to resolve alleged AML compliance failures.[5]

By providing a concise examination of the AML laws applicable to the gaming industry, this chapter is designed to serve as a resource to the business lawyer. The chapter begins by providing an overview of legal gambling operations, which consists of traditional land-based casinos and the growing prevalence of Internet gaming.[6] In order to present a coherent study of AML obligations, this chapter next defines the "problem" (i.e., money laundering) and explores the history and policy of AML laws as applied to the gambling industry. It is helpful to step back and gain an understanding of the perceived social harm and policy goals of AML laws in order to better comprehend the applicable legal requirements. After exploring the perceived social harm of money laundering and the policy goals behind AML laws, the relevant U.S. AML laws are discussed.[7] These laws are primarily found in two statutory sources: the Bank Secrecy Act[8] and the USA PATRIOT Act of 2001.[9]

---

2. Notably, government investigations include the Volkswagen Group diesel emissions scandal, which resulted in a $2.8 billion criminal fine and $1.5 billion in civil penalties. *See* U.S. Department of Justice, *Volkswagen AG Agrees to Plead Guilty and Pay $4.3 Billion in Criminal and Civil Penalties* (Jan. 11, 2017), https://www.justice.gov/opa/pr/volkswagen-ag-agrees-plead-guilty-and-pay-43-billion-criminal-and-civil-penalties-six. *See also* Joseph Rillotta, *Beyond the SAR-C: Best Practices for Gaming Companies to "Know Their Customer" and Avoid Organizational Money Laundering Liability in the Post-Sands Climate*, 5 UNLV Gaming L.J. 145, 151 (2014).

3. Rillotta, *supra* note 2, at 151.

4. *See id.* at 153. The former chairman of the Nevada Gaming Control Board is on record as stating that a violation of federal law could serve as the basis for disciplinary action under Nevada gaming laws.

5. *See* U.S. Department of Justice, *U.S. Attorney's Office Central District of California, Operator of Venetian Resort in Las Vegas Agrees to Return of $47 Million after Receiving Money Under Suspicious Circumstances* (August 27, 2013), https://www.justice.gov/usao-cdca/pr/operator-venetian-resort-las-vegas-agrees-return-over-47-million-after-receiving-money.

6. Internet gaming is interchangeably referred to as "I-gaming" or "Internet-based gaming" throughout this chapter.

7. AML laws have received widespread international attention. Most foreign jurisdictions have adopted comprehensive AML requirements applicable to financial institutions. AML standards have been a focus of the international community, particularly with respect to the Internet gaming industry.

8. 31 U.S.C. § 5311, et seq (2018).

9. Pub. L. No. 107-56, 115 Stat. 272 (2001), as amended by Pub. L. No. 109-177, Pub. L. No.109-178, Pub. L. No.112-3, Pub. L. No. 111-141, and Pub. L. No.112-14. The USA PATRIOT Act amended several different statutory regimes. The statutory text of USA PATRIOT Act, the various amendments, and other related resources can be found online at https://it.ojp.gov/PrivacyLiberty/authorities/statutes/1281.

II. AN INTRODUCTION TO THE GAMBLING INDUSTRY

Historically, gaming in the United States has been confined to state-operated lotteries and brick-and-mortar, land-based casinos.[10] Land-based gaming is conducted under three different regulatory environments: state-authorized commercial gaming, state-conducted lottery offerings, and Indian gaming conducted by Indian tribes.[11] As land-based gaming has proliferated across the United States, new mediums of gambling offerings have developed. The new mediums principally have been in the form of Internet-based gaming.[12]

It is helpful to offer an elementary overview of the operating models for gaming operations in order to appreciate the AML obligations of gaming properties. A comprehensive discussion of gaming operating models is well beyond the scope of this chapter.

A. Overview of Land-Based Gaming

The hallmark of land-based gaming is a physical location that houses the gambling activity. Land-based gaming typically offers electronic gaming devices (e.g., slot machines) and may also offer table games. Patrons place wagers in person. In the United States, land-based gaming is offered by commercial casinos, Indian tribal casinos, and state lottery games, such as video lottery terminals.[13]

B. Overview of the I-Gaming Business Model

The Internet gaming business model differs from other forms of gambling.[14] Capital needs, operating costs, the role of suppliers, and staff needs all substantially differ from the brick-and-mortar gaming industry. Moreover, the medium by which games

---

10. Nevada was the first state to authorize gaming in the United States. *See, e.g.*, Robert W. Stocker II & Peter J. Kulick, *Chapter 11 Cases Involving Gambling Casinos in* COLLIER GUIDE TO CHAPTER 11 (Alan N. Resnick & Henry J. Sommer, eds. 2015). As of 2018, twenty-four states have authorized some form of commercial casino gaming, which generated $40.28 billion in gaming revenue. *See* American Gaming Ass'n, *2018 State of the States: the AGA Survey of the Commercial Casino Industry* 4 (2018).

11. The legal and regulatory framework for Indian tribal gaming is set forth in the Indian Gaming Regulatory Act of 1988, 25 U.S.C. §§ 2701–2721 (2018). Indian tribal gaming has evolved into a substantial segment of the U.S. gaming industry, contributing over $30 billion in gaming revenue. *See* Alan Meister, *The Economic Impact of Tribal Gaming: A State-by-State Analysis*, AM. GAMING ASS'N (2017). For a discussion of the economic impact of Indian gaming, see Alan P. Meister, Kathryn R.L. Rand, & Steven Andrew Light, *Indian Gaming and Beyond: Tribal Economic Development and Diversification*, 54 S.D. L. REV. 375 (2009).

12. There is also a widespread market of unregulated gaming, which spans the spectrum of Internet cafes, purported skill-based gaming, and fantasy sports. *See, e.g.*, Marc W. Dunbar & Daniel R. Russell, *The History of Internet Cafes and the Current Approach to their Regulation*, 3 UNLV GAMING L.J. 243 (2012). Although daily fantasy sports offerings have gained incredible popularity, the legality of daily fantasy sports under state antigambling laws is still very much the subject of legal debate. *See* Jake Lestok, *Tackling Daily Fantasy Sports in the States*, 26 NAT'L CONFERENCE OF STATE LEGISLATURES 1 (Jan. 2018), http://www.ncsl.org/research/civil-and-criminal-justice/tackling-daily-fantasy-sports-in-the-states.aspx.

13. *See, e.g.*, I. Nelson Rose, *Gambling and the Law: The Third Wave of Legal Gambling*, 17 VIL. SPORTS & ENT. L.J. 361, 363–64 (2010); Joseph M. Kelly, *U.S. Land-Based and Internet Gaming; Would You Bet on a Rosy Future?* 17 VIL. SPORTS & ENT. L.J. 339, 341–44 (2010).

14. *See generally* Kulick, *supra* note 1, at 57–64 for an overview of Internet gaming business models.

are offered and the anonymity by which gaming takes place in an online environment differs from land-based gaming. The differences in the business model and the offering medium leads to tailoring AML compliance programs to match the risk profile unique to I-gaming operations.

The flow of money in I-gaming illustrates the differences in money-laundering risks vis-à-vis land-based gaming. Typically, a player will use a credit or debit card to transfer money to an account held in the name of the Internet gaming operator. The credit or debit card transfer will be effectuated by a money processor, which may or may not be directly affiliated with the I-gaming operator. The funds will be held on account for the player with the I-gaming operators. The funds held on deposit in a financial institution may be placed in a segregated account or commingled with funds of other players or even other funds of the I-gaming operators.

Like any other business, including land-based gaming operators, there is no one-size-fits-all organizational structure for I-gaming. The three categories of providers operating within the I-gaming sphere are business-to-business (B2B), business-to-consumer (B2C), and business-to-government (B2G).

Internet gaming operations normally encompass eight distinct activities: (1) the game software, (2) the gaming license granted by a licensing jurisdiction, (3) payment processing, (4) liquidity management, (5) site hosting, (6) customer service, (7) marketing, and (8) back-end support. The activities that the licensee assumes will depend upon the business model adopted. The business model that an Internet gaming licensee adopts will depend on a variety of business factors, such as in-house IT capabilities and payment processing expertise.

III. A HISTORY OF MONEY LAUNDERING AND POLICY GOALS OF AML LAWS

Understanding the historical context behind AML laws is beneficial in order to gain an appreciation of the legal obligations AML laws impose on the gaming industry. Fundamentally, AML efforts are designed to snuff out other criminal activity, such as terrorism financing, drug trafficking, fraud, or political corruption.[15] Thus, AML laws seek to identify and report transactions that have a likelihood to involve proceeds from, or funds to be used in furtherance of, criminal activities.

A. What Is Money Laundering?

The motivation to engage in the act of money laundering is obvious. As one author succinctly noted:

> When there are no records of substantial income, but an individual is able to maintain a large pool of assets, authorities often question the legitimacy of the sources

---

15. Brittany Yantis, Monica Attia, & Georgina Lethouris, *Money Laundering*, 55 Am. Crim. L. Rev. 1469, 1470 (2018).

of the assets. Money laundering seeks to solve this problem by creating seemingly legitimate revenue streams in an effort to prevent authorities from taking notice.[16]

Accordingly, from a definitional standpoint, money laundering is the act of disguising the source of funds earned in an illegal activity in an effort to make it appear as if the funds are derived from a legitimate activity.

Money laundering is accomplished through three stages: placement, layering, and integration.[17] Placement involves "the launderer plac[ing] criminally-derived money into a legitimate enterprise."[18] Layering involves the process of "plac[ing] the money in various pretextual transactions to obscure the original source."[19] Finally, integration consists of transforming "the funds into non-cash instruments recognized in the legitimate financial world, such as bank notes, loans, letters of credit, or any number of recognizable financial instruments."[20] Accordingly, the act of money laundering is an effort to disguise the source of funds derived from an illegal activity in an effort to legitimatize the funds.

B. Policy Goal and Substance of AML Laws

The overriding policy goal of AML laws is to limit, or eliminate, criminal activity.[21] AML laws attempt to eliminate criminal activity by attacking criminals where it hurts the most: their pocketbook. Specifically, AML laws accomplish this goal by attempting to limit criminals' access to the financial services system.[22] By limiting access to the legitimate financial world, the underlying criminal activity can be limited. AML laws further offer the opportunity to identify potential criminal activity by identifying and reporting suspicious financial transactions to law enforcement.[23] Procedurally, AML laws function to achieve the underlying policy goal by requiring certain persons involved in the financial services industry to maintain records and report information that may be useful in criminal, tax, or other regulatory investigations.[24]

---

16. Norm Keith, *Anti-Money Laundering: A Comparative Review of Legislative Development*, 19 Bus. L. Int'l 245, 272 (2018).
17. *Id.* at 249–50.
18. Yantis, *supra* note 15, at 1469.
19. *Id.*
20. *Id.*
21. *Id.*
22. *See* Keith, *supra* note 16, at 246–48. Historically, "bank secrecy was a fundamental principle of business." *Id.* at 248. Consequently, criminals could effectively use bank secrecy policies to obfuscate the source of funds and further criminal activities.
23. *See* 31 U.S.C. § 5311 (2018) ("It is the purpose of [the Bank Secrecy Act] to require certain reports or records where they have a high degree of usefulness in criminal, tax, or regulatory investigations or proceedings, or in the conduct of intelligence or counterintelligence activities, including analysis, to protect against international terrorism."). *See also* Leonard C. Senia, *Bank Secrecy Act Requirements* in Regulating Land-Based Casinos 213 (Cabot & Pindell, eds. 2014). As Senia points out, "[A]nti-money laundering laws and regulations assist law enforcement in controlling criminal activities by requiring financial institutions and other regulated entities to prevent, detect, and report money laundering activities."
24. *See* Senia, *supra* note 23, at 214.

The primary source of federal law that imposes AML obligations on financial institutions is the Bank Secrecy Act of 1970 (BSA).[25] The BSA imposes three requirements on "financial institutions":[26] reporting certain identified transactions,[27] recordkeeping,[28] and adopting AML compliance programs.[29] As discussed below, it is the definition of a financial institution that ultimately brings most casinos within the purview of the BSA.[30]

Congress and the Department of the Treasury have refined and expanded the scope of the BSA since 1970 to further combat money-laundering activities.[31] Two significant AML developments were the enactment of the Money Laundering Control Act of 1986[32] and the USA PATRIOT Act of 2001.[33]

The Money Laundering Control Act established the crime of money laundering,[34] which is a felony offense and subject to significant criminal penalties.[35] The crime of money laundering is defined to mean conducting, or attempting to conduct, a financial transaction with the *proceeds of an unlawful activity* with the *intent* to either (1) promote the carrying on of a specified unlawful activity, (2) engage in tax evasion, or (3) avoid currency transaction reporting.[36]

C. AML Laws and the Gaming Industry

In the United States, the gambling industry is heavily regulated.[37] Furthermore, the growing trend in the United States among casino operators is to be publicly traded, which introduces further regulatory requirements.[38] As publicly traded businesses,

---

25. 31 U.S.C. § 5311, et seq (2018). Extensive regulations have been promulgated by the U.S. Department of the Treasury. To add a layer of confusion, the BSA regulations were originally codified in 31 C.F.R. § 103. In 2010, FinCEN issued a final rule transferring and reorganizing the BSA regulations to a new chapter in the Code of Federal Regulations. *See* 75 Fed. Reg. 65806-1 (Oct. 26, 2010). The BSA regulations, as codified in 31 C.F.R. § 103, are still made publicly available on official government information portals.
26. *See* 31 U.S.C. § 5312 (2018); *see also* 58 Fed. Reg. 13538, 13550 (Mar. 12, 1993).
27. As discussed *infra*, reporting is accomplished by filing current transaction reports, suspicious activity reports, or both.
28. The BSA reporting and recordkeeping obligations are procedures that are designed to be effective in criminal enforcement activities.
29. AML compliance programs help ensure that financial institutions have effective procedures in place to comply with BSA reporting and recordkeeping obligations.
30. *See* 18 U.S.C. § 5312(a)(2)(X) (2018) (defining a financial institution to mean, inter alia, "a casino, gambling business, or gaming establishment with an annual gaming revenue of more than $1,000,000" that is licensed by a state or operated under the Indian Gaming Regulatory Act).
31. For a detailed history of the BSA and its evolution, see Senia *supra* note 23, at 217–22.
32. 18 U.S.C. §§ 1956–1957 (2018).
33. *See* PATRIOT Act, *supra* note 9.
34. 18 U.S.C. § 1956 (2018).
35. The criminal penalties include a fine of the greater of $500,000 or twice the value of the property involved in the transaction and imprisonment of up to twenty years. 18 U.S.C. § 1956 (2018).
36. *Id.* (emphasis added).
37. Chapter 3 of this book provides a comprehensive outline of the forms of regulation of gaming in the United States. *See also*, Stocker & Kulick, *supra* note 10, at ¶ 25.03[2].
38. The Securities Act of 1933 and the Securities Exchange Act of 1934 establish a mandatory disclosure system in the United States for publicly traded companies. The Sarbanes-Oxley Act of 2002 introduced additional financial disclosure and reporting obligations on public companies.

management ultimately answers to shareholders.[39] Thus, at first blush, it would appear that imposing AML obligations on casinos is an overreaction to the history of the mob within the casino industry. However, by taking a step back and examining *how* casinos generate revenue and the services offered by casinos, it becomes apparent that the AML compliance focus is not aimed at any remaining mob influence in casino ownership. Rather, the concern with AML in the casino setting lies with how gambling is conducted and the services casinos offer to their patrons.

Casinos are largely cash businesses. The activity on the casino floor is fast-paced, with numerous transactions occurring simultaneously each second of the day.[40] The pace of play and transactions occurring in the I-gaming universe share a similar characteristic. Casinos provide financial services that are similar to depository institutions. For example, casinos accept customer deposits, transmit money, and offer check-cashing services and currency exchange services.[41] Internet gaming customers must establish deposit accounts, which is often accomplished remotely and through an online environment. Gambling businesses can thus be attractive vehicles for criminals to launder money.

IV. CASINO AML LEGAL OBLIGATIONS

The BSA goals are noble to assist in the prevention of crime and combat terrorism. The obligations imposed on covered persons under the BSA are onerous. Noncompliance can result in draconian penalties.[42] As a result, there is an incentive to fall outside the scope of those statutorily required to comply with the BSA.

A covered person under the BSA generally includes any financial institution.[43] Therefore, the threshold question to be addressed is whether casinos are financial institutions for purposes of the BSA. As initially enacted in 1970, the BSA defined a financial institution much as one would expect: traditional banks and money transmitters. Casinos were not expressly included within the initial definition of a financial institution.

While the original version of the BSA did not expressly pull casinos within its purview, the BSA did grant regulatory authority to the Department of the Treasury to designate other persons as a financial institution based on two separate standards.[44] First, the Treasury could designate a person as a financial institution if the

---

39. Casino operations are no longer the province of organized crime. For a history of organized crime in the casino industry, see Jerome H. Skolnick & John Dombrink, *The Limits of Gaming Control*, 12 Conn. L. Rev. 762, 763–67 (1979).
40. *See* Peter J. Kulick, *Auditing and Accounting of Casino Revenues*, *in* Regulating Land-Based Casinos 305, 314–18 (Anthony Cabot & Ngai Pindell, eds. 2014).
41. The scope of financial services offered by casinos quickly reveal that casinos are very much participating in the financial services industry.
42. *See* 31 U.S.C. § 5321 (2018); *see also* 31 C.F.R. § 1010.820 (identifying civil penalties) and 31 C.F.R. § 1010.830 (identifying criminal penalties).
43. 31 U.S.C. § 5312 (2018).
44. *See id.*

person is engaged in activities that are similar to, related to, or a substitute for activities of covered businesses. Alternatively, the Treasury was granted the authority to designate a person as a financial institution for BSA purposes if the business engaged in cash transactions that have a high degree of usefulness in criminal, tax, or regulatory matters. Casinos would seem to fit the bill for the type of persons that the Treasury could designate as a financial institution under the BSA. In fact, the Treasury did just that in regulations promulgated in 1985.[45]

In 1994, Congress ended any debate by adding casinos to the list of financial institutions covered by the BSA.[46] Specifically, the BSA now provides in relevant part that a

> "financial institution" means . . . (X) a casino, gambling casino, or gaming establishment with an annual gaming revenue of more than $1,000,000 which—
> (i) is licensed as a casino, gambling casino, or gaming establishment under the laws of any State or any political subdivision of any State; or
> (ii) is an Indian gaming operation conducted under or pursuant to the Indian Gaming Regulatory Act other than an operation which is limited to class I gaming (as defined in section 4(6) of such Act).[47]

As a result, most legal gaming operations, whether commercial or Indian casinos, are financial institutions for BSA purposes and, accordingly, are subject to the BSA obligations.[48] Card clubs, which typically offer only card games, are also treated as financial institutions for BSA purposes.[49]

Not all gambling businesses fall within the scope of the BSA casino rules. By the plain language of the statute, certain casinos will necessarily fall outside the scope of the definition of a financial institution. Specifically, small casinos—those with annual gaming revenue of $1,000,000 or less—and Indian gaming operations that are limited to Class I gaming fall outside the statutory definition. Horse racing tracks that offer pari-mutuel wagering or other forms of wagering solely on races are

---

45. *See* 50 Fed. Reg. 5065 (1985).
46. *See* 18 U.S.C. § 5312(a)(2)(X) (2018). The Money Laundering Suppression Act of 1994 added casinos to the list of financial institutions under the BSA.
47. *Id.*; *see also* 31 C.F.R. § 1010.100(t)(5) (defining a casino) and § 1010.100(t)(6) (defining a card club).
48. FinCEN has released a series of frequently asked questions, which address casino recordkeeping, reporting, and compliance program requirements. In FIN-2007-G005 (Nov. 14, 2007), FinCEN offered informal guidance with respect to its view of the gaming institutions subject to the BSA casino requirements:

> **Question 1: What gaming institutions are subject to the BSA casino regulatory requirements?**
> **Answer 1:** A casino or a card club that is duly licensed or authorized to do business as such, and has gross annual gaming revenue in excess of $1 million, is a "financial institution" under the BSA. The definition applies to both land-based and riverboat operations licensed or authorized under the laws of a state, territory, or tribal jurisdiction, or under the Indian Gaming Regulatory Act. Tribal gaming establishments that offer slot machines, video lottery terminals, or table games, and that have gross annual gaming revenue in excess of $1 million are covered by the definitions. Card clubs generally are subject to the same rules as casinos, unless a different treatment for card clubs is explicitly stated in 31 C.F.R. Part 103 (citations omitted).

49. *See* 31 C.F.R. § 1010.100(t)(6). Card clubs are largely prevalent in California.

not considered casinos and are thus exempt from the BSA casino rules.[50] Although horse racing tracks are not considered to be a casino with respect to the BSA casino-specific rules, they could still fall within BSA reporting obligations applicable to the receipt of currency in a trade or business.[51]

After concluding that most casinos are covered persons under the BSA, the analysis turns to the obligations imposed by the BSA. The BSA imposes three categories of obligations upon covered persons: reporting certain financial transactions, recordkeeping, and establishing a compliance program.

A. BSA Reporting Requirements

Information reporting serves as the backbone of the AML laws by assisting law enforcement in identifying criminal activities and supporting active criminal investigations.[52] There are two types of reports casinos may be required to file with the U.S. Department of the Treasury Financial Crimes Enforcement Network (FinCEN) pursuant to the BSA: (1) a Currency Transaction Report (CTR) for currency transactions that exceed $10,000 and (2) a Suspicious Activity Report (SAR).

1. Currency Transaction Reporting

The obligation to file a CTR is a bright-line standard. A CTR must be filed with FinCEN for each currency transaction involving *more than* $10,000 by the same person during a twenty-four-hour period. Casino CTR reporting applies to "each transaction in currency, involving either cash in or cash out, of more than $10,000."[53]

The regulations promulgated under the BSA enumerate several cash-in and cash-out transactions that may be subject to BSA reporting.[54] "Transactions in currency involving *cash in*" include, for example, purchases of chips, tokens, or other gaming instruments; front money deposits; safekeeping deposits; payments on markers; and bets placed in cash.[55] "Transactions in currency involving *cash out*" are the reverse side of cash-in transactions.[56] Thus, examples of cash-out transactions include redemptions of chips, tokens and other gaming instruments, front money

---

50. *See* 61 Fed. Reg. 7054-5056 (Feb. 23, 1996); *see also* FIN-2007-G005 (Nov. 14, 2007).
51. *See* 31 U.S.C. § 5331 (2018); *see also* 31 C.F.R. § 1010.330 (2018). Specifically, Example 2 of 31 C.F.R. § 1010.330(c)(13)(iii) addresses currency transaction reporting by a racetrack. While the example concludes a CTR was not required under the particular facts of the example, the example demonstrates that a racetrack could still be subject to the trade or business reporting obligation under certain circumstances.
52. *See Prepared Remarks of FinCEN Director Kenneth A. Blanco, delivered at the 11th Annual Las Vegas Anti-Money Laundering Conference and Expo*, FinCEN (Aug. 14, 2018), https://www.fincen.gov/news/speeches/prepared-remarks-fincen-director-kenneth-blanco-delivered-11th-annual-las-vegas-1. Blanco noted that BSA information reporting "1) provides leads; 2) helps expand cases and puts together pieces of the puzzle or networks we would not otherwise see; and 3) helps alert us to trends in illicit activity so that we can get ahead of them, deter the activity, or prevent harm from spreading."
53. 31 C.F.R. § 1021.311 (2018).
54. *See* 31. C.F.R. § 1021.311(a) and (b).
55. 31 C.F.R. § 1021.311(a) (emphasis added).
56. 31 C.F.R. § 1021.311(b) (emphasis added).

withdrawals, advances on markers, check cashing, and travel and complimentary expenses and gaming incentives.[57]

Multiple currency transactions by or for the same person are aggregated to determine if the $10,000 threshold is met during a twenty-four-hour period.[58] The regulations require aggregation of currency transactions into a single transaction where the casino has knowledge that the transactions are by or for the same person and result in cash in or cash out exceeding $10,000.[59] The twenty-four-hour period, referred to as a "gaming day" in the regulations, used by a casino to test currency transactions generally is the same period the casino uses for business, accounting, and tax purposes.[60]

If a casino determines that a CTR is required to be filed, it must obtain and verify "know your customer" information from the patron,[61] prior to concluding the transaction.[62] Similar to traditional financial institutions, the information that casinos are required to collect and verify includes the name, address, account number, and social security number or taxpayer identification number of the customer.[63]

Reportable currency transactions are filed on FinCEN Form 112. A CTR must be filed within fifteen days following the reportable currency transaction.[64] Casinos are obligated to maintain CTRs for a period of five years after the date of the CTR.[65]

The regulations exempt four categories of casino transactions from currency transaction reporting requirements.[66] This includes any "cash out transactions to the extent that the currency is won in a money play and is the same currency the customer wagered in the money play."[67] Similarly, cash-out transactions involving

---

57. *See id.*
58. *See* 31 C.F.R. § 1021.313.
59. *See id.*
60. *See* 31 C.F.R. § 1021.100(d). The regulation provides that a "[g]aming day means the normal business day of a casino." The regulations accommodate casinos by recognizing that most casinos operate twenty-four hours a day. Thus, the regulations specify that for casinos operating twenty-four hours a day, the gaming day is the "24 hour period by which the casino keeps its books and records for business, accounting, and tax purposes."
61. *See* 31 C.F.R. § 1010.312.
62. *See id.*
63. *See id.*
64. *See* 31 C.F.R. § 1010.306(a)(1).
65. *See id.*
66. *See* 31 C.F.R. § 1021.311(c).
67. *See* 31 C.F.R. § 1021.311(c)(2). For an interesting discussion of the 2006 FinCEN proposed regulations applicable to casino reporting obligations, see Comment Letter from the Nevada Gaming Control Board (May 17, 2006), https://www.fincen.gov/sites/default/files/shared/neilander2.pdf. From a compliance standpoint, the Nevada Gaming Control Board offered a succinct argument with respect to why currency transaction reporting offered little additional benefit to FinCEN for cash-out transactions involving the same money wagered and electronic gaming device drops. Essentially, the Nevada Gaming Control Board observed that many cash-out transactions involving the same money wagered is never part of the casino's "drop" (i.e., never recorded as a receipt of money wagered by the casino), and many of the transactions never involve more than $10,000 from a patron. With respect to electronic gaming devices, suspect transactions are more likely to be identified and reported under the suspicious transaction regime.

the same currency wagered in a money play at table games are exempt from CTR reporting.[68] The regulations also exempt from currency transaction reporting jackpots winnings from slot machines or video lottery terminals.[69]

2. Suspicious Activity Reporting

In contrast to CTRs, the standard to file a SAR is not a bright-line standard. Rather, the SAR filing obligation arises when a casino knows, suspects, or has reason to believe that a transaction, or pattern of transactions, that involves at least $5,000 of funds or other assets is either derived from illegal activities, designed to evade reporting requirements, has no business or apparent lawful purpose, or facilitates criminal activity.[70]

Suspicious activity reporting is based on an analysis of facts and circumstances to determine whether a transaction meets the "suspicious" standard. Suspicious behaviors that can prompt a filing of a SAR generally include structuring transactions, minimal or no casino play, false or altered identification, or fraudulent conduct. FinCEN has published guidance that offers useful details in identifying red flags that may indicate suspicious activities, thereby prompting the need to further investigate.[71] At a 2010 congressional hearing, FinCEN officials detailed common behaviors and activities that have prompted casinos to file a SAR:[72]

- Structuring transactions—60 percent of the SAR reports identified structuring transactions as a suspicious activity. Examples of structuring transactions included:
  o cash-outs followed by cash buy-ins and payments on markers;
  o reducing the number of chips or tokens to be cashed out at the cage to slightly below $10,000 when identification was requested;
  o reducing cash buy-ins at pits to avoid providing identification;
  o use of agents to cash out chips;
  o engaging in a pattern of cashing out chips multiple times a day or at different cages;
  o requesting payouts over $10,000 to be paid in multiple checks; and
  o splitting the purchase of chips at the cage and pit.

---

68. *See id.*
69. *See* 31 C.F.R. § 1021.311(c)(4) ("[C]asinos are exempted from reporting [CTR] obligations . . . for the following transactions in currency or currency transactions: . . . (4) Jackpots from slot machines or video lottery terminals."). The risk of suspected money laundering associated with jackpots is likely minimal. Moreover, casinos are required to report jackpot payouts that are over $1,200 for income tax purposes. *See* 26 U.S.C. § 6041 (2018); Treas. Reg. § 7.6041-1.
70. *See* 31 C.F.R. § 1021.320(a)(2).
71. *See* Rillotta, *supra* note 2, at 154 ("[T]here are no hard-and-fast formulas or algorithms for detecting potential money laundering. . . . Ultimately, at the granular level, there are few if any 'one size fits all' rules.").
72. *Statement of Charles Steele, Deputy Director of Financial Crimes Enforcement Network, United States Department of the Treasury*, FIN. CRIMES ENFORCEMENT NETWORK (May 10, 2010), https://www.fincen.gov/news/testimony/statement-charles-m-steele-deputy-director-financial-crimes-enforcement-network.

- Minimal or no casino play. FinCEN has stated that approximately 30 percent of the SAR identified minimal or no casino play as a suspicious activity. Specific examples identified by FinCEN include:
  - cashing out chips in instances when the casino did not have a record of the patron buying or playing the chips;
  - buying chips with cash, casino credit, credit card advances, or wired funds followed by little or no play and leaving the casino without redeeming the chips;
  - requesting funds received by wire transfer to be wired by the casino to a second bank account without casino play;
  - frequent deposits of money orders or casino checks into accounts followed by minimal play and cashing out via a casino check; and
  - converting cash into ticket-in, ticket-out (TITO) vouchers and then cashing out the TITO vouchers.
- Use of false, expired, altered, or stolen identifications, typically in the form of social security numbers and driver's licenses.
- Fraudulent conduct perpetrated against casinos. Fraudulent activity has included the use of counterfeit money and misusing player's club points.

These examples, taken from a FinCEN study,[73] offer guidance for land-based casinos with respect to common categories of activities that have prompted filing a SAR. An important point to note is that the behaviors identified in the FinCEN study may not, as singular events, appear suspicious in isolation; however, when viewed collectively or over a period of time along with other events, the behavior may constitute reportable suspicious activities. By understanding frequent patterns of suspicious activities, casinos can develop effective policies and procedures to combat money laundering and other criminal activities. Properly training front-line staff is one of the fundamental responsibilities of a casino in demonstrating compliance with AML requirements.

FinCEN issued an advisory in 2009, FIN-2009-A003, "to remind casinos and card clubs that structuring is unlawful, and that such activity can give rise to significant civil and criminal penalties under the BSA." FIN-2009-A003 identified four common scenarios of structuring transactions intended to evade BSA reporting or recordkeeping requirements:

- A premium player inducing casino personnel to divide transactions into multiple transactions in order to fall below the currency transaction reporting threshold
- Persuading casino personnel to alter or omit relevant information, such as player rating records or identification information

---

73. *Id.* Mr. Steele's prepared statement included a summary of FinCEN's analytical study on SAR reporting trends in the gambling industry. FinCEN collects data and prepares studies to aid in law enforcement activities. Mr. Steele's testimony in 2010 summarized the key findings from FinCEN's studies.

- Cage personnel advising patrons to reduce chip redemptions to fall below the currency transaction reporting threshold
- Obtaining the assistance of a pit boss to coordinate buy-ins to span two gaming days

Enforcement actions can also serve as a useful tool to identify situations that may prompt the filing of a SAR. As discussed in greater detail below, the recent settlement between Las Vegas Sands and FinCEN offers several examples of missed red flags.[74] The "irregularities" that should have prompted action from Las Vegas Sands consisted of a high-roller patron's

> use of different financial accounts, held in different, seemingly unrelated names; his tendency to break wire transfer up in to smaller tranches, without a coherent, legitimate explanation; his failure to designate himself as a wire transfer beneficiary; his routing of wire transfers through foreign jurisdictions; and perhaps most significantly, his insistence on the use of a name-neutral account to receive the funds.[75]

The Las Vegas Sands enforcement action reveals that money-laundering risks can arise at even the most profitable casino patrons. Moreover, efforts to accommodate profitable patrons can compromise awareness of conduct that should have triggered SAR reporting.

Casinos file a SAR electronically on FinCEN Form 111. The SAR must be filed within thirty days after the initial detection of the suspicious activity.[76] The thirty-day filing period can be extended by an additional thirty days if no suspect is identified on the date of the initial transaction.[77] The requirement that casinos report suspicious transactions comes with an important protection. Casinos that file a SAR are not liable to any person who might feel aggrieved by the filing of the SAR.[78] Removing the threat of liability promotes the interest of having casinos report suspicious activities without fear of being sued. Another important feature of the SAR reporting is that a casino may not notify a person involved in a suspicious activity that a SAR has been filed.[79] Casinos may share the fact that a SAR was filed with other business locations of the casino, its parent, or an affiliate of the casino within the United States.[80]

---

74. See Rillotta, *supra* note 2, at 146–53 for a detailed overview of the Las Vegas Sands matter.
75. *Id.* at 149.
76. *See* 31. C.F.R. § 1021.320(a)(3).
77. *See id.*
78. *See* 31 U.S.C. § 5318(g)(3) (2018).
79. *See* 31 U.S.C. § 5318(g)(2)(A). Furthermore, the regulations reiterate the confidentiality obligation by providing that "[n]o casino, and no director, officer, employee, or agent of any casino, shall disclose a SAR or any information that would reveal the existence of a SAR." 31 C.F.R. § 1021.320(e). The confidentiality requirements do not prevent disclosure of the SAR or the facts surrounding the SAR to law enforcement agencies or federal or state regulatory bodies that conduct BSA-compliance investigations.
80. *See* FIN-2017-G001 (Jan. 4, 2017).

B. BSA Recordkeeping Requirements

The BSA generally imposes recordkeeping requirements on all financial institutions subject to the BSA. These regulations include a rule that details when recordkeeping requirements are triggered and what records casinos are required to be maintained.[81]

Generally under the BSA regulations, casinos are required to maintain certain information relating "to each deposit of funds, account opened or life of credit extended."[82] The record content generally includes know-your-customer information. Specifically, the regulations require a casino to "secure and maintain a record of the name, permanent address, and social security number of the person involved."[83] The casino must verify the information provided by customers.[84] Casinos must use reasonable efforts to obtain the requisite information.[85] If an account is established in the name of multiple persons, the casino must obtain the required information and maintain records for each person having a financial interest in the deposit, account, or line of credit.[86]

In addition, the BSA regulations require a casino to maintain either an original, microfilm, or other copy or reproduction of certain information relating to customer deposit accounts.[87] The scope of the records required to be maintained include those relating to extensions of credit, deposits of funds, know-your-customer information, player rating records, government required records, and written compliance program records.[88] A casino must maintain the required records for five years. The recordkeeping requirements often parallel state gaming regulatory requirements.[89]

---

81. *See* 31 C.F.R. § 1021.410; *see also Frequently Asked Questions: Casino Recordkeeping, Reporting, and Compliance Program Requirements*, Fin. Crimes Enforcement Network, https://www.fincen.gov/frequently-asked-questions-casino-recordkeeping-reporting-and-compliance-program-requirements-0.

82. 31 C.F.R. § 1021.410(a).

83. *See id.* For nonresidents, the regulations contemplate that the casino will obtain the nonresident person's passport number or a description of some other government document used to verify identity.

84. *See id.*

85. Under the BSA regulations, a casino is not deemed to violate the recordkeeping requirements if it uses reasonable efforts to obtain a social security number and maintains a list of the names and addresses of those individuals. *See* 31 C.F.R. § 1021.410(a).

86. *See* 31 C.F.R. § 1021.410(a). There are many unique business-operation aspects of a casino. Casinos often will bring in multiple guests as part of a "junket." Casinos may receive a single deposit of funds for multiple patrons participating in a junket. A question could arise whether the casino would need to maintain records of each person included in the junket and what records should be maintained. FinCEN guidance concludes that a junket account is effectively a front-money account. Therefore, the casino would need to obtain the required information from each patron prior to allowing a junket participant to conduct wagers through the account. *See* FIN-2012-GOO4 (Aug. 13, 2012).

87. *See* 31 C.F.R. § 1021.410(b).

88. *See id.* The records required to be maintained under 31 C.F.R. § 1021.410(b) are comprehensive. For example, casinos must maintain a record of each transaction involving instruments having a face value of $3,000 or more, including personal checks, cashier checks, promissory notes, or money orders. *See* 31 C.F.R. § 1021.410(b)(9). The scope of the information content extends to "all reference numbers (e.g., casino account number, personal check number, etc.); and the name of the casino license number of the casino employee who conducted the transaction." 31 C.F.R. § 103.36(b)(ii); *see also* FIN-2012-GOO4 (Aug. 13, 2012).

89. *See* Kulick *supra* note 40, at 326–28 (discussing internal controls and regulatory recordkeeping requirements).

C. AML Compliance Program

The USA PATRIOT Act requires financial institutions, including casinos, to establish written AML programs "reasonably designed to assure and monitor compliance with the requirements set forth [in the BSA] and the regulations [promulgated under the BSA]."[90] Written compliance procedures are a form of internal control systems (ICS).[91] ICS have several functions, including to "provide reasonable assurances to either prevent or allow for the timely detection of unauthorized transactions involving company assets that could have a material effect on financial statements."[92] AML compliance programs are risk-based—that is, a covered business must adopt an AML compliance program that takes into account the risks posed by the financial services and products provided by the specific business.

The BSA regulations offer the general contours for the content required to be included in AML compliance programs.[93] The contours of AML compliance programs consist of providing for an ICS, independent testing of internal controls for compliance, adequate training, designating individual(s) responsible for compliance, and maintaining records.[94]

D. Penalties for Noncompliance

Failure to comply with BSA requirements can lead to significant civil monetary penalties. Under 31 U.S.C. § 5321(a)(1), the federal government may impose "a civil penalty of not more than the greater of the amount (not to exceed $100,000) involved in the transaction (if any) or $25,000" on a financial institution—and its directors, officers, or employees—for any willful violation of the BSA. Civil monetary penalties can also be imposed on any failure to file a report or filing a report with a material omission or statement.[95]

In recent years, there has been an uptick of criminal investigations of business entities. In many respects, the United States' legal system is largely based on self-certification and compliance self-reporting.[96] While self-reporting is a hallmark of the U.S. legal system, the government ordinarily has investigative powers to assess compliance. Moreover, there are significant legal penalties—both civil and criminal—for noncompliance.[97]

---

90. 31. C.F.R. § 1021.210(b).
91. ICS are ordinarily pronounced phonetically precisely as one would expect: literally it is pronounced "icks." Chapter 3 sets out the requirements imposed on casinos regarding internal control standards.
92. Kulick, *supra* note 1, at 69.
93. *See id.*
94. *See id.*
95. 31 U.S.C. § 5321(a)(2) (2018).
96. One need only look to the federal tax laws and the obligation of taxpayers to voluntarily file returns and pay the corresponding tax. The self-certification/self-reporting model is in contrast to mandatory government audits on an ongoing basis. For an overview of mandatory government audits in the casino gaming industry, see generally Kulick, *supra* note 1.
97. *See* Rillotta, *supra* note 2.

What does this mean for the casino gaming industry? FinCEN has increasingly focused enforcement actions on casinos.[98] Enforcement actions have principally centered on failures to file SARs and failures to maintain and implement AML programs designed to ensure and monitor compliance with the BSA.[99] In 2015, FinCEN imposed a $75 million fine on the Tinian Dynasty Hotel & Casino for "willful and egregious violations of the [BSA]."[100] Even large, well-known casinos have not been immune to BSA enforcement activity. Las Vegas Sands Corp. agreed to pay a $47.4 million fine for failing to file a SAR.[101] As recently as 2017, FinCEN imposed an $8 million fine on a California card club for violations of the BSA.[102]

The Las Vegas Sands enforcement action presents an interesting case study. As detailed earlier, the alleged failures of the Las Vegas Sands appeared to consist of compliance breakdowns at several levels. The casino was presented a golden "whale": an individual who quickly became the casino's most profitable patron over a very short period of time. The Las Vegas Sands matter focused on the curious relationship with a Mexican national, Zhenli Ye Gon, who quickly became one of the Las Vegas Sands' largest whales.[103] Ye Gon appeared to be a legitimate businessman, owning a chemical company in Mexico. It turned out that he was in the chemical business but was supplying ingredients to manufacture methamphetamine.[104]

The nonprosecution agreement offers far-reaching details of the compliance missteps:[105]

- A failure to investigate Ye Gon, his business interests, or his sources of funds
- A failure to comprehend the layered manner in which Ye Gon wire transferred funds
- Lack of suspicion to Ye Gon's use of multiple third-party sources of funds
- Ye Gon's use of multiple Mexican money-exchange houses, known as *casas de cambios*[106]

---

98. *See, e.g.*, Kathleen E. Brody & Grace C. Rebling, *Show Me the Money: Casinos' Anti-Money-Laundering Obligations and Enforcement*, FED. LAWYER (Aug. 2015).

99. The focus of FinCEN enforcement activity is not entirely surprising, especially because SAR reporting is risk-based.

100. *See In re* Hong Kong Entertainment (Overseas) Investments, Ltd, Untied States Department of the Treasury, FinCEN No. 2015-07 (June 3, 2015).

101. *See* Brody & Rebling, *supra* note 98.

102. *FinCEN Issues $8 Million Penalty on California for Willful Violation of Anti-Money Laundering Controls*, Fin. Crimes Enforcement Network (Nov. 17, 2017), https://www.fincen.gov/news/news-releases/fincen-issues-8-million-penalty-california-card-club-willful-violation-anti.

103. *See Operator of Venetian Resort in Las Vegas Agrees to Return Over $47 Million After Receiving Money Under Suspicious Circumstances*, U.S. ATTORNEY'S OFFICE CENT. DISTRICT OF CAL. (Aug. 27, 2013), https://www.justice.gov/usao-cdca/pr/operator-venetian-resort-las-vegas-agrees-return-over-47-million-after-receiving-money. Over a two-year period, Ye Gon wired approximately $45 million to Las Vegas Sands properties.

104. *See id.* Ye Gon was apparently enlisted by drug cartels to launder money from illicit activities.

105. A copy of the Las Vegas Sands nonprosecution agreement is reprinted in 17 GAMING L. REV. & ECON. 584 (2013).

106. FinCEN had previously issued an advisory warning financial institutions about financial transactions involving *casas de cambios*. *See* FIN-2012-A002 (July 28, 2012).

- Failing to have appropriate suspicion to the fact that a Las Vegas Sands' casino property's own diligence could not link Ye Gon to all the companies he claimed to own or control that sent wire transfers to the casino
- Routing of payments through Las Vegas Sands' Hong Kong subsidiary
- Ye Gon's request to use non-casino name accounts

The consequences to Las Vegas Sands were significant. Not only did it face the threat of a criminal prosecution, but it also faced the very real risk of attendant state gaming regulatory disciplinary action. Once the federal government and state government take enforcement action, it is only a matter of time before the civil lawsuits start searching for their pound of flesh. Ultimately, the Las Vegas Sands entered into to a nonprosecution agreement, which imposed extensive obligations on the casino: enhancing the casino's compliance program, incorporating AML and BSA compliance performance as a factor in employee bonuses, maintaining know-your-customer guidelines and controls designed to detect and prevent money laundering, enhancing suspicious activity reporting protocols, and forfeiting $47,400,300.[107]

In an environment of growing government enforcement actions, there is a substantial incentive to develop and implement comprehensive AML compliance programs. The BSA and its implementing regulations identify AML compliance as obligations of casino gaming businesses.

V. CONCLUSION

We began our journey on the casino floor by establishing that casinos are financial institutions. While casinos may not operate like a bank, we now understand when casinos are considered financial institutions (when the BSA tells us so!) and the obligations that arise from this designation. Casinos operate in a cash-intensive environment. Not only are patrons placing wagers, sometimes in significant dollar amounts, but casinos also offer a bevy of ancillary financial services such as check cashing, deposit accounts, and currency exchanges. As a result, casinos can be the unknowing targets of money-laundering activities.

The BSA is designed to prevent criminal activity by limiting criminals from accessing the financial services industry and to identity suspect transactions. The BSA specifically includes casinos as financial institutions, thus formally dragging casinos into the gambit of the BSA requirements. As discussed above, the BSA operates by imposing reporting, recordkeeping, and compliance-program obligations on financial institutions. The BSA buttresses its obligations by including the power to impose significant monetary penalties for failures to comply with its requirements.

---

107. *See supra* note 105.

Chapter 5

Corporate Reorganizations, Bankruptcy, and Restructuring

Sean McGuinness and Adam M. Langley

I. GENERALLY

The gaming market, like any business, is not immune to insolvency risks. The Bankruptcy Code (Title 11 of the United States Code) applies standard rules and procedures for insolvent businesses and offers no special provisions for insolvent gaming businesses. Nevertheless, when considering gaming insolvencies, the unique nature of the businesses in the gaming industry and the detailed and specific regulatory processes they are subject to creates issues that warrant special attention. This chapter will examine the basic structure of the Bankruptcy Code and its application to the gaming industry.

II. THE BASICS OF CHAPTER 7 AND CHAPTER 11 OF THE BANKRUPTCY CODE

The Bankruptcy Code creates two mechanisms for an insolvent business: liquidation and reorganization. Liquidation, governed by Chapter 7 of the Bankruptcy Code, is the traditional mechanism whereby a debtor's assets are liquidated and the liquidation proceeds are distributed to creditors pro rata according to priority.[1]

---

1. *See Chapter 7—Bankruptcy Basics*, U.S. Courts, https://www.uscourts.gov/services-forms/bankruptcy/bankruptcy-basics/chapter-7-bankruptcy-basics.

Liquidations in the gaming industry are not unprecedented, and they include the Maxim Hotel and Casino,[2] Fitzgeralds Reno,[3] Klondike Sunset Casino,[4] and the Lucky Dragon Hotel & Casino.[5]

In contrast to a liquidation, reorganization under the Bankruptcy Code is a more complex mechanism. Reorganizations, governed by Chapter 11 of the Bankruptcy Code, are intended to preserve a business while maximizing returns to creditors.[6] As one court stated:

> Whereas, the aim of a Chapter 7 liquidation is the prompt closure and distribution of the debtor's estate, Chapter 11 provides for reorganization with the aim of rehabilitating the debtor and avoiding forfeitures by creditors. In overseeing this latter process, the bankruptcy courts are necessarily entrusted with broad equitable powers to balance the interests of the affected parties, guided by the overriding goal of ensuring the success of the reorganization.[7]

While there is considerable variation among reorganizations, generally there are two classes of reorganizations: (1) continued operation of the business under a plan of reorganization[8] or (2) a sale of the business through either a plan of reorganization[9] or a special sale process known as a Section 363 sale.[10]

Gaming companies' use of the reorganization provisions of the Bankruptcy Code has been a frequent occurrence. Examples of gaming debtors that formulated a plan of reorganization and continued operations include Caesars Entertainment,[11] Herbst Gaming,[12] Station Casinos,[13] the Riviera,[14] Stratosphere Casino and Hotel,[15] Hard Rock Hotel & Casino Biloxi,[16] Fitzgeralds Gaming Corporation,[17]

---

2. *In re* Premier Interval Resorts, Inc., No. 99-38340-HCA-11, 2003 WL 145069 (N.D. Tex. 2003).
3. *In re* Fitzgeralds Reno, Inc., No. 00-33469 (Bankr. D. Nev. 2011).
4. *In re* Nevada Gaming Partners, LLC, No. 16-15521 (Bankr. D. Nev. 2016).
5. *In re* Lucky Dragon Hotel & Casino, LLC, No. 2:18-BK-10792 (Bankr. D. Nev. 2018).
6. *See Chapter 11—Bankruptcy Basics*, U.S. Courts, https://www.uscourts.gov/services-forms/bankruptcy/bankruptcy-basics/chapter-11-bankruptcy-basics.
7. Pioneer Inv. Services Co. v. Brunswick Associates Ltd. Partnership, 507 U.S 380, 389 (1993).
8. 11 U.S.C. §§ 1108; 1123(a)(5)(A) (2018) (authorizing the continued operation of the debtor's business and the retention and use of assets through a Chapter 11 plan); *see, e.g.*, N.L.R.B. v. Bildisco and Bildisco, 465 U.S. 513, 528 (1984) (citing H.R. Rep. No. 95-595, p. 220 [1977]) ("The fundamental purpose of reorganization is to prevent a debtor from going into liquidation, with an attendant loss of jobs and possible misuse of economic resources.").
9. 11 U.S.C. § 1123(a)(5)(B), (C), and (D) (allowing for a Chapter 11 plan to transfer or sell all property or effectuate a merger or consolidation).
10. 11 U.S.C. § 363(b); *see, e.g.*, Stephens Indus., Inc. v. McClung, 789 F.2d 386, 390 (6th Cir. 1986) ("[A] bankruptcy court can authorize a sale of all a Chapter 11 debtor's assets under § 363(b)(1) when a sound business purpose dictates such action.").
11. *In re* Caesars Entertainment Operating Company, Inc., No. 15-01145 (Bankr. N.D. Ill. 2015).
12. *In re* Herbst Gaming Inc., No. 09-50752-GWZ (Bankr. D. Nev. 2012).
13. *In re* Station Casinos, Inc., No. 09-52477-GWZ (Bankr. D. Nev. 2010).
14. *In re* Riviera Holdings Corp., No. 10-22910-LBR, 2011 WL 4520494 (Bankr. D. Nev. 2011).
15. *In re* Stratosphere Corp., No.2:97-BK-20554 (Bankr. D. Nev. 2004).
16. *In re* Premier Entertainment Biloxi, LLC, 445 B.R. 582 (Bankr. S.D. Miss. 2010).
17. *In re* Fitzgeralds Gaming Corp., No. BK-00-33467-GWZ (Bankr. D. Nev. 2003).

Trump Hotels & Casino Resorts,[18] Trump Entertainment Resorts,[19] and the Aladdin Casino and Hotel.[20]

There are also numerous examples of entities that went through the sale process. This includes Revel Casino Hotel Atlantic City,[21] the Resort at Summerlin,[22] Stateline Casino,[23] and Sands Hotel & Casino.[24] In addition to the two traditional reorganizations, courts may allow debtors to confirm Chapter 11 plans that simply liquidate the gaming debtor's assets. An example of a liquidating plan is the Atlantic Club Casino Hotel.[25] Also, it is not uncommon for a gaming debtor that fails to reorganize under Chapter 11 to be converted to Chapter 7 for liquidation.[26]

Because reorganization rights are statutorily defined and subject to established case law, sophisticated debtors and creditors, and those who represent them, usually understand the economic realities of the insolvent business and the rights that each hold under the Bankruptcy Code. This predictability is intended to facilitate consensual restructurings of debt without the need for a bankruptcy proceeding. In the setting of the gaming industry, as elsewhere, parties are well-advised to restructure consensually and avoid the costs and formalities of filing a bankruptcy petition.

If the majority of creditors reach a deal with the debtor but there are some holdouts preventing a consensual resolution, a debtor may be forced to file bankruptcy to get approval of the pre-bankruptcy plan. This is commonly referred to as a "prepackaged plan."[27]

At other times, exigencies arising from negative cash flow, ongoing disputes, threatening creditors, or other business realities may make consensual resolutions or prepackaged plans impossible and jeopardize the going concern value of the business. Here, gaming debtors will seek bankruptcy protection to obtain a breathing spell to stabilize operations and restructure. In describing this process, one court stated, "[A] central purpose of the Code is to provide a procedure by which certain insolvent debtors can reorder their affairs, make peace with their creditors, and enjoy 'a new opportunity in life with a clear field for future effort, unhampered by the pressure and discouragement of preexisting debt.'"[28]

---

18. *In re* Trump Hotels & Casino Resorts, Inc., No. 04-46898/JHW (Bankr. D.N.J. 2008).
19. *In re* Trump Entertainment Resorts, Inc., 526 B.R. 116 (Bankr. D. Del. 2015).
20. *In re* Aladdin Gaming LLC, No. 2:01-BK-20141 (Bankr. D. Nev. 2010).
21. *In re* Revel AC, LLC, Case No. 1:13-BK-16255 (Bankr. D.N.J. 2014).
22. *In re* The Resort at Summerlin, Ltd., No. 2:00-BK-18878 (Bankr. D. Nev. 2006).
23. *In re* State Line Casino, No. 02-50081 (Bankr. D. Nev. 2005).
24. *In re* Greate Bay Hotel and Casino, Inc., Case No. 98-10001 (Bankr. D.N.J. 2000).
25. *In re* RIH Acquisitions NJ, LLC, 551 B.R. 563 (Bankr. D.N.J. 2016).
26. Czyzewski v. Jevic Holding Corp., 137 S. Ct. 973, 979 (2017) (acknowledging that "conversion in effect confesses an inability to find a plan").
27. *In re* Pioneer Fin. Corp., 246 B.R. 626, 630 (Bankr. D. Nev. 2000) ("With a 'prepackaged' plan, . . . a plan proponent has negotiated a plan and solicited votes prior to the filing of a Chapter 11 petition and before there is a hearing to determine the adequacy of the disclosure.").
28. Grogan v. Garner, 498 U.S. 279, 286–87 (1991) (quoting Local Loan Co. v. Hunt, 292 U.S. 234, 244 [1934]).

III. RIGHTS IN CHAPTER 11 REORGANIZATION CASES

A. Filing a Petition

A business commences a Chapter 11 bankruptcy case by filing a bankruptcy petition in a U.S. Bankruptcy Court with proper jurisdiction. Generally, a business may file in the jurisdiction in which it is incorporated, its principal place of business, or where its principal assets are located.[29] The District of Delaware and the Southern District of New York are well known for their experience in Chapter 11 reorganizations. The District of Nevada has considerable experience with gaming debtors due to the volume of gaming operations located within the state. While these districts may be the most common courts for significant Chapter 11 litigation or gaming cases, there may be strategic and equitable benefits to filing in other districts, depending on the specific circumstances of a case.[30]

B. Consequences of a Filed Petition

The filing of a bankruptcy petition automatically triggers important protections and safeguards.[31] First, the filing of a petition constitutes an order for relief and automatically operates as a stay of several actions:

1. Litigation and other administrative and judicial proceedings
2. The enforcement of a judgment
3. Any act to obtain possession or control property
4. Any act to create, perfect, or enforce a lien
5. Any act to collect, assess, or recover a claim against the debtor that arose before the case commenced
6. The setoff of debt

This stay is referred to as the "automatic stay."[32] Second, the petition creates a bankruptcy estate that includes all legal and equitable interests of the debtor, wherever located and by whomever held.[33]

---

29. 28 U.S.C. § 1408 (2018).
30. *See, e.g., In re* Patriot Coal Corp., 482 B.R. 718, 747 (Bankr. S.D.N.Y. 2012) (finding the transfer of a case filed in the Southern District of New York to the Eastern District of Missouri was in the interest of justice and served the convenience of the parties). The *Caesars Entertainment* case, which was filed in the Northern District of Illinois, serves as an example of a major gaming case that was handled outside of Nevada, Delaware, or New York.
31. Czyzewski v. Jevic Holding Corp., 137 S. Ct. 973, 978–79 (2017). "Filing for Chapter 11 bankruptcy has several relevant legal consequences. First, an estate is created comprising all property of the debtor. § 541(a)(1). Second, a fiduciary is installed to manage the estate in the interest of the creditors. §§ 1106, 1107(a). This fiduciary, often the debtor's existing management team, acts as 'debtor in possession.' §§ 1101(1), 1104. It may operate the business, §§ 363(c)(1), 1108, and perform certain bankruptcy-related functions, such as seeking to recover for the estate preferential or fraudulent transfers made to other persons, § 547 (transfers made before bankruptcy that unfairly preferred particular creditors); § 548 (fraudulent transfers, including transfers made before bankruptcy for which the debtor did not receive fair value). Third, an 'automatic stay' of all collection proceedings against the debtor takes effect. § 362(a)."
32. 11 U.S.C. § 362(a) (2018).
33. *Id.* § 541.

Furthermore, the commencement of a bankruptcy case imposes immediate restrictions on the debtor. The debtor must now seek court approval to employ professionals;[34] incur secured debts or debts outside the ordinary course of business;[35] use, sell, or lease property outside the ordinary course of business;[36] and use cash collateral.[37] Along with the automatic stay, these restrictions could quickly damage the business of a gaming debtor. Without relief from these restrictions, the gaming debtor cannot operate its casino floor, sports book, and cash management systems; pay employees, suppliers, customers, and other stakeholders; or honor room reservations and convention contracts.[38] A bankruptcy petition should never be filed on behalf of a casino client until the debtor's counsel has prepared and is ready to file emergency motions for specific relief from these restrictions. These emergency motions are colloquially called "first day motions."[39]

The courts are prepared to hear and decide the first day motions on an emergency basis. First day motions will be expected to include a request to allow the debtor to pay employees, trade creditors, and tax authorities; to honor room reservations, convention contracts, and deposits; to use the existing cash management system; to retain attorneys and other advisors; to use cash collateral; and to obtain interim financing. This request for relief needs to specify that gaming chips, tokens, and vouchers may be honored in the ordinary course of business along with sports book wagers and deposits, prepetition charge cards, travel commitments, and other prepetition room deposits. Other examples of typical first day motions include:

- motion to employ professionals;
- motion to continue use of debtor's cash management system and bank accounts;
- motion to use cash collateral;
- motion to pay critical vendors;
- motion to pay prepetition employee wages and benefits;
- motion to pay and maintain utilities;
- motion to maintain and administer customer programs;
- motion to honor certain prepetition obligations;
- motion to pay certain prepetition taxes and fees;
- motion to continue prepetition insurance coverage; and
- motion for debtor in possession financing.

---

34. *Id.* § 327.
35. *Id.* § 364.
36. *Id.* § 363(b).
37. *Id.* § 363(c)(2).
38. *See* Dawn M. Cica & Laury M. Macauley, *When Gaming Goes Heads Up with the Bankruptcy Code: Unique Restructuring Issues for Gaming Businesses in Difficult Economic Times*, 3 UNLV Gaming L.J. 23, 32 (2012).
39. Joan N. Feeney, Michael G. Williamson, & Michael J. Stepan, 2 Bankruptcy Law Manual § 11:16 (5th ed.) (2019) (discussing first day motions and orders).

Most bankruptcy courts have adopted local rules, procedures, or orders that allow for expedited hearings on first day motions with special noticing procedures.[40] As stated earlier, these motions are critical for the continued operation, survival, and reorganization of the bankrupt business.

C. Cash and Debtor in Possession Financing

A debtor in possession will need cash flow in order to operate its business, administer the Chapter 11 bankruptcy estate, and confirm a plan. The debtor may have either cash on hand or the debtor's operations may be able to generate cash flows, especially if certain debts are not currently being paid. However, the use of this cash faces two problems: (1) if pledged as collateral, the cash cannot be used absent authorization from the secured creditor or the bankruptcy court, and (2) even if authorized to use cash collateral or if cash is unencumbered, the cash may be insufficient to fund continued operations while paying the administrative costs of the bankruptcy case. The debtor needs to seek authorization from the court to use cash collateral and to obtain post-petition financing (aka *debtor in possession financing* or *DIP financing*).[41]

Section 363 of the Bankruptcy Code governs the use, sale, and lease of the debtor's estate property. The debtor may continue to use, sell, or lease estate property in the ordinary course of business, except for cash collateral.[42] Use of cash collateral must be authorized by the secured creditor holding the collateral or by the bankruptcy court.[43]

Section 364(a) of the Bankruptcy Code authorizes the debtor to obtain unsecured credit and incur unsecured debts in the ordinary course of business unless the court orders otherwise. The reality is that lenders and vendors are not willing to extend unsecured credit to a bankrupt business absent adequate assurance of repayment. The Bankruptcy Code recognizes this reality and authorizes a bankruptcy court to allow the debtor to obtain financing that is (1) granted administrative expense status, (2) granted super-priority administrative expense status, (3) secured by a lien on unencumbered property, or (4) secured by a priming lien.[44] These heightened priorities and priming liens incentivize DIP financing to further the fresh start policy so that a going-concern business can allow creditors to recover more than a liquidated business.

Together, the use of cash collateral and post-petition financing should be tailored to allow the debtor to continue gaming operations, pay bankruptcy professionals, and formulate and confirm a plan of reorganization. Many institutional lenders

---

40. *See, e.g.*, U.S. Bankruptcy Court Northern District of Texas, *General Order Regarding Procedures for Complex Chapter 11 Cases*, N. District of Tex. (Jan. 13, 2006), https://www.txnb.uscourts.gov/sites/txnb/files/basic/2006-02rev2.pdf.
41. 11 U.S.C. § 364 (2018).
42. *Id.* §§ 363(c)(1); 1108.
43. *Id.* § 363(c)(2).
44. *Id.* § 364(b), (c), and (d).

are sophisticated at DIP financing, while other DIP financing can come from private equity, stalking horse bidders, related parties, or any number of other sources of funds.

1. 363 Sales

The Bankruptcy Code allows gaming debtors to continue operations of their business in the ordinary course, except for the use of cash collateral, which, as noted above, must be approved by the court.[45] Transactions outside the ordinary course of business must be approved by the bankruptcy court after notice and a hearing.[46]

Bankruptcy sales outside the ordinary course of business take their name—363 sales—from this bankruptcy subsection. A 363 sale ordinarily can be made free and clear of any interest in the property being sold.[47] This protection provides a significant incentive for a debtor seeking to dispose of assets to file bankruptcy. A good-faith buyer that purchases assets in a fair 363 sale process is usually protected from the liabilities of the debtor and any successor liabilities.[48] The buyer takes the estate's assets, and the court issues an order indicating that the assets were acquired free and clear.

A 363 sale can be for all of a debtor's assets if the debtor can demonstrate that there is a sound business purpose for the transaction. Courts weigh a number of factors to determine whether a sound business purpose exists. These factors would include, among others, the following:

- Whether the sale is in the best interest of the estate
- Whether it was negotiated at arm's length, and whether the property is increasing or decreasing in value
- Whether competitive bidding was facilitated
- Whether the property has been fairly marketed, who the beneficiaries from the proposed sale are, what the proportionate value to the estate as a whole is, and the timing of the motion
- Whether there is evidence of a need for speed, and the likelihood of a successful reorganization
- The proceeds resulting from the sale
- The burdens on the estate[49]

Almost all bankruptcy sales are subject to bid procedures for a public auction because of the fairness and integrity that such a process confers onto the sale.

Asset sales of a gaming debtor pose unique regulatory hurdles. The buyer must not only navigate through the bankruptcy procedures, hearings, and rules but also

---

45. *Id.* § 1108.
46. *Id.* § 363(b).
47. *Id.* § 363(f).
48. *Id.* §§ 363(f) and (m).
49. *See, e.g., In re* Lionel Corp., 722 F.2d 1063, 1071 (2d Cir. 1983) (citing factors); *In re* 9 Houston LLC, 578 B.R. 600, 611 (Bankr. S.D. Tex. 2017) (analyzing factors).

must obtain licensing approval from gaming regulators. The buyer of gaming assets will need a bankruptcy court order and also either gaming approval or a license. Gaming regulators oversee the integrity of the gaming industry and act to protect gaming consumers. Licensing is a fundamental mechanism used by gaming regulators to further their policy obligations. Only a licensed person may own and operate certain gaming assets.

A buyer of gaming assets, therefore, must anticipate and understand the licensing process. Failure to do so may frustrate or delay the 363 sale. Gaming regulators will need to perform a gaming license investigation. A new investigation will usually be required for a buyer without a prior gaming license, while a buyer with a prior license will likely only be subjected to an updated investigation. Obviously, a new investigation will be more involved and take more time. This licensing hurdle causes many debtors to identify and solicit buyers who are already licensed.

Buyers may also attempt to structure their purchasing entity in a way that it is exempt from licensing. Depending on the jurisdiction, licensing exemptions may exist for public companies, institutional investors, or nonvoting stockholders, among other exemptions. The gaming regulations add additional planning and strategy for both gaming debtors and buyers.[50]

2. Chapter 11 Plan Process

A Chapter 11 plan typically either proposes an asset sale in a manner similar to a 363 sale or fosters the continued operations and reorganization of the debtor. The debtor has the exclusive right to propose a plan during the first 120 days of a case.[51] This exclusivity period may be extended for cause up to eighteen months after the petition date.[52] After a debtor's plan is proposed, the debtor has 180 days after the petition date to have the bankruptcy court confirm the plan.[53] This 180-day period may be extended for cause up to twenty months after the petition date.[54] If a debtor cannot propose a plan within the exclusivity period or get a plan confirmed within the applicable deadline, any party in interest may propose a plan.[55]

At a minimum, a Chapter 11 plan must be proposed in good faith, be feasible, comply with the Bankruptcy Code and applicable non-bankruptcy law, and pay creditors at least as much as each would receive under a Chapter 7 liquidation.[56] It is particularly important in the gaming setting that the means of implementing the

---

50. See John M. Czarnetzky, *When the Dealer Goes Bust: Issues in Casino Bankruptcies*, 18 Miss. C. L. Rev. 459, 461 (1998) (discussing state regulation of casino debtors in bankruptcy); Robert W. Stocker II & Peter J. Kulick, *Gambling with Bankruptcy: Navigating A Casino Through Chapter 11 Bankruptcy Proceedings*, 57 Drake L. Rev. 361, 373 (2009) (discussing the interaction of state gaming regulation and Chapter 11 bankruptcy proceedings).
51. 11 U.S.C. § 1121(b) (2018).
52. *Id.* § 1121(d)(2)(A).
53. *Id.* § 1121(c)(3).
54. *Id.* § 1121(d)(2)(B).
55. *Id.* § 1121(c).
56. *Id.* § 1129(a).

Chapter 11 plan is not forbidden by gaming regulations. Gaming debtors proposing a Chapter 11 plan will need to work with gaming regulators to ensure the proposed plan adequately complies with gaming regulations. If a Chapter 11 plan disregards gaming laws and regulations, gaming regulators will have standing and good cause to object to the plan.

A Chapter 11 plan must also designate classes of claimants and interest holders.[57] These classes must contain claims or interests that are substantially similar, and the plan must deem each class as either impaired or unimpaired based on the proposed treatment of each class. A class is impaired if the plan does not leave unaltered the legal, equitable, and contractual rights of the claimant or interest holder.[58] The plan must also provide adequate means for the plan's implementation, which may be done by allowing the debtor to do the following: retain property of the estate, transfer property of the estate, merge or consolidate, sell property of the estate, distribute property of the estate, satisfy or modify liens, extend maturity dates or change interest rates of debts, or by other allowable means.[59]

Prior to a plan proponent soliciting votes on a plan, or a bankruptcy court conducting a confirmation hearing, the plan proponent must prepare a disclosure statement approved by the bankruptcy court.[60] A disclosure statement must contain adequate information, which means information of a kind and in sufficient detail to enable a hypothetical investor to make an informed judgment about the plan.[61] Adequate information for a gaming debtor will necessarily require specific information regarding the gaming industry and gaming regulations.

Each creditor or interest holder may vote to accept or reject a plan as a member of its designated class. The Bankruptcy Code concerns itself with class acceptance or rejection rather than individual creditor or interest holder votes. A class of claims votes to accept a Chapter 11 plan if creditors holding two-thirds in the amount and more than one-half in number of the allowed claims of such class held by such creditors vote to accept.[62] For a Chapter 11 plan to be confirmed, at least one class that is impaired must vote for the plan.[63] If all of the impaired classes accept a plan, the plan is confirmed consensually. However, if some classes reject a plan while at least one accepts, a debtor may still "cramdown" a plan on creditors so long as the plan is found to be fair and equitable.[64]

Fair and equitable is a statutory term of art that means the plan must satisfy the absolute priority rule.[65] The absolute priority rule is a statutory scheme of priorities that must be followed in order for cramdown to be allowed. Specifically, a secured

---

57. *Id.* § 1122.
58. *Id.* § 1124.
59. *Id.* § 1123.
60. *Id.* § 1125.
61. *Id.* § 1125(a)(1)
62. *Id.* § 1126.
63. *Id.* § 1129(a)(10).
64. *Id.* § 1129(b).
65. *Id.* § 1129(b)(2) (defining the absolute priority rule).

creditor must (1) retain its lien and receive deferred cash payments equal to the allowed amount of its claim, (2) receive the proceeds from the sale of its collateral, or (3) realize the indubitable equivalent of its claim.[66] After secured creditors are treated fairly and equitably, priority creditors must be paid in full as of the effective date of the plan.[67] After priority creditors are paid, unsecured creditors must be paid either in full or pro rata.[68] Unless unsecured creditors are paid in full, interest holders cannot be paid.[69] If these priorities are followed, a Chapter 11 plan may be crammed down over the dissent of objecting classes.

D. Special Concerns Regarding Native American Gaming

While casino gaming conducted on Native American tribal lands in the United States has a large market presence (particularly in Arizona, California, Michigan, Minnesota, New Mexico, and Oklahoma), these casinos are not immune to restructuring and reorganization issues. Indian casinos do look to traditional financial markets to finance their operations, and as such, they are subject to the same insolvency risks as their commercial counterparts. There is a major difference in how these issues get resolved, however. That is because there is a judicial split on the applicability of the Bankruptcy Code to Native American tribes.

On February 26, 2019, the Sixth Circuit upheld a ruling that Native American tribes have sovereign immunity, which exempts tribes from jurisdiction under the Bankruptcy Code.[70] This ruling was consistent with a 2016 ruling from the Seventh Circuit.[71] In contrast, the Ninth Circuit ruled in 2004 that Native American tribes do not have sovereign immunity from the Bankruptcy Code.[72]

Native American tribes have consistently taken strong positions to maintain their sovereign status and sovereign immunity. Indeed, the federal Indian Gaming Regulatory Act (IGRA),[73] which establishes the framework for Native American gaming, provides for Native American tribes to enter into tribal-state compacts with the states (where tribal lands are located) as equal sovereigns. In addition, no Native American tribe has ever voluntarily attempted to utilize the Bankruptcy Code. To do so might erode tribal sovereign immunity rights.

As a practical matter, this means that financial restructuring in a Native American casino setting takes place in the form of a negotiated transaction outside of

---

66. *Id.* § 1129(b)(2)(A).
67. *Id.* § 1129(a)(9)(C).
68. *Id.* § 1129(b)(2)(B).
69. *Id.* § 1129(b)(2)(C).
70. *In re* Greektown Holdings, LLC, 917 F.3d 451 (6th Cir. 2019).
71. Meyers v. Oneida Tribe of Indians of Wisconsin, 836 F.3d 818 (7th Cir. 2016).
72. Krystal Energy Co. v. Navajo Nation, 357 F.3d 1055 (9th Cir. 2004), *as amended on denial of reh'g* (Apr. 6, 2004).
73. 25 U.S.C. § 2701 et seq (2018). Chapter 9 of this book looks into the details of IGRA and issues of tribal sovereignty.

court (federal, state, or tribal). The certainty of timing with the reorganization process is not present, so the parties involved have to work together to resolve the outstanding issues. In essence, this is the equivalent of a pre-bankruptcy negotiation in a Chapter 11 prepackaged bankruptcy where the borrower and main creditors agree on terms of reorganization. The difference is that no bankruptcy proceeding follows the negotiated transaction.

Chapter 6

Gaming Contracts

Keith C. Miller

I. INTRODUCTION

There are several ways in which contract law is implicated in a gaming setting. In some respects, these contract issues are no different than those that business lawyers would find themselves dealing with generally. But in other instances, the peculiar nature of regulated gambling presents wrinkles in the law that warrant special attention. This chapter seeks to sensitize the business lawyer to the sometimes-subtle issues that arise when contract law enters the world of regulated gambling. Several problem areas will be considered.

First, there is the matter of the contract between the player and the casino when the player wants to place a wager. It is in every sense an adhesion, take-it-or-leave-it contract. If casinos entered agreements altering the rules that give them the statistical edge that exists in their favor, they wouldn't be profitable. Nevertheless, questions about how the contract is formed, the contract terms, who the offeror and offeree are, and how performance is executed can raise problems.

Second, the wager itself is not the only contract between the player and the casino. In many states, casinos are allowed to extend credit to a player who can use the funds to gamble. The process by which the credit is granted involves the player signing a "marker," a countercheck that, if properly prepared, is a negotiable instrument. If the player fails to pay back the debt, the casino may present the negotiable instrument to the bank it is drawn on. But what if there are no funds in the player's account? Can the dishonored negotiable instrument representing a gambling debt be enforced in court as any dishonored negotiable instrument is? What defenses can be raised to enforcement?

Third, what happens when a player says the casino has breached the contract it has with the player by not paying, for example, a casino jackpot that the player says he is entitled to? What is the process for determining whether there is a "breach" of the contract between bettor and casino?

Examination of these issues will give the business lawyer a foundation for recognizing and handling some of the basic contract issues in the gaming field.

II. THE WAGERING CONTRACT

At a fundamental level, the wager between the player and the casino is a contract. As such, the typical elements of offer, acceptance, and consideration will be present. It is generally accepted that in a wagering situation, the player is the offeror and the casino is the offeree.[1] The bettor makes the offer by, for example, placing a wager on the designated area of a blackjack table, and the casino accepts the wager by either acknowledging the bet or starting the game.[2] Given the nature of casino gambling where many bets may be placed, won, and lost in a short period of time, it makes sense that the contracts formed through the wagers are not subject to negotiation.

One case that illustrates the player-as-offeror principle is *Campione v. Adamar of New Jersey*.[3] The casino posted a sign indicating that the maximum bet was $100, a lower amount that had been previously in force.[4] The casino reduced the maximum bet in order to thwart a blackjack player who was "counting cards." Despite the sign indicating the lower limits, the bettor placed a $350 bet, the casino did not object, the hand was played, and the player won.[5] The casino, however, refused to pay the bettor $350, instead maintaining that the $100 maximum limit sign limited its liability to that amount.[6] In ruling in favor of the player, the court stated:

> When [the player] placed a bet of $350 on the table after the casino employee had lowered the maximum bet to $100, he presented an offer to the casino. The casino then had the option to reject the offer by informing [the player] that he had bet above the limit established for the table, and requesting that he lower his bet to a maximum of $100. No casino employee did so. As a result, when the casino allowed [the player] to pursue the hand with his $350 bet, this constituted an acceptance of [the player's] offer. Therefore, a binding contract was formed between [the player] and the casino, and the casino was obliged to pay [the player] the full amount of his winning bet.[7]

The game layout indicating maximum bets and other information is not an offer being made to the bettor by the casino; rather, it is the solicitation of an

---

1. *See* Campione v. Adamar of New Jersey, 643 A.2d 42, 46 (N.J. Super. Ct. App. Div. 1993), *rev'd on other grounds*, 694 A.2d 1045 (N.J. Super. Ct. App. Div. 1997); Anthony Cabot & Robert Hannum, *Advantage Play and Commercial Casinos*, 74 Miss. L.J. 681, 722 (2005); Jordan T. Smith, *Cheater's Justice: Judicial Recourse for Victims of Gaming Fraud*, 7 UNLV Gaming L.J. 61, 76 (2017); *contra* Blackford v. Prairie Meadows Racetrack and Casino, 778 N.W.2d 184, 190 (Iowa 2010).
2. Cabot & Hannum, *supra* note 1, at 723–724.
3. *Campione*, 643 A.2d at 42.
4. *Id.* at 46.
5. *Id.*
6. *Id.*
7. *Id.* at 49.

offer by the casino to the bettor to place a wager. The casino may choose not to accept the offer (i.e., the bet), but once accepted, a valid contract is formed. In one case, a bettor argued that advertisements by a casino relating to playing blackjack constituted an offer to the player,[8] but the casino rejected the player's bet because it suspected he was a card counter.[9] The player sued the casino on the basis he had accepted the casino's offer by placing a bet.[10] Rejecting this argument, the court held that the casino advertisements did not constitute an offer and were at most "invitations to make an offer, enter into negotiations, or to patronize [the casino]. Because there was no offer, there could be neither an acceptance nor a breach of contract."[11]

Some of the terms of the wagering contract are expressly stated. For example, on a blackjack table, there may be a written statement that *Blackjack Pays 3:2* or *Blackjack Pays 6:5*. This means, respectively, that a person receiving a blackjack—an ace accompanied by a 10, jack, queen, or king on the first two cards dealt to them—would win $30 for the $20 wagered or $24 for the $20 wagered. There may be other implied terms that involve the rules of the game that, while not written down, are still a part of the contract. "For example, a craps table does not tell you that if you roll a seven after rolling a point, you lose; however, this rule is commonly understood and forms the basis for the game of craps."[12]

It is a bit misleading to emphasize the primacy of the wagering contract between the bettor and the casino, however. There is a reason the term *regulated gambling* is used. The specific terms of the wagering contract are fundamentally affected by the statutes and regulations that a state uses to regulate gambling games. These provisions dictate the way games are played and consequently supply specific terms of the wagering contract that the parties would not be allowed to alter. In this regard, the notion that the player and the casino are free actors who are setting the terms of their contest is a fiction. As one court stated, because "every aspect of the relationship between the gambler and the casino is minutely

---

8. Ziglin v. Players MH, L.P., 36 S.W.3d 786 (Mo. Ct. App. 2001).
9. *Id.* at 788. The power of casinos to exclude players who are, or are suspected to be, counting cards is a controversial one. Card counting is a type of advantage play in blackjack where the player keeps mental track of cards that have been played to determine whether high-value cards, face cards, and aces make up a significant part of the cards remaining toward the end of a deck or number of decks. If that is the case, the player may have a statistical edge against the house if he or she increases the bet substantially. No court has ever ruled that card counting is cheating, and the player is not altering the "selection of criteria which determine . . . [t]he result of a game," the classic definition of cheating. Casinos may be concerned, however, that the card counter will reduce or even eliminate the statistical advantage the house has in the game. These concerns are especially acute where "teams" of card counters work together, as popularized by movies such as *21* (Relativity Media 2008). Despite the fact that card counting is not cheating, most states, most notably Nevada, have not prevented casinos from excluding suspected card counters. This is often based on the common law "right to exclude." For discussion of the advantage play exclusion issues, see Cabot & Hannum, *supra* note 1; Tom Julian, *Exclusions and Countermeasures: Do Card Counters Have a Right to Play?* 9 Gaming L. Rev. 165 (2005).
10. *Ziglin*, 36 S.W.3d at 789.
11. *Id.* at 790.
12. Cabot & Hannum, *supra* note 1, at 725.

regulated by the state," it is fair to conclude that "there is little freedom of contract in the usual sense."[13] The interplay of the express and implied terms of the wagering contract, including the relevant statutes and regulations, often play a role in the resolution of disputes between a player and a casino. This is addressed later in this chapter.[14]

III. CASINO CREDIT AND THE COLLECTION OF GAMBLING DEBTS

A. The Granting of Casino Credit

Casino gambling is historically a cash game. When a player sits down at a gaming table and wishes to place a wager, the house takes cash from the player and gives the player denominated chips to use in wagering. States with casino gambling do not permit a player to place a bet using a credit or debit card,[15] though the player can use those items to obtain cash.[16] However, while casino gambling is a cash game, the cash may not always come from money the bettor has brought with him to the casino. In many states, casinos are permitted to extend credit to the player so the player can draw on that credit to make wagers.[17] Credit play in some casinos amounts to more than 50 percent of the amount of money wagered. If a business lawyer is contacted by a person who has a gambling debt, or alleged gambling debt, owed to a casino, careful attention is required, as several policy questions and legal and practical problems are implicated by this practice.

Perhaps the most obvious policy issue regarding the extension of credit to a player by a casino is whether it is a good idea in the first place. Those in the problem gambling treatment community claim that casino credit provides too easy of an

---

13. Tose v. Greate Bay Hotel & Casino Inc., 819 F. Supp. 1312, 1316 n.8 (D.N.J. 1993); *see also* Blackford v. Prairie Meadows Racetrack & Casino, Inc., 778 N.W.2d 184, 189 (Iowa 2010) (stating statutory and regulatory restrictions are part of the parties' gaming contract); Cabot & Hannum, *supra* note 1, at 726; Smith, *supra* note 1, at 76.

14. *See* section IV discussing Patron Disputes.

15. *See* Michelle Crouch, *10 Things You Can't (Easily) Buy with Credit Cards*, CreditCards.com (Oct. 14, 2011), https://www.creditcards.com/credit-card-news/10-things-credit-cards-wont-easily-buy-1267.php.

16. Some states regulate the placement and number of ATMs and cash advance machines by not allowing them in gaming areas. *See* Iowa Code § 99 F.7 (2019).

> 10.b. A licensee shall not permit a financial institution, vendor, or other person to dispense cash or credit through an electronic or mechanical device including but not limited to a satellite terminal, as defined in section 527.2, that is located on the gaming floor.

Iowa Code 99 F.1 defines "gaming floor" by giving the Iowa Racing and Gaming Commission authority to designate an area that is a gaming floor.

17. According to the American Gaming Association, as of 2018, a bit more than half the states with casino gambling allow for casinos to extend credit (14 out of 23). *State of the States* 2018: *The AGA Survey of the Commercial Casino Industry*, Am. Gaming Ass'n (2018), http://www.americangaming.org/sites/default/files/AGA%202018%20State%20of%20the%20States%20Report_FINAL.pdf; *see also* Alvin J. Hicks, *No Longer the Only Game in Town: A Comparison of the Nevada and New Jersey Regulatory Systems of Gaming Control*, 12 Sw. U. L. Rev. 620 (1981). Missouri and several other states prohibit the use of credit altogether; Robert D. Faiss, *Nevada Gaming Industry Credit Practices and Procedures*, 3 Gaming L. Rev. 145 (1999).

opportunity for players to lose more than they can truly afford.[18] Concerns may also exist about collection tactics being heavy-handed, though this may not reflect the modern casino industry. The argument in favor of casinos granting credit is that it allows people to gamble at casinos without having to carry a large amount of money on their person. This, it is argued, is a matter of convenience and safety.[19] The fact that approximately half the states that offer casino gambling allow for casino credit illustrates the division of opinion on the issue.[20]

The process of granting credit begins quite unremarkably with a player submitting an application to the casino asking for credit. An application for casino credit resembles credit applications one would see outside the gaming context, although some of the inquiries are a bit more specific.[21] The application will likely ask for information regarding:

- personal information such as name, address, social security number, date of birth, passport, driver's license number, or a physical description of height, weight, and eye color;
- employment information, including the position held, length of employment, and annual income; and
- financial information, including the name and routing number of the applicant's bank, applicant's account number and type of account (there may be the opportunity to list more than one bank).

In addition to requiring the applicant to supply information, a credit application will also provide information about the credit application process. The casino may be authorized "to obtain consumer reports, to contact financial institutions, and to check my consumer credit, employment, bank and gaming history in order to evaluate [the] credit application as well as to update and/or review [the] account to provide services requested by [the applicant], as necessary or as required by law."[22] Significantly, the applicant "releases and waives" any claims relating to the credit investigation and "the collection, processing, and transmission" of the applicant's information and data.[23]

What if the credit application is approved? Is there anything in particular the applicant should know before drawing on the credit line? Indeed, there is. The document the bettor signs to draw on the credit is often referred to as a marker. The marker looks like a normal check. A credit application will make one thing very

---

18. *See* Florida Council on Compulsive Gambling, Inc., *Gambling on Credit: Exploring the Link between Compulsive Gambling and Access to Credit*, GAMBLINGHELP (May 2006), https://gamblinghelp.org/assets/research_pdfs/Gambling_on_Credit.pdf.
19. *See* I. Nelson Rose, *Gambling and the Law: The Role of Credit in the Third Wave of Legal Gambling*, WHITTIER LAW SCHOOL (1998), https://govinfo.library.unt.edu/ngisc/meetings/11nov98/rose.pdf.
20. *See State of the States 2018*, *supra* note 17 for a listing of states that allow or disallow credit.
21. One example of a credit application is *Caesars Palace Credit Application*, CAESARS PALACE https://nccreports.com/application/?caesarspalace.
22. *Id.*
23. *Id.*

clear: the executed marker is a negotiable instrument. Here is what a typical application will tell the bettor who draws on the credit line:

- If there is information missing on the marker, such as the name of the payee, missing amounts, the date, the name of the bank and relevant account information, or electrical encoding of information, the applicant authorizes the casino to complete that information.[24]
- The applicant agrees that the laws of a particular state, such as Nevada, apply to any dispute, and that the casino may bring the action in any court, state or federal, in that state.
- The applicant consents to the jurisdiction of any of the courts listed.
- The applicant agrees to pay interest, such as 18 percent per year, on the marker that is the subject of the dispute, as well as attorney fees and costs.
- Last but not least, applicants are told that if they willfully draw or pass the marker with an intent to defraud, including knowing there are insufficient funds in the account, they are subject to criminal prosecution as well as civil liability.

As is evident, the credit process is a serious, arm's-length transaction that no person should consider without careful thought. Even if the ability to draw on a credit line is a convenience, the consequences of not paying are significant. In a typical case, a bettor visiting from out of town who draws on credit while gambling will pay back the amount borrowed before leaving town, or shortly after. Industry practice is that a bettor with an outstanding credit marker will be contacted by the credit department of the casino at some time shortly after the marker has been issued, or after the bettor has returned home, to inquire about repayment. This query is typically not designed to be adversarial. As a matter of best practices, it is usually in the casino's interest to be flexible in making arrangements with the player to repay the marker because the bettor is a customer the casino would like to have return (and bet and lose more). At some point, however, the casino may lose patience and give up on the prospect of the bettor paying back the debt. The casino may do exactly what it is authorized to do with this credit instrument drawn on a bank—present it for payment. If there are sufficient funds, the casino is paid back what it is owed. But what happens if the account is closed, or there is not sufficient funds? What are the options the casino has?

B. Collection of Casino Debts

1. The General Legal Background of Casino Debt Collection

Among the many ways in which gaming contracts differentiate themselves from contracts generally is in the collection of debts. The enforceability of gambling debts

---

24. New Jersey does not allow for information such as the date to be filled in at a later time, and the process of granting and extending credit in that state differs considerably from Nevada. *See* discussion in immediately following section on collections.

has an interesting history in the United States. A 1950 Nevada case is notable.[25] Leonard Wolff signed three checks (i.e., markers) for a total of $86,000 drawn on the respondent bank in order to play 21.[26] When Wolff died, the checks were presented for payment to the bank, but the bank did not honor the instruments. The casino sued the administrator of Wolff's estate in a Nevada court seeking to collect on the markers. The administrator resisted, asserting that the sole consideration for the checks was money won by the casino from gambling games. Consequently, the debt was unenforceable.[27]

One important question to ask is whether gambling was legal at this time in Nevada. Yes, as part of what has sometimes been called the Wide Open Gambling Law of 1931, gambling was legal in the state. So what possible objection could exist to the enforcement of an otherwise valid gambling debt? The answer is found in an obscure English law known as the Statute of Anne.

In seventeenth- and eighteenth-century England, gambling, both legal and illegal, was popular. However, large gambling debts often led to transfers of property, which "disrupted England's land-based aristocracy."[28] This prompted Queen Anne to sign the statute named for her that made gambling debts in excess of 10 pounds unenforceable.[29] Losers of more than 10 pounds could recover their gambling losses if they brought an action within three months of their losses.[30] If they didn't bring such an action, any other person could sue and recover treble damages.[31]

But what is the relevance of an English statute in the United States, a country established in rebellion from the former's rule? When colonies and then states established their legal systems, they "received" (that is, incorporated) the common law of England.[32] A revolution was fought to win independence, but the legal system established was the one most familiar to those in the newly established country. Therefore, until a court or legislature determined that the common law of the state departed from that prescribed in the Statute of Anne, the prohibition against enforcing gambling debts remained in place.[33]

In the case of Nevada, however, that shouldn't have been a problem. After all, in 1931, Nevada had gone all in by passing a statute called a *wide-open gambling law*,[34]

---

25. West Indies, Inc. v. First National Bank of Nevada, 214 P.2d 144 (Nev. 1950).
26. *Id.* at 145.
27. *Id.*
28. Ronald J. Rychlack, *Lotteries, Revenues and Social Costs: A Historical Examination,* 34 B.C.L. Rev. 11, 19 (1992). Citing other sources, the author notes that similar concerns about transfers of wealth and property from gambling debts existed in France and in the American South. *Id.* at n. 42.
29. *Id.* at 19; *see also* Smith, *supra* note 1.
30. Rychlack, *supra* note 28, at 19.
31. *Id.*
32. *See* William B. Stoebuck, *Reception of English Common Law in the American Colonies,* 10 William & Mary L. Rev. 393 (1968) (discussing different theories that explain reception process).
33. Note that the Statute of Anne didn't make gambling illegal; it simply made gambling debts unenforceable. On the other hand, all gambling in the United States in the nineteenth century was regarded as illegal.
34. Despite Nevada's reputation as the center of U.S. gambling, it wasn't until 1931 that gambling was firmly established as legal.

and gambling was spreading across the state. By 1950, when the *West Indies, Inc. v. First National Bank of Nevada* case was decided, no plausible argument could be made that gambling offended public policy and that gambling debts shouldn't be enforced.

Or so it seemed. The Nevada Supreme Court acknowledged that the 1931 law opening Nevada to wide-open gambling indicated that public opinion on gambling had "changed toward liberality." But nothing in the 1931 law specifically provided for the enforceability of gambling debts, and because the statute was in derogation of the common law, it was subject to a strict construction. Moreover, gambling laws passed after the 1931 statute likewise made no reference to gambling debts. The result was that despite the acceptance of gambling within Nevada, the Statute of Anne continued to operate and preclude the enforcement of gambling debts.[35] Interestingly, this did not change in Nevada until 1983.[36]

A similar result was reached in a 1993 California case,[37] where the court expressed concerns about the problems associated with credit play. A California resident incurred debts of $22,000 at a casino in Lake Tahoe, Nevada. The California player stopped payment on the markers representing the debts. Caesars Tahoe assigned the debt to a collection agency, which, in turn, sued the player. The California court held that it would not require the player to repay the debt.[38] The court was not persuaded by the plaintiff's argument that, despite the fact California had historically refused to enforce gambling debts, the recent proliferation of legal gaming in California should cause the court to come to a different conclusion now. The court reasoned that California's rule against enforcing gambling debts has never depended upon the criminalization of gambling itself; instead, the court viewed gambling on credit as the real culprit. Shifting public attitudes about gambling itself hadn't changed this. The court noted, "If Californians want to play, so be it. But, the law should not invite them to play themselves into debt. The judiciary cannot protect pathological gamblers from themselves, but we can refuse to participate in their financial ruin."[39]

In the cases just discussed, the irony of the court's refusal to enforce a gambling debt lawfully incurred in another state was that the nonenforcing state itself offered gambling. It is an easier case when the state asked to enforce the gambling debt does *not* offer gambling. For example, in *Resorts International Hotel, Inc. v. Agresta*, the gambler signed three drafts totaling $10,000 payable to the casino for his gambling losses incurred in New Jersey.[40] When the bank dishonored the drafts, the casino brought a diversity of citizenship action in a federal court in Virginia, where the gambler was a resident, seeking payment of the drafts.

---

35. West Indies, Inc. v. First National Bank of Nevada, 214 P.2d 144 (Nev. 1950).
36. Nev. Rev. Stat. § 463.368, which sets out the process for gambling debt collection, was passed in 1983.
37. Metropolitan Creditors Service v. Soheil Sadri, 15 Cal. App. 4th 1821 (1993).
38. *Id.* at 1828.
39. *Id.* at 1830.
40. 569 F. Supp. 24 (E.D. Va. 1983).

The court noted that the law of Virginia controlled the substantive issues in the case, and that contracts valid in the state where made were enforceable under Virginia law "unless such contract or liability is contrary to morals, public policy, or the positive law" of Virginia.[41] New Jersey permitted gambling and the contract was presumably valid in that state, leaving only the question of whether Virginia's principles of public policy would be offended by enforcement of the gambling debt. For several reasons, they would be, the court ruled.

First, there were a number of criminal prohibitions against gambling and operating a gambling business in Virginia. These prohibitions were reinforced by a Virginia statute, which stated that contracts to repay money lent for the purpose of gaming were "utterly void."[42] Moreover, the Virginia Supreme Court had ruled that statute should be construed strictly and that the "plain and unambiguous language" of the statute indicated that "the State court system [was] unavailable to unpaid gambling winners."[43] In light of that, the conclusion that Virginia's public policy would be offended by the enforcement of the gambling debt was unmistakable.

This result has been followed by a number of courts.[44] Thus, in jurisdictions that refuse to enforce gambling debts, the reason may be either that the state has a strong public policy against gambling generally or finds the granting of credit to be so subject to abuse that it should be discouraged. Even if a jurisdiction doesn't prohibit the granting of credit, it may employ other regulatory strategies to curb excessive or indiscriminate credit practices. For example, New Jersey regulations cap the percentage of credit that can be written off as uncollectable. A casino cannot include in its deductible operating expenses "losses on bad debt instruments from gaming operations in excess of the lesser of such instruments actually uncollected or 4% of gross revenues."[45] This requires the casinos to be more selective and conservative in the granting of credit. A second strategy is to allow the casinos only to accept checks from the player, rather than using counterchecks prepared by the casino that are drawn on the player's bank account.

When it comes to collecting gambling debts, however, casinos have learned there is more than one way to skin a cat. This is illustrated by a 1991 North Carolina case, with the court's recitation of facts relating a story that may support those who believe casino credit is a bad idea:

> [I]n June 1989 defendant traveled to Las Vegas, Nevada, where he visited plaintiff's casino. . . . On 7 June he "commenced to gamble with dice, the dice, or crap table, provided by the Plaintiff." Defendant lost all his cash, $2,700.00, but was advised by plaintiff's agent that credit was available to him if he would make application.

---

41. *Id.* at 25.
42. *Id.* (citing Va. Code § 11-14 [1982]).
43. *Id.* at 26.
44. *See* Gulf Collateral, Inc. v. Morgan, 415 F. Supp. 319 (D. Ga. 1976); Condado Aruba Caribbean Hotel, N.V. v. Tickel, 561 P.2d 23 (Colo. App. 1977); Hilton of San Juan, Inc. v. Lateano, 305 A.2d 538 (Conn. Cir. 1972).
45. *See* N.J. Stat. § 5:12-147 (2013).

Defendant went to an office on plaintiff's premises, completed some forms and was told to return the next day to determine if credit would be available to him. On 8 June defendant returned to the casino and was told credit was available; all he had to do was sign a marker signifying the amount of credit he desired. On that same day, over the course of several hours during which he lost $20,000.00 at the dice table, defendant signed ten markers, each in the amount of $2,000.00.[46]

The gambler paid off some of his debt, but the casino sued him for the unpaid balance, and a default judgment was entered against Holz for $14,000, plus prejudgment interest, costs, and an attorney's fee of $3,500. Holz returned to North Carolina, and armed with the default judgment that the court had entered against him, the casino followed. The casino registered its judgment in accordance with the Uniform Enforcement of Foreign Judgments Act. Holz resisted the action, however, pointing to North Carolina law that declared contracts to repay gambling debts void[47] and the North Carolina iteration of the Uniform Act, which stated that foreign judgments that were contrary to the law of North Carolina would not be enforced.[48] The law of North Carolina forbidding gambling was every bit as emphatic as that of Virginia considered in the *Agresta* case, noted previously. So why didn't this public policy against gambling and gambling debts help the defendant?

The answer to that question is found in the case *Fauntleroy v. Lum*, a 1908 decision of the Supreme Court.[49] A Missouri judgment based on a gambling transaction in cotton futures was presented for enforcement to a Mississippi court, a state where these transactions were void. But the Court held that fact wasn't of consequence. No jurisdictional defect was claimed in the Missouri action, the Court ruled, and that meant the judgment could not "be impeached in Mississippi."[50]

What the "*Fauntleroy* Doctrine" established was the principle that when an otherwise valid judgment from one state is presented to another state for enforcement, the Full Faith and Credit Clause of the U.S. Constitution requires the state to enforce the judgment.[51] Later Supreme Court cases addressed the issue of whether a state had to enforce a foreign judgment when the public policy of the state was offended by the underlying cause of action. The North Carolina court noted that the *Fauntleroy* decision had "narrow[ed] almost to the vanishing point the area of state public policy relief from the mandate of the Full Faith and Credit Clause—at least so far as the judgments of sister states are concerned."[52] The court stated that it was "aware of no such exception in the case of a money judgment rendered in a civil suit," and

---

46. MGM Desert Inn, Inc v. Holz, 411 S.E.2d 399 (N.C. App. 1991).
47. *Id.* at 400.
48. *Id.*
49. 210 U.S. 230 (1908).
50. *Id.* at 237.
51. The Full Faith and Credit Clause is in Article IV, Section 1 of the Constitution and provides: "Full Faith and Credit shall be given in each State to the public Acts, Records, and judicial Proceedings of every other State. And the Congress may by general Laws prescribe the Manner in which such Acts, Records and Proceedings shall be proved, and the Effect thereof."
52. *Holz*, 411 S.E.2d at 402.

that it knew of no considerations of local policy or law that impaired the force and effect of the clause.[53]

There is a limitation to the constitutional requirement: a defect in personal or subject matter jurisdiction can be raised and, if established, supplies a basis for the court not to enforce the sister state's judgment. Apart from that, however, there is no public policy exception to the Full Faith and Credit Clause. The jurisdictional point must be emphasized. In *Holz*, the plaintiff-casino sued Holz in Nevada, the state where he incurred the gambling debt. How had they obtained personal jurisdiction over him sufficient to obtain an *in personam* judgment if he was not a resident of Nevada? Remember, the provisions of the credit instrument, the marker, typically state that the gambler agrees that an action to enforce the marker can be brought in the state where the debt is incurred and that he agrees both to submit to the jurisdiction of the courts of that state and that the laws of that state—here, Nevada—apply.[54]

To summarize:

- *Holz* differs from *Agresta* in one important way. The casino sued the debtor in the state where the gambling debt was incurred, rather than the state where the debtor resides.
- Jurisdiction over the gambler was established by the gambler's consent, as evidenced by the language on the casino marker.
- In addition to personal jurisdiction being properly exercised over the gambler, valid service of process has to be achieved.
- After jurisdiction is established and service confirmed, the court in the state where the gambling debt was incurred may go forward with the case against the gambler and, if the gambler doesn't appear, enter a default judgment against him or her.
- The casino then will take the valid judgment and register it in the state where the gambler resides, seeking to enforce the judgment there.
- As the *Holz* case makes clear, the fact that the gambler/judgment debtor's state has a strong public policy against gambling, or against gambling debts, does not matter. The judgment must be enforced pursuant to the Full Faith and Credit Clause of the U.S. Constitution.
- Although courts may offer dicta to the contrary, there is no recognized public policy exception to the Clause, at least insofar as a civil money judgment is involved.

Other courts have recognized the *Fauntleroy* Doctrine and the principle expressed in *Holz*.[55] The lesson to the gambler is clear: when you execute the casino

---

53. *Id.*
54. *See* discussion of provisions of marker, *supra* part III.A.
55. *See* Coghill v. Boardwalk Regency Corp., 396 A.2d 838 (Va. 1990); Marina Assocs. v. Barton, 563 N.E.2d 1110 (Ill. App. 1990); M & R Investments, Co. v. Hacker, 511 So. 2d 1099 (Fla. App. 1987); GNLV Corp. v. Jackson, 736 S.W.2d 893 (Tex. App. 1987).

marker, you are signing a negotiable instrument and consenting to the jurisdiction of the court in the state where the casino is located. Running home to your state that abhors gambling or casino credit won't save you. Once you are served with process, expect to be hearing from the casino or its collectors again soon.[56]

There is another controversial tactic that casinos in Las Vegas have used to obtain assistance in the gaming debt collection process. Because the dishonored marker is tantamount to a normal check being returned by a bank, state law provisions making the passing of bad checks a criminal offense may be invoked. The Nevada Code states that a person who willfully and with the intent to defraud draws a check to obtain casino credit with insufficient funds to cover the draft is guilty of a felony if the amount is $1,200 or more.[57] Casinos in Las Vegas frequently refer unpaid marker cases to the Clark County district attorney for prosecution under this statute. Objections have been raised that this amounts to the district attorney acting as a collection agent for the casino. As one commentator put it, "This situation evokes a troubling image. Casinos have no need for a bagman if they can refer the debt to the public prosecutor to collect under threat of a criminal trial leading to imprisonment. The seemingly distant memory of debtors' prisons suddenly returns as an all-too-vivid reality."[58]

Despite the apparent concerns regarding the law, the Nevada Supreme Court ruled in 2015 that it did not violate the Nevada constitution.[59] The court also held that a casino's actual knowledge that the gambler had insufficient funds in his bank accounts negated the "intent to defraud" requirement of the statute.[60] However, in the particular situation, there was insufficient evidence to support a conclusion that the casino knew of the insufficiency of funds at the time the markers were executed, so no instruction on that point was needed.[61]

2. Enforcing Gaming Debts in Foreign Countries

Casinos in the United States have different problems when they seek to enforce gambling debts incurred by players who reside in foreign countries. The casinos don't have the benefit of constitutional full faith and credit principles when seeking to enforce a judgment against a gambler in a foreign country. Principles of "comity"

---

56. Issues raised by the enforceability of gambling debts have been addressed by many commentators. *See* Anthony N. Cabot, *Casino Collection Lawsuits: The Basics*, 4 Gaming L. Rev. 319 (2000); Note, *A Continuing Debate: Public Policy and Welfare Versus Economic Interests Regarding Enforcement of Gambling Debts in* State v. Dean, 46 Loy. L. Rev. 299 (2000); Jeffrey R. Soukup, *Rolling the Dice on Precedent and Wagering on Legislation: The Law of Gambling Debt Enforceability in Kentucky After* Kentucky Off-Track Betting, Inc. v. McBurney *and KRS § 372.005*, 95 Ky. L.J. 529 (2007).

57. *See* Nev. Rev. Stat. § 205.130 (2019). The amount that converts the crime to a felony was raised from $650 to $1,200 in 2019.

58. Francis J. Mootz III, *Even Moe Dalitz Would Blush: Why the District Attorney Has No Business Collecting Unpaid Casino Markers*, 3 UNLV Gaming L.J. 59, 60 (2012). The author also argues that casino markers aren't subject to the bad check statute.

59. Zahavi v. State of Nevada, 343 P.3d 595 (Nev. 2015).

60. *Id.* at 600.

61. *Id.* at 601–602.

may cause a foreign jurisdiction to enforce the U.S. judgment, as may the terms of a treaty between the United States and the foreign country, but the collection process is far more nuanced than when a domestic judgment is involved. While there may not be a public policy exception to the Full Faith and Credit Clause, foreign jurisdictions not bound by that provision may very well refuse to enforce the U.S. gambling debt on just that basis.[62]

One particularly challenging issue is presented by the gambling debts incurred in Las Vegas casinos by Chinese residents. Unquestionably, gamblers from China have been important to the success of Las Vegas casinos. The game favored by Chinese gamblers is baccarat.[63] In fact, one report stated that Asians "account for as much as 90% of baccarat gambling in Las Vegas, with the majority being Chinese."[64] When one considers the size of the baccarat market, the problem comes clearly into focus: in 2018, for Las Vegas strip casinos alone, baccarat produced winnings of nearly $1.2 billion, by far the biggest money winners for the casinos there.[65] If the great majority of baccarat players are Chinese, questions of debt collection are of great importance.

In fact, the legal wrinkles in dealing with Chinese resident gamblers begins at an early stage for U.S. casinos. Nevada Gaming Regulations, like the regulations of some other states, require casinos to take certain steps to determine the creditworthiness of any gambler seeking credit.[66] While these measures are familiar to U.S. residents, they are less feasible when applied to a foreign country, especially one where few residents have credit scores.[67] The problem is raised to another level when gamblers seeking credit submit a completed credit application though they don't read or speak English.[68]

From the standpoint of gambling debt collection, the Chinese example can present daunting challenges. First, Chinese law prohibits their citizens from transferring

---

62. The enforceability of judgments in foreign countries based on gambling debts has been the subject of considerable study. *See, e.g.*, Joseph Kelly, *Caught in the Intersection between Public Policy and Practicality: A Survey of the Legal Treatment of Gambling-Related Obligations in the United States*, 5 CHAP. L. REV. 87 (2002) (containing an appendix detailing international treatment of gaming debts); Maria Angela Jardim de Santa Cruz Oliveira, *Recognition and Enforcement of United States Money Judgments in Brazil*, 19 N.Y. INT'L. L. REV. 1 (2006).

63. *See* I. Nelson Rose, *What China Means to Las Vegas*, ASIAN GAMING LAWYER (May 2017).

64. Joel Schechtman & Koh Gui Qing, *Shill Game—Vegas Casino's Attempt to Collect a Debt Exposes World of Chinese High-Rollers*, REUTERS (Sep. 30, 2016), https://www.reuters.com/investigates/special-report/usa-vegas-shell/.

65. David G. Schwartz & Autumn Bassett. *Nevada Gaming Win 2018*, LAS VEGAS: CENTER FOR GAMING RES., UNIV. LIBRARIES, UNIV. OF NEVADA LAS VEGAS (2019).

66. NEV. GAMING COMM'N REG. § 6.120.2 (2018). N.J. ADMIN. CODE § 13:69D-1.27 (2018). New Jersey also has statutory requirements for the opening of accounts if the person is not a U.S. citizen. N.J. STAT. ANN. § 5:12-101.1 (2018).

67. *See* Bruce Einhorn, *Credit Scores Come to Debt-Leery Chinese—To Boost Consumption, the Government Wants More Borrowers*, BLOOMBERG BUSINESS WEEK (July 2, 2015), https://www.bloomberg.com/news/articles/2015-07-02/china-credit-scores-come-to-a-debt-leery-culture.

68. *See* Jeffrey B. Setness, *Chinese Gamblers—The Rewards and Challenges Facing Las Vegas Casinos*, NEV. GAMING LAWYER 55 (Sep. 2017).

more than $50,000 per year out of the country.[69] These currency control regulations can hamper collection of amounts from the Chinese resident. Second, gambling is illegal in China, and one running a gambling house can be imprisoned.[70] As one commentator understatedly put it, in light of that, "it would seem that the Chinese government may not be thrilled with the prospect of Chinese citizens transferring substantial sums of money out of China to pay gambling debts owing to Las Vegas casinos."[71] Finally, the Chinese government can act without warning to further limit the flow of cash out of the country, adding even more unpredictability to the process.[72] The overall issue reflects the fact that business judgments will be the driver of how the industry will respond: though the collection and enforcement issues can be treacherous, casinos have a difficult time not seeking that revenue.

3. Avoiding the Debt: Nevada and New Jersey Models

Gamblers have attempted many tactics to evade having to pay the outstanding credit markers casinos hold. Some of those efforts relate to supposed flaws with the credit instrument or collection process. This is a setting where one finds a significant difference between the two largest gaming jurisdictions, Nevada and New Jersey. Both jurisdictions have extensive and specific requirements a casino must follow when granting credit to a player.[73] But what happens if a casino in one of those states does not follow the procedures set out in the state's code and regulations?

Nevada law does not allow a casino licensee to escape consequences from this, but the consequences are regulatory in nature. The Nevada statute states that a person who doesn't follow the prescriptions of section 463.368 "is subject *only* to the penalties provided in NRS 463.310 to 463.318."[74] The word *only* is important here because the statute continues: "The failure of a person to comply with the provisions of this section or the regulations of the Commission does not invalidate a credit instrument or affect the ability to enforce the credit instrument or the debt that the credit instrument represents."[75] In other words, a casino can be in trouble with regulators if it doesn't follow the rules governing the granting of credit and collection of debts based on the granting of credit, but the debt itself stands. This is, as discussed below, of no small consequence in collection actions.

New Jersey presents a very different picture. As one commentator put it, "There are many endeavors where close is good enough. The extension of credit and collection practices under the New Jersey Casino Control Act do not fall in

---

69. *Id.* at 56. The discussion relates to China's State Administration of Foreign Exchange (SAFE).
70. *See* Criminal Law of the People's Republic of China, art. 303.
71. Setness, *supra* note 68, at 56.
72. *Id.*
73. For New Jersey, see N.J. Stat. Ann. 5:12-101 (2018) and N.J. Admin. Code §§ 13:69D–1.27-13:69D-1.29 (2018); in Nevada, see Nev. Gaming Comm. Reg. § 6.120 (2018) and Nev. Rev. Stat. § 463.368 (2018).
74. Nev. Rev. Stat. § 463.368.7 (2018) (emphasis added).
75. *Id.*

the category, however."[76] Indeed, in a number of cases, casinos that have run afoul of the statutory and regulatory provisions on credit have found they were unable to collect on the debt. The application of this principle goes back at least to 1981. In *Resorts International Hotel, Inc. v. Salamone*,[77] the casino had extended $1,500 in credit to a player through three $500 counterchecks drawn on the player's bank. When the checks were returned unpaid, the casino sought to collect the money.

The court noted two problems with the transaction between the player and the casino. First, one of the three checks was undated at the time it was written, and it was not until several weeks later that the casino's cage manager filled in the date.[78] Second, the checks were not deposited until almost four weeks after they were written.[79] Both actions were in violation of New Jersey law: one provision required checks to be "dated, but not postdated,"[80] and another required that checks of $500 had to be deposited within seven banking days.[81]

The casino argued that "a mere 'blemish' in the handling of the check should not avoid the underlying obligation to repay consideration given in good faith."[82] The court disagreed. "We merely hold that casinos must comply with the Legislature's strict control of credit for gambling purposes. Unless they do, the debts reflected by the players' checks will not be enforced in our courts."[83] In other words, the court was saying that not only were the checks unenforceable, the *underlying obligation itself* was likewise void. "Voiding the check would be meaningless if the obligation it represents remains."[84]

New Jersey courts have consistently reinforced this principle set forth in *Salamone*.[85] Limits have been set, however. When a gambler established violations of the laws and regulations concerning casino credit, a court held that would invalidate the casino debt, but it did not create a private, implied cause of action whereby the gambler could sue the casino to recover damages.[86] Given the extraordinary and extensive regulation of casinos by the legislature, the court held if the legislature had wanted such a cause of action to exist, it would have created it.[87]

In contrast to the dramatic consequences for failing to comply with the statutory and regulatory particulars of casino credit in New Jersey, the more forgiving attitude of Nevada law is illustrated by several cases. In one, the gambler maintained

---

76. Lloyd D. Levenson, *Casino Credit and Collections in New Jersey—An Overview*, 4 Gaming L. Rev. 413 (2000).
77. 429 A2d 1078 (N.J. Super. 1981).
78. *Id.*
79. *Id.*
80. *Id.* at 1080.
81. *Id.*
82. *Id.*
83. *Id.* at 1082.
84. *Id.*
85. *See, e.g.,* Miller v. Zoby, 595 A.2d 1104 (N.J. Super. Ct. App. Div. 1991).
86. *Id.*
87. *Id.* at 577.

that the casino's failure to present the markers against those accounts specified by the gambler in his credit application was a material breach of the credit application agreement and relieved him of the contractual obligation to perform under the marker agreements.[88] In affirming the trial court, the Ninth Circuit held that the signed markers authorized the casino "to debit *any* of Morales's bank accounts, whether or not he specified them in his credit application."[89] Moreover, even if the casino's action amounted to a breach of contract, no reasonable jury could find the breach was so material it relieved the gambler of his duty to pay. "Debiting the wrong account is, at best, tangential to the primary object of the parties' credit agreement: the loan of money and the repayment of that money."[90]

In another case, a casino extended a gambler $3 million in chips on credit—known as "rim credit"—as part of an agreement they had whereby he applied for credit and represented he was good for the losses and would sign casino markers if he lost the money.[91] Lose the money he did—all $3 million of it. But he refused to sign the markers that would obligate him to pay the casino back, and the casino sued to compel him to sign the markers as the agreement required.[92]

The case really turned on the characterization of the casino's cause of action. The gambler said there was a long-time policy in Nevada not to enforce gaming debts in court, and that was the essence of the casino's claim. As the casino, and the court, viewed it, however, the casino was seeking not enforcement of a gaming debt but enforcement of the promise to sign credit instruments that then would allow the casino to enforce the gaming debt. This meant that the casino was "attempting to do precisely what the Nevada legislature said it could: extend credit first and get a signed credit instrument later."[93] Consequently, the court granted the casino's motion for summary judgment and ordered the gambler to "specifically perform his promise by promptly executing in full a credit instrument in the amount of $3,000,000, which represents the outstanding rim debt that Caesars issued to him on September 20–21, 2014."[94]

The matter didn't end there, however. In a subsequent proceeding in the same court, the court ruled that the gambler was in contempt for refusing to comply with the earlier order to sign the documents and that he was equitably estopped from raising the argument that his gaming debt was unenforceable without an executed instrument. In addition, the court awarded damages to the casino for the gambler's repeated refusal to sign the markers.[95]

---

88. Morales v. Aria Resort and Casino, LLC, 995 F. Supp. 2d 1176 (D. Nev. 2014), *aff'd*, 646 Fed. Appx. 545 (9th Cir. 2016).
89. Morales v. Aria Resort and Casino, LLC, 646 Fed. Appx. 545 (9th Cir. 2016).
90. *Id.* at 546.
91. Desert Palace, Inc. v. Michael, 2:16-cv-00462-JAD-GWF, 2017 WL 2695296 (D. Nev. 2017).
92. *Id.*
93. *Id.*
94. *Id.*
95. Desert Palace, Inc. v. Michael, 370 F. Supp. 3d 1177 (D. Nev. 2019).

These statutes, regulations, and cases from New Jersey and Nevada reflect a very different regulatory orientation toward credit issues.[96] They also illustrate the balancing act casinos must do in handling the credit process. As is evident, this is by no means risk free, but for some casinos, credit play supplies a large portion of overall gaming revenues.[97] If an attorney represents a person who has been sued for a gambling debt, it is critical to remember that this may not be treated as just any other type of debt. States following a New Jersey approach will make the casino pay dearly for mistakes in the process. On the other hand, representing a gambling debtor in a jurisdiction with more of a Nevada orientation offers fewer avenues of escape from the debt.

4. Avoiding the Debt: Diminished Capacity

Another type of case where a gambler seeks to avoid the payment of gambling losses is characterized by claims of diminished capacity, often due to intoxication or a mental or behavioral disorder of some type. Sometimes the assertion is that the gambler had a gambling disorder of which the casino was aware. In this situation, it is helpful to separate the defenses offered.

Generally speaking, a gambler who alleges his losses were attributable to the casino serving him excessive alcohol that impaired his judgment has little chance of recovery. For example, in *Hakimoglu v. Trump Taj Mahal Associates*,[98] the Third Circuit analyzed whether New Jersey law allowed recovery for losses caused by the alcohol served to the gambler by the casino after it was evident the gambler was intoxicated. While noting there were conflicting district court opinions on the issue,[99] the Third Circuit predicted New Jersey courts would not recognize such a claim. New Jersey courts had not expanded dram shop liability beyond injuries directly related to drunken driving and barroom brawls.[100] Also, given the extensive regulation of gaming by the state, if there was a belief such a claim should

---

96. Not all Nevada cases reflect this bias in favor of the industry. In Zoggolis v. Wynn Las Vegas, LLC, 768 F.3d 919 (9th Cir. 2014), a gambler claimed that he had directed the casino not to let his credit line exceed $250,000 and that the casino had committed in writing to doing that. The casino failed to do that, and the gambler executed markers exceeding $1,000,000. Predictably, the gambler argued that because the casino had not limited his credit line as it promised, any debt over $250,000 was discharged. In reviewing the trial court's ruling that the gambler needed first to exhaust administrative remedies before filing his action, the Ninth Circuit disagreed. Nevada law did not require exhaustion when gaming debts evidenced by credit markers were in question nor did it deprive debtors of litigating these disputes.

97. Elena Holodny, *Here's How the Real High-Rolling VIPs Gamble*, Business Insider (Sep. 15, 2015), https://www.businessinsider.com/how-high-rollers-vips-gamble-casinsos-2015-9 (noting marker play in Las Vegas can be up to two-thirds of total gaming play).

98. 70 F.3d 291 (3d Cir. 1995).

99. *Compare* GNOC Corp. v. Aboud, 715 F. Supp. 644 (D.N.J. 1989) (finding casino had duty to refrain from knowingly permitting patron to gamble if patron was obviously and visibly intoxicated or under influence of narcotic substance) *with* Hakimoglu v. Trump Taj Mahal Associates, 876 F. Supp. 625 (D.N.J. 1994) (disagreeing with other district court decisions predicting New Jersey courts would impose duty on casino in such cases).

100. *Hakimoglu*, 70 F.3d at 293.

be permitted, that policy would have been positively enacted.[101] Finally, causation problems posed impossible challenges in these cases; a drunk gambler doesn't necessarily lose and a sober gambler doesn't necessarily win. The potential for a fabricated cause of action was substantial.[102]

A distinction needs to be made in this situation, however. If a gambler were able to establish that his mind "was so disqualified by excessive and complete intoxication that he was at the time mentally incapable of understanding the subject of the agreement, its nature and probable consequences,"[103] a basic contract defense might be established. This sets a very high standard of proof for gamblers, however, as they would need to show they were incapable of understanding the nature and consequences of the transaction.

Mental states, such as depression, may be alleged as a defense in debt collection cases.[104] Nevada addresses the broader issue of mental disorders, including gambling disorder, in the set of statutes dealing with the enforceability of casino debts. The law provides that:

> 6. A patron's claim of having a mental or behavioral disorder involving gambling:
> (a) Is not a defense in any action by a licensee or a person acting on behalf of a licensee to enforce a credit instrument or the debt that the credit instrument represents.
> (b) Is not a valid counterclaim to such an action.[105]

A New Jersey court recently considered the issue of whether a claim of compulsive gambling addiction could be a valid defense to a collection case.[106] The court ruled it wasn't, as compulsiveness alone did not establish an incapacity to enter into a credit arrangement with the casino. Unless the debtor could establish a defense of duress—that is, the casino exerted wrongful pressure to overcome the free will of the gambler—the debt was still valid. Moreover, the court ruled, the casino had no duty to deny the gambler credit, as the relationship between the casino and the gambler was "built on enabling gaming, not withholding it."[107] Further, it made no difference whether the casino knew the defendant was a compulsive gambler, particularly in a case where the gambler "assured the casino he had ample funds to support his gambling and did not request to suspend his casino credit privileges."[108]

---

101. *Id.* at 294.
102. *Id.*
103. *See* Levenson, *supra* note 76, at 415.
104. *See* Harrah's Club v. Van Blitter, Civ. R-85-267 (D. Nev. 1988), discussed in Anthony N. Cabot, *Casino Collection Lawsuits: The Basics*, 4 Gaming L. Rev. 319, 327 (2000).
105. Nev. Rev. Stat. § 463.368.6 (2017).
106. Harrah's Atlantic City Operating Co. v. Dangelico, No. A-2158-17T3, 2019 WL 1869008 (N.J. Super. Ct. 2019) (unpublished opinion).
107. *Id.* at *2.
108. *Id.* at *3.

There is a significant consensus in the courts that supports the New Jersey and Nevada approach.[109] Ultimately, the efforts of gamblers to assert defenses to a gambling debt is an uphill struggle when they allege some diminished capacity falling short of complete incapacity. This is true regardless of whether the casino is aware of intoxication, a gambling addiction, or some other mental condition.

IV. PATRON DISPUTES

Another way the contract between a gambler and a casino gets tested is when there are disputes regarding the rules of the game, employee mistakes, and machine malfunctions. This is an area where a business lawyer might well be contacted by a person who says he or she has been unfairly denied a jackpot payout by a casino. Indeed, the facts of the situation might suggest the casino is wrongly failing to pay the gambler. As is often the case, however, this type of case is not low-hanging fruit, and an attorney needs to proceed cautiously before taking on such cases.

Recall that the contract between the gambler and the casino is formed when the gambler makes an offer—a wager—that is accepted by the casino. Both express and implied terms apply to the situation, and statutory provisions can supersede the contractual obligations and rights of the parties. Not all disputes between the gambler and casino lead to court actions, and informal means of resolution are common. The discussion below also illustrates the administrative process for resolving disputes that some states have established.

A. Disputed Jackpots — Review Process

If a substantial jackpot is apparently won by a gambler but the casino refuses to pay, it is no surprise that the gambler will turn to the legal process. At a basic level, these cases implicate contract principles in a number of ways.

In *Erickson v. Desert Palace Inc.*,[110] Kirk Erickson, then nineteen, won a jackpot of $1,061,812. The casino refused to pay him because he was under twenty-one as required by Nevada law. As a matter of contract law, this is a relatively

---

109. *See* Merrill v. Trump Indiana, Inc., 320 F.3d 729, 733 (7th Cir. 2003) (concluding that Indiana law would not impose a duty on a casino to prevent a compulsive gambler from causing himself financial harm); Rahmani v. Resorts Int'l Hotel, Inc., 20 F. Supp. 2d 932, 937 (E.D. Va. 1998) (finding a casino had no duty, under New Jersey law, to prevent a compulsive gambler from playing); Logan v. Ameristar Casino Council Bluffs, 185 F. Supp. 2d 1021 (S.D. Iowa 2002) (finding no duty of "good faith and fair dealing" existed between casino and gambler, even if casino was told of gambling addiction and alcoholism of gambler); Duff v. Harrah South Shore Corp., 125 Cal. Rptr. 259, 260–61 (Ct. App. 1975) (finding a Nevada-based casino had no duty to limit a decedent's check-cashing ability); Stevens v. MTR Gaming Grp., Inc., 788 S.E.2d 59, 66 (W.Va. 2016) (holding casinos featuring video lottery terminals have no duty of care "to protect users from compulsively gambling"); Caesars Riverboat Casino, LLC v. Kephart, 934 N.E.2d 1120, 1123 (Ind. 2010) (holding that a comprehensive regulatory scheme governing riverboat gaming abrogated any common law duty that might exist "to refrain from attempting to entice or contact gamblers that it knows or should know are compulsive gamblers").

110. 942 F.2d 694 (9th Cir. 1991).

straightforward case, as a minor would not have the capacity to enter into a contract with the casino. Given the amount of money involved, however, it is not surprising that the family sued the casino, alleging breach of contract, the existence of a quasi-contract, fraud and cheating, and interference with contractual relations. The case is instructive because it illustrates how some states deal with such disputes.

Nevada law provides that "an unpaid slot machine jackpot is a gaming debt not evidenced by a credit instrument."[111] This is in contrast to gaming debts represented by a credit instrument—that is, a marker.[112] As such, the unpaid jackpot is "void and unenforceable and do[es] not give rise to any administrative or civil cause of action,"[113] "except as provided in NRS 463.361 to 461.366."[114] Those latter provisions allow for the dispute to be considered by the state Gaming Control Board, with review by a state district court and the Nevada Supreme Court.[115] As the court in *Erickson* stated, this review is the exclusive method for review and resolution of a disputed jackpot case.[116]

The Ericksons initially filed a complaint with the Gaming Control Board. The board ruled that young Erickson was prohibited from collecting the slot jackpot due to his age, and no contract between the casino and Erickson could change that. Further, the casino had taken sufficient steps to warn those under twenty-one of their ineligibility to win a jackpot, so no fraud existed. Unjust enrichment remedies were also inapplicable because the casino had only benefited from the $3 that had been wagered, and the plaintiffs were seeking payment of the jackpot. These findings were affirmed by the district court and state supreme court. In the meantime, the plaintiffs had filed an action in federal court. The Ninth Circuit ruled that the Nevada process was applicable to the plaintiffs' claims because a gambling debt was involved; therefore, there was no basis for the federal court action.

A Mississippi case offers a helpful analysis of the manner in which state administrative bodies handle these disputes.[117] In *Eash v. Imperial Palace of Mississippi, LLC*, Eash was playing a $5 Double Top Dollar slot machine. She testified that it was her first time playing the machine and that she did not read the instructions or the description of the possible awards listed on the front of the machine before playing. After several plays, Eash hit a winning combination—three double diamond symbols lined up on the single pay line and the following words scrolled across the electronic display on the machine: "Hand Pay Jackpot 200,000 credits." The keypad showed that the winnings totaled $1,000,000. Understandably, Eash thought that she had won $1,000,000. But that was quickly thrown into doubt.

---
111. *Id.* at 695.
112. *See* discussion of casino credit and markers, *supra* Part III.A.
113. Nev. Rev. Stat. § 463.361 (2017).
114. *Id.*
115. *Erickson*, 942 F.2d at 695.
116. *Id.*
117. Eash v. Imperial Palace of Miss., LLC, 4 So. 3d 1042 (Miss. 2009).

Staff members of the casino approached Eash, and a staff member cleared the keypad showing the $1,000,000 win. The staff members informed Eash that she would be paid only $8,000 for her win. This was based on the fact the "awards glass" displayed the permanent rules and instructions of the game, and it stated that the maximum award on that particular machine was $8,000. Eash, not liking the reduced prize, initiated a patron dispute claim with the casino.

An agent ran a battery of tests on the machine and reviewed the videotape of the incident. He concluded that the International Game Technology (IGT) programmer who set up the machine mistakenly entered $1,000,000 as the jackpot, rather than $8,000. The machine was also mistakenly programmed as a "Stand Alone Progressive" machine, although nothing on the exterior of the machine indicated that it was a progressive machine. The complaint process went forward.

Whatever flaws there might have been in that process, no one could claim the dispute did not receive considerable attention. Before the Mississippi Supreme Court ruled on the case, the following action was taken:

- The executive director of the state's Gaming Commission issued a written decision stating that Eash was entitled to $1,000,000.
- The casino filed a petition to reconsider the decision, requesting a hearing before a hearing examiner. After conducting a hearing, the hearing examiner reversed the executive director's decision and ruled that Eash was entitled only to $8,000.
- Eash appealed that decision to the Gaming Commission, which reinstated the executive director's decision awarding her $1,000,000.
- The casino then appealed to a state circuit court, and at the conclusion of a hearing, the court ruled in favor of the casino, awarding Eash only the $8,000.

Finally, the case reached the Mississippi Supreme Court.

The court noted that Mississippi prescribes a "deferential standard of review" for actions of the Gaming Commission. The decisions of that body would be reversed only if "the substantial rights of the petitioner have been prejudiced" because, for example, the decision was "not in accordance with the law." In this instance, the ruling in fact did not properly apply principles of contract law, the court ruled. The unambiguous language on the permanent signage of the machine indicated the most that could be won was $8,000. As the court put it:

> Contract law dictates that when Eash put her money into the . . . machine, she and [the casino] entered into a contract whereby [the casino] would pay her $8000 if her ten-dollar wager resulted in three double diamond symbols lining up on the single pay line. Since her play resulted in that winning combination, Eash is entitled to $8000.

But what about the keypad display that indicated Eash had won $1,000,000? Wasn't that part of the contract that existed between her and the casino? No, the court ruled, these "secondary indicators" could not alter the fact that there was no question *ex ante* that the maximum amount that could be won was $8,000. These were the terms of the contract between the parties, despite the "regrettable programming error that led Eash to believe she had won $1,000,000."

There are cases where courts have awarded gamblers a jackpot greater than what the casino said the machine should have paid. In one case, the gambler was playing a video poker machine and hit a descending sequential royal flush—ace, king, queen, jack, and 10 of hearts. She alleged this entitled her to the "primary progressive jackpot," which was the advertised award for such a hand. The machine maker, however, claimed this jackpot was intended only for *ascending* royal flushes, and the player instead was entitled only to a secondary progressive jackpot. The court held that the signage on the machine was ambiguous and did not specify the requirement of the ascending royal flush for the primary progressive jackpot. As a matter of basic contract construction, the court stated, ambiguities in a written contract are resolved unfavorably to the contract drafter. In light of this principle, the player was entitled to the primary jackpot.[118]

The court decisions discussed above emerged from administrative proceedings provided for in state law. This is not uncommon, as a number of states have established such procedures.[119] If a state does not provide an administrative path for these disputes, the matter is likely relegated to the court system. Cases then are decided by applying contract principles, subject to regulatory and statutory provisions relating to gaming transactions. In these cases, the regulatory body may play a role in investigating the dispute but only in the framework of determining whether the casino, a licensee, has complied with gaming provisions.

In *McKee v. Isle of Capri Casinos, Inc.*,[120] plaintiff was playing a Miss Kitty penny slot machine when the machine displayed a message stating that she had won a "Bonus Award" of approximately $42 million. Iowa does not have an administrative process for resolving patron disputes, but the Iowa Racing and Gaming Commission investigated the dispute from a licensure perspective and determined the bonus was invalid. The casino then refused to pay the award.

After the casino's refusal to pay and because of the absence of an administrative process, the player sued. The Iowa Supreme Court affirmed the summary judgment the trial court had granted in favor of the casino. The court ruled that the rules of

---

118. *See also* Ledoux v. Grand Casino-Coushatta, 954 So. 2d 902, 909 (La. App. 2007) (noting that though the casino argued that the maximum payout for a "three 7 s bonus" was clearly set out on the machine and this limited the gambler's recovery, the court disagreed, holding that "[n]owhere [did] any language appear on the slot machine that the *maximum* payout [was] fixed by [those] numbers"); *Cf* Marcangelo v. Boardwalk Regency, 847 F. Supp. 1222 (D.N.J. 1994) (finding player's court action against casino for disputed jackpot was preempted by requirement that commission approve all signage; however, *even if* the court were to recognize this cause of action, the gambler would not prevail. As a unilateral mistake, he could merely collect his initial $1.25, not the difference between the primary and secondary progressive jackpots).

119. In addition to Nevada and Mississippi, see 68 INDIANA ADMIN. CODE § 18-1-2 (2018) (Patron Dispute Process).

120. 864 N.W.2d 518 (Iowa 2015).

the Miss Kitty game were clear, and the plaintiff had an express contract with the casino according to the rules of the machine, regardless of whether or not she actually read the rules. Neither the rules of the game nor its pay-table, both of which could be displayed and read by tapping a "Touch Game Rules" button, mentioned any sort of jackpots, prizes, or bonuses that a player could win. Consequently, the plaintiff had no contractual right to the bonus because the rules, and thus the contract, did not describe any bonuses available to players. The plaintiff was limited to winnings of $1.85. The question of whether there was a machine malfunction was not relevant. "[W]hen the machine, as here, generates an award that is not within the rules of the game, isolating the cause of what happened is not necessary. It is sufficient for present purposes that the award was erroneous in the sense that it was not a part of the game."[121]

As the *McKee* case suggests, a state regulatory body that investigates a dispute to determine only whether the casino complied with the law can still do damage to a gambler's case against the casino. If the regulators determine the casino was acting appropriately in not paying a jackpot, that finding may or may not be admissible in a subsequent court proceeding. Regardless of that, once a casino receives a regulator's determination that it has not acted improperly, it is far less likely to pay the player the jackpot. A finding that the casino was acting improperly, of course, could have the opposite effect.

B. Machine Malfunctions

One of the biggest obstacles to a player winning a disputed jackpot is the standard industry practice to place on slot machines a sign or legend saying, MALFUNCTION VOIDS ALL PAYS AND PLAYS. Where a slot machine's reels operate irregularly, an error code is displayed, or noises, alerts, or displays indicate a malfunction, the casino will be able to invoke the VOIDS ALL PAYS AND PLAYS language to refuse to pay an apparent jackpot. In short, the statement on the machine becomes a term of the contract between the player and the casino when the player puts money into the machine.

One example of a malfunction situation is *Senegl v. IGT*.[122] The gambler was playing a slot machine that stopped abruptly when it received an error code. A "tilt code" appeared on the machine, the light on top of the machine indicated a maintenance issue, no sirens or music came from the slot machine, and no jackpot win registered on the interlinked computer system.[123] But the gambler argued there was no malfunction because the machine acted exactly the way it was designed to operate. It stopped when it received an error code, and the machine displayed a result on the reels that was a winning result. Because the machine functioned as designed, he argued, there was no malfunction.

---

121. *Id.* at 530.
122. 2 P.3d 259 (Nev. 2000).
123. *Id* at 259.

The court noted that it gives "great deference" to the rulings of the Nevada Gaming Control Board on such matters. The board decision will be upheld unless it is arbitrary or capricious, unsupported by evidence, or otherwise contrary to law. That was not the case here. The court noted evidence that the machine was designed to produce jackpots through its random number generator, not through a sudden stoppage produced by an error code. Several indicators of a malfunction were evident, including that the machine itself registered a malfunction and that the winning symbols were not evenly aligned on the pay line. An uneven alignment did not constitute a jackpot even if it had not been caused by a malfunction. The board, the court held, had a reasonable basis for ruling as it did.

One important point that plays a fundamental role in this and many cases is the manner of operation of a slot machine. Simply put, the results of a wager made on a slot machine are determined by a random number generator (RNG) inside the machine. The RNG is perpetually operating, and when a wager is made, it picks a random number for each reel with the number matching a "stop" on the reel. It is critical to understand the following about slot machines: by the time the reels are spinning, the RNG has already determined whether the wager is a winner or loser. The spinning of the reels has nothing to do with determining wins and losses; that is the function of the RNG. The reels spin for entertainment and perhaps as a way of suggesting to a player that they were "close" to winning. In fact, slot machines could operate without reels because they only display what the RNG has already picked. A gambler could put money in, activate the game, and the machine could instantly tell the gambler whether he or she won or lost. But what fun would that be?[124]

The reason this is important is because many claims brought by gamblers that allege they are being unfairly denied a jackpot emphasize that the machine readout clearly indicated they had won a jackpot. For example, in *Eash*, the readouts indicated a $1,000,000 win and "hand pay 200,000 credits."[125] But courts state that these are only secondary indicators, and whether a malfunction has occurred can often only be determined by a forensic examination of the RNG. This is a concept that gamblers may not fully comprehend; after all, the machine is displaying a jackpot win.

One rather subtle point to consider is what is the definition of a malfunction? In *Eash*, the court referred to a "regrettable programming error."[126] By definition, however, a programming error is a mistake in design; a computer that operates exactly the way it was designed to operate really isn't malfunctioning. The result may not be what the casino had in mind, but it is difficult to categorize that programming error as a malfunction.

---

124. See Pickle v. IGT, 830 So. 2d 1214, 1217–18 (Miss. 2002) for a discussion of the slot machine's functioning.
125. Eash v. Imperial Palace of Miss., LLC, 4 So. 3d 1042, 1043 (Miss. 2009).
126. *Id.* at 1048.

A related issue is whether the casino should be required to identify a specific malfunction in order to make use of the malfunction defense. In one case,[127] a casino claimed that the machine had malfunctioned but was unable to locate a specific malfunction or replicate the player's winning scenario. When the machine was returned to service and another jackpot was hit, the casino sent the machine to a testing lab. The lab conducted extensive testing but was still unable to locate a specific malfunction or to replicate the players' results, and it could not determine whether the alleged malfunction was in the machine's hardware or software.[128] "Notwithstanding its negative results, [the lab] concluded that the slot machine 'must have malfunctioned' because it was not programmed to pay out that much money."[129] The lab officially reported that the "cause of the malfunction was indeterminate."[130]

The court rejected the casino's malfunction claim. Nothing in the machine's behavior suggested a malfunction, and experts were unable to find a specific malfunction or even duplicate the machine's mechanics.[131] The court stated, "[W]here there [is] no apparent malfunction indication *by the slot machine itself*, a casino may not rely on the argument that the machine was not intended to register the particular jackpot to deny payment."[132] Moreover, without objective proof of a malfunction, a casino was incentivized to declare a malfunction for any win. As for the concept of a malfunction:

> The functioning of software reflects the ingenuity of the designer-programmer. Who is to say that this software did not behave as it was intended to behave? A result undesirable from the Casino's standpoint does not necessarily mean that a malfunction caused it. It might have been that the result was programmed accidentally, or even purposely. It cannot be inferred that simply because the machine paid out more than it was believed to have been designed and programmed to pay out, there was a malfunction.[133]

The *Ledoux v. Grand Casino-Coushatta* case does give gamblers challenging the malfunction claim by the casino some support if the malfunction is not one accompanied by clearly evident error codes, misaligned reels, or a specific identification of a malfunction. Attorneys considering involvement with such cases should proceed carefully, however. The weight of cases on the malfunction issue definitely favors casinos,[134] though there are some cases in the gambler's favor.[135]

---

127. Ledoux v. Grand Casino-Coushatta, 954 So. 2d 902 (La. App. 2007).
128. *Id.* at 911.
129. *Id.*
130. *Id.* at 909.
131. *Id.* at 910.
132. *Id.* at 912 (emphasis added).
133. *Id.* at 911, n. 7.
134. *See e.g.*, Pickle v. IGT, 830 So. 2d 1214 (Miss. 2002); Dockery v. Sam's Town, No. 06-1293, 2007 WL 3023928 (W.D. La. 2007); Griggs v. Harrah's Casino, 929 So. 2d 204 (La. App. 2006).
135. *See e.g.*, *Ledoux*, 954 So. 2d at 902 (holding in favor of the patron because the casino could not prove a malfunction); Grand Casino Biloxi v. Hallman, 823 So. 2d 1185 (Miss. 2002) (holding for the player because the casino failed to preserve evidence of the malfunction).

V. CONCLUSION

This chapter illustrates an area of gaming law that many business lawyers feel comfortable handling. After all, contract issues are the bread and butter of a business practice. Many of the contract issues raised are relatively straightforward, and a capable business lawyer will be in his or her element. On the other hand, there are many areas where the subtleties of gaming law influence the contract issues enough that a business lawyer will want to proceed with some circumspection. It is hoped that this discussion of contract issues in the gaming area has supplied helpful guidance to attorneys presented with these disputes.

Chapter 7

Problem Gambling and the Business Lawyer

Stacey A. Tovino

Individuals who have problem gambling experience adverse consequences as a result of their gambling.[1] Individuals with gambling disorder exhibit (1) persistent and recurrent problematic gambling behavior leading to clinically significant impairment or distress and (2) four or more of nine diagnostic criteria over a period of twelve months.[2] This chapter is designed to familiarize business lawyers with several common legal issues faced by individuals with problem gambling or gambling disorder, including those relating to health insurance coverage of gambling-related treatments and services (Part I), the availability of disability nondiscrimination protections (Part II), and professional discipline due to gambling-related behavior (Part III).[3]

---

1. *What Is Problem Gambling or Gambling Disorder*, Nat'l Ctr. Resp. Gaming, http://www.ncrg.org/press-room/media-kit/faq/what-problem-or-pathological-gambling (defining problem gambling).
2. Am. Psych. Ass'n, Diagnostic and Statistical Manual of Mental Disorders (5th ed. 2013) [hereinafter DSM-5] (identifying nine diagnostic criteria, including (1) "Needs to gamble with increasing amounts of money in order to achieve the desired excitement"; (2) "Is restless or irritable when attempting to cut down or stop gambling"; (3) "Has made repeated unsuccessful efforts to control, cut back, or stop gambling"; (4) "Is often preoccupied with gambling (e.g., having persistent thoughts of reliving past gambling experiences, handicapping or planning the next venture, thinking of ways to get money with which to gamble)"; (5) "Often gambles when feeling distressed (e.g., helpless, guilty, anxious, depressed)"; (6) "After losing money gambling, often returns another day to get even ('chasing' one's losses)"; (7) "Lies to conceal the extent of involvement with gambling"; (8) "Has jeopardized or lost a significant relationship, job, or educational or career opportunity because of gambling"; and (9) "Relies on others to provide money to relieve desperate financial situations caused by gambling").
3. The author has written several prior law review articles comprehensively addressing the intersection of problem gambling, gambling disorder, health law, and professional responsibility law. These articles include Stacey A. Tovino, *The House Edge: On Gambling and Professional Discipline*, 91 Wash. L. Rev. 1253 (2016); Stacey A. Tovino, *Gambling Disorder, Vulnerability, and the Law: Mapping the Field*, 16 Hous. J. Health L. & Pol'y 102 (2016); Stacey A. Tovino, *Introduction: Problem Gambling and the Law*, 6 UNLV Gaming L.J. iii (2015); and Stacey A. Tovino, *Lost in the Shuffle: How Health and Disability Laws Hurt Disordered Gamblers*, 89 Tulane L. Rev. 191 (2014). With the permission of the author, and with updates and conforming amendments, much of this chapter is taken from these prior articles.

I. HEALTH INSURANCE COVERAGE ISSUES

An individual with problem gambling or gambling disorder may wish to obtain treatment or therapy to help stop gambling only to be told by a health insurer that it (1) will not cover the requested treatment or therapy because the health insurance policy or plan contains an exclusion for gambling-related treatments and services, or (2) will cover the requested treatment or therapy but the coverage will be more expensive compared to coverage of a traditional physical health condition, such as cancer. Both of these insurer responses can be illegal in some health plan contexts, and business lawyers should be aware of illegal health insurer behavior vis-à-vis individuals with problem gambling and gambling disorder.

As background, many public health care programs and private health plans traditionally distinguished between physical and mental disorders and provided inferior insurance benefits for all mental disorders, including gambling disorders. For example, Medicare Part B formerly imposed a 50 percent beneficiary coinsurance on outpatient mental health services, including individual, family, and group psychotherapy services, compared to the 20 percent beneficiary coinsurance traditionally applied to nonmental health outpatient services.[4] Many private health plans also formerly provided inferior health insurance benefits for individuals with mental disorders by completely excluding their treatments and services from coverage or by providing less comprehensive coverage of their treatments and services.

For example, Kaiser Permanente's 2012 Small Group Colorado Health Benefit Plan (Kaiser Plan) provided insurance coverage of "biologically-based mental illnesses," but the Kaiser Plan only included six illnesses (schizophrenia, schizoaffective disorder, bipolar affective disorder, major depressive disorder, specific obsessive-compulsive disorder, and panic disorder) within that definition.[5] Gambling disorder was not included. Likewise, UnitedHealthcare's traditional Certificate of Coverage provided coverage for "biologically-based mental illnesses," but it also defined the phrase to include schizophrenia, bipolar disorder, pervasive

---

4. *See* Medicare Improvements for Patients and Providers Act of 2008, Pub. L. No. 110-275, § 102, 122 Stat. 2494, 2498 (codified as amended at 42 U.S.C. §1395*l*[c] [2012]) (calculating Medicare incurred expenses as only 62.5 percent of the outpatient expenses associated with the treatment of mental, psychoneurotic, and personality disorders). Until 2010, Medicare was thus responsible for only 50 percent (i.e., 62.5 percent × 80 percent, with 80 percent being the Medicare approved amount) of the cost of most outpatient mental health services, and the Medicare beneficiary was responsible for the remaining 50 percent. In 2008, President George W. Bush signed into law the Medicare Improvements for Patients and Providers Act of 2008, Section 102 of which increased Medicare's portion of incurred expenses for outpatient mental health services to 68.75 percent in 2010 and 2011 (resulting in a 45 percent beneficiary coinsurance), 75 percent in 2012 (resulting in a 40 percent beneficiary coinsurance), 81.25 percent in 2013 (resulting in a 35 percent beneficiary coinsurance), and 100 percent in 2014 and thereafter (resulting in a 20 percent coinsurance). Since 2014, Medicare has been paying 80 percent of (and Medicare beneficiaries are only paying a 20 percent coinsurance on) all outpatient mental health services.

5. *See* KAISER PERMANENTE, 2012 *Colorado Health Benefit Plan Description Form Kaiser Foundation Health Plan of Colorado Plan 230 HMO—City and County of Denver, Group #00075 Denver/Boulder—Large Group* n. 9 (2012) (defining biologically based mental illness).

developmental disorder, autism, paranoia, panic disorder, obsessive-compulsive disorder, and major depressive disorder.[6] Again, gambling disorder was not included in this definition.

Some private health plans went further by specifically excluding gambling disorder from coverage. For example, a prior version of Wellmark South Dakota's Blue Priority HSA Plan expressly excluded "pathological gambling" from coverage.[7] Similarly, the 2013–2014 Student Injury and Sickness Insurance Plan for students attending Embry-Riddle Aeronautical University in Florida also expressly excluded from coverage treatments and services for gambling.[8] The University of Pittsburgh Medical Center's health plan likewise excluded gambling disorder from coverage.[9] Although many states had enacted parity laws designed to put mental health conditions on equal footing with physical health conditions, some of these parity laws specifically excluded gambling disorder from protection as well. As an illustration, New Mexico's long-standing parity law requires group health plans in New Mexico to provide "mental health benefits" and to provide them at parity with "medical and surgical benefits."[10] However, the New Mexico law specifically excludes treatments for gambling addiction from the definition of "mental health benefits."[11]

During the past twenty-five years, developments in health insurance law have eliminated some, but not all, of these mental health benefit disparities, including gambling disorder benefit disparities. The federal government took its first step toward establishing mental health parity on September 26, 1996, when President Bill Clinton signed the federal Mental Health Parity Act (MHPA) into law.[12] As originally enacted, the MHPA prohibited large group health plans that offered medical and surgical benefits as well as mental health benefits from imposing more stringent lifetime and annual spending limits on their offered mental health benefits.[13] For example, the MHPA would have prohibited a covered, large group health plan from imposing a $20,000 annual cap or a $100,000 lifetime cap on mental health care if the plan had no annual or lifetime caps for medical and surgical care or if the plan had

---

6. *See Certificate of Coverage* 17–18, UNITEDHEALTHCARE INS. CO., https://www.uhc.com/content/dam/uhcdotcom/en/Legal/PDF/MY-7.pdf.

7. *See* Wellmark S.D., *BluePriority HSA Health Plans for Individuals and Families*, WELLMARK 8 (2012), https://www.ehealthinsurance.com/ehealthinsurance/benefits/ifp/WellmarkBCBS/SD-BluePriority HSA_1-11.pdf (excluding certain mental health and chemical dependency services, including "[i]mpulse-control disorders [such as pathological gambling]").

8. *See* UNITEDHEALTHCARE INS. CO., *Certificate of Coverage: 2013–2014 Student Injury & Sickness Insurance Plan* 16 (2013) (excluding coverage for "treatment, services or supplies for . . . [a]ddiction, such as . . . nicotine addiction, except as specifically provided in the policy and caffeine addiction; non-chemical addiction, such as . . . gambling, sexual, spending, shopping, working and religious; [and] codependency").

9. *See* UPMC HEALTH PLAN, *Exclusions* 1 (excluding from insurance coverage "[t]welve step model programs as sole therapy for conditions, including, but not limited to . . . addictive gambling").

10. *See* N.M. STAT. ANN. § 59 A-23E-18(A) (1978 & Supp. 2000).

11. *Id.* § 59 A-23E-18(F).

12. *See* Mental Health Parity Act of 1996, Pub. L. No. 104-204, 110 Stat. 2944 (codified as amended at 29 U.S.C. § 1185a (2012); 42 U.S.C. § 300gg-26 [2012]) [hereinafter Mental Health Parity Act].

13. *See id.* § 712(a)(1)–(2).

higher caps, such as a $50,000 annual cap or a $500,000 lifetime cap, for medical and surgical care.[14]

One problem with the MHPA was that its application and scope were very limited. As originally enacted, the MHPA regulated only insured and self-insured group health plans of large employers, then defined as those employers that employed an average of fifty-one or more employees.[15] The MHPA thus did not apply to the group health plans of small employers.[16] In addition, the MHPA did not apply to individual health plans, the Medicare Program, Medicaid nonmanaged care plans, or any self-funded, nonfederal governmental plan whose sponsor opted out of the MHPA.[17] Finally, the MHPA contained an "increased cost" exemption for covered group health plans or health insurance coverage offered in connection with those plans if the application of the MHPA resulted in an increase in the cost under the plan of at least 1 percent.[18] By November 1998, over two years after the MHPA's enactment, only four plans across the United States had obtained exemptions due to cost increases of 1 percent or more.[19]

In terms of its substantive provisions, the MHPA was neither a mandated offer nor a mandated benefit law; that is, nothing in the MHPA required a large group health plan to actually offer or provide any mental health benefits for conditions such as gambling disorder.[20] Thus, health plans were free, even after the enactment of the MHPA, to simply not provide any benefits for gambling disorder or any other mental health condition.[21] As originally enacted, the MHPA also was not a comprehensive parity law because it expressly excluded from protection individuals with substance use and addictive disorders.[22] Finally, the MHPA did not require parity between medical and surgical benefits and mental health benefits in terms of deductibles, copayments, coinsurance, inpatient day limitations, or outpatient visit limitations.[23]

---

14. *See id.*

15. *See id.* § 712(c)(1)(A)–(B) (applying in each case to "a group health plan [or health insurance coverage offered in connection with such a plan]").

16. *See id.* (exempting from the MHPA application group health plans of small employers; defining small employers as those "who employed an average of at least 2 but not more than 50 employees on business days during the preceding calendar year and who employs at least 2 employees on the first day of the plan year").

17. *See* 42 U.S.C. § 300gg-21(a)(2)(A) (2012) (statutory provision permitting sponsors of self-insured nonfederal governmental health plans to opt out of particular federal requirements); 45 C.F.R. § 146.180(a)(1)(v) (2015) (regulatory provision permitting sponsors of self-insured, nonfederal governmental health plans to opt out of federal mental health parity requirements).

18. Mental Health Parity Act, *supra* note 12, § 712(c)(2).

19. Colleen L. Barry, *The Political Evolution of Mental Health Parity*, 14 Harv. Rev. Psychiatry 185, 187 (2006).

20. *See* Mental Health Parity Act, *supra* note 12, § 712(b)(1) ("Nothing in this section shall be construed . . . as requiring a group health plan [or health insurance coverage offered in connection with such a plan] to provide any mental health benefits.").

21. *See id.*

22. *See id.* § 712(e)(4) ("The term 'mental health benefits' means benefits with respect to mental health services, as defined under the terms of the plan or coverage [as the case may be], but does not include benefits with respect to treatment of substance abuse or chemical dependency.").

23. *See id.* § 712(b)(2) ("Nothing in this Section shall be construed . . . as affecting the terms and conditions [including cost sharing, limits on numbers of visits or days of coverage, and requirements relating to medical necessity] relating to the amount, duration, or scope of mental health benefits under the plan or coverage.").

Because of these limitations, President George W. Bush expanded the MHPA twelve years later by signing into law the Paul Wellstone and Pete Domenici Mental Health Parity and Addiction Equity Act of 2008 (MHPAEA).[24] The MHPAEA built on the MHPA by expressly protecting individuals with substance-related and addictive disorders and by imposing comprehensive parity requirements on large group health plans.[25] In particular, the MHPAEA provided that any financial requirements (including deductibles, copayments, coinsurance, and other out-of-pocket expenses)[26] and treatment limitations (including inpatient day and outpatient visit limitations as well as nonquantitative treatment limitations such as medical necessity requirements)[27] that large group health plans imposed on mental health and substance use disorder benefits must not be any more restrictive than the predominant financial requirements and treatment limitations imposed by the plan on substantially all medical and surgical benefits.[28] The MHPAEA thus would have prohibited a large group health plan from imposing higher deductibles, copayments, and coinsurances or lower inpatient day and outpatient visit maximums on individuals seeking care for any mental health or substance use disorder listed in the current edition of the American Psychiatric Association's *Diagnostic and Statistical Manual of Mental Disorders* (DSM) or the World Health Organization's *International Classification of Diseases* (ICD).[29] The previous sentence is very important: If a large group health plan actually provided insurance benefits for gambling disorder, then the *DSM*'s and the *ICD*'s recognition and listing of gambling disorder meant that the health plan would be prohibited from imposing higher financial requirements or more stringent treatment limitations on individuals seeking services for these conditions.

Like the MHPA, the MHPAEA's application and scope were initially very limited. As originally enacted, the MHPAEA regulated only insured and self-insured group

---

24. Paul Wellstone and Pete Domenici Mental Health Parity and Addiction Equity Act of 2008, Pub. L. No. 110-343, 122 Stat. 3881 (codified as amended at 26 U.S.C. § 9812 [2012]; 29 U.S.C. § 1185a [2012]; 42 U.S.C. § 300gg-26 [2012]) [hereinafter MHPAEA].

25. *See id.* § 512(a)(4) (adding a new definition of "substance use disorder benefits"); *see also id.* § 512(a)(1) (regulating the financial requirements and treatment limitations that are applied to both mental health and substance use disorder benefits).

26. *See id.* § 512(a)(1) (including within the definition of "financial requirements" deductibles, copayments, coinsurance, and out-of-pocket expenses).

27. *See id.* (including within the definition of "treatment limitations" limits on the frequency of treatment, number of visits, days of coverage, and "other similar limits on the scope or duration of treatment").

28. *See id.* (requiring both financial requirements and treatment limitations applicable to mental health and substance use disorder benefits to be "no more restrictive than the predominant financial requirements" and treatment limitations "applied to substantially all [physical health benefits] covered by the plan").

29. *See, e.g.*, Final Rules Under the Paul Wellstone and Pete Domenici Mental Health Parity and Addiction Equity Act of 2008, 78 Fed. Reg. 68,240, 68,242 (Nov. 13, 2013) (to be codified at 45 C.F.R. pts. 146 and 147) (adopting 45 C.F.R. § 146.136, a federal regulation implementing the MHPAEA that requires a plan's definition of "mental health benefits" and "substance use disorder benefits" to be "consistent with generally recognized independent standards of current medical practice [for example, the most current version of the Diagnostic and Statistical Manual of Mental Disorders [DSM], the most current version of the ICD, or State guidelines]").

health plans of large employers, defined as those employers that employ an average of fifty-one or more employees.[30] The MHPAEA, like the MHPA, did not apply to small group health plans, individual health plans, the Medicare Program, Medicaid nonmanaged care plans, or any self-funded, nonfederal governmental plans whose sponsors had opted out of the MHPAEA.[31] In terms of its substantive provisions, the MHPAEA also was neither a mandated offer nor a mandated benefit law; nothing in the MHPAEA required a covered group health plan to actually offer or provide any benefits for conditions such as gambling disorder.[32] Like the MHPA, the MHPAEA also contained an "increased cost" exemption for covered group health plans and health insurance coverage offered in connection with such plans, but under the MHPAEA, the amount of the required cost increased, at least for the first year.[33] That is, a covered plan that could demonstrate a cost increase of at least 2 percent in the first plan year and 1 percent in each subsequent plan year of the actual total costs of coverage with respect to medical and surgical benefits and mental health and substance use disorder benefits would be eligible for an exemption from the MHPAEA for that year.[34] The MHPAEA required determinations of exemption-qualifying cost increases to be made and certified in writing by a qualified and licensed actuary who is a member in good standing of the American Academy of Actuaries.[35]

To summarize thus far, before President Barack Obama signed the Affordable Care Act into law in 2010, mental health insurance benefits were regulated by the MHPA and were expanded by the MHPAEA, as well as by more stringent state law.[36]

---

30. MHPAEA, *supra* note 24; 29 U.S.C. § 1185a (2012); 42 U.S.C. § 300gg-26 (2012) (stating that the MHPAEA applies only to "group health plan[s] or [health insurance coverage offered in connection with such . . . plan(s)]").

31. *See, e.g.*, CTRS. FOR MEDICARE & MEDICAID SERVS., CTR. FOR CONSUMER OVERSIGHT & INS. OVERSIGHT, *The Mental Health Parity and Addiction Equity Act* ("MHPAEA does not apply directly to small group health plans"). The Centers for Medicare and Medicaid Services has explained that Medicare and Medicaid are not issuers of health insurance: "They are public health plans through which individuals obtain health coverage. . . . Medicaid benchmark benefit plans, [however,] . . . require compliance with certain requirements of MHPAEA." "Non-Federal governmental employers that provide self-funded group health plan coverage to their employees [coverage that is not provided through an insurer] may elect to exempt their plan [opt-out] from the requirements of MHPAEA." *See also* Colleen L. Barry et al., *A Political History of Federal Mental Health and Addiction Insurance Parity*, 88 MILBANK Q. 404, 407 (2010) (explaining that MHPAEA applies to Medicare Advantage coverage offered through a group health plan, Medicaid managed care, the State Children's Health Insurance Program, and state and local government plans, but not Medicaid nonmanaged care plans).

32. MHPAEA, *supra* note 24, § 512(a)(1) (regulating only those group health plans that offer both physical health and mental health benefits); SUBSTANCE ABUSE & MENTAL HEALTH SERVS. ADMIN., *Implementation of the Mental Health Parity and Addiction Equity Act* (MHPAEA) (noting that "[s]elf-insured non-federal government employee plans can opt out of the federal parity law" and that the MHPAEA's requirements do not apply to "[s]mall employer plans created before March 23, 2010," "[c]hurch-sponsored plans and self-insured plans sponsored by state and local governments," "[r]etiree-only plans," TriCare, Medicare, and "[t]raditional Medicaid [fee-for-service, non-managed care]").

33. *See* MHPAEA, *supra* note 24, § 512(a)(3)(2)(A) (establishing new cost exemption provisions).

34. *Id.* § 512(a)(3)(2)(A)–(B).

35. *Id.* § 512(a)(3)(2)(C).

36. *See* Stacey A. Tovino, *Reforming State Mental Health*, 11 HOU. J. HEALTH L. & POL'Y 461–78 (2011) (describing the patchwork of state mental health parity law and providing examples of state laws that are more and less stringent than federal law).

Unless a more stringent state law required a health plan to provide gambling disorder benefits (and research revealed no state law that did so), a health plan was not required to provide such benefits. In late March 2010, however, President Obama responded to this limitation by signing the Patient Protection and Affordable Care Act and the Health Care and Education Reconciliation Act (HCERA) into law (as consolidated, the Affordable Care Act [ACA]).[37] Best known for its controversial (and now repealed) individual health insurance mandate,[38] the ACA has two other sets of provisions that relate to mental health parity and mandatory mental health and substance use disorder benefits. As of this writing, the U.S. District Court for the Northern District of Texas has issued an opinion striking down the entire Affordable Care Act, including the two sets of provisions discussed below.[39] If the U.S. Court of Appeals for the Fifth Circuit and/or the U.S. Supreme Court affirms this district court opinion, these ACA provisions will become irrelevant and any analysis of health insurer obligations with respect to individuals with gambling disorder will depend only on MHPA, MHPAEA, and more stringent state law, as discussed above.

That said, the first set of ACA provisions extends MHPA's and MHPAEA's mental health parity provisions to the individual and small group health plans offered on and off the ACA-created health insurance exchanges.[40] Now many individual and small group health plans that previously discriminated against individuals with gambling disorder through higher deductibles, copayments, and coinsurance rates, as well as lower inpatient day and outpatient visit limitations, must comply with the MHPA and MHPAEA.

The second set of relevant ACA provisions requires certain health plans to actually provide mental health and substance use disorder benefits. That is, the ACA now requires individual and small group health plans,[41] exchange-offered qualified health plans,[42] state basic health plans,[43] and Medicaid benchmark plans[44] to offer

---

37. *See* Patient Protection and Affordable Care Act, Pub. L. No. 111-148, 124 Stat. 119 (2010) (codified as amended in scattered sections of 26 and 42 U.S.C.) [hereinafter ACA].

38. *Id.* § 5000 A, 124 Stat. at 244 (adding the following to the Internal Revenue Code: "An applicable individual shall for each month beginning after 2013 ensure that the individual, and any dependent of the individual who is an applicable individual, is covered under minimum essential coverage for such month").

39. Texas v. United States, No. 4:18-CV-00167-O, 2018 WL 6589412, *26 (Dec. 14, 2018) ("In sum, the Individual Mandate 'is so interwoven with [the ACA's] regulations that they cannot be separated. None of them can stand.'") (internal citations omitted); (declaring the ACA's individual mandate unconstitutional and further declaring the remaining provisions of the ACA "inseverable" and therefore "invalid").

40. ACA, *supra* note 37, §1311(j) ("[MHPAEA] shall apply to qualified health plans in the same manner and to the same extent as such section applies to health insurance issuers and group health plans"); *see also id.* § 1562(c)(4) (identifying the conforming and technical changes that will be made to former 42 U.S.C. 300gg-5, now codified at 42 U.S.C. § 300gg-26); *see also* Ctr. for Consumer Info. & Ins. Oversight, *Essential Health Benefits Bulletin* 12 (2011) ("The Affordable Care Act also specifically extends MHPAEA to the individual market.").

41. *See* ACA, *supra* note 37, § 1201(2)(A) (noting amendments to the Public Health Service Act § 2707[a]) (codified at 42 U.S.C. § 300gg-6[a]).

42. *Id.* § 1301(a)(1)(B) (adding new 42 U.S.C. § 18021[a][1][B]).

43. Individuals eligible for state basic health plan coverage include individuals who are not eligible for Medicaid and whose household income falls between 133 percent and 200 percent of the federal poverty line for the family involved as well as low-income legal resident immigrants. § 1331(e).

44. *Id.* § 2001(c)(3) (adding new 42 U.S.C. § 1396u-7[b][5]–[6]).

"[m]ental health and substance use disorder services, including behavioral health treatment" in addition to nine other categories of essential health benefits (EHBs).[45] Unfortunately, not every individual with health insurance will benefit from these ten required EHB categories because some health plans, including self-insured health plans and grandfathered health plans, are exempt from the requirement to provide the ten EHBs.[46] In some states, such as Nevada, only a small percentage of state residents are covered by a health plan that must comply with the ACA's EHB mandate, leaving the vast majority of residents without federally mandated mental health and substance use disorder benefits.[47]

For those health plans that must provide benefits within the ten EHB categories, the statutory EHB requirements were unclear as to whether particular benefits, such as gambling disorder benefits, were included. As a result, the federal Department of Health and Human Services (HHS) issued its first set of final regulations implementing the ACA's EHB requirements on February 25, 2013 (2013 Final Regulations).[48] The 2013 Final Regulations required states to select (or be defaulted into) a benchmark plan[49] that was sold in 2012 and that provided coverage for the ten EHB categories, including mental health and substance use disorder services,[50] and that served as a reference plan for health plans in each state. According to the 2013 Final Regulations, health plans in the state to which the EHB requirements applied were required to provide health benefits substantially equal to those provided by

---

45. *Id.* § 1302(b)(1)(A)–(J).
46. *See* Interim Final Rules for Group Health Plans and Health Insurance Coverage Relating to Status as a Grandfathered Health Plan Under the Patient Protection and Affordable Care Act, 75 Fed. Reg. 34,538, 34,562 (June 17, 2010) (to be codified at 29 C.F.R. pt. 2590) (adopting 29 C.F.R. § 2590.715-1251[a], which defines "grandfathered health plan coverage" as "coverage provided by a group health plan, or a health insurance issuer, in which an individual was enrolled on March 23, 2010"); *id.* at 34,559 (explaining that Public Health Service Act § 2707 does not apply to grandfathered health plans); *id.* at 34,567–68 (adopting 29 C.F.R. § 2590.715-1251(c)(1), which states that "the provisions of PHS Act section . . . 2707 . . . do not apply to grandfathered health plans"); *Application of the New Health Reform Provisions of Part A of Title XXVII of the PHS Act to Grandfathered Plans*, U.S. Dep't Labor 1 (2010), https://www.dol.gov/sites/dolgov/files/EBSA/laws-and-regulations/laws/affordable-care-act/for-employers-and-advisers/grandfathered-health-plans-provisions-summary-chart.pdf (explaining ACA's essential benefit package requirement is not applicable to grandfathered plans); Inst. of Med. et al., Essential Health Benefits: Balancing Coverage and Cost 19 (2012) (listing the health plan settings to which ACA's EHB requirement do not apply); Sara Rosenbaum, *The Essential Health Benefits Provisions of the Affordable Care Act: Implications for People with Disabilities*, Commonwealth Fund 3 (2011), https://www.commonwealthfund.org/publications/issue-briefs/2011/mar/essential-health-benefits-provisions-affordable-care-act ("The act exempts large-group health plans, as well as self-insured [Employee Retirement Income Security Act] plans and ERISA-governed multiemployer welfare arrangements not subject to state insurance law, from the essential benefit requirements.").
47. *See* e-mail from Glenn Shippey, Nev. Div. of Ins., to Stacey Tovino, Univ. of Nev., Las Vegas (Apr. 8, 2016, 3:33 PM PT) ("Please note that fewer than 10% of Nevadans are covered under an individual or small group policy in the state, and large employers are not required to provide coverage for essential health benefits") (on file with author) [hereinafter Shippey e-mail].
48. Patient Protection and Affordable Care Act; Standards Related to Essential Health Benefits, Actuarial Value, and Accreditation, 78 Fed. Reg. 12,834 (Feb. 25, 2013) (to be codified at 45 C.F.R. pts. 147, 155, and 156).
49. *Id.* at 12,866 (adopting 45 C.F.R. § 156.100).
50. *Id.* (adopting 45 C.F.R. § 156.110[a][5]).

the state's benchmark plan, including the benchmark plan's covered benefits and excluded benefits.[51] Thus, the question of whether a particular health insurance policy or plan was responsible for providing (between years 2014 and 2016) benefits for a particular mental disorder, such as gambling disorder, required an analysis of the applicability of the ACA's EHB provision to the policy or plan as well as the content of the state's selected benchmark plan.

The state of Nevada's first benchmark plan can be used to illustrate the application of these rules. Nevada's first benchmark plan was the Health Plan of Nevada Point of Service Group 1 C XV 500 HCR Plan (Nevada's First Benchmark Plan).[52] If Nevada's First Benchmark Plan included gambling disorder benefits, then individual, small group, and other ACA-covered health plans in Nevada were responsible for providing these benefits in years 2014, 2015, and 2016.[53] On the other hand, if Nevada's First Benchmark Plan did not include gambling disorder benefits on March 31, 2012, then benefits for this disorder were not considered EHBs in Nevada, and individuals with gambling disorder did not have coverage in years 2014, 2015, and 2016 unless their health plans voluntarily included such benefits[54] or they accessed separate state funds (only available in some states) for relevant treatments and services.[55]

Nevada's First Benchmark Plan excluded coverage for a class of mental health conditions known as the "impulse control disorders."[56] Because the then-current edition of the *DSM*—the *DSM-IV-TR*—classified "pathological gambling" as an impulse-control disorder, Nevada's First Benchmark Plan excluded coverage for treatments of gambling disorders in years 2014, 2015, and 2016. In other words, during these three years, Nevada residents and residents of other states with similar benchmark plan limitations[57] did not benefit from any mandatory gambling disorder benefits and only had them to the extent their health plans voluntarily provided gambling disorder benefits, or they were able to access state-funded gambling disorder benefits (only available in some states).

---

51. *Id.* at 12,867 (adopting 45 C.F.R. § 156.115[a]).
52. Health Plan of Nevada Point of Service Group 1 C XV 500 HCR Plan (eff. 2014–2016).
53. *See* Shippey e-mail, *supra* note 47 (explaining the application of the EHB requirements in the state of Nevada).
54. *See* Amanda Cassidy, *Essential Health Benefits. States Have Determined the Minimum Set of Benefits to be Included in Individual and Small-Group Insurance Plans. What's Next?*, 2 Health Aff. (May 2, 2013) (noting that HHS has indicated that the benchmark plan approach may be changed in 2016 and in future years based on evaluation and feedback).
55. *See, e.g.*, Bo J. Bernhard & Sarah St. John, Problem Gambling and Treatment in Nevada (Dmitri N. Shalin ed., 2012) (discussing problem gambling treatments that are partially or fully supported by the state of Nevada).
56. Shippey e-mail, *supra* note 47 (noting the Nevada Benchmark Plan's exclusion of impulse control disorders).
57. *See, e.g.*, *Iowa EHB Benchmark Plan* 4, Ctrs. for Medicare & Medicaid Servs., https://www.cms.gov/cciio/resources/data-resources/ehb.html (referencing Iowa's benchmark plan, which excludes from coverage "[c]ommunication disorders, impulse control disorders, sexual identification or gender disorders, and residential facility services").

However, due to the fifth edition of the *DSM*'s reclassification in May 2013 of gambling disorder from the Impulse Control Disorders section to the Substance-Related and Addictive Disorders section, the result has changed in some jurisdictions. In ACA regulations published on February 27, 2015 (the 2015 Final Regulations), HHS required states to select a new benchmark plan that was sold in 2014 and that would be in effect for years 2017, 2018, and 2019 (the Second Benchmark Plan).[58] The deadline for states to select that Second Benchmark Plan was June 1, 2015.[59] Nevada, for example, selected the Health Plan of Nevada Solutions Health Maintenance Organization Platinum 15/0/90% Plan.[60] This plan included coverage of "mental/behavioral health services" other than the "impulse control disorders."[61] Because the *DSM-5* no longer categorized gambling disorder as an impulse-control disorder, inpatient and outpatient treatments for gambling disorder were considered EHBs in Nevada in years 2017, 2018, and 2019.

This result was both historically significant and frustratingly limited at the same time. In terms of its significance, the ACA now required some health plans to provide gambling disorder benefits in some states, such as Nevada. After decades without medical recognition and health insurance coverage of their conditions, some individuals with gambling disorder now have health insurance benefits for medically necessary treatments and services, including counseling and cognitive behavioral therapy. This result would have been thought impossible twenty years earlier.

In terms of its limitations, the ACA's EHB requirements still did not help the tens of millions of Americans who were enrolled in grandfathered health plans, self-insured health plans, and other health plans that were not required to comply with the EHB mandate. In Nevada, less than 10 percent of residents are enrolled in a plan required to comply with the EHB mandate, leaving the vast majority of Nevadans without mandatory mental health and substance use disorder benefits, including gambling disorder benefits.[62] The ACA's EHB requirement also did not help residents of states with benchmark plans that specifically excluded gambling disorder alone (versus excluding the impulse-control disorders more generally). For example, the Second Benchmark Plan of Nebraska specifically excludes coverage of treatments and services for gambling disorders, regardless of how or where the disorder is

---

58. *See* Patient Protection and Affordable Care Act; HHS Notice of Benefit and Payment Parameters for 2016, 80 Fed. Reg. 10,750, 10,812 (Feb. 27, 2015).

59. *See, e.g.*, JoAnn Volk, *States Need to Select Essential Health Benefit Benchmark Plans for 2017 Soon!*, Geo. U. Health Pol'y Inst., Ctr. for Children & Families (May 7, 2015) (referencing the June 1, 2015, deadline for states to select an EHB benchmark for small employer and individual coverage available in 2017); Dep't Bus. & Industry, *Essential Health Benefits*, Nev. Div. of Ins., http://doi.nv.gov /Healthcare-Reform/Individuals-Families/Essential-Health-Benefits/ (identifying Nevada's benchmark plan selections).

60. Health Plan of Nevada Solutions Health Maintenance Organization Platinum 15/0/90% Plan.

61. *Id.*

62. *See* Shippey e-mail, *supra* note 47 ("Please note that fewer than 10% of Nevadans are covered under an individual or small group policy in the state, and large employers are not required to provide coverage for essential health benefits.").

classified in the *DSM* or the *ICD*.⁶³ Interestingly, one state's (North Dakota's) Second Benchmark Plan specifically includes coverage of treatments and services for gambling disorder.⁶⁴

On April 17, 2018, HHS published a third final rule on this topic (the 2018 Final Regulations) giving states the option to select a new (i.e., third) benchmark plan that would become effective in 2020. However, the 2018 Final Regulations took a slightly different approach than did the 2013 and 2015 Final Regulations.⁶⁵ In particular, the 2018 Final Regulations gave each state the flexibility to change its Second Benchmark Plan by (1) selecting another state's Second Benchmark Plan, (2) replacing one or more categories of the state's current EHBs with the same category or categories of EHBs set forth in another state's Second Benchmark Plan, or (3) selecting an entirely new benchmark plan so long as the new benchmark plan did not exceed the generosity of the most generous among a set of comparison plans, including the state's Second Benchmark Plan and any of the state's options for a Second Benchmark Plan.⁶⁶ Interestingly, only one state (Illinois) selected a new (i.e., third) benchmark plan as permitted by the 2018 Final Rule; however, Illinois's new plan continues to cover all mental illnesses so long as they are listed anywhere in the current edition of the *DSM*.⁶⁷ All of the other states kept their Second Benchmark Plans, which will now remain in effect through the end of year 2020 or until the U.S. Court of Appeals for the Fifth Circuit and/or the U.S. Supreme Court, as appropriate, affirms the opinion by the U.S. District Court for the Northern District of Texas striking down the entire ACA.⁶⁸

The extent to which a health insurance policy or plan must provide coverage for gambling-related treatments and services following President Obama's ACA and President Trump's to-date incremental health care reforms is, thus, extraordinarily complex. On the one hand, unrepealed portions of the ACA continue to require certain, but not all, health plans to offer essential health benefits, including essential mental health and substance use disorder benefits. However, the ACA deferred to the states, through their selected benchmark plans, to define the scope of the required EHBs, and state benchmark plans vary widely on the question of coverage for gambling-related treatments and services. For example, Nebraska's Second Benchmark Plan, now effective through 2020, expressly *excludes* coverage of gambling-related treatments and services. On the other hand, North Dakota's

---

63. Nebraska Benchmark Plan (2017–2019), BCBS of Nebraska—Blue Pride Plus, at 28 (excluding "[p]rograms that treat obesity or gambling addiction").
64. North Dakota Benchmark Plan (2017–2019), North Dakota Benchmark Plan (2017–2020) BCBS North Dakota—Blue Care Gold 90 500, at 29 ("Benefits include diagnostic, evaluation and treatment services provided by a Physician, Licensed Clinical Psychologist or Licensed Addiction Counselor, including for gambling addiction.").
65. Patient Protection and Affordable Care Act; HHS Notice of Benefit and Payment Parameters for 2019, 83 Fed. Reg. 16,930 (Apr. 17, 2018) (to be codified at 45 C.F.R. pt. 147, 153–58).
66. *Id.* at 17,068 (creating new 45 C.F.R. § 156.111[a]).
67. Illinois Access to Care and Treatment Plan at 8 (defining mental illness).
68. *See* Texas v. United States, No. 4:18-CV-00167-O, 2018 WL 6589412, *26 (Dec. 14, 2018).

Second Benchmark Plan, also effective through 2020, expressly *requires* coverage of gambling-related treatments and services.

In summary, business lawyers who counsel their clients and colleagues regarding health insurance coverage of gambling-related treatments and services should first consult the health insurance policy or plan at issue. If the policy or plan covers gambling-related treatments and services but the insurer continues to refuse to pay for such services, then a traditional action for breach of insurance contract may be appropriate. If the policy or plan is required to comply with the EHBs but does not cover gambling-related treatments and services, and the U.S. Court of Appeals for the Fifth Circuit and/or the U.S. Supreme Court reverses the opinion of the U.S. District Court for the Northern District of Texas, then the business lawyer should check the state's current benchmark plan to see whether the state benchmark plan requires coverage of gambling-related treatments and services. If the benchmark plan requires coverage, the business lawyer should consider complaining to (1) the sponsor of the health plan or the issuer of the health insurance policy that the plan or policy does not comply with federal law, with the hope of achieving voluntary compliance, or (2) federal government or state division of insurance with the goal of enforcement. Finally, if the health plan or health insurance policy is not required to comply with the EHBs and also does not cover gambling-related treatments and services, or the U.S. Court of Appeals for the Fifth Circuit and/or the U.S. Supreme Court affirms the opinion of the U.S. District Court for the Northern District of Texas striking down the entire ACA, the business lawyer (and the lawyer's client or colleague) may be out of luck.

The above discussion focuses on the minimum benefits that must be offered by health plans and health insurance policies that are required to comply with the EHB requirements set forth in the ACA. Of course, many health plans and health insurance policies voluntarily provide benefits above the federal minimum without regard to statutory or regulatory requirements. For example, the current Tufts Health Plan Coverage Guidelines for Outpatient Psychotherapy (Coverage Guidelines) allows for coverage of psychotherapy when "clinical data provide clear evidence of signs and symptoms consistent with a mental health or substance use disorder as defined in the most recent DSM."[69] These Coverage Guidelines further state, "Medically Necessary Outpatient psychotherapy services are covered for the diagnosis and treatment of mental health and substance abuse disorders specified in the most recent Diagnostic and Statistical Manual (DSM)."[70] Gambling disorder would be covered under these Coverage Guidelines because gambling disorder is included in the most recent edition of the *DSM*.[71] Indeed, a condition called "pathological gambling" has been included in the *DSM* since its third edition, published in 1980.[72]

---

69. TUFTS HEALTH PLAN, COVERAGE GUIDELINES: OUTPATIENT PSYCHOTHERAPY 1 (2016).
70. *Id.*
71. DSM-5, *supra* note 2, at 585.
72. AM. PSYCH. ASS'N, DIAGNOSTIC AND STATISTICAL MANUAL OF MENTAL DISORDERS 291 (3d ed. 1980) [hereinafter *DSM-III*].

II. PROTECTION UNDER DISABILITY NONDISCRIMINATION LAWS

Although health insurance coverage of treatments and services for gambling disorder has improved in part due to the development of federal mental health parity law and the ACA-required EHBs, the status of individuals with gambling disorder has not improved under federal and state disability nondiscrimination laws. A business lawyer who has a client with problem gambling or gambling disorder may be tasked with determining whether the client is eligible for protection or relief under disability nondiscrimination laws. Likewise, a business lawyer who has an employee with problem gambling or gambling disorder may wonder whether the lawyer can terminate the employee for illegal gambling-related behavior (e.g., misappropriation of law firm trust accounts to support the colleague's gambling) or behavior prohibited by law firm or other company policy (e.g., a prohibition against using law firm hardware or software for gambling activity during work hours). As discussed in more detail below, individuals with problem gambling and gambling disorder generally are not entitled to protection under disability nondiscrimination laws because these conditions do not fall within statutorily protected definitions of disability.

As background, a range of antidiscrimination protections and accommodations are available to qualified individuals who have physical and mental disabilities under a variety of federal and state laws. Signed into law by President Richard Nixon on September 26, 1973, Section 504 of the Rehabilitation Act prohibits employers and organizations that receive federal financial assistance from discriminating on the basis of disability against qualified individuals with disabilities.[73] The original Americans with Disabilities Act (ADA), signed into law by President George H. W. Bush on July 26, 1990, prohibits certain employers, state and local government agencies, and places of public accommodation from discriminating on the basis of disability against qualified individuals with disabilities.[74] The ADA Amendments Act of 2008 (ADAAA), signed into law by President George W. Bush on September 25, 2008, clarifies that the ADA's definition of disability should be broadly construed in favor of individuals with physical and mental impairments who seek protection and generally shall not require extensive analysis.[75] State laws such as the California Fair Housing and Employment Act also provide individuals with protection from harassment and discrimination in the contexts of housing and employment because of physical or mental disability.[76] A major theme underlying these federal and state

---

73. Rehabilitation Act of 1973, § 504, Pub. L. No. 93-112, 87 Stat. 394 (Sept. 26, 1973), *codified at* 29 U.S.C. § 701 et seq. ("No otherwise qualified handicapped individual in the United States . . . solely by reason of his handicap, be excluded from the participation in be denied the benefits of, or be subjected to discrimination under any program or activity receiving Federal financial assistance.").

74. Americans with Disabilities Act of 1990, Pub. L. No. 101-336 (July 26, 1990), *codified at* 42 U.S.C. §§ 12101–12150 [hereinafter ADA].

75. The ADA Amendments Act of 2008, Pub. L. No. 110-325 (Sept. 25, 2008), *codified at* 42 U.S.C. 12101 [hereinafter ADAAA].

76. Cal. Gov't Code § 12940 (2007).

statutes is that it is wrong to discriminate against individuals because of their physical and mental disabilities and that it is right to accommodate them to help them participate more fully in society.[77]

To determine whether an individual with problem gambling or gambling disorder is entitled to protection under one or more of these statutes, each statute's definition of disability must be examined. For example, the original ADA defined a disability as, "[W]ith respect to an individual—(A) a physical or mental impairment that substantially limits one or more of the major life activities of such individual; (B) a record of such an impairment; or (C) being regarded as having such an impairment."[78] The regulations implementing the original ADA defined "physical or mental impairment" to include, in relevant part, "any physiological disorder, or condition . . . affecting . . . the . . . neurological [system]" or "[a]ny mental or psychological disorder, such as mental retardation, organic brain syndrome, emotional or mental illness, and specific learning disabilities."[79] However, the ADA specifically excluded compulsive gambling from the definition of disability.[80] Case law interpreting the original ADA confirms that individuals with gambling disorder are not protected.[81]

The reason for the ADA's exclusion of compulsive gambling from the definition of disability is unclear, although the exclusion may have its origins in *Rezza v. United States Department of Justice.*[82] In *Rezza,* a special agent of the FBI named Anthony Rezza was employed as an FBI agent beginning in 1964.[83] On July 11, 1985, Mr. Rezza drove an FBI vehicle to Atlantic City, where he gambled with and lost $2,000 in government funds received by him as part of an undercover assignment.[84] On July 12, 1985, Mr. Rezza entered a twenty-two-day treatment program and then returned to active duty on September 3, 1985.[85] Thereafter, Mr. Rezza performed his job duties satisfactorily while attending twice-weekly Gamblers Anonymous meetings and

---

77. *See, e.g.,* Timothy P. Ward, *Needing a Fix: Congress Should Amend the Americans with Disabilities Act of 1990 to Remove a Record of Addiction as a Protected Disability,* 36 RUTGERS L.J. 683, 719 (2005) ("Implicit in Congress's legitimate goal of protecting the disabled from discrimination is the idea that discrimination against disabled persons is unfair because it is wrong to treat a person differently based on circumstances or conditions over which he has no control.").
78. ADA, *supra* note 74, 42 U.S.C. § 12102.
79. 29 C.F.R. § 1630.2(h)(1), (2).
80. ADA, *supra* note 74, 42 U.S.C. § 12211(b)(2).
81. *See, e.g.,* Trammell v. Raytheon Missile Systems, 721 F. Supp. 2d 876, 878 (D. Ariz. 2010) (stating "Congress expressly excluded compulsive gambling, along with various sexual disorders, kleptomania, pyromania, and psychoactive substance use disorders resulting from current drug use, from the ADA's definition of disability"; and rejecting the plaintiff's theory that compulsive gambling is synonymous with depression "given the ADA's expression exclusion of compulsive gambling as a disability"); Labit v. Akzo-Nobel Salt, Inc., No. 99-30047, 2000 WL 284015, at *2 & n. 13 (5th Cir. 2000) ("Congress specifically excluded compulsive gambling as a disability under the Act.").
82. *See* Rezza v. U.S. Dept. of Justice, No. 87-6732, 1988 WL 48541, *2–*3 (E.D. Pa. 1988) [hereinafter Rezza I] (unpublished decision), *reconsideration denied,* Rezza v. U.S. Dep't of Justice, 698 F. Supp. 586 (1988) [hereinafter Rezza II].
83. Rezza I, at *1.
84. *Id.*
85. *Id.*

remaining abstinent from gambling.[86] The FBI terminated Mr. Rezza's employment on August 15, 1986.[87]

Following his termination, Rezza sued the FBI, the Department of Justice, and other defendants, arguing that he was a compulsive gambler and that his termination resulted from an incident caused by his compulsive gambling in violation of Section 504 of the Rehabilitation Act of 1973 (Section 504).[88] Rezza then filed a motion for summary judgment, contending that under Section 504, compulsive gambling is a protected disability.[89] The Eastern District of Pennsylvania relied on the APA's inclusion of "pathological gambling" in the then-current edition of the *DSM* (the *DSM-III-R*) to state that Rezza's compulsive gambling "may" come within the abstract definition of "psychological impairment" necessary for a "mental impairment."[90] However, the court ultimately denied Rezza's motion for summary judgment due to the existence of a material fact issue as to whether Rezza was "otherwise qualified" to be an FBI agent.[91]

Rezza's complaint, filed in 1986 and adjudicated and ultimately settled in 1988—prior to the 1990 enactment of the ADA—may be the source of the ADA's exclusion of "compulsive gambling" from the ADA's definition of disability. Indeed, at least one ADA historian has stated that the conditions that are excluded from the definition of disability, including the impulse-control disorder exclusions, were "reportedly derived from court cases regarding similar legislation."[92]

The ADA's complete exclusion of compulsive gambling from the definition of disability also may be due to its original classification as an impulse control disorder. As discussed in Part I, the APA initially classified pathological gambling as an impulse-control disorder (alongside kleptomania,[93] pyromania,[94] and intermittent explosive disorder[95]) in the *DSM-III*, published in 1980. As late as 2000, in the *DSM-IV-TR*, the APA continued to classify pathological gambling as an impulse-control disorder (still alongside kleptomania, pyromania, intermittent explosive disorder, and trichotillomania[96]). Not until May 2013, in the *DSM-5*, did the APA rename the

---

86. *Id.*
87. *Id.*
88. Rezza II, at 587.
89. *Id.*
90. Rezza I, at *3.
91. *Id.* at *3, *6.
92. RUTH COLKER, THE DISABILITY PENDULUM, THE FIRST DECADE WITH THE AMERICANS WITH DISABILITIES ACT 41 (2005).
93. Kleptomania, according to the *DSM-III*, is the recurrent failure to resist impulses to steal objects not for immediate use or their monetary value. *DSM-III*, *supra* note 72, at 293.
94. Pyromania, according to the *DSM-III*, is the recurrent failure to resist impulses to set fires and intense fascination with setting fires and seeing them burn. *Id.* at 294.
95. Intermittent explosive disorder, according to the *DSM-III*, is characterized by several discrete episodes of loss of control of aggressive impulses that result in serious assault or destruction of property. *Id.* at 295.
96. Trichotillomania, according to the *DSM-5*, is the recurrent pulling out of one's hair for pleasure, gratification, or relief of tension that results in noticeable hair loss. *DSM-5*, *supra* note 2, at 663.

condition gambling disorder and reclassify it as a non-substance-related disorder.[97] Gambling disorder certainly may have suffered in its treatment by Congress due to the disorder's linkage to the other impulse-control disorders. Stated another way, stealing, fire setting, and hair pulling may not have sounded as much like a disability as other traditional neurological and psychiatric conditions.

By 2008, Congress had grown weary of the limitations placed by courts on the classes of individuals eligible to receive protections under the ADA, including individuals with mental health conditions.[98] On September 25, 2008, President George W. Bush signed the ADAAA into law.[99] The ADAAA continued to use a three-prong definition of disability, including, with respect to an individual, (1) a physical or mental impairment that substantially limits one or more major life activities of the individual, (2) a record of such an impairment, or (3) being regarded as having such an impairment.[100] The ADAAA clarified, however, that the definition of disability "shall be construed in favor of broad coverage of individuals . . . to the maximum extent permitted by the terms of [the ADAAA]."[101] Indeed, the ADAAA expanded the list of activities that constituted major life activities by adding "concentrating" and "thinking"[102] as well as the "operation of a major bodily function," which was defined in relevant part to include "neurological [and] brain . . . functions,"[103] and implementing regulations followed suit.[104]

That said, Congress continued to exclude certain conditions from the definition of disability, including compulsive gambling, kleptomania, and pyromania.[105] Many state laws also continue to exclude individuals with gambling disorder from protected status. For example, the California Fair Employment and Housing Act,[106] which was designed to protect and safeguard the right and opportunity of all persons to seek, obtain, and hold employment without discrimination or abridgment on account of physical disability, mental disability, and other indicators,[107] continues to exclude compulsive gambling from the definition of both mental disability[108] and physical disability.[109]

---

97. *Id.*
98. ADAAA, *supra* note 75, § 2 (a)-(b).
99. *Id.* § 1.
100. *Id.* § 3.
101. *Id.*
102. The regulations implementing the original ADA only included "caring for oneself, performing manual tasks, walking, seeing, hearing, speaking, breathing, learning, and working" within the list of "major life activities." *See* 29 C.F.R. § 1630.2(i) (2007).
103. ADAAA, *supra* note 75, § 3.
104. Regulations to Implement the Equal Employment Provisions of the Americans With Disabilities Act, as Amended; Final Rule, 75 Fed. Reg. 16978 (Mar. 25, 2011).
105. *See* 42 U.S.C. § 12211(b)(2).
106. Cal. Gov't Code § 12900 (2017).
107. *Id.* § 12920.
108. *Id.* § 12926(j) ("'Mental disability' does not include sexual behavior disorders, compulsive gambling, kleptomania, pyromania, or psychoactive substance use disorders resulting from the current unlawful use of controlled substances or other drugs.").
109. *Id.* § 12926(m)(6) ("'Physical disability' does not include sexual behavior disorders, compulsive gambling, kleptomania, pyromania, or psychoactive substance use disorders resulting from the current unlawful use of controlled substances or other drugs.").

In summary, the status of individuals with problem gambling and gambling disorder has not improved under federal and state disability nondiscrimination laws. In particular, individuals with problem gambling and gambling disorder do not fall within current and statutorily protected definitions of disability. Because individuals with problem gambling and gambling disorder may have other physical or mental disabilities that are protected, however, business lawyers should carefully analyze the protected status of each physical and mental health condition claimed by the client or employee.

III. PROFESSIONAL DISCIPLINE

In addition to situations involving health insurance and disability nondiscrimination, business lawyers also may find themselves involved in professional discipline cases. That is, a business lawyer may have a client with problem gambling or gambling disorder who has a license to practice a profession, such as architecture, law, or medicine, and the client's licensing board may have revoked the client's license following unprofessional or illegal gambling-related behavior. The business lawyer may be asked to represent the client in the client's petition for license reinstatement. Although a review of all gambling-related discipline cases across all professions is beyond the scope of this chapter, this part does provide several examples of professional discipline cases involving attorneys who lost their licenses to practice law following their misappropriation of client trust funds to support their gambling. As discussed in more detail below, a business lawyer may be able to assist a rehabilitated attorney in regaining the lost license, although the former attorney will be required to complete several different steps and procedures.

As background, the law of professional responsibility requires an attorney to deposit any funds received or held for the benefit of a client, including advances for costs and expenses, in one or more identifiable bank accounts designated as a client trust account.[110] An attorney has a fiduciary duty to safeguard a client's trust funds.[111] An attorney generally may not commingle the attorney's own funds with a client's trust funds.[112] In addition, an attorney may not withdraw funds from a client trust account unless the attorney is withdrawing earned legal fees, incurred legal expenses, or is delivering funds owed or due to the client.[113] Upon receiving funds or other property in which a client has an interest, such as a settlement check, the attorney must promptly notify the client of the funds received and deliver the funds to the client.[114] An attorney is required to maintain detailed records regarding each

---

110. *See, e.g.*, La. Rules Prof'l Conduct R. 1.15 (2015); Nev. Rules Prof'l Conduct R. 1.15(a) (2015).
111. *See, e.g., In re* Deschane, 527 P.2d 683, 684 (Wash. 1974) ("[A] lawyer, as a fiduciary, owes the highest duty to his clients as a matter of law."); *id.* at 683 (referencing the defendant attorney's "high duties and responsibilities in dealing with trust funds").
112. *See, e.g.*, La. Rules Prof'l Conduct R. 1.15(a) (2017).
113. *See, e.g., id.* R. 1.15(c).
114. *See, e.g., id.* R. 1.15(d).

client trust account, including records of account withdrawals and other payments, for a period of time, including up to seven years in some states, after termination of the representation.[115] Upon request, an attorney must promptly provide the client a full accounting of his or her trust funds.[116]

An attorney who fails to safeguard client trust funds in accordance with the law of professional responsibility may be sanctioned. Depending on the jurisdiction, sanctions may include admonition, censure, restitution, diversion, probation, interim suspension, suspension for a fixed period of time, disbarment, or a combination of these.[117] Regional and state disciplinary boards and, on appeal, state supreme courts consider a range of factors when recommending and ordering sanctions, including, but not limited to, whether the attorney has violated a duty owed to a client, the public, the legal system, or the profession; whether the attorney acted intentionally, knowingly, or negligently; the amount of the actual or potential injury caused by the attorney's misconduct; and the existence of any aggravating or mitigating factors.[118] To illustrate the application of state disciplinary procedures to attorneys who have misappropriated client trust funds to finance their gambling, this part will discuss four cases: *In re Michael Reilly*, *In re Danny Winder*, *In re Samuel Bellicini*, and *In re Douglas Crawford*. This part will also show how licensure reinstatement is possible in some cases.

---

115. *See, e.g.*, Ill. Rules Prof'l Conduct R. 1.15(a) (requiring Illinois attorneys to maintain client trust found account records for seven years).

116. *See, e.g.*, La. Rules Prof'l Conduct R. 1.15(a) (2017).

117. *See, e.g.*, La. Sup. Ct. R. XIX § 10(A) (2015) (stating that attorney misconduct in Louisiana may result in one or more of the following sanctions: permanent disbarment; suspension for a fixed period of time not in excess of three years; probation not in excess of two years; public reprimand; private admonition; restitution to persons financially injured by the attorney's actions or omissions; limitation on the nature or extent of the attorney's future practice; and diversion); Nev. Sup. Ct. R. 102 (2015) (stating that attorney misconduct in Nevada may result in one or more of the following sanctions: permanent, irrevocable disbarment; suspension for a fixed period of time; temporary restraining order regarding funds; temporary suspension precluding the attorney from accepting new cases but allowing the attorney to continue to represent existing clients for fifteen days; public or private reprimand, with or without conditions; and a letter cautioning the attorney against specific conduct).

118. *See, e.g.*, La. Sup. Ct. R. XIX, § 10(C) (2015). Depending on the jurisdiction, aggravating factors may include prior disciplinary offenses, dishonest or selfish motive, a pattern of misconduct versus one instance of misconduct, multiple offenses, bad faith obstruction of the disciplinary proceeding, submission of false evidence or statements during the disciplinary proceeding, refusal to acknowledge the wrongful nature of conduct, vulnerability of the victim, substantial experience in the practice of law, indifference to making restitution, and illegal conduct, including illegal conduct involving the use of controlled substances. *See, e.g.*, Nev. Sup. Ct. R. 102.5(1)(a)–(k) (2015). Depending on the jurisdiction, mitigating factors may include absence of a prior disciplinary record, absence of a dishonest or selfish motive, personal or emotional problems, timely good faith effort to make restitution or to rectify consequences of misconduct, full and free disclosure to disciplinary authority or cooperative attitude toward proceeding, inexperience in the practice of law, character or reputation, physical disability, mental disability or chemical dependency ("including alcoholism or drug abuse when: (1) there is medical evidence that the respondent is affected by chemical dependency or a mental disability; (2) the chemical dependency or mental disability caused the misconduct; (3) the respondent's recovery from the chemical dependency or mental disability is demonstrated by a meaningful and sustained period of successful rehabilitation; and (4) the recovery arrested the misconduct and recurrence of that misconduct is unlikely"), delay in disciplinary proceedings, interim rehabilitation, imposition of other penalties or sanctions, remorse, and remoteness of prior offenses. *Id.* § 102.5(2)(a)–(n).

A. *In re Michael Reilly*

First licensed to practice law in Nebraska in 1982, Michael Reilly was a well-respected attorney who later gained admission to the Iowa Bar and subsequently misappropriated over $96,000 of an Iowa resident's personal injury settlement funds to feed his gambling disorder.[119] Following an investigation, the Grievance Commission of the Iowa Supreme Court found that Reilly had violated the Iowa Rules of Professional Conduct, including rules prohibiting attorneys from withdrawing client trust funds for personal use and prohibiting attorneys from engaging in conduct that is illegal, involves dishonesty, and adversely reflects on attorney's fitness to practice law.[120] The commission recommended that the Iowa Supreme Court suspend Reilly's license to practice law for a period of three years.[121]

In its January 13, 2006, opinion reviewing the commission's recommendations, the Iowa Supreme Court respectfully considered the commission's recommendation but ultimately imposed a greater sanction: license revocation.[122] The court reasoned that it considered trust fund misappropriation to be a "particularly reprehensible" ethical violation that "almost universally" called for license revocation.[123] The court also reasoned that it had ordered license revocation in prior cases involving relatively smaller (e.g., $1,500) misappropriations as well as in prior cases in which attorneys had returned the misappropriated funds to their clients' trust accounts before the clients discovered the wrongful takings.[124] According to the court, the only prior trust fund misappropriation cases that had not resulted in license revocation were those in which the attorney had a colorable claim to the client funds at issue, such as in earned fee disputes, as well as cases in which the attorney had not taken the funds for his or her own use.[125] In its conclusion, the Iowa Supreme Court stated that Reilly's "fall from grace was precipitated by an uncontrollable gambling habit that left him constantly in need of funds."[126] The court further stated that although Reilly's gambling habit was "regrettable and cause for sympathy," the habit did not "obviate the seriousness of the improper attorney conduct that ha[d] occurred."[127]

Reilly filed applications for reinstatement in January 2009 and again in November 2015.[128] In response to the second application for reinstatement, the Iowa Supreme Court Attorney Disciplinary Board urged the Supreme Court to deny it, arguing that revocation is "indisputably the appropriate sanction for conduct involving the

---

119. *See* Iowa Sup. Court Attorney Disciplinary Bd. v. Reilly, 708 N.W.2d 82, 83 (Iowa 2006); Nebraska v. Reilly, 712 N.W.2d 278, 278 (Neb. 2006).
120. Reilly (Iowa), 708 N.W.2d at 82–84.
121. *Id.* at 82.
122. *Id.* at 82, 84, 85.
123. *Id.* at 84.
124. *Id.*
125. *Id.*
126. *Id.* at 85.
127. *Id.*
128. Iowa Sup. Court Attorney Disciplinary Bd. v. Reilly, No. 05-1365, at 3–4 (Sept. 2, 2016), https://law.justia.com/cases/iowa/supreme-court/2016/051365.html (referencing the applications for reinstatement).

conversion of client funds to which an attorney has no colorable future claim."[129] Although the board acknowledged that Reilly had a gambling addiction, it felt that the addiction was irrelevant "because no illness, regardless of its severity, can excuse an attorney's dishonest conduct."[130] The board specifically argued that Reilly's trust fund misappropriation was "fundamentally dishonest and worthy of a permanent sanction, not a temporary one."[131]

On September 2, 2016—more than ten years following his license revocation—the Iowa Supreme Court issued an unexpected opinion provisionally granting Reilly's application for reinstatement.[132] Before Reilly could be formally reinstated, he was required to complete thirty hours of continuing legal education and to take and pass the Multistate Professional Responsibility Examination.[133] In the opinion, the Iowa Supreme Court stated that Reilly's gambling addiction "[did] not obviate the seriousness of his improper conduct" but felt that the evidence Reilly submitted together with his second application for reinstatement demonstrated his sincere acceptance of responsibility for his wrongful actions, his successful treatment, and his sustained commitment to recovery.[134]

B. *In re Danny Winder*

First licensed to practice law in 1984, Nevada attorney Danny Winder ran a successful general law practice in northern Nevada throughout the mid to late 1980s.[135] In April 1990, less than six years into his practice, Winder misappropriated a client's $9,000 personal injury settlement check to feed his gambling disorder and substance-related disorders.[136] On July 11, 1990, Winder tendered a conditional plea of guilty to the disciplinary matters then pending against him.[137]

On December 23, 1990, the Supreme Court of Nevada issued an order indefinitely suspending Winder's license to practice law and precluding him from applying for reinstatement for a period of at least two and a half years.[138] In its order, the court stated that any reinstatement would be subject to Winder's compliance with numerous conditions precedent to reinstatement set forth in his conditional guilty plea.[139] These conditions included, but were not limited to, (1) paying restitution, including interest, to his injured client; (2) refraining from gambling, alcohol, and drugs for at

---

129. *Id.* at 7.
130. *Id.*
131. *Id.* at 10.
132. *Id.* at 20.
133. *Id.* at 19–20.
134. *Id.* at 18–19.
135. *Find an Attorney, Danny Winder*, STATE BAR OF NEV., https://www.nvbar.org/find-a-lawyer/?usearch=winder+danny(stating that Danny Winder was admitted to the State Bar of Nevada on October 1, 1984).
136. Conditional Guilty Plea in Exchange for a Stated Form of Discipline at 1–2, State Bar v. Winder, No. 90-50-139 (St. Bar. Nev., N. Nev. Disc. Bd., July 11, 1990) [hereinafter Winder Conditional Guilty Plea].
137. *Id.*
138. Order of Suspension at 1, State Bar v. Winder, No. 20984 (Nev. Sup. Ct. Dec. 23, 1990).
139. *Id.*

least two and a half years; (3) submitting to random urinalysis or blood testing for alcohol and drugs; (4) attending at least three Gamblers Anonymous (GA) meetings per week for the first three months of his suspension, attending at least two GA meetings per week for the second six months of his suspension, and providing proof of attendance to Bar Counsel; (5) attending at least three Alcoholics Anonymous (AA), Lawyers Concerned for Lawyers (LCL), or similar organizational meetings per week for the first three months of his suspension; attending at least two AA, LCL, or similar organizational meetings per week for the second six months of his suspension; and providing proof of attendance to Bar Counsel; and (6) attending counseling or other therapy sessions for gambling addiction with a licensed psychologist or psychiatrist approved by Bar Counsel for a period of two and a half years.[140] In 1998, Winder petitioned for reinstatement.[141] After a hearing on the issue, a panel of the Northern Nevada Disciplinary Board recommended that Winder's petition be denied without prejudice because he had not satisfied certain conditions in his guilty plea, including paying full restitution, abstaining from drugs for a period of two and a half years, and completing two and a half years' worth of gambling counseling.[142] Following the denial of his petition for reinstatement, Winder relocated to southern Nevada.[143]

In 2001, Winder again petitioned for reinstatement.[144] This time, a panel of the Southern Nevada Disciplinary Board found that Winder had satisfied all of the conditions precedent to reinstatement set forth in his 1990 guilty plea and recommended reinstatement subject to a one-year probationary period with several conditions:[145] Winder was to (1) continue to attend LCL and Narcotics Anonymous (NA) meetings during the probationary period and provide proof of attendance to Bar Counsel; (2) complete all continuing legal education requirements and attend a Bridge the Gap program offered by the State Bar of Nevada; (3) submit his general operating and trust account records to Bar Counsel for inspection upon request at any time during the probationary period; and (4) submit to random alcohol and drug testing upon Bar Counsel request at any time.[146]

On May 9, 2002, eleven and a half years following his initial license suspension, the Supreme Court of Nevada reinstated Winder's license to practice law.[147] Today, Winder has a busy solo practice in Las Vegas and is a member in good standing of the State Bar of Nevada.

---

140. *See* Winter Conditional Guilty Plea, *supra* note 136, at 2–4 (listing the conditions precedent to reinstatement).
141. Order of Reinstatement at 1, *In re* Reinstatement of Danny Winder, No. 38723 (Nev. Sup. Ct. May 9, 2002).
142. *Id.* at 1–2, nn.1–3.
143. *Id.* at 2.
144. *Id.*
145. *Id.*
146. *Id.* at 2–3.
147. *Id.* at 1, nn.2, 3.

C. *In re Samuel Bellicini*

On May 7, 1991, Samuel Bellicini was admitted to the State Bar of California.[148] Two years later, Bellicini misappropriated approximately $3,520 in client trust funds to feed his gambling disorder and alcohol use disorders.[149] On September 28, 1993, Bellicini voluntarily surrendered his license with disciplinary charges pending.[150]

On May 15, 2001, almost eight years after surrendering his law license, Bellicini experienced his first full day of recovery from alcohol and gambling.[151] Three days later, on May 18, 2001, Bellicini enrolled in Kaiser Permanente's two-year Chemical Dependency Recovery Program (CDRP), which provided intensive education regarding the physiological and emotional bases of alcoholism, daily group therapy sessions, and weekly individual visits with a psychologist.[152] Sixty days after enrolling in CDRP, Bellicini's wife and son went on vacation, and Bellicini felt the urge to drink again. Bellicini told his therapist about his helpless feelings toward alcohol and the therapist referred him to AA, in which fellow participants assist each other with their sobriety efforts.[153] During the next year, Bellicini continued to attend CDRP and AA meetings on a regular basis.[154] By July 2003, Bellicini had paid restitution to his former clients and outstanding sanctions.[155]

On September 17, 2003, Bellicini petitioned for reinstatement and, on August 24, 2004, a hearing on Bellicini's petition commenced.[156] On December 21, 2004, the hearing judge decided that Bellicini had demonstrated by clear and convincing evidence that he was rehabilitated and that he possessed the moral qualifications necessary for reinstatement, which the judge recommended.[157]

On March 6, 2006, the Review Department of the State Bar of California issued an opinion reviewing the hearing judge's decision and recommendation.[158] The department's opinion commended Bellicini's incredible recovery efforts but reversed the decision of the hearing judge, reasoning that Bellicini's period of sustained exemplary conduct (i.e., the thirty-nine-month period beginning May 15, 2001, Bellicini's first day of recovery, and ending August 24, 2004, the first day of Bellicini's hearing)

---

148. *In re* Samuel C. Bellicini, No. 03-R-03728, 2006 WL 541224, at *1 (Rev. Dep't, St. Bar Ct. Cal. Mar. 6, 2006).
149. *See id.* at *3 ("In one matter, after petitioner retained $2,962.20 in client funds for payment to a client's doctor, petitioner failed to make that payment and instead used the funds to gamble and purchase alcohol.").
150. *Id.* at *1.
151. *See id.* at *7 ("Although petitioner resigned in 1993, he continued to drink alcohol until he enrolled in a recovery program in 2001. As discussed in greater detail, *post*, we measure petitioner's rehabilitation from this point.").
152. *Id.* at *4.
153. *Id.*
154. *Id.*
155. *Id.* at *5.
156. *Id.*
157. *Id.* at *7.
158. *Id.* at *1.

was insufficient to demonstrate his overall rehabilitation from his past misconduct.[159] The department noted the lack of any other cases granting reinstatement following only thirty-nine months of recovery.[160]

On July 27, 2007, Bellicini applied for reinstatement for the second time, and on July 14, 2008, the State Bar of California Hearing Department found that Bellicini had clearly and convincingly satisfied the requirements for reinstatement and recommended reinstatement.[161] The department reasoned that Bellicini had now been sober for seven years, had abstained from gambling for six years, and had demonstrated a sustained commitment to his sobriety through his participation and volunteer work in AA and other chemical-dependency treatment programs.[162] The State Bar of California officially reinstated Bellicini's license on October 15, 2008.[163]

D. *In re Douglas Crawford*

On September 30, 1985, Douglas Crawford was admitted to the State Bar of Nevada.[164] Over the following decade, Crawford built a lucrative family law and criminal defense practice in Las Vegas, grossing shy of $1 million per year[165] and accumulating more than $1.5 million in assets, including a lavish home, automobile, and downtown office.[166] Due in part to the stress associated with his successful practice as well as the departure of key employees who helped him run his practice, Crawford suffered a mental breakdown in 2006.[167] Part of that mental breakdown was associated with his addiction to gambling, resulting in the loss of $1.5 million of his own assets and his subsequent misappropriation of approximately $398,345 in client trust funds between late 2005 and 2007, as well as Crawford's co-occurring mental health conditions, including substance abuse and depression.[168]

On May 1, 2007, the State Bar of Nevada temporarily suspended Crawford's license to practice law pending the resolution of formal disciplinary proceedings

---

159. *Id. See also id.* at *14 ("We commend petitioner's efforts in overcoming his addictions that caused him to commit serious ethical violations early in his legal career and which plagued him for many years thereafter"; and "Having viewed the evidence in its totality, we conclude that petitioner's rehabilitative showing is insufficient at this time to establish his overall rehabilitation from his past misconduct over an extended period of time.").

160. *Id.* at *11–13.

161. *In re* Samuel C. Bellicini, No. 07-R-12922-LMA, at 5 (St. Bar. Ct. Cal., Hearing Dep't San Fran. July 14, 2008).

162. *Id.* at 15–16.

163. Attorney Search: *Samuel Christian* #152191, State Bar Of Cal., http://members.calbar.ca.gov/fal/Member/Detail/152191.

164. *Find a Lawyer, Douglas C. Crawford*, State Bar Of Nev., https://wr.perma-archives.org/public/t3l6-atg2/im_/https://www.nvbar.org/find-a-lawyer/?usearch=douglas+crawford.

165. *See* Opening Brief of Douglas C. Crawford at 14, State Bar v. Crawford, No. 51724, at 6 (Nev. July 30, 2008) [hereinafter Crawford Opening Brief].

166. *Id.* at 6.

167. *Id.* at 7.

168. *Id.* at 8.

against him.[169] In June and September 2007, the state bar filed two complaints against Crawford.[170] Shortly thereafter, Crawford entered a conditional plea of guilty, admitting to sixty-five violations of the Nevada Rules of Professional Conduct and agreeing to seek not less than a five-year suspension.[171] In exchange, the state bar retained the right to seek a suspension lasting longer than five years, including disbarment.[172] A final recommendation as to Crawford's discipline was left to a future hearing panel of the Southern Nevada Disciplinary Board.[173]

In the meantime, on October 8, 2007, Crawford experienced his first full day of recovery from gambling, alcohol, and drugs.[174] One day of recovery led to a second and soon Crawford had completed six weeks of intensive inpatient treatment for gambling disorder; hundreds of weekly therapy sessions, "aftercare" sessions, and "friends and family" sessions; and thousands of GA meetings.[175]

On March 26, 2008, a hearing was held before a panel of the Southern Nevada Disciplinary Board to determine Crawford's sanction. On April 24, 2008, the board unanimously recommended disbarment.[176] An automatic de novo appeal to the Nevada Supreme Court followed. In his opening appellate brief, Crawford argued that he should be suspended for five years, not permanently disbarred, because his trust fund misappropriations occurred as a result of his gambling disorder, a disease of the brain.[177] In its answering brief, the state bar supported the board's order of disbarment, arguing that Crawford's conduct was too egregious, even with mitigation, to allow for a lesser sanction.[178] In its brief, the state bar also referred to Crawford's gambling, substance abuse and depression as "bad habits"[179] and "personal demons."[180]

On February 18, 2009, the Nevada Supreme Court sided with Crawford, suspending him for a period of five years but not disbarring him.[181] Relying on Nevada Supreme Court Rule 102.5, which identifies several mitigating and aggravating

---

169. Order of Temporary Suspension at 2, *In re* Discipline of Douglas C. Crawford, No. 49333, at 2 (Nev. May 1, 2007).
170. Crawford Opening Brief, *supra* note 165, at 4–5.
171. Order of Suspension at 1–2, *In re* Discipline of Douglas C. Crawford, No. 51724 (Nev. Sup. Ct. Feb. 18, 2009) [hereinafter Crawford Order of Suspension].
172. *Id.* at 2.
173. *Id.*
174. Crawford Opening Brief, *supra* note 165, at 14; Motion to Assign Douglas C. Crawford to a Program for the Treatment of Problem Gambling Pursuant to NRS 458 A.200 through 458 A.260 at 9, in State v. Crawford, Case No. C-11-275513-1 (Dist. Ct., Clark Cty., Nev. Dec. 22, 2011).
175. Crawford Opening Brief, *supra* note 165 at 14.
176. Order of Disbarment at 2, line 28, State Bar of Nevada v. Douglas C. Crawford (S. Nev. Disc. Bd. Apr. 24, 2008) [hereinafter 2008 Panel Decision].
177. Crawford Opening Brief, *supra* note 165 at 18.
178. State Bar of Nevada's Answering Brief at 17, State Bar of Nevada v. Douglas Crawford (Nev. Sup. Ct. Sept. 8, 2008).
179. *Id.* at 24, line 3.
180. *Id.* at 19, line 6.
181. *See* Crawford Order of Suspension, *supra* note 171.

circumstances that may be considered in sanction determinations,[182] the court found that a number of mitigating circumstances existed, including personal and emotional problems, good character and reputation, restitution, remorse, and "most importantly according to Crawford, mental disabilities of depression and gambling addiction."[183] The court also identified, however, several aggravating circumstances, including prior attorney discipline matters, selfish motive for the misconduct, multiple offenses, and substantial experience as an attorney.[184] The court concluded that Crawford's mitigating circumstances outweighed his aggravating circumstances and that the appropriate sanction was a five-year suspension rather than permanent disbarment.[185] Bar counsel also agreed that the five-year suspension should be retroactive to May 1, 2007, the date the state bar first (temporarily) suspended Crawford's license.[186]

In its order of suspension, the court imposed numerous conditions on any future application by Crawford for reinstatement.[187] According to the court, Crawford would be required to (1) take and pass the Nevada State Bar Examination and the Multistate Professional Responsibility Examination again; (2) maintain his "gambling recovery efforts . . . including attending his weekly gamblers anonymous and 12-step program meetings along with continued weekly meetings with his psychiatrist"; (3) not engage in the unlicensed practice of law or handle client trust funds during his five-year suspension; (4) agree to mentorship and refrain from handling client trust funds for a period of time after reinstatement, if reinstated; (5) pay restitution to his former clients for the trust funds he misappropriated; and (6) pay restitution to the Nevada Clients' Security Fund for the amounts the fund paid to Crawford's former clients.[188]

On March 22, 2012, Crawford petitioned for reinstatement.[189] A hearing panel of the Southern Nevada Disciplinary Board subsequently recommended reinstatement subject to seven conditions. These conditions required Crawford to: (1) refrain from abusing alcohol and drugs and from gambling for as long as he wishes to practice law in Nevada; (2) submit to mentoring by attorney Robert Dickerson or an alternate mentor and cooperate with such mentoring for three years; (3) submit semiannual reports to the State Bar of Nevada until full restitution has been made, including an oath stating that he has abstained from all substance abuse and gambling; (4) refrain from the solo practice of law, work in affiliation with and under the

---

182. *See* Nev. Sup. Ct. R. 102.5(1), (2) (2015) (listing dozens of aggravating and mitigating circumstances that may be relevant to an attorney sanction determination).
183. Crawford Order of Suspension, *supra* note 171 at 3 (citing Nev. Sup. Ct. R. 102.5[1]).
184. Crawford Order of Suspension, *supra* note 171 at 3 (citing Nev. Sup. Ct. R. 102.5[2]).
185. Crawford Order of Suspension, *supra* note 171 at 3–4.
186. Petition for Extraordinary Relief and Motion for Modification of Order of Suspension and for Conditional Reinstatement to the Practice of Law at 2, *In re* Discipline of Douglas C. Crawford (Nev. Sup. Ct. Mar. 22, 2012) [hereinafter Crawford Petition for Reinstatement]; Crawford Opening Brief, *supra* note 165 at 5.
187. Crawford Order of Suspension, *supra* note 171 at 4.
188. *Id.*
189. Crawford Petition for Reinstatement, *supra* note 186 at 2.

supervision of an established law office, and refrain from signing any trust or operating accounts for two years following reinstatement; (5) allow a mentor to review his trust accounts, operating accounts, and adherence to salary restrictions on a regular basis thereafter, if he wishes to open a solo practice; (6) adhere to an annual salary cap of $25,000 until full restitution is made and pay income received above the cap towards restitution; and (7) pay the costs of the reinstatement proceeding within one year of reinstatement.[190]

On June 18, 2015, over eight years after the State Bar of Nevada first suspended Crawford's license, the Nevada Supreme Court issued an order reinstating Crawford to the rolls of the Nevada Bar.[191] In its order of reinstatement, the court agreed with the latest recommendations and conditions of the board but added two additional conditions: (1) he must continue his gambling recovery efforts, including regularly attending GA, alumni, and aftercare meetings, and (2) report his attendance to the State Bar of Nevada in semiannual reports.[192] In a social media post made on September 28, 2018, Crawford announced that he had made full and final payment of restitution to his former clients and the State Bar of Nevada Client Security Fund.[193] Crawford celebrated the eleventh anniversary of his recovery one and a half weeks later.[194]

E. Trends in Attorney Disciplinary Proceedings

The detailed description of the four cases set forth above was intentional and designed to reveal several trends in attorney license reinstatement cases. First, it is possible for an attorney who has lost a license due to gambling-related behavior to regain that license; however, the attorney (with the assistance of the attorney's business lawyer) will likely have to clear many hurdles including, and depending on the state, (1) pursuing and achieving recovery from gambling as well as other potentially associated behaviors or substances, including alcohol and drugs; (2) continuing gambling and other substance and behavioral addition recovery efforts; (3) retaking and passing the state's bar examination; (4) retaking and passing the Multistate Professional Responsibility Examination; (5) completing additional hours of continuing legal education; (6) working under the supervision of another attorney in good standing for a period of time; (7) not having access to client trust fund accounts for a period of time; (8) making full (or partial and ongoing) restitution to injured clients or the state bar's client recovery fund; and (9) submitting regular reports to the state's bar regarding all of the foregoing. A business lawyer who represents an attorney who is petitioning

---

190. *See* Order of Reinstatement at 4, *In re* Reinstatement of Douglas C. Crawford, No. 65284, at 2-3 (Nev. June 18, 2015) (summarizing the board's recommendations).
191. *See id.* at 4.
192. *Id.* at 3–4.
193. Facebook post by Douglas Crawford (Sept. 28, 2018).
194. *Id.* (Oct. 8, 2018).

for license reinstatement should counsel the attorney regarding the clearance of these hurdles and, in court documents, should consider analogizing the attorney's progress to the successful licensure reinstatement cases of Michael Reilly (Iowa), Danny Winder (Nevada), Samuel Bellicini (California), and Douglas Crawford (Nevada).

Second, a review of state court rules governing attorney reinstatement reveals that many such rules provide specific, helpful guidelines for suspended attorneys with alcohol use disorder and drug use disorder but not suspended attorneys with gambling disorder or other mental health conditions. Louisiana Supreme Court Rules, for example, allow attorneys with alcohol or drug use disorder to be considered for reinstatement so long as they have "pursued appropriate rehabilitative treatment," "abstained from the use of alcohol or other drugs for at least one year," and are "likely to continue to abstain from alcohol or other drugs."[195] Likewise, North Dakota Supreme Court Rules provide that, "where alcohol or drug abuse was a causative factor in the lawyer's misconduct, the petitioner must show that the petitioner has been successfully rehabilitated or is pursuing appropriate rehabilitative treatment."[196] South Carolina Supreme Court Rules also provide that where alcohol or drug abuse is a causative factor in the attorney's misconduct, the attorney may be reinstated if the attorney "has pursued appropriate rehabilitative treatment"; "has abstained from the use of alcohol or other drugs for at least [one] year or the period of suspension, whichever is shorter"; and "is likely to continue to abstain from alcohol or other drugs."[197] Research did not reveal one state court rule that provided similar, specific guidance for individuals with problem gambling, gambling disorder, or any other behavioral problems or addictions, thus raising the question why individuals in recovery from addictions other than alcohol and drugs are not treated like individuals in recovery from alcohol and drugs. Business lawyers who counsel and represent attorneys with problem gambling or gambling disorder thus have less specific support in state rules of professional conduct for the clients' restatement; that said, the cases of Michael Reilly, Danny Winder, Samuel Bellicini, and Douglas Crawford reveal that licensure reinstatement efforts involving individuals with gambling struggles can be successful.

IV. CONCLUSION

This chapter has carefully outlined several common legal issues faced by individuals with problem gambling and gambling disorder. These legal issues relate to health insurance coverage of gambling-related treatments and services, the availability of disability nondiscrimination protections, and professional discipline due to gambling-related behavior. Business lawyers who represent individuals with

---

195. La. Sup. Ct. R. XIX § 24(E)(3) (2015).
196. N.D. Sup. Ct. R. 4.5(F)(4) (2015).
197. S.C. Sup. Ct. R. 33(f)(3)(A)–(C) (2015).

problem gambling and gambling disorder should be familiar with these legal issues. In some cases, and depending on the particular facts and circumstances of each case, individuals who struggle with gambling may be eligible for health insurance coverage of gambling-related treatments and services and license reinstatement. However, currently, individuals with problem gambling or gambling disorder (standing alone) are not protected under federal and state disability nondiscrimination laws, although disability nondiscrimination laws should be monitored for changes on this point.

PART III

Other Forms of Gambling

Chapter 8

Tribal Gaming

Kathryn R. L. Rand and Steven Andrew Light

I. INTRODUCTION

The U.S. casino gaming industry is comprised of two major markets: the commercial sector and the American Indian tribal sector.[1] In 2017, some 460 commercial casinos—347 land-based casinos, 63 riverboat casinos, and 50 racinos—were authorized in twenty-four states. In 2017, the commercial casino industry earned $40.3 billion in gross gaming revenue, the highest amount in history, and a year-over-year increase of 3.4 percent.[2] At the same time, 242 tribes owned and operated 494 tribal casinos in twenty-eight states. In 2017, the Indian gaming industry also marked record revenue, earning $32.4 billion, a 3.9 percent increase from the prior year.[3]

While tribal gaming as a whole is the largest segment of the U.S. casino industry,[4] national figures alone obscure the wide range of profitability by state and tribe. Location, customer base, competition and market saturation, number and types of games offered, and destination amenities all contribute to profit. On one end of what we have labeled the "spectrum of success,"[5] tribal gaming in just two states— California and Oklahoma—accounts for more than 40 percent of total tribal gaming

---

1. The first major market, casinos operated by commercial operators, includes land-based casinos such as those in Las Vegas or Atlantic City, riverboat casinos such as those in Illinois and Mississippi, and racinos, or race tracks that offer both pari-mutuel betting on horse or dog racing along with casino games. The second major market, casinos operated by American Indian tribal governments, includes both Class II and Class III gaming facilities regulated pursuant to the federal Indian Gaming Regulatory Act (IGRA), 25 U.S.C. §§ 2701-21, discussed below.

2. *2018 State of the States Report*, Am. Gaming Ass'n, 14 (2018), https://www.americangaming.org/sites/default/files/AGA%202018%20State%20of%20the%20States%20Report_FINAL.pdf.

3. *See 2017 Indian Gaming Revenues Increase 3.9% to $32.4 Billion*, NIGC (June 26, 2018), https://www.nigc.gov/news/detail/2017-indian-gaming-revenues-increase-3.9-to-32.4-billion.

4. In 2016, tribal gaming accounted for about 45 percent of the casino industry's revenue, while commercial casinos accounted for approximately 43 percent, with the remainder of revenue generated by racinos. Alan Meister, Casino City's Indian Gaming Industry Report 13 (2018).

5. *See* Steven Andrew Light & Kathryn R.L. Rand, Indian Gaming and Tribal Sovereignty: The Casino Compromise 9-11 (2005).

revenue nationwide; the top ten states (California, Oklahoma, Florida, Washington, Arizona, Connecticut, Minnesota, Michigan, Wisconsin, and New York, by rank) account for 84 percent of national revenue. The remaining 16 percent is spread across eighteen states and many tribes.[6] Profitability also varies by facility; relatively few tribal casinos are true destination casino-resorts akin to the casino properties on the Las Vegas strip. More typically, tribal casinos are smaller, have limited amenities, and are located in rural areas. As shown in Table 8.1, just under 7 percent of tribal casinos earned $250 million or more in 2017, and these accounted for over 45 percent of total tribal gaming revenue. On the other end of the spectrum, nearly 40 percent of tribal casinos earned $10 million or less, accounting for just over 2 percent of national revenue. Unlike the commercial sector, tribal casino profits flow directly to tribal governments.

Table 8.1. Range of Revenue for Tribal Gaming Facilities 2017[7]

Revenue Range	Number of Facilities	Revenue	Percent of Facilities	Percent of Revenue
Over $250M	33	$15.017B	6.7	46.3
$100M–$250M	56	$9.059B	11.3	28
$50M–$100M	54	$3.767B	10.9	11.6
$25M–$50M	68	$2.383B	13.8	7.4
$10M–$25M	91	$1.495B	18.4	4.6
$3M–$10M	89	$0.575B	18	1.8
Under $3M	103	$0.109B	20.9	0.3
Total	494	$32.404B	100	100

The laws and regulations—as well as the regulatory authorities—governing each sector are distinct. As explained in other chapters of this book, commercial casinos generally are subject to state law and regulation with applicability of some federal laws. Casinos and other gaming operations owned and operated by American Indian tribal governments generally are subject to tribal and federal law and regulation with applicability of some state laws, particularly through tribal–state gaming compacts. As casino gaming continues to spread in the United States, with both commercial and tribal operators seeking new markets, business lawyers must understand important distinctions between the two sectors of the U.S. casino industry.

Among the areas of gaming law, the navigation of issues arising with Indian gaming can be especially challenging and complex. The articulation of particular public policy goals underlying tribal gaming has resulted in a highly particularized set of legal and regulatory requirements. As will be discussed, the concept

---

6. MEISTER, *supra* note 4, at 13 (analyzing proprietary data from calendar year 2016).

7. *FY13–FY17 Gaming Revenues by Range*, NIGC (2017), https://www.nigc.gov/images/uploads/reports/Chart2017GamingRevenuesbyRange.pdf.

of tribal sovereignty injects complexity, and often an element of uncertainty, into many transactions. Accordingly, in addition to familiarity with gaming law, the business lawyer has to be alert to the subtleties of federal Indian law as well as tribal law.

In this chapter, we set forth a short overview of tribal gaming law and regulations, highlighting key areas of distinction between Indian gaming and commercial gaming. We then outline several recent cases and issues specific to tribal gaming and particularly relevant to business lawyers in the areas of Indian lands, tribal–state compacts, management contracts, labor and employment, and tribal sovereign immunity.

II. OVERVIEW OF TRIBAL GAMING REGULATION

The law and policy governing commercial and tribal casinos differ in important ways. First, and most significantly, tribal casinos are rooted in tribes' authority within, and outside, the U.S. constitutional and governmental system. Tribal governments may conduct gambling on reservations not because a state or Congress has authorized them to do so but because Indian gaming is an aspect of tribal sovereignty.[8] Second, as Indian gaming is conducted by tribal governments, it is distinct from both commercial and charitable gaming and is more (but not wholly) akin to state lotteries. Third, as Indian gaming is a tool to achieve the stated public policy goal of promoting tribal economic development, self-sufficiency, and strong tribal governments, regulation of tribal casinos is designed to serve this goal. Regulation of Indian gaming reflects both distinct legal foundations and a markedly different intent as compared to the regulation of commercial gaming.

A. The Indian Gaming Regulatory Act and Gaming Classifications

While state law governs commercial casinos, tribal casinos are governed primarily by federal and tribal law under the federal Indian Gaming Regulatory Act of 1988 (IGRA).[9] Importantly, IGRA created an independent, federal regulatory agency within the Department of the Interior, the National Indian Gaming Commission (NIGC).[10] As defined by IGRA, Indian gaming is gaming conducted by an Indian tribe on Indian lands in states whose public policy allows for such gaming.[11] Through IGRA, Congress intended to balance tribal sovereignty, self-determination, and economic

---

8. California v. Cabazon Band of Mission Indians, 480 U.S. 202 (1987).
9. 25 U.S.C. §§ 2701–2721 (2018). For an in-depth account of relevant law and policy governing tribal gaming, see Kathryn R.L. Rand & Steven Andrew Light, Indian Gaming Law & Policy (2d ed. 2014).
10. 25 U.S.C. §§ 2704–2708 (2018). NIGC regulations are found in 25 C.F.R. pts. 500–599.
11. 25 U.S.C. §§ 2703(5), 2703(4) (2018).

development on reservations with state interests in controlling the crime assumed to be associated with high-stakes casino gambling.[12] Thus, the congressional purposes served by IGRA were to codify tribes' right to conduct gaming on Indian lands as a means of promoting tribal economic development, self-sufficiency, and strong tribal governments, while providing sufficient regulation to ensure legality and to protect the financial interests of the tribes.[13] IGRA's statements of public policy and statutory purpose, along with its comprehensive (and, to date, unrevised) statutory regulatory framework, distinguish it from the often unsystematic and frequently-in-flux approach reflected in many states' gaming laws.

The hallmark of IGRA's regulatory framework is its categorization of three classes of gaming, as summarized in Table 8.2. Class I gaming includes social and traditional games for minimal prizes associated with Native American ceremonies. Class I gaming is subject to exclusive tribal jurisdiction on tribal lands; IGRA's provisions do not apply to Class I gaming.[14]

Class II gaming includes bingo and its variants, as well as non-house-banked card games, such as poker, that meet certain state provisions. Class II gaming specifically excludes house-banked card games, slot machines, and other electronic facsimiles of games of chance.[15] The tribe must adopt a tribal gaming ordinance governing its Class II gaming.[16] Class II gaming is legal only in states that "permit such gaming," meaning a state must have authorized bingo or another Class II game "for any purpose by any person."[17] Tribes may regulate Class II gaming with oversight by the NIGC. Other than the initial question of state public policy, there is no role for state regulation of Class II gaming.

Class III gaming is a residual category, including all other types of gaming not included in Class I or Class II.[18] The catch-all nature of Class III gaming heightens the stakes of defining Class II gaming, as any game that does not qualify as Class II will fall within Class III. Class III games, typically high-stakes, include slot machines, house-banked card games, pari-mutuel betting, sports betting, roulette, craps, and other casino games. As with Class II, Class III gaming is legal only in states that "permit such gaming," and it requires the same kind of tribal ordinance, as well as a valid tribal–state compact.[19] Unlike Class I or Class II, Class III gaming creates a regulatory role for the states through the tribal–state compact requirement, the centerpiece of Class III regulation.

---

12. *See* RAND & LIGHT, *supra* note 9.
13. 25 U.S.C. § 2702 (2018).
14. *Id.* §§ 2702(6), 2710(a)(1).
15. *Id.* § 2702(7).
16. A tribe's gaming ordinance must be approved by the NIGC, the federal regulatory agency authorized by IGRA. IGRA's requirements for the tribal ordinance are broad. *See id.* at § 2710(b)(2); *see also Model Tribal Gaming Ordinance*, NIGC (Jan. 2018), https://www.nigc.gov/images/uploads/bulletins/Bulletin_2018-1_Revised_Model_Ordinance.pdf.
17. 25 U.S.C. §§ 2710(b)(1)(A).
18. *Id.* § 2702(8).
19. *Id.* § 2710(d)(1)(B).

Table 8.2. Summary of IGRA's Gaming Classes and Regulatory Framework

Gaming Class	Type of Games	Regulatory Authority	General Requirements	Statutory Provisions
Class I	Social and traditional games associated with tribal ceremonies	Exclusive tribal authority; IGRA does not apply	None	25 U.S.C. §§ 2702(6); 2710(a)(1)
Class II	Bingo and similar games, as well as non-house-banked card games that meet certain state provisions; specifically excludes house-banked card games, slot machines, and other electronic facsimiles of games of chance	Primary tribal authority, subject to IGRA's provisions and NIGC oversight	– Indian tribe – Indian lands – State permits such gaming – Approved tribal ordinance – Compliance with tribal and NIGC regulations	25 U.S.C. §§ 2702(7); 2710(a)(2); 2710(b) & (c)
Class III	All forms of gaming that are not Class I or II	Tribal and state authority per required tribal–state compact	– Indian tribe – Indian lands – State permits such gaming – Approved tribal ordinance – Approved and valid tribal–state compact – Compliance with tribal regulations and compact	25 U.S.C. §§ 2702(8); 2710(d)

B. The Tribal–State Compact Requirement

For Class III gaming, Congress intended the compact requirement to encourage states and tribes to negotiate, on a government-to-government basis, issues related to the regulation of casino-style gaming on tribes' reservations. Without a compact, a tribe cannot legally conduct Class III gaming; the compact also allows the state to negotiate regulatory and other conditions and limits on casino-style gaming.[20] As an enforcement mechanism initially intended to overcome state resistance to tribal gaming, IGRA's compact requirement imposes a duty on states to negotiate in good

---

20. *Id.* § 2710(d)(3).

faith with tribes toward reaching a Class III compact.[21] IGRA requires that compacts be reviewed and approved (or disapproved) by the U.S. Secretary of the Interior.[22]

Initially, in order to trigger the state's duty to negotiate in good faith, the tribe must formally request that the state enter into compact negotiations. If 180 days pass without a response from the state or without successful negotiation of a compact, then a cause of action accrues, and the tribe may file suit against the state in federal district court. IGRA sets forth highly detailed procedures governing a tribe's cause of action against the state for its failure to negotiate in good faith.[23]

In *Seminole Tribe v. Florida*, the U.S. Supreme Court invalidated the tribe's cause of action against the state for failure to negotiate in good faith.[24] In 1991, the Seminole Tribe filed a suit against Florida and its governor under IGRA, alleging that the state had refused to negotiate a tribal–state compact that allowed the tribe to offer Class III games on its reservation. Florida moved to dismiss the tribe's action, asserting its state sovereign immunity under the Eleventh Amendment. The Supreme Court ruled that Congress's constitutional power with regard to tribes did not extend to abrogation of state sovereign immunity. State sovereignty, said the Court, "is not so ephemeral as to dissipate when the subject of a suit is an area, like the regulation of Indian commerce, that is under the exclusive control of the Federal Government."[25] Accordingly, the *Seminole Tribe* decision held that a state could not be sued in federal court by a tribe under IGRA without the state's consent, effectively invalidating Congress's statutory compromise among state, tribal, and federal interests over Indian gaming.[26]

The Supreme Court's decision in *Seminole Tribe* left open the question of what should happen when a state fails to negotiate with a tribe, in good faith, toward reaching a tribal–state compact. While the state could waive its sovereign immunity and consent to be sued in federal court under IGRA's cause of action (as California has done), the more likely occurrence is that the state would invoke its Eleventh Amendment immunity under *Seminole Tribe*, and the suit would be dismissed,

---

21. *Id.* As enforcement mechanisms for the compact requirement, IGRA authorizes three federal causes of action. First, a tribe may sue a state in federal court for failing to negotiate a tribal–state compact in good faith. Second, the U.S. Secretary of the Interior may sue to enforce the gaming procedures promulgated through a tribe's suit against the state. Third, either a tribe or a state may sue to stop a Class III gaming activity that violates the governing tribal–state compact. *Id.* § 2710(d)(7)(A).

22. *Id.* § 2710(d)(8).

23. *Id.* § 2710(d)(7)(B). For a comprehensive overview, see Rand & Light, *supra* note 9, at 60–65.

24. 517 U.S. 44 (1996).

25. *Id.* at 72. The Court also held that because IGRA's cause of action against the state is narrower that the general remedy allowed under the *Ex parte Young* doctrine, that exception does not apply to suits under IGRA. *Id.* at 73–76.

26. IGRA contains a severability clause. 25 U.S.C. § 2721 (2018) ("In the event that any section or provision of this chapter, or amendment, made by this chapter, is held invalid, it is the intent of Congress that the remaining sections or provisions or this chapter, and amendments made by this chapter, shall continue in full force and effect."). Most courts and commentators agree that the severability clause protects IGRA's remaining provisions, such that *Seminole Tribe* invalidates only the tribe's cause of action against the state rather than the entire act or the entire section addressing Class III gaming. As the Eleventh Circuit Court of Appeals noted, "IGRA contains an explicit severability clause and we find no 'strong evidence' to ignore that plain congressional directive." Seminole Tribe v. Florida, 11 F.3d 1016, 1029 (11th Cir. 1994), *aff'd*, 517 U.S. 44 (1996).

leaving the tribe without a remedy for the state's alleged breach of the good-faith duty. The resulting legal uncertainty prompted the Secretary of the Interior to promulgate regulations, the "Part 291" or "secretarial procedures" that took effect in 1999, to issue "administrative gaming procedures" for Class III gaming. If the tribe's cause of action accrues under IGRA but is dismissed based on the state's assertion of sovereign immunity, then the regulations are triggered and the Secretary of the Interior can issue gaming procedures that allow the tribe to conduct Class III gaming in the absence of a tribal–state compact.[27]

Two federal circuit courts have held that the administrative procedures are invalid. In the Fifth Circuit, the case arose from the Kickapoo Traditional Tribe of Texas's unsuccessful efforts to negotiate a Class III gaming compact with the state. Following the dismissal of the tribe's lawsuit on state sovereign immunity grounds, the tribe filed an application for administrative gaming procedures under Part 291. The state filed suit in federal court challenging the secretarial procedures. The district court dismissed the state's challenge on ripeness grounds but opined that it appeared the procedures were an appropriate exercise of the Secretary's authority under IGRA, as well as 25 U.S.C. §§ 2 and 9.[28]

The Fifth Circuit reversed. After determining that the issue was ripe for review, the court first reasoned that Congress, through IGRA, intended to "permit[] limited secretarial intervention only as a last resort, and only after the statute's judicial remedial procedures have been exhausted." The court stated that "the Secretarial Procedures stand in direct violation of IGRA . . . insofar as they may authorize Class III gaming without a compact."[29] As the court concluded, IGRA "does not guarantee an Indian tribe the right to conduct Class III gaming" but only "grants tribes the right to negotiate the terms of a tribal-state compact."[30]

In 2017, the Tenth Circuit reached the same conclusion in similar circumstances. In New Mexico, the Pueblo of Pojoaque and the state reached a stalemate when the tribe refused to agree to increased revenue payments to the state. After the tribe's lawsuit against New Mexico was dismissed on state sovereign immunity grounds, the tribe sought administrative procedures to conduct Class III gaming. New Mexico responded with its own lawsuit challenging the secretarial procedures. The court concluded that the "specific and detailed" statutory process for resolving a state's failure to negotiate in good faith left no ambiguity that might permit the Secretary

---

27. 25 C.F.R. pt. 291. The regulations essentially follow the mediated negotiation process set forth in IGRA, with the important exception that the administrative process is triggered by the dismissal of the tribe's lawsuit on state sovereign immunity grounds, whereas the statutory process is triggered by the court's finding that the state failed to negotiate in good faith. *See* 25 U.S.C. § 2710(d)(7)(B)(iii) (2018).

28. Texas v. U.S., 362 F. Supp. 2d 765, 770–71 (W.D. Tex. 2004).

29. Texas v. U.S., 497 F.3d 491, 503–07 (5th Cir. 2007). Nor did 25 U.S.C. §§ 2 and 9 provide sufficient support for the regulations, as those statutes delegated authority to the Secretary only to promulgate "regulations that . . . are consistent with other relevant federal legislation." Because the court saw the Part 291 regulations as inconsistent with IGRA, sections 2 and 9 could not provide authority. *Id.* at 507–09.

30. *Id.* at 509–11. The dissenting opinion noted that the state's "stonewalling" by refusing to negotiate effectively blocked the application of IGRA as Congress intended. *Id.* at 511 (Dennis, J., dissenting).

of the Interior to issue "gaming procedures outside of" the "narrow circumstances" delineated in IGRA—that is, a court's finding that the state failed to negotiate in good faith and the state's subsequent failure to consent to a compact.[31]

Spanning nine states and dozens of tribes, the decisions in the Tenth Circuit and the Fifth Circuit have widespread impact. As noted above, few states have opted to waive sovereign immunity.

III. INDIAN LANDS

IGRA authorizes Class II and Class III gaming only on Indian lands. Indian lands are defined as reservation lands, as well as trust and restricted lands over which a tribe exercises governmental authority.[32] The NIGC's Office of General Counsel makes initial determinations whether land qualifies as Indian lands.[33] For most tribes with reservations, the question of whether a location qualifies as Indian lands is straightforward. Two less-than-straightforward situations, one concerning newly acknowledged (or recognized) tribes and the other newly (or after) acquired lands, are worth discussion here.

A. Newly Acknowledged Tribes

Through the 1934 Indian Reorganization Act (IRA),[34] Congress authorized the Secretary of the Interior to take land into trust for the benefit of federally acknowledged tribes. The U.S. Supreme Court's 2009 decision in *Carcieri v. Salazar*, however, significantly limited the Secretary of the Interior's ability to take land into trust for tribes recognized after 1934. The case concerned the Narragansett Tribe, which achieved federal acknowledgment in 1983. When the Secretary approved the tribe's application to take into trust a parcel of land owned by the tribe in Charleston, Rhode Island, the state sued. Both a federal district court and the First Circuit found in favor of the tribe, but the Supreme Court reversed.[35]

---

31. New Mexico v. U.S. Dep't of Interior, 854 F.3d 1207, 1224 (10th Cir. 2017). The court was not persuaded that its outcome left tribes without a remedy, as the state could choose to waive its sovereign immunity or the federal government could sue the state as a tribal trustee to "sidestep[ ] the sovereign immunity defense." *Id.* at 1235.

32. 25 U.S.C. § 2703(4) (2018). Until the introduction of the term *Indian lands* in IGRA, most federal laws used the term *Indian country*, with a similar definition. *See* 18 U.S.C. § 1151 (2018) (defining Indian country). Because Congress chose to use a different term with a different definition in IGRA, it is plain that *Indian lands* and *Indian country* are not necessarily the same; that is, lands that qualify as Indian country may not qualify as Indian lands under IGRA. For analyses of whether non-reservation lands qualify as Indian lands, *see, e.g.,* Kansas v. U.S., 249 F.3d 1213 (10th Cir. 2001); Rhode Island v. Narragansett Indian Tribe, 19 F.3d 685 (1st Cir. 1994); Cheyenne River Sioux Tribe v. South Dakota, 830 F. Supp. 523 (D.S.D. 1993).

33. The NIGC makes its land determinations available through its website. *See Indian Land Opinions*, NIGC, https://www.nigc.gov/general-counsel/indian-lands-opinions.

34. Wheeler-Howard (Indian Reorganization) Act, Pub. L. No. 73-383, 48 Stat. 984 (1934) (codified as amended at 25 U.S.C. §§ 461–479 [2006]).

35. Carcieri v. Kempthorne, 497 F.3d 15 (1st Cir. 2007), *rev'd sub nom.*, Carcieri v. Salazar, 555 U.S. 379 (2009).

The Court's analysis largely turned on its reading of the 1934 statutory language authorizing the Secretary to take land into trust for the benefit of a "recognized Indian Tribe now under Federal jurisdiction."[36] In the decades since the IRA's passage, the Department of the Interior has held land in trust for tribes federally acknowledged after 1934, whether by Congress or administratively.[37] Lower federal courts had held that the meaning of *now* in the IRA was ambiguous enough to warrant deferring to the Secretary's interpretation of that word.[38]

The Supreme Court in *Carcieri*, however, found the meaning of *now* to be clearly understood by its dictionary definition: "the present time; at this moment; at the time of speaking." The Court therefore concluded that "the term 'now under Federal jurisdiction' . . . unambiguously refers to those tribes that were under the federal jurisdiction of the United States when the IRA was enacted in 1934."[39]

Accordingly, in order for the Secretary to acquire land under the IRA for a tribe, the tribe must have been "under federal jurisdiction" in 1934. The majority opinion, however, was limited to the first definition of Indian in the IRA and did not further elaborate on the meaning of "under federal jurisdiction," a phrase pre-dating the modern tribal acknowledgment process.[40]

In 2014, the Interior Department's Office of the Solicitor released a guidance memorandum addressing these issues. After extensive analysis, the memorandum concluded that the meaning of "under federal jurisdiction" is ambiguous, thus requiring agency interpretation. The memorandum set forth a two-part inquiry to determine whether a tribe was under federal jurisdiction in 1934. The first question looks for evidence that the tribe was under federal jurisdiction by or before 1934:

> [W]hether the United States had, in 1934 or at some point in the tribe's history prior to 1934, taken an action or series of actions—through a course of dealings or other relevant acts for or on behalf of the tribe or in some instance tribal members—that are sufficient to establish, or that generally reflect federal obligations, duties, responsibility for or authority over the tribe by the Federal Government.[41]

---

36. Section 5 of the IRA authorizes the Secretary of the Interior to acquire interests in land for the purpose of providing land for Indians, defined in Section 19 as "persons of Indian descent who are members of any recognized Indian tribe now under Federal jurisdiction." Wheeler-Howard (Indian Reorganization) Act, *supra* note 34. The *Carcieri* Court did not address taking land into trust for groups that fall under other definitions of Indian in Section 19 of the IRA. *See* Carcieri v. Salazar, 555 U.S. 379 (2009).
37. *See* 25 C.F.R. pt. 83.
38. *See* Chevron U.S.A. Inc. v. Natural Resources Defense Council, Inc., 467 U.S. 837, 843 (1984).
39. *Carcieri*, 555 U.S. at 395.
40. *See* 25 C.F.R. pt. 83. Pursuant to the Federally Recognized Indian Tribe List Act of 1994 (Pub. L. 103-454; 108 Stat. 4791, 4792), the Bureau of Indian Affairs annually publishes a list of federally acknowledged tribes in the Federal Register. No such comprehensive list exists for tribes under federal jurisdiction in 1934, raising the question of what evidence would demonstrate that a tribe was under federal jurisdiction at that time.
41. Office of the Solicitor, *The Meaning of "Under Federal Jurisdiction" for Purposes of the Indian Reorganization Act*, U.S. Dep't of the Interior (Mar. 12, 2014), https://www.doi.gov/sites/doi.opengov.ibmcloud.com/files/uploads/M-37029.pdf.

Examples include treaty negotiations, administration of reservations, enforcement of federal laws relating to tribes, or the provision of educational, social, or health services to a tribe. "Once having identified that the tribe was under federal jurisdiction prior to 1934, the second question is to ascertain whether the tribe's jurisdictional status remained intact in 1934." Both questions are tribe-specific, factual inquiries.[42]

Two cases subsequent to *Carcieri* offer elaboration on some of the issues raised by the Court's decision. In *Match-E-Be-Nash-She-Wish Band of Pottawatomi Indians v. Patchak*, the Supreme Court held that a citizen had standing to challenge the Secretary's decision to take land into trust.[43] The case involved the Match-E-Be-Nash-She-Wish Band of Pottawatomi Indians (Gun Lake Tribe). The tribe achieved federal recognition in 1999, and the Secretary of the Interior placed in trust a tract of land for the tribe's future casino, located halfway between Grand Rapids and Kalamazoo, Michigan, and near the home of David Patchak. While the Supreme Court ruled that Patchak could proceed with his challenge under *Carcieri*, in the meantime Congress passed the Gun Lake Trust Land Reaffirmation Act, ratifying the Secretary's decision to take the land into trust. The 2014 act directed that any legal action pertaining to the tribe's trust land "shall not be filed or maintained in a Federal court and shall be promptly dismissed."[44] Patchak's suit was dismissed accordingly, and the Supreme Court affirmed.[45]

In *Big Lagoon Rancheria v. California*, the Ninth Circuit, sitting en banc, held that the state could not collaterally launch an untimely *Carcieri* challenge to avoid its duty to negotiate in good faith, effectively reversing an earlier decision in the case.[46] The Big Lagoon Rancheria has been federally recognized since at least 1979.[47] In the late 1990s, the tribe negotiated with California regarding a casino on a tract of land placed into trust by the Secretary of the Interior in 1994. Negotiations broke down by 1999, and the tribe sued, alleging bad faith on the state's part. In that litigation, California questioned whether "the lands on which Big Lagoon proposed to build its casino were Indian lands over which Big Lagoon properly had jurisdiction to conduct gaming activities," but the lawsuit eventually was dismissed without prejudice after the tribe and the state reached a compact. The state legislature failed to ratify the compact, however, and subsequent negotiations between the tribe and the state once again reached a stalemate. The tribe sued California a second time in 2009, resulting in the district court's finding that the state had failed to negotiate in

---

42. *Id.*; *see also* Stand Up for California! v. U.S. Dep't of the Interior, 879 F.3d 1177 (D.C. Cir. 2018) (upholding the Secretary of the Interior's decision to take land into trust for the North Fork Rancheria of Mono Indians).
43. 567 U.S. 209 (2012) (hereinafter *Patchak I*). The Court held that the suit was authorized under the Administrative Procedures Act and was not barred by the "Indian lands exception" of the Quiet Title Act, *see* 28 U.S.C. § 2409a(a).
44. Pub. L. 113–179, 128 Stat. 1913 (2014).
45. Patchak v. Zinke, 138 S. Ct. 897 (2018) (hereinafter *Patchak II*).
46. 741 F.3d 1032 (9th Cir. 2014), *rev'd en banc and as amended on denial of further rehearing en banc*, 789 F.3d 947 (9th Cir. 2015).
47. *See Big Lagoon Rancheria*, 789 F.3d at 750–51 (summarizing the tribe's history).

good faith. On appeal, the state argued that because the Secretary lacked authority to take the land into trust under *Carcieri*, the state had no duty to negotiate in good faith, as the land in question was not "Indian lands" under IGRA.[48]

Initially, the three-judge panel of the Ninth Circuit concluded:

> [A] predicate to the right to request negotiations under the IGRA is jurisdiction over the Indian lands upon which a tribe proposes to conduct class III gaming. . . . *Carcieri* holds that the [Interior Secretary's] authority to take lands in trust for a tribe extends only to tribes under federal jurisdiction in 1934. [We conclude] that Big Lagoon is not such a tribe [and thus] cannot demand negotiations to conduct gaming on the [land], and cannot sue to compel negotiations if the State fails to negotiate in good faith.[49]

Sitting en banc, the Ninth Circuit reversed. As the Ninth Circuit acknowledged, *Carcieri* "involved a timely administrative challenge" while California's challenge "is a belated collateral attack."[50] Allowing such an untimely challenge "would constitute just the sort of end-run that we have previously refused to allow, and would cast a cloud of doubt over countless acres of land that have been taken into trust for tribes recognized by the federal government." California also challenged Big Lagoon Rancheria's status as a federally recognized tribe. This, too, was time-barred for the same reasons. The Ninth Circuit warned, however, that "[w]hile the State's claims fail in this case, such considerations might not be irrelevant in a [good-faith duty] case involving a timely . . . claim."[51]

B. Newly Acquired Lands

IGRA includes a general prohibition against tribal gaming on trust lands acquired after the statute's date of enactment: "Except as provided in subsection (b) of this section, gaming regulated by this chapter shall not be conducted on lands acquired by the Secretary in trust for the benefit of an Indian tribe after October 17, 1988."[52] Such lands are commonly referred to as "newly acquired" or "after acquired" lands. There are, however, several general, state-specific, and tribe-specific exceptions. These exceptions and the related issue of the location of tribal casinos are among the most controversial issues in the field of Indian gaming.

First, a tribe may conduct gaming on newly acquired lands that are located within the tribe's existing reservation or that are contiguous to the reservation's boundaries.[53] Second, for tribes without reservations as of October 17, 1988, gaming

---

48. *See* Guidiville Band of Pomo Indians v. NGV Gaming, Ltd., 531 F.3d 767, 778 (9th Cir. 2008) (stating that IGRA requires a tribe "show that it has 'Indian lands' as defined by IGRA at the time of filing [suit for failure to negotiate in good faith]"); Match-E-Be-Nash-She-Wish Band of Pottawatomi Indians v. Engler, 304 F.3d 616, 618 (6th Cir. 2002) ("[I]t is clear that the State does not have an obligation to negotiate with an Indian tribe until the tribe has Indian lands.").
49. 741 F.3d at 1045.
50. 789 F.3d at 953.
51. *Id.* at 955.
52. 25 U.S.C. § 2719 (2018).
53. *Id.* § 2719(a)(1).

is not prohibited on newly acquired lands if the lands are within the tribe's last recognized reservation and within the state in which the tribe currently resides.[54] A special exception applies to tribes without reservations that have acquired trust lands in Oklahoma. Gaming is allowed on newly acquired lands in Oklahoma if the lands are within the tribe's former reservation or if the lands are contiguous to the tribe's current trust or restricted lands.[55] This first set of exceptions sometimes is referred to as the "reservation exemptions," as the general prohibition against gaming on newly acquired lands does not apply.

Third, an exception is made when gaming on newly acquired lands is "in the best interest of the tribe and its members, and would not be detrimental to the surrounding community."[56] Called the "best interest" exception or the "two-part determination," this provision requires the Secretary of the Interior to consult with the tribe, the state, local officials, and officials of nearby tribes and then determine that gaming on the newly acquired lands would be in the best interest of the tribe and its members and would not be detrimental to the surrounding community. Importantly, the state's governor must concur with the Secretary's determination—essentially providing state veto power over tribal gaming under this exception.[57] Fourth, gaming is allowed on newly acquired lands when the lands are placed in trust as a settlement of a land claim, as the initial reservation of a federally recognized tribe, or as the restoration of lands for a tribe whose federal recognition is restored.[58]

Though the term *off-reservation gaming* is often used to refer to gaming under any of these exceptions, the Interior Department generally uses the term *off-reservation* to refer to land that is neither within or contiguous to existing reservation boundaries. Further, the best-interest exception is the only exception that does not require some historical tie or legal claim to the land in question.[59]

In addition to meeting the requirements of IGRA, the tribe also must satisfy the requirements of the land-into-trust process.[60] While some acquisitions by the Secretary

---

54. *Id.* § 2719(a)(2)(B).
55. *Id.* § 2719(a)(2)(A).
56. *Id.* § 2719(b)(1)(A).
57. *See* Lac Courte Oreilles Band of Lake Superior Chippewa Indians of Wisconsin v. U.S., 367 F.3d 650 (7th Cir. 2004) (addressing several challenges to the gubernatorial concurrence requirement). For useful and practical analyses of the best-interest exception, see Heidi McNeil Staudenmaier & Brian Daluiso, *Current Battles and the Future of Off-Reservation Indian Gaming*, 12 INDIAN GAMING LAWYER (Spring 2017); Heidi McNeil Staudenmaier, *Off-Reservation Native American Gaming: An Examination of the Legal and Political Hurdles*, 4 NEV. L.J. 301 (2004).
58. 25 U.S.C. § 2719(b)(1)(B) (2018). Finally, IGRA includes specific exceptions for the St. Croix Chippewa Indians in Wisconsin and the Miccosukee Tribe of Indians in Florida. *Id.* § 2719(b)(2). These tribe-specific exceptions also reference particular lands.
59. For a recent secretarial determination under the best interest exception, see *Secretarial Determination for the Shawnee (Loyal) Tribe*, BUREAU OF INDIAN AFFAIRS (Jan. 19, 2017), https://www.bia.gov/sites/bia.gov/files/assets/as-ia/oig/gaming-applications/2017.01.19%20Shawnee%20sigd%20%28cover%20letter%20with%202%20Part%29.pdf. Oklahoma governor Mary Fallin concurred in the Secretary's determination.
60. 25 C.F.R. pt. 151. At the time of this writing, the Interior Department was pursuing revisions to the fee-to-trust process (updated information available at https://www.indianaffairs.gov/as-ia/raca/regulations-development-andor-under-review/fee-trust-regulations-25-cfr-151).

are nondiscretionary, such as those mandated by a federal statute or court decision directing the Secretary to place land into trust, the Secretary generally may exercise discretion when deciding to grant or deny an application to take land into trust for a tribe. The Secretary has promulgated regulations governing both on-reservation and off-reservation land acquisitions, which require consideration of the impact on local and state governments as well as opportunity for public comment.[61]

IV. TRIBAL–STATE COMPACTS

If a tribe wants to conduct Class III gaming, it first must formally request that the state enter into compact negotiations. Once the state receives the tribe's request, "the State shall negotiate with the Indian tribe in good faith to enter into such a compact."[62] Which state official or branch of state government has authority to negotiate and enter into a compact on behalf of the state is not addressed by IGRA; it therefore is a question of state law and relevant separation-of-powers principles.[63]

The Interior Secretary has the power to approve or disapprove a tribal–state compact, whether reached through amicable negotiations between the state and the tribe or through the tribe's cause of action in federal court. The Secretary may disapprove a compact for any of three reasons: (1) the compact violates one or more of IGRA's provisions; (2) the compact violates federal law, other than the federal law allocating jurisdiction over gambling on reservation lands; or (3) the compact violates the federal government's trust obligation to the tribes.[64]

There are hundreds of gaming compacts now in effect; many are based on "model" compacts such that the compact provisions are the same or similar for all tribes within a particular state, while others are more individualized.[65] Some compacts are complex while others are relatively straightforward—compare, for example, tribal–state compacts in California to those in Minnesota. A general rule of thumb for the practitioner is that compact complexity tends to increase with tribal gaming revenue, particularly in states that also have commercial gaming,

---

61. *See* 25 C.F.R. §§ 151.10 (on-reservation acquisitions), 151.11 (off-reservation acquisitions).

62. 25 U.S.C. § 2710(d)(3)(A) (2018).

63. *See, e.g., Florida House of Representatives v. Crist*, 999 So. 2d 601 (Fla. 2008) (holding that compact terms exceeded governor's authority and thus were invalid under state law); *Panzer v. Doyle*, 680 N.W.2d 666 (Wis. 2004) (detailing state law concerning governor's authority to negotiate compacts and to agree to certain provisions); *Saratoga County Chamber of Commerce v. Pataki*, 798 N.E.2d 1047 (N.Y. 2003) (holding that compact negotiations involve policymaking and thus fall within the state legislature's authority).

64. 25 U.S.C. § 2710(d)(8) (2018). If the Secretary takes no action on a tribal–state compact within forty-five days of its submission, the compact automatically will be approved. This "pocket" approval is limited to the extent that the compact's provisions comport with IGRA. *Id.* § 2710(d)(8)(C). Notices of approved tribal–state compacts are published in the Federal Register, and a compact becomes effective upon such publication. *Id.* §§ 2710(d)(8)(D), 2710(d)(3)(B).

65. For a (mostly up-to-date) list and links to compacts, see Indian Affairs, *Indian Gaming Compacts*, U.S. Dep't of the Interior, https://www.bia.gov/as-ia/oig/gaming-compacts. Many states make gaming compacts publicly available; *see, e.g., Tribal Compacts and Amendments*, Wisc. Dep't of Admin., https://doa.wi.gov/Pages/AboutDOA/TribalCompactsAndAmendments.aspx.

tribal–state revenue sharing, or both. Another factor in compact complexity is the degree to which negotiations were politically or legally fraught.

A. Compact Provisions

Under IGRA, tribal–state compact provisions, and thus their negotiation, are categorically prescribed. Such provisions may include (1) the application of the state's and the tribe's criminal and civil laws and regulations "that are directly related to, and necessary for, the licensing and regulation" of Class III games; (2) allocation of criminal and civil jurisdiction between the state and the tribe "necessary for the enforcement of such laws and regulations"; (3) payments to the state to cover its costs of regulating the tribe's Class III games; (4) tribal taxation of Class III gaming, limited to amounts comparable to the state's taxation of similar activities; (5) remedies for breach of contract; (6) operating and facility maintenance standards, including licensing; and (7) "any other subjects that are directly related to the operation of gaming activities."[66]

A typical compact, then, might include such provisions as a list or other designation of allowed Class III games, hardware and software requirements for slot machines and other electronic gaming machines, tribal and state licensing of casino employees and vendors, application of state liquor or food safety standards, minimum age requirements for casino employees and patrons, application of state or federal standards for commercial facilities and workplace safety, tribal participation in state workers' compensation programs, and so on. Compacts generally include specific remedies and procedures for resolving disputes over the compact's terms, as well as a "sunset" or expiration clause, or other mechanism to facilitate renegotiation.

IGRA allows states to negotiate tribal reimbursement for state regulatory costs associated with Indian gaming. States also may negotiate tribal payments to offset the costs of law enforcement; noise, pollution, or traffic abatement; environmental impacts; infrastructural improvements, such as utility, sewer, or road construction; and gambling disorder education and treatment programs.

Although IGRA does not dictate that a tribal–state compact must provide for state regulation of Class III gaming, compacts typically have done so, though to widely varying extents. Some compacts provide for a robust state role in regulating tribal casinos, including assigning primary regulatory authority to a state agency, while other compacts rely primarily on tribal regulation or incorporate selected aspects of state law, such as hours for serving alcohol.[67] At the same time, a tribe's

---

66. 25 U.S.C. § 2710(d)(3)(C) (2018).
67. In 2015, the U.S. Government Accounting Office (GAO) conducted an extensive review of tribal–state gaming compacts with regard to regulatory authority. The GAO found that the "24 states with class III gaming operations vary in their approach for regulating Indian gaming. Specifically, based on the extent and frequency of state monitoring activities, GAO categorized 7 states as having an active regulatory role, 11 states with a moderate role, and 6 states with a limited role." *Indian Gaming: Regulation and Oversight by the Federal Government, States, and Tribes*, GOVERNMENT ACCOUNTING OFFICE 1 (GAO-15-355, June 2015), https://www.gao.gov/assets/680/670603.pdf.

own ordinances and regulatory commission also provide day-to-day oversight, as the tribe retains the right to concurrent regulation of its Class III gaming, so long as tribal regulation is not inconsistent with or less stringent than the state's regulation as provided in the compact.[68] Notably, the NIGC has limited authority over Class III gaming.[69]

B. Revenue Sharing

IGRA explicitly prohibits states from imposing a direct "tax, fee, charge, or other assessment" on tribes or tribal casinos as a precondition for signing a tribal-state compact.[70] In practice, however, the Secretary of the Interior, in exercising authority to approve or disapprove tribal-state compacts, has interpreted IGRA as allowing tribes to make payments to states in return for additional benefits beyond the right to operate Class III gaming. This type of payment is usually referred to as *revenue sharing*. If the state provides to the tribe a "valuable economic benefit," typically substantial exclusivity in the gaming market, a revenue-sharing agreement where the tribe makes payments to the state generally will not run afoul of IGRA, as interpreted by the Secretary.[71]

There is no "bright-line" legal definition or test for the balance between the state's concessions and the economic benefit to the tribe, and what rate of revenue sharing is therefore permissible. The Interior Secretary's articulation of this standard has evolved into a two-part analysis: first, the compact must include the state's significant or meaningful concessions over which it is not required to negotiate in good faith under IGRA, and second, the state's concessions must result in substantial and quantifiable economic benefits to the Indian tribe that justify the amount of the payments to the state.[72] Over time, the Interior Secretary has proffered case-specific answers to that question in the form of its actions on submitted tribal-state compacts.

There is relatively little case law in this area; the most significant developments have arisen out of the tribal-state compacts in California. In 2003, the Ninth Circuit decided *In re Indian Gaming Related Cases*, which concerned the revenue-sharing provisions in the model compacts negotiated under Governor Gray Davis in 1999.

---

68. 25 U.S.C. § 2710(d)(5) (2018).
69. In Colorado River Indian Tribes v. Nat'l Indian Gaming Comm'n, 466 F.3d 134 (D.C. Cir. 2006), a federal appeals court held that the NIGC did not have authority to issue minimum internal control standards (MICS) for Class III gaming. In response, the NIGC recently released nonbinding MICS for Class III gaming. *See Bulletin No. 2018-3, Guidance on the Class III Minimum Internal Control Standards*, NIGC (Aug. 14, 2018), https://www.nigc.gov/images/uploads/bulletins/ClassIIIMICSBulletin201803.pdf.
70. 25 U.S.C. § 2710(d)(4) (2018).
71. *See* Aurene M. Martin, Statement Before the U.S. Senate Committee on Indian Affairs on the Indian Gaming Regulatory Act (July 9, 2003); *see also* Steven Andrew Light, Kathryn R.L. Rand, & Alan P. Meister, *Spreading the Wealth: Indian Gaming and Revenue-Sharing Agreements*, 80 N.D. L. Rev. 657 (2004).
72. *See, e.g.,* Comanche-Oklahoma Compact Approval Letter (2004); Viejas Band of Kumeyaay Indians-California Compact No Action Letter (2014), both available at Office of Indian Gaming, Indian Gaming Compacts, https://www.bia.gov/as-ia/oig/gaming-compacts.

The court adopted the Interior Secretary's general approach to reviewing revenue-sharing provisions and upheld the provisions in question in light of the state's concessions, as well as the provisions' consistency with IGRA's goals.[73]

Shortly thereafter, then-governor Arnold Schwarzenegger set about renegotiating the compacts, offering to increase the number of slot machines allowed in exchange for a larger state share of tribal gaming revenue. In response, the Rincon Band of Luiseno Mission Indians filed suit in federal court alleging that the state's revenue-sharing demands were in bad faith. Under its 1999 compact, the tribe operated 1,600 slot machines. The tribe sought to increase its slot limit to 2,500 machines, and in return the state sought 15 percent of the net win on each of the additional 900 machines as well as an additional annual flat-fee payment—in all, the state's revenue sharing demand amounted to nearly $38 million each year to be paid into the state's general fund. The state's own expert, the highly respected gambling studies scholar William R. Eadington, estimated that the additional slot machines would increase the tribe's annual profits by $39 million, but after paying the state's revenue-sharing demands, the tribe's net would drop to $1.7 million. In ruling that the state had negotiated in bad faith, the Ninth Circuit was skeptical of the value of the concessions offered by the state in light of the 37-to-1 ratio of the state's financial benefit over the tribe's: "[T]he relative value of the demand versus the concession here strongly suggests the State was improperly using its authority over compact negotiations to impose, rather than negotiate for, a fee." The court concluded, "The State's demand for 10-15% of Rincon's net win, to be paid into the State's general fund, is simply an impermissible demand for the payment of a tax by the tribe. None of the State's arguments suffices to rebut the inference of bad faith such an improper demand creates."[74] While the decision resulted in administrative gaming procedures being established for the Rincon Band, the court's decision impacted revenue-sharing negotiations across the country.

Nationally, only a relatively few states require revenue sharing beyond defraying regulatory costs. Of these ten or so states, the majority set payment amounts based on a percentage of gaming revenues, whether via a fixed percentage or a sliding percentage scale contingent on varying criteria established within the compact. Some tribes make revenue-sharing payments to local (rather than state) governments, and some contribute to special state or community funds that have a particular public policy rationale.[75]

The negotiation of new or amended compact terms related to revenue sharing is among the most fraught issues an attorney may face in compact negotiations. The establishment of fair terms that are palatable to the state and to the tribe, to any commercial interests, and ultimately, to the Interior Secretary requires attention to detail that includes a balancing of legal, market, and political considerations.

---

73. *In re* Indian Gaming Related Cases, 331 F.3d 1094 (9th Cir. 2003).
74. Rincon Band of Luiseno Mission Indians v. Schwarzenegger, 602 F.3d 1019 (9th Cir. 2010), *cert. denied*, 564 U.S. 1037 (2011); *see also In re* Indian Gaming Related Cases, 331 F.3d 1094 (9th Cir. 2003).
75. *See* MEISTER, *supra* note 4, at 85–90.

V. MANAGEMENT CONTRACTS AND COLLATERAL AGREEMENTS

While IGRA requires that a tribe has "sole proprietary interest and responsibility" for its gaming operations,[76] it also permits tribes to enter into limited management contracts, if approved by the NIGC. The chair has the power to approve management contracts for the operation and management of both Class II and Class III gaming. Although one might assume that such Class II and Class III contracts are governed by the same or substantially similar sections of IGRA, there are some distinctions.[77] IGRA and NIGC regulations set forth extensive requirements for submission and approval of management contracts.[78] The chair typically requires modifications to a submitted contract to achieve approval.[79]

NIGC regulations define a management contract as "any contract, subcontract, or collateral agreement between an Indian tribe and a contractor . . . if such contract or agreement provides for the management of all or part of the gaming operation."[80] Collateral agreements are defined as

> any contract, whether or not in writing that is related, either directly or indirectly, to a management contract, or to any rights, duties or obligations created between the tribe (or any of its members, entities, or organizations) and a management contractor or subcontractor (or any person related to a management contractor or subcontractor).[81]

If a management contract is not approved by the NIGC chair, it is invalid. This extends to the full range of contracts and agreements included in the regulatory

---

76. 25 U.S.C. § 2710(b)(2)(A) (2018).
77. The authorization for Class II management contracts is found, logically, in the section titled "Management Contracts," 25 U.S.C. § 2711; the authorization for Class III managements contracts is found in § 2710(d)(9), which states, "An Indian tribe may enter into a management contract for the operation of a class III gaming activity if such contract has been submitted to, and approved by, the Chairman." Section 2710(d)(9) goes on to require that the chair's review and approval of Class III management contracts "shall be governed by the provisions of subsections (b), (c), (d), (f), (g), and (h) of section 2711," omitting subsections 2711(a), (e), and (i). Subsection (a) includes submission requirements, including the obligation of the tribe to disclose information on individuals with a direct financial interest in or management responsibility for the contract; subsection (e) outlines the circumstances under which the chair must disapprove the contract; and subsection (i) requires the NIGC to charge to the contractor the fees necessary to cover the cost of an investigation to determine whether any of the circumstances in (e) are present. Thus, the statutory requirements for Class III management contracts are less stringent than those for Class II management contracts.
78. 25 U.S.C. § 2711 (2018); 25 C.F.R. pts. 531 (Content of Management Contracts), 533 (Approval of Management Contracts), 535 (Post-Approval Procedures), 537 (Background Investigations for Persons or Entities with a Financial Interest in, or Having Management Responsibility for, a Management Contract). For useful, practice-oriented overviews, see Kevin K. Washburn, *The Mechanics of Indian Gaming Management Contract Approval*, 8 Gaming L. Rev. 333 (2004); Heidi McNeil Staudenmaier, *Negotiating Enforceable Tribal Gaming Management Agreements*, 7 Gaming L. Rev. 31 (2003).
79. *See* Washburn, *supra* note 78, at 334.
80. 25 C.F.R. § 502.15.
81. *Id.* § 502.5. Definitions for other key terms related to management contracts also are found in 25 C.F.R. pt. 502. For commentary on the requirements for approving collateral agreements, see Matthew D. Craig, *The Negative Effects of Confusion Over Collateral Agreements Under the Indian Gaming Regulatory Act: Which Agreements Need Review?*, 8 UNLV Gaming L.J. 185 (2018).

definition and is the case even if the parties did not consider the contract to constitute a management contract under IGRA. For this reason, attorneys representing commercial entities conducting business with tribes should be aware of IGRA's and the NIGC's requirements for submission and approval of potential management contracts or related agreements, as the consequences can be steep.

In *Wells Fargo Bank v. Lake of the Torches Economic Development Corporation*, the Seventh Circuit invalidated a $50 million tribal bond indenture on grounds that the indenture was an unapproved management contract.[82] The case concerned the Lac du Flambeau Band of Lake Superior Chippewa Indians in Wisconsin, which, through the tribally chartered Lake of the Torches Economic Development Corporation, owns and operates the Lake of the Torches Resort Casino. To secure funding for a gaming-related economic development investment and to refinance $27.8 million of existing debt, Lake of the Torches issued $50 million in taxable gaming revenue bonds, which were purchased by a private equity firm. The bonds were secured by the revenue and assets of the tribe's casino and were accompanied by a trust indenture naming Wells Fargo as trustee. Not long afterward, the tribe's planned investment went south and the tribe repudiated its obligations under the bonds. Wells Fargo then filed suit for breach of the indenture.

The terms of the indenture included several provisions that, in the court's view, transferred management authority from the tribe's economic development corporation to the bondholders: oversight and control of casino gross revenues; limitations on capital expenditures without bondholder consent; mandatory retention of an independent management consultant under certain circumstances; limitations on changes to key casino management personnel without bondholder consent; and, in the event of default, the ability of the bondholder to select new management. Together, the provisions "transfer[red] significant management responsibility to Wells Fargo and the bondholder and therefore render the Indenture a management agreement subject to the approval of the [NIGC] Chairman. . . . The parties' failure to secure such approval renders the Indenture void in its entirety. . . ."[83]

The failure to obtain NIGC approval of management contracts and collateral agreements can have a devastating effect on an entity doing business with an Indian tribe. Scrupulous attention must be given to the requirements of these agreements contained in IGRA. Moreover, even when the attorney is awaiting

---

82. 658 F.3d 684 (7th Cir. 2011). The court also held that the tribe's waiver of sovereign immunity in the bond indenture could not be severed from the invalid agreement, thus precluding suit against the tribal development corporation.

83. *Id.* A California appellate court reached a similar conclusion in Sharp Image Gaming, Inc. v. Single Springs Band of Miwok Indians, 15 Cal. App. 5th 391 (2017), reversing a $30 million judgment against the tribe for breach of an equipment leasing agreement and promissory note. For an analysis of *Wells Fargo Bank v. Lake of the Torches Economic Development Corporation* from a bankruptcy law perspective, see Michael M. Eidelman, Terence M. Dunleavy & Stephanie K. Hor-Chen, *Dealing with Troubled Tribal Casinos*, 6 Pratt's J. Bankr. L. 302 (2010).

approval of the contract or agreement by the NIGC and assumes that approval is forthcoming, moving forward without approval actually being granted may expose the client to significant risk. While historically the NIGC's formal review and approval of management contracts has taken a year or more,[84] the agency also offers an expedited, courtesy initial review to determine whether formal review is required. This initial review process, which takes about a month to complete, focuses on two questions: is the agreement a management contract, and does it violate the statutory requirement that the tribe maintain sole proprietary interest in the tribe's gaming operation?[85] If the answer to both questions is no, then the NIGC will issue a declination letter indicating no further review or approval of the agreement is required. Agreements submitted for initial review might include loan agreements, security agreements, promissory notes, bond indentures, employment agreements, independent contractor agreements, and depository account agreements.[86]

VI. LABOR AND EMPLOYMENT

Most federal labor and employment statutes are of general applicability and thus are silent as to whether they apply to Indian tribes or tribal business enterprises, while others, such as Title VII of the 1964 Civil Rights Act, specifically exempt tribes.[87] Generally speaking, a tribe's "commercial activities,"[88] as opposed to tribal government functions, are more likely to be subject to federal labor and employment statutes of general applicability. Tribal casinos in particular have triggered significant and ongoing adjudication of this issue with differing and evolving results, so business attorneys are wise to research the applicable law in their jurisdictions.[89]

---

84. Washburn, *supra* note 78, at 334.
85. *See* 25 U.S.C. § 2710(b)(2)(A) (2018).
86. For more on the NIGC's expedited initial review process and declination letters, see *Declination Letters*, NIGC, https://www.nigc.gov/general-counsel/management-review-letters.
87. *See* 42 U.S.C. § 2000e(b) (2018) (providing that the term *employer* does not include "the United States, a corporation wholly owned by the government of the United States, Indian Tribe, or any department or agency of the District of Columbia"). Further, Title VII expressly permits certain employers to give preference to Indians in employment decisions. *Id.* § 2000e-2(i). Section 7(b) of the Indian Self-Determination and Education Assistance Act of 1975, 25 U.S.C. § 450e(b), requires the inclusion of Indian preference provisions in certain federal contracts and grants. To implement the tribal preference, tribes typically enact a Tribal Employment Rights Ordinance (TERO) that requires all employers operating a business on the tribe's reservation to give preference to qualified Indians in all aspects of employment, contracting, and other business activities.
88. As governments, tribes engage in activities, including gaming operations, that generate revenue. Though commonly described as commercial activities, a tribe's business endeavors are distinct from private, for-profit commercial entities. *See, e.g.*, Padraic I. McCoy, *Sovereign Immunity and Tribal Commercial Activity: A Legal Summary and Policy Check*, Fed. Law. 41, 42–43 (Mar./Apr. 2010), http://www.fedbar.org/Resources_1/Federal-Lawyer-Magazine/2010/The%20Federal%20Lawyer%20%20-%20March%20and%20April%202010/Features/Sovereign-Immunity-and-Tribal-Commercial-Activity.aspx?FT=.pdf.
89. For useful overviews, *see, e.g.*, Richard G. McGee, A Guide to Tribal Employment (2008); Gregory S. Arnold, *Employment Law in Indian Country: Finding the Private-Action Jurisdictional Hook Is Not Easy*, Fed. Law. 3 (Apr. 2015).

One of the most significant issues relating to labor and employment law is the status of tribal casinos under the National Labor Relations Act (NLRA). In 2007, in *San Manuel Indian Bingo & Casino v. NLRB*, the federal appeals court upheld the National Labor Relations Board's (NLRB) ruling that the NLRA applies to tribal enterprises. The NLRB's ruling reversed its earlier position that tribal businesses were exempt from the NLRA, along with the federal government, states, and political subdivisions. The agency instead concluded that because tribes were not expressly included in the statutory exemption provision, "Congress purposely chose not to exclude Indian tribes from the Act's jurisdiction." The D.C. Circuit agreed, holding that the NLRA is a statute of general application and therefore applies to tribal commercial enterprises.[90]

The Sixth and Ninth Circuits reached similar conclusions. In 2015, the Sixth Circuit issued two decisions extending the NLRA to tribal casinos. In *Little River Band of Ottawa Indians v. NLRB*, the court upheld an NLRB decision requiring the tribe to stop enforcing a tribal law that restricted union powers at its casino in Michigan.[91] In *Soaring Eagle Casino & Resort v. NLRB*, the court ruled that the NLRB could order a casino owned and operated by the Saginaw Chippewa Indian Tribe of Michigan to reinstate a housekeeper who was fired for soliciting union support.[92] Most recently, in 2018, the Ninth Circuit upheld the NLRB's determination that the Pauma Band of Mission Indians committed unfair labor practices by attempting to stop distribution of union leaflets to customers in certain areas of the tribe's casino.[93]

With three federal circuits—the D.C., Sixth, and Ninth Circuits—in agreement, the NLRB's position that the NLRA applies to tribes has gained strength. In 2011, the Interior Department's Deputy Solicitor for Indian Affairs urged the NLRB to return to its original position exempting tribes from the NLRA, and various legislative "fix" bills were introduced in Congress. In 2018, the proposed Tribal Labor Sovereignty Act, which would have amended the NLRA to exclude tribes and tribal enterprises on tribal land from the act's requirements for employers, passed the House but was defeated in the Senate.[94] Without a legislative amendment to the NLRA, the NLRB continues to apply the act's requirements to tribal casinos.

VII. TRIBAL SOVEREIGN IMMUNITY

Like states and the federal government, and stemming from the same legal principles, tribal governments have sovereign immunity against suit in tribal, state, and federal courts. Under this doctrine, a federally recognized tribe cannot be sued by

---

90. San Manuel Indian Bingo & Casino v. NLRB, 475 F.3d 1306 (D.C. Cir. 2007).
91. 788 F.3d 537 (6th Cir. 2015).
92. 791 F.3d 648 (6th Cir. 2015).
93. Pauma v. National Labor Relations Board, 888 F.3d 1066 (9th Cir. 2018).
94. *See* H.R. 986, 115th Congress (2017–2018).

a private party, a state, or other entity, unless the tribe expressly waives its sovereign immunity or Congress abrogates it.[95] Tribal sovereign immunity extends to tribal officials and employees acting in their official capacity and within the scope of their employment. Tribal sovereign immunity also extends to a tribe's commercial activities,[96] including gaming operations. Although not required to do so, tribes can waive sovereign immunity and often do in the context of negotiating contracts related to the tribe's business endeavors. The particulars of the waiver, including the scope of waiver, applicable law, and forum for resolution of conflicts, are subject to negotiation.[97]

While a full discussion of tribal sovereign immunity is beyond the scope of this chapter, the business lawyer representing an entity doing business with a tribe should never underestimate the importance of determining whether a tribe or tribal entity has validly waived its immunity, and to what extent, to avoid disputes should they later develop. Here we focus on a few recent and illustrative cases addressing tribal sovereign immunity that are particularly relevant to tribal gaming operations, including the applicability of federal bankruptcy laws to tribal casinos.

A. Generally

In *Michigan v. Bay Mills Indian Community*,[98] the state attempted to stop the tribe from operating a second casino on newly acquired lands off its reservation. Relying on IGRA's cause of action that allows a state to sue in federal court "to enjoin a class III gaming activity located on Indian lands and conducted in violation" of a tribal–state compact,[99] the state alleged that the tribe's new casino was not, in fact, located on Indian lands and therefore was in violation of the tribal–state compact. Relying both on the plain language of the statute and the Court's prior cases, the Supreme Court held that the state's suit was outside the cause of action authorized by IGRA. "[W]e have time and again treated the 'doctrine of tribal immunity [as] settled law' and dismissed any suit against a tribe absent congressional authorization

---

95. *See* C & L Enterprises, Inc. v. Citizen Band Potawatomi Indian Tribe of Oklahoma, 532 U.S. 411 (2001); Kiowa Tribe v. Manufacturing Technologies, 523 U.S. 751 (1998).

96. *See supra* note 88.

97. In addition, in order to be valid, waivers of immunity must be made by tribal officials with the appropriate authority to bind the tribe to such waivers. For an overview and critique of recent cases involving tribal sovereign immunity, see Hunter Malasky, *Tribal Sovereign Immunity and the Need for Congressional Action*, 59 B.C.L. Rev. 2469 (2018). For helpful resources geared toward practitioners, *see, e.g.*, Gabriel S. Galanda, *Deal or No Deal? Understanding Indian Country Transactions*, Bus. L. Today (Nov./Dec. 2008) (including additional resources at the end of the article), https://www.americanbar.org/groups/business_law/publications/blt/2008/11/01_galanda/; Heidi McNeil Staudenmaier & Ruth K. Khalsa, *Theseus, the Labyrinth, and the Ball of String: Navigating the Regulatory Maze to Ensure Enforceability of Tribal Gaming Contracts*, 40 J. Marshall L. Rev. 1123 (2007); Gabriel S. Galanda, *Getting Commercial in Indian Country*, Bus. L. Today (July/Aug. 2003).

98. 572 U.S. ___, 134 S. Ct. 2024 (2014).

99. 25 U.S.C. § 2710(d)(7)(A)(ii) (2018).

(or a waiver)."[100] Here, while IGRA authorized a state to sue to enjoin tribal gaming "on Indian lands," it did not allow a state to sue to enjoin tribal gaming outside of Indian lands. Such a circumstance may violate IGRA and state law and thereby trigger other possible penalties for the tribe, but it does not fall within the statute's partial abrogation of tribal sovereign immunity.

The Court also rejected the state's argument that the tribe's second casino was an extension of the tribe's gaming activity on its reservation, as the tribe authorized and operated the casino from its reservation. "[T]hat argument comes up snake eyes," said the Court, "because numerous provisions of IGRA show that 'class III gaming activity' means just what it sounds like—the stuff involved in playing class III games," not the administrative actions required to license and conduct them.[101] The Court concluded, "If Congress had authorized this suit, Bay Mills would have no valid grounds to object. But Congress has not done so: The abrogation of immunity in IGRA applies to gaming on, but not off, Indian lands."[102]

In a different context, the Tenth Circuit applied the reasoning of *Bay Mills* to require a slip-and-fall case to be tried in tribal court. The Navajo Nation's compact with New Mexico included the tribe's agreement to waive its sovereign immunity for personal injury lawsuits arising from the tribe's casino and to allow such claims to be tried in state court—"unless it is finally determined by a state or federal court that IGRA does not permit the shifting of jurisdiction over visitors' personal injury suits to state court." After a guest slipped on a wet floor in the casino, he sued the tribe in state court. But the tribe filed its own suit in federal court to enjoin the state court proceedings, arguing that neither IGRA nor Navajo law permitted shifting jurisdiction from the tribe to the state. The Tenth Circuit held in the tribe's favor, concluding that IGRA did not authorize tribes to shift tort jurisdiction to states. As the court reasoned,

> [A]bsent clear congressional authorization, state courts lack jurisdiction to hear cases against Native Americans arising from conduct in Indian country. . . . [C]ongressional approval is necessary—i.e., it is a threshold requirement that must be met—before states and tribes can arrive at an agreement altering the scope of a state court's jurisdiction over matters that occur on Indian land.[103]

Turning to IGRA, the court examined the subsection outlining permissible compact provisions, which includes "the application of the criminal and civil laws . . . of the Indian tribe or the State that are directly related to, and necessary for, the licensing and regulation of such activity," "the allocation of criminal and civil jurisdiction between the State and the Indian tribe necessary for the enforcement of such laws and regulations," and, in the subsection's final clause, "any

---

100. *Bay Mills*, 134 S. Ct. at 2030–31 (quoting *Kiowa Tribe*, 523 U.S. at 756).
101. *Id.* at 2032.
102. *Id.* at 2039. The Court also declined to limit the reach of tribal sovereign immunity with regard to off-reservation commercial activities, affirming its prior holding in *Kiowa Tribe*. *Id.* at 2036–39.
103. Navajo Nation v. Dalley, 896 F.3d 1196, 1204–05 (10th Cir. 2018).

other subjects that are directly related to the operation of gaming activities."[104] The Tenth Circuit concluded that "the Court's analysis in *Bay Mills* leads us to the clear conclusion" that the statute's reference to "the licensing and regulation of such activity"

> relates only to activities actually involved in the playing of the game and not activities occurring in proximity to, but not inextricably intertwined with, the betting of chips, the folding of a hand, or suchlike. . . . It necessarily follows that the allocation of civil jurisdiction referenced in [the first two clauses] pertains solely to the allocation that is "necessary for the enforcement of the laws and regulations" that are "directly related to, and necessary for, the licensing and regulation of" the playing of Class III games—and not for the enforcement of laws and regulations pertaining to such tangential matters as the safety of walking surfaces in Class III casino restrooms.[105]

As for the final clause, "any other subjects that are directly related to the operation of gaming activities," the court construed the clause as excluding the topics expressly included in the provision, therefore effectively excluding any allocation of jurisdiction between tribes and states other than as specifically allowed in the preceding clauses.[106]

The 2017 case of *Lewis v. Clarke*[107] involved a car accident caused by a limousine driver employed by the Mohegan Tribal Gaming Authority (MTGA), a tribal entity, while he was driving customers home from the tribe's casino. The plaintiffs sued the driver in his individual capacity in state court, and the driver moved for dismissal based on tribal sovereign immunity. Under the tribe's constitution, the MTGA consented to suit in tribal court, but neither the tribe nor the MTGA waived tribal sovereignty to allow claims arising under state law. Relying on the distinction between individual-capacity and official-capacity suits under general sovereign immunity law,[108] the Supreme Court determined that the action was against the

---

104. 25 U.S.C. § 2710(d)(3)(C) (2018).
105. *Navajo Nation*, 896 F.3d at 1210.
106. *Id.* at 1212–16. The court did not reach the issue of whether Navajo law authorized a waiver of tribal sovereign immunity to permit state jurisdiction:

> Because Congress, through IGRA, has not authorized tribes to enter into compacts with states allocating jurisdiction to state courts over tort claims arising on Indian land . . . whether . . . Navajo law would have permitted such a jurisdictional transfer is immaterial. In other words, because we conclude that Congress has not authorized the shifting of jurisdiction over the tort claims at bar by way of IGRA, our analysis is at an end; we need not decide more because "the negotiated terms of the Compact cannot exceed what is authorized by the IGRA."

Id. at 1205 n.4 (quoting Pueblo of Santa Ana v. Nash, 972 F. Supp. 2d 1254, 1266 [D.N.M. 2013]). As other tribal–state compacts have been held invalid by state courts on state law grounds, particularly the governor's ability to bind the state to the terms of the compact (*see* note 63 *supra*), it should follow that tribal law similarly may be a basis for invalidation of a compact.

107. 581 U.S. ___, 137 S. Ct. 1285 (2017).
108. *See, e.g.*, Hafer v. Melo, 502 U.S. 21 (1991).

driver in his individual capacity, and therefore he was not entitled to invoke tribal sovereign immunity:

> This is a negligence action arising from a tort committed by Clarke on an interstate highway within the State of Connecticut. The suit is brought against a tribal employee operating a vehicle within the scope of his employment but on state lands, and the judgment will not operate against the Tribe. This is not a suit against Clarke in his official capacity. It is simply a suit against Clarke to recover for his personal actions. . . . Clarke, not the Gaming Authority, is the real party in interest.[109]

B. Federal Bankruptcy Laws

A key issue concerning tribal sovereign immunity in the context of gaming is the applicability of federal bankruptcy laws. Tribal casinos typically are financed through traditional banks, private equity, syndications, public debt, or some combination of these. While real estate serves as collateral in other contexts, tribes generally are unable to encumber tribal lands[110] and instead rely on other property, such as slot machines, gaming tables, or even future gaming revenue streams, to secure financing.[111] Business law attorneys frequently assist in establishing these terms. What happens if things go south down the road?

In 2004, the Ninth Circuit held that tribes, as "domestic dependent nations," are domestic governments within the category of governmental units under the federal bankruptcy code, so the code's abrogation of sovereign immunity for governmental units applies to tribes.[112] "Congress explicitly abrogated the immunity of any 'foreign or domestic government.' Indian tribes are domestic governments. Therefore, Congress expressly abrogated the immunity of Indian tribes."[113] The Ninth Circuit was the first federal circuit court to directly address the issue of tribal sovereign immunity under federal bankruptcy law. Since that time, a few bankruptcy cases

---

109. 137 S. Ct. at 1292. As the Court determined,

> In ruling that Clarke was immune from this suit solely because he was acting within the scope of his employment, the [state supreme] court extended sovereign immunity for tribal employees beyond what common-law sovereign immunity principles would recognize for either state or federal employees. The protection offered by tribal sovereign immunity here is no broader than the protection offered by state or federal sovereign immunity.

Id. at 1292–93 (citation omitted). The Court also held that the fact that the tribe was legally obligated to indemnify the driver under tribal law did not alter its determination that the suit was against the driver in his individual capacity. *Id.* at 1293–95.

110. Most tribal lands are held in trust by the federal government; trust lands cannot be encumbered or sold by the tribe without federal approval. *See* 25 C.F.R. § 151.3.

111. *See* Steven T. Waterman, *Tribal Troubles—Without Bankruptcy Relief*, Am. Bankr. Inst. J. (Dec./Jan. 2009).

112. *See* 11 U.S.C. § 106(a) (2018) ("[S]overeign immunity is abrogated as to a governmental unit to the extent set forth in this section."); *id.* § 101(27) ("The term 'governmental unit' means United States; State; Commonwealth; District; Territory; municipality; foreign state; department, agency, or instrumentality of the United States [but not a United States trustee while serving as a trustee in a case under this title], a State, a Commonwealth, a District, a Territory, a municipality, or a foreign state; or other foreign or domestic government.").

113. Krystal Energy Co. v. Navajo Nation, 357 F.3d 1055 (9th Cir. 2004).

involving tribal casinos' sovereign immunity have been decided. An Eighth Circuit bankruptcy appellate panel declined to follow the Ninth Circuit's decision as inconsistent with the required "unequivocally expressed" congressional abrogation of tribal immunity. Relying on foundational federal Indian law, the court concluded that tribes' status as domestic dependent nations was in fact a unique governmental status distinct from either domestic or foreign governments.[114] A 2017 case involved a tribal casino's claims against the debtor. The Chapter 11 trustee sought avoidance of preferential transfers to a tribal casino. The court dismissed the preference action based on tribal sovereign immunity.[115]

Another key question is whether tribes are eligible for bankruptcy protection. At the height of the economic downturn, the casino industry had shed its recession-proof reputation. At the time, there was very little precedent to guide what would or could happen when a tribe defaulted on a debt, as tribes are not mentioned in the definition of debtor under the federal bankruptcy code.[116] This area of law remains largely untested, and thus unclear.

The Mashantucket Pequot Tribal Nation's Foxwoods Resort Casino, billed as the largest casino in the Western Hemisphere, was over $2 billion in debt; in 2013, the tribe successfully negotiated an agreement with more than 100 creditors.[117] In 2007, the Iipay Nation of Santa Ysabel opened a small casino near San Diego. With the recession, the casino reported losses of $24 million in its first three years. The tribe filed for bankruptcy, but the court summarily dismissed the tribe's application as ineligible.[118] In a case related to extensive litigation over the Grand Canyon Skyway, Sa'Nyu Wa, Inc., a tribally chartered corporation wholly owned by the Hualapai Indian Tribe in Arizona, filed a Chapter 11 bankruptcy petition on the basis of its status as a corporation.[119] The tribal corporation's eligibility was not challenged by

---

114. Whitaker v. Dakota Finance, 474 B.R. 687, 693–95 (B.A.P. 8th Cir. 2012).
115. *In re* Money Center of America, Docket No. 14-10603 (Bankr. D. Del. Feb. 28, 2017).
116. *See* 11 U.S.C. § 109(a) (2018) ("Notwithstanding any other provision of this section, only a person that resides or has a domicile, a place of business, or property in the United States, or a municipality, may be a debtor under this title."); *see also* Ji Hun Kim & Christopher S. Koenig, *Rolling the Dice on Debtor Eligibility: Native American Tribes and the Bankruptcy Code*, AM. BANKR. INST. J. (June 2015); Eidelman, et al., *supra* note 83. For in-depth analysis of whether tribes may be debtors under the federal bankruptcy code, *see, e.g.*, Stephen A. Hoover, *Forcing the Tribe to Bet on the House: The Limited Options and Risks to the Tribe When Indian Gaming Operations Seek Debtor Relief*, 49 CAL. W. L. REV. 269 (2013); Corina Rocha Pandeli, *When the Chips Are Down: Do Indian Tribes with Insolvent Gaming Operations Have the Ability to File for Bankruptcy Under the Federal Bankruptcy Code?*, 2 UNLV GAMING L.J. 255 (2011). *See also* discussion in Chapter 5.
117. Michael Sokolove, *Foxwoods Is Fighting for Its Life*, N.Y. TIMES (Mar. 14, 2012).
118. Order to Dismiss at 2, *In re* Santa Ysabel Resort and Casino, No. 12-09415-PB 11 (Bankr. S.D. Cal. Sept. 11, 2012), ECF No. 98. In 2014, the tribe's casino closed. *See* J. Harry Jones, *Santa Ysabel Casino Goes out of Business*, SAN DIEGO UNION-TRIB. (Feb. 3, 2014). The tribe also pursued an ultimately unsuccessful Class II online gaming operation. *See* California v. Iipay Nation, 898 F.3d 960 (9th Cir. 2018) (holding that even if IGRA permits an Indian tribe to offer online gaming, the Unlawful Internet Gambling Enforcement Act, 31 U.S.C. § 5361, et seq., bars the tribe's online gaming).
119. *In re* 'SA' NYU WA, Inc., BK 2:13-02972-MBW (Bankr. D. Ariz., Mar. 4, 2013). Under § 109, a "person" may be a debtor; the definition of person includes corporations. *See* 11 U.S.C. § 101(41) (2018) ("The term 'person' includes individual, partnership, and corporation, but does not include governmental unit. . . ."). For additional background, see Tim O'Reiley, *Legal Battle Surrounding Grand Canyon Skywalk Still Flares*, LAS VEGAS REV.-J. (Jan. 2, 2014).

any party-in-interest, and the case proceeded normally until it was consensually dismissed through a settlement agreement.[120]

VIII. CONCLUSION

The fact that there are nearly 500 tribally owned and operated casinos in twenty-eight states means that business lawyers are likely to encounter an opportunity to practice in the area. At the intersection of federal Indian law and gaming law, tribal gaming law and regulation is a complicated area. Business lawyers are advised to do their research specific to both tribal gaming and tribal governments, as well as to consider whether a specialist familiar with a particular jurisdiction or area of practice is warranted as an additional resource. The benefits of conducting business with American Indian tribes are numerous, and the area of practice is gratifying, so long as one follows the appropriate roadmaps for navigating complex terrain.

---

120. *See* Kim & Koenig, *supra* note 116.

Chapter 9

Internet Gambling

Karl Rutledge, Glenn Light,
Mary Tran, and Jason Bacigalupi

I. INTRODUCTION

This chapter will address the current legal and regulatory framework for different forms of Internet gambling in the United States. Also, it will look to the future development of Internet gambling and the potential barriers to that development.

Generally speaking, like most other forms of gambling, Internet gambling is regulated at the state level. Each state has the authority to determine what forms of gambling to authorize within its borders. This power is not absolute, however, as it is subject to certain restrictions established by federal gambling laws that will be discussed.

Because of the broad authority given to states, it is unsurprising that authorized Internet games or activities vary considerably from state to state. As of April 2019, the most authorized type of online wagering is on horse races, which is legal in more than two dozen states. This is followed by (1) Internet fantasy sports contests (eighteen states); (2) lottery (seven states); (3) sports wagering (six states); and (4) casino games, poker, or both (forty-five states).[1]

Recent developments in gaming law have created both opportunity and uncertainty in the Internet gambling industry, as well as the gaming industry in general. Two events in particular stick out. First, in May 2018, the U.S. Supreme Court struck down the Professional and Amateur Sports Protection Act (PASPA),[2] which had prohibited states from legalizing (or expanding currently legalized)

---

1. *U.S. Internet Gambling Regulatory Tracker*, GAMBLING COMPLIANCE (Apr. 2, 2019), https://gamblingcompliance.com/premium-content/research_report/us-internet-gambling-regulatory-tracker.
2. Murphy v. NCAA, 138 S. Ct. 1641 (2018).

sports betting.[3] Since then, a number of states have joined Nevada and passed laws or adopted regulations to allow for Internet or mobile sports wagering. By the time this book is published, it is likely that several more states will have legalized some form of sports betting, almost all including sports betting online.[4]

The event with the most dramatic impact on Internet gambling relates to the federal Wire Act.[5] In an opinion released January 14, 2019 (and dated November 2, 2018), the Office of Legal Counsel (OLC) for the U.S. Department of Justice (DOJ) announced that the federal Wire Act applied to *all* forms of betting, not just sports wagering (the 2018 Opinion). This constituted a reversal of a 2011 OLC Opinion that concluded the language and the legislative history of the Wire Act indicated it applied only to sports betting. As part of the 2018 Opinion, the OLC also offered controversial views on the topic of "intermediate routing," which is discussed later in this chapter. Unsurprisingly, the 2018 Opinion immediately spurred litigation, and on June 3, 2019, the U.S. District Court rejected the 2018 Opinion and ruled that the Wire Act applies only to sports gambling (the "New Hampshire litigation").[6] The DOJ is now evaluating its options and has extended the deadline to implement its reinterpretation of the Wire Act to December 31, 2019, or sixty days after entry of final judgment in the New Hampshire litigation, whichever is later.[7] These events have roiled the online gambling world, and it may be that it will take a case decided by the U.S. Supreme Court to resolve the turmoil and uncertainty.

---

3. 28 U.S.C. §§ 3701–3704 (2018). PASPA makes it unlawful for:

(1) a government entity to sponsor, operate, advertise, promote, license, or authorize by law or compact, or
(2) a person to sponsor, operate, advertise, or promote, pursuant to the law or compact of a governmental entity, a lottery, sweepstakes, or other betting, gambling, or wagering scheme based, directly or indirectly (through the use of geographical references or otherwise), on one or more competitive games in which amateur or professional athletes participate, or are intended to participate, or on one or more performances of such athletes in such games.

Id. § 3702. Because some states already had state-authorized sports wagering, exceptions were crafted to allow them to continue. These exceptions applied to the states of Nevada, Oregon, Delaware, and Montana.

4. *See U.S. Internet Gambling Regulatory Tracker, supra* note 1. As of June 2019, fifteen states have authorized legal sports wagering, nine of which have also authorized mobile or online wagering.

5. 18 U.S.C. § 1084 (2018).

6. The court stated:

In sum, while the syntax employed by the Wire Act's drafters does not suffice to answer whether § 1084(a) is limited to sports gambling, a careful contextual reading of the Wire Act as a whole reveals that the narrower construction proposed by the 2011 OLC Opinion represents the better reading. The Act's legislative history, if anything, confirms this conclusion. Accordingly, I construe all four prohibitions in § 1084(a) to apply only to bets or wagers on a sporting event or contest.

N.H. Lottery Comm'n v. Barr, No. 19-CV-163-PB, 2019 WL 2342674, at *18 (D.N.H. June 3, 2019).

7. *See Updated Directive Regarding Applicability of the Wire Act, 18 U.S.C. § 1084, to Non-Sports Gambling*, U.S. DOJ (June 12, 2019), https://www.justice.gov/opa/press-release/file/1172726/download [hereinafter *Updated Directive*].

II. THE FEDERAL LEGAL AND REGULATORY FRAMEWORK OF INTERNET GAMBLING

On the federal level, Internet gambling is generally governed by a series of laws passed in the early 1960s and 1970s to combat organized crime. These include the Wire Act, noted above; the Interstate Transportation of Wagering Paraphernalia Act of 1961 (18 U.S.C. § 1953); the Travel Act (18 U.S.C. § 1952); and the Illegal Gambling Business Act (18 U.S.C. § 1955). Of course, these laws were all enacted long before the development of the Internet. A more recent law that is specific to the Internet is the Unlawful Internet Gambling Enforcement Act.[8] With the exception of the Wire Act, these federal gambling laws merely prohibit certain forms of gambling activity that violate underlying *state* laws. In other words, instead of creating new criminal offenses, the policy of the federal gambling laws is to assist states in enforcing their own gambling laws.

On the state level, laws and state constitutions can address gambling directly by authorizing or prohibiting certain forms of gambling, including Internet gambling. The laws can also place limitations or other requirements on how gambling is conducted. Other than Utah and Hawaii, every state has some form of authorized gambling, and several of those states authorize (or prohibit) certain forms of Internet gambling, including horse racing, lotteries, fantasy contests, casino games, poker, and sports wagering.

In most instances, it is clear what is authorized or prohibited in each state. However, there is some ambiguity in states that do not specifically address, whether in a criminal or civil context, certain forms of gambling. In other words, while the activity is not authorized by law, the activity is also not *prohibited* by law. This creates a gray area, as there is conflicting case law regarding whether engaging in an activity that is neither specifically authorized nor prohibited is considered legal for the purpose of applying federal gambling laws.

A. Wire Act

The Wire Act is the federal law cited most often as having direct applicability to Internet gambling. Subsection (a) sets forth the Wire Act's basic prohibitions:

> Whoever being engaged in the business of betting or wagering knowingly uses a wire communication facility for the transmission in interstate or foreign commerce of bets or wagers or information assisting in the placing of bets or wagers on any sporting event or contest, or for the transmission of a wire communication which entitles the recipient to receive money or credit as a result of bets or wagers, or for information assisting in the placing of bets or wagers, shall be fined under this title or imprisoned not more than two years, or both.[9]

---

8. 31 U.S.C. §§ 5361–5367 (2018).
9. 18 U.S.C. § 1084(a) (2018).

Subsection (b) contains a "safe harbor" provision, which states:

> Nothing in this section shall be construed to prevent the transmission in interstate or foreign commerce of information . . . assisting in the placing of bets or wagers on a sporting event or contest from a State or foreign country where wagering on that sporting event or contest is legal into a State or foreign country in which such wagering is legal.[10]

Congress enacted the Wire Act in the early 1960s as part of a series of laws aimed at organized crime and racketeering.[11] Attorney General Robert F. Kennedy, whose disdain for organized crime was well known, first introduced the Wire Act in 1961 as part of a comprehensive plan aimed at curbing the illegal activities on which organized crime thrived. Specifically, Kennedy explained, "The people who will be affected are the bookmakers and the layoff men, who need incoming and outgoing wire communication in order to operate."[12]

The legislative history of the Wire Act further supports the view that it was directed at criminal elements, not the states. According to a House report, the Wire Act was enacted in response to "modern bookmaking" in order to "assist the various States and the District of Columbia in the enforcement of their laws pertaining to gambling, bookmaking, and like offenses" and "to aid in the suppression of organized gambling activities" nationally by "prohibiting the use of wire communication facilities . . . for the transmission of bets or wagers. . . ."[13] Similarly, a Senate Report noted that the Wire Act "deals primarily with the question of 'bookmaking' where there is a violation of the law of a particular State insofar as a business is concerned, and as a continuing operation," and "would prevent the use of the wire services to carry on such business."[14]

1. Interpretation of the Wire Act

Despite the rather clear indications of intent from the Wire Act's legislative history, the structure and language of the law itself are anything but clear, and this has produced inconsistent interpretations of the Wire Act. Much of this is likely due to the fact that § 1084(a), which specifies the activity that violates the Wire Act, is a single-sentence paragraph that includes several clauses that can be interpreted differently, along with key terms that are not defined within the Wire Act.

This imperfect statutory draftsmanship has led to considerable debate and confusion over the application and scope of three portions of the Wire Act: First, what does it mean to say one is in the "business of betting or wagering"? Second, what qualifies as "information assisting" in placing bets or wagers? And third, and perhaps most significantly, is the Wire Act limited to sports wagering? Each of these issues warrants special attention.

---

10. 18 U.S.C. § 1084(b) (2018).
11. *See* S. Rep. No. 87-588, at 3 (1961).
12. *The Attorney General's Program to Curb Organized Crime & Racketeering: Hearings on S. 1656 Before the S. Comm. on the Judiciary*, 87th Cong. 12 (1961) (statement of Robert F. Kennedy, Att'y Gen. of the United States).
13. H.R. Rep. No. 87-967, at 1–2 (1961), *reprinted in* 1961 U.S.C.C.A.N. 2361, 2361.
14. 107 Cong. Rec. 15,503, 16,534 (1961).

a. "Business of Betting or Wagering."

The Wire Act applies to those "in the business of betting or wagering," yet it does not define the term *business*. Therefore, courts must interpret what activity rises to the level of being in business. Generally, courts have found this requires that a person be engaged in the "sale of a product or service for fee" and that the person also be engaged in a "continuing course of conduct."[15] Accordingly, where operators charge their customers a fee for their services consistently over a period of time, they would likely be "engaged in the business of betting or wagering."[16] What is clear is that the Wire Act is not directed at the casual bettor.[17]

b. "Information Assisting" in Placing Bets or Wagers

The Wire Act also does not define the term *information assisting*, nor does it elaborate on what constitutes wagering information. Moreover, as the Wire Act has been subject to few judicial interpretations, there is less predictability than when courts have given statutory provisions more frequent construction.

The legislative history provides limited clarification on the subject. One House report, for example, stated "the immediate receipt of information as to results of a horserace permits a bettor to place a wager on a successive race," which is the type of information that would assist the placing of bets or wagers.[18]

Although precedent is limited, courts have held that the providing of line information, weather conditions, player injury, handicapping, and similar information can qualify as "information assisting in the placing of bets" if *received or transmitted* by someone engaged in the business of betting or wagering.[19] In one instance, a court reviewing the phrase *information assisting in the placing of bets* found that most prosecutions under this statute likely reference the information typically offered by bookies, such as the odds on a particular sporting event.[20]

---

15. *See* United States v. Barborian, 528 F. Supp. 324, 329 (D.R.I. 1981).
16. United States v. Scavo, 593 F.2d 837, 842 (8th Cir. 1979).
17. *See Barborian*, 528 F. Supp. at 329.
18. *Id.; see* H.R. Rep. No. 87-967, at 1–2 (1961), *reprinted in* 1961 U.S.C.C.A.N. 2631, 2631–32 (citing "the immediate receipt of information as to results of a horse-race" as an example of "'rapid transmission of gambling information' by wire communication facilities").
19. *See* United States v. Corrar, 512 F. Supp. 2d 1280, 1288 (N.D. Ga. 2007) (noting most prosecutions under this statute likely reference the information typically offered by bookies, such as the odds on a particular sporting event).
20. *See* United States v. Reeder, 614 F.2d 1179 (8th Cir. 1980). The defendant—clearly a bookmaker who accepted and placed bets, published a line, and charged bettors a 10 percent juice if they lost their bets—challenged his conviction for violating § 1084(a) on the grounds that the information he received from sports information service providers could not assist in the placing of bets or wagers on sports events. Defendant made this contention, despite the testimony of two sports information service providers who testified their services provided sports scores of games in progress, final scores, overnight wrap-up stories, and general late-breaking sports news, including features on the best pick in certain games. The court concluded that the jury was properly instructed so that they could draw reasonable inferences from the facts, and certainly the evidence adduced was adequate to show the recorded information, whether it concerned stories on the status of athletes, picked game favorites, or simply provided scores, could assist the defendant in the placing and accepting of bets and wagers.

Information assisting in the placing of bets, however, has also been construed more broadly. For example, even when a court acknowledged that information assisting in the placing of bets most likely relates to information typically offered by bookies, such as the odds on a particular sporting event, it could also include providing account numbers that allow a patron to place bets.[21] In that case, the defendant provided another individual with account numbers allowing that person to place bets with PlayWithAl.com (PWA), an Internet sports book operating out of the Netherlands Antilles. In denying the defendant's motion for acquittal after he was convicted by a jury of violating the Travel Act and the Wire Act, the district court declined to rule "that a defendant who provides the account numbers that make a bettor's subsequent wager possible has not provided 'information.' Certainly, these account numbers are not only helpful, but are required to place a bet with PWA."[22]

Given the dearth of precedent and the fact that existing precedent predates the current proliferation of legalized and regulated Internet gambling, uncertainty and ambiguity exists as to what the phrase *information assisting in the placing of a bet or wager* fully entails. As a result, Internet gambling businesses are forced to navigate an unclear legal landscape that fails to clearly delineate between administrative activities and transmissions that involve information assisting in the placing of a bet or wager.

c. Limitation to Sports Wagering

At the core of the 2018 Opinion was its pronouncement that the 2011 OLC Opinion was mistaken when it declared the Wire Act applied only to sports wagering. In opining that the Wire Act applied to all types of online gambling, the OLC injected considerable uncertainty into the scope of the Wire Act and into the future of online gambling generally. When one examines the case precedent and the two OLC Opinions on this point, the differences in analysis are stark.

i. Case law. There is a case to be made that the plain language and legislative history of the Wire Act strongly suggest the law applies only to sports betting. Notably, the law specifies that its focus is on a "sporting event or contest," with the word *sporting* predicating both the word *event* and *contest*. This interpretation of the Wire Act has been adopted by both the First and Fifth Circuits.

In the First Circuit case, *United States v. Lyons*,[23] the court considered two defendants' challenges to their convictions under, among other statutes, the Wire Act.[24] The defendants worked for a gaming business based in Antigua and conducted their operations in the United States, providing information to customers, taking bets, and distributing winnings. Their employer, Sports Off Shore (SOS), mainly took bets on team sports but sometimes also took bets on horse racing or on casino games. On appeal of their convictions under the Wire Act, the defendants argued that

---

21. *Corrar*, 512 F. Supp. 2d at 1288.
22. *Id.* at 1288.
23. United States v. Lyons, 740 F.3d 702, 718 (1st Cir. 2014).
24. *Id.*

because SOS accepted both sports bets *and* other types of bets, such as on casino games that were not covered by the Wire Act, they had not committed an offense under the Wire Act.

The court rejected the defendants' argument but not because the Wire Act applies to nonsports gaming. In fact, citing the statute and the Fifth Circuit's decision in *In re MasterCard Int'l, Inc.*, 313 F.3d 257 (5th Cir. 2002), the court held, "The Wire Act applies only to 'wagers on any sporting event or contest,' that is, sports betting."[25] Nonetheless, the defendants' convictions stood because "nothing in the statute limits its reach to entities devoted exclusively to sports betting any more than a bank robber gets off if he also withdraws money properly from an ATM."[26] The court concluded that because there was evidence that SOS had "advertised itself as a place to bet on sports, it published odds for sports bets, and its customer-witnesses testified that they placed bets on sports and paid their losses to" the defendants, there was sufficient evidence to sustain the convictions.[27]

The only other court of appeals decision addressing whether the Wire Act's application extends beyond sports betting is a Fifth Circuit case relied upon in the First Circuit's *Lyons* case, *In re MasterCard Int'l, Inc.*[28] In that case, the court likewise concluded that "the Wire Act does not prohibit non-sports internet gambling."[29] The court of appeals decision affirmed the thorough analysis of the lower court, which had reasoned that "a plain reading of the statutory language clearly requires that the object of the gambling be a sporting event or contest."[30]

In addition to these two courts of appeals decisions, several district courts have also concluded the Wire Act is limited to sports betting. In *United States v. Kaczowski*, a district court in the Western District of New York held that the Wire Act prohibits "the placing of bets or wagers on any sporting event or contest."[31] Twelve years later, a court in the Eastern District of New York similarly held that the "[Wire] Act applies only to wagering on sporting events."[32]

Not all courts agree, however, with this reading of the Wire Act. In *United States v. Lombardo*, the U.S. District Court for the District of Utah concluded the second and third prohibited uses of a wire communication facility under § 1084(a) do not require that the bets or wagers to which those uses relate be limited to bets or wagers placed on sporting events or contests alone.[33] As the court concluded:

> The phrase "sporting event or contest" modifies only the first of these three uses of a wire communication facility. Giving effect to the presumably intentional exclusion

---

25. *Id.*
26. *Id.*
27. *Id.*
28. *In re* MasterCard Int'l Inc., 313 F.3d 257 (5th Cir. 2002).
29. *Id.* at 262–63.
30. *In re* MasterCard Int'l, Inc., 132 F. Supp. 2d 468, 480 (E.D. La. 2001).
31. 114 F. Supp. 2d 143, 153 (W.D.N.Y. 2000).
32. United States v. DiChristina, 886 F. Supp. 2d 164, 215 (E.D.N.Y. 2012).
33. 639 F. Supp. 2d 1271, 1281 (D. Utah 2007).

of the "sporting event or contest" qualifier from the second and third prohibited uses indicates that at least part of § 1084(a) applies to forms of gambling that are unrelated to sporting events.[34]

Therefore, while the weight of precedent supports the argument that the Wire Act is limited to wagering on sporting events or contests, there is case law on both sides of the issue. This split of opinion is also reflected in the executive branch, where the OLC of the DOJ has taken different positions on the subject.

ii. 2011 DOJ Opinion. On December 23, 2011, the DOJ published an administrative opinion that had been originally issued on September 20, 2011 (the 2011 Opinion).[35] The 2011 Opinion concluded that the Wire Act applies only to interstate transmissions of wire communications that relate to wagering on a sporting event or contest. Accordingly, the Wire Act did not apply to other forms of gambling, including poker, traditional casino gaming, and lotteries.

The 2011 Opinion was issued in response to a question posed by the New York and Illinois state lotteries in 2009. The lotteries sought clarification from the DOJ regarding the legality of Internet sales of lottery tickets to persons within their state but where lottery data was transmitted to transaction processors across state lines. For over a decade, the DOJ had read the Wire Act as applying to all forms of wagering, including Internet transactions, and even when the operator's server and the player's computer or other device were in the same state.[36] In the 2011 Opinion, the scope of the Wire Act was reanalyzed, and the DOJ's prior position was reversed. The Wire Act, the 2011 Opinion declared, was limited to sports betting. The immediate impact of this opinion was that states were free to authorize intrastate Internet gambling on any nonsports-related wagering, including lotteries, casino games, and poker.

The 2011 Opinion determined that the DOJ's prior misreading of the law stemmed from a misreading of syntax. The earlier DOJ Opinion determined that the phrase *of bets or wagers or information assisting in the placing of bets or wagers* was a ban on all types of interstate gambling, not just sports. But according to the 2011 Opinion:

> Reading subsection 1084(a) to contain some prohibitions that apply solely to sports-related gambling activities and other prohibitions that apply to all gambling activities, . . . would create a counterintuitive patchwork of prohibitions. If the provision's second clause is read to apply to all bets or wagers, subsection 1084(a) as a whole would prohibit using a wire communication facility to place bets or to provide

---

34. *Id.*
35. Office of Legal Counsel, *Whether Proposals by Illinois and New York to Use the Internet and Out-of-State Transaction Processors to Sell Lottery Tickets to In-State Adults Violates the Wire Act*, DEP'T OF JUSTICE (Sep. 20, 2011), https://www.justice.gov/sites/default/files/olc/opinions/2011/09/31/state-lotteries-opinion.pdf [hereinafter 2011 Opinion].
36. *See U.S. House of Reps. Comm. on the Judiciary Hearing on Establishing Consistent Enforcement Policies in the Context of Online Wagers*, 110th Cong., (2007) (testimony of Catherine Hanaway, U.S. Attorney (E.D. Mo.), Dept. of Justice).

betting information only when sports wagering is involved, but would prohibit using a wire communication facility to transmit any and all money or credit communications involving wagering, whether sports-related or not.[37]

The 2011 Opinion concluded Congress was unlikely in 1961 to "have intended to allow the transmission of information assisting in the placing of bets or wagers on non-sporting events, but then prohibit transmissions entitling the recipient to receive money or credit for the provision of information assisting in the placing of those lawfully-transmitted bets."[38] Rather, reading "on any sporting event or contest" to modify "the transmission . . . of bets or wagers" produces the more logical result, the Opinion stated. Based on the text of the Wire Act and the relevant legislative materials, the Opinion concluded that the Wire Act's prohibitions applied only to sports-related gambling activities in interstate and foreign commerce.

In reaching this conclusion, the DOJ reasoned it was "more natural to treat the phrase 'on any sporting event or contest' in subsection 1084(a)'s first clause as modifying both 'the transmission of interstate or foreign commerce of bets or wagers' and 'information assisting in the placing of bets or wagers.'"[39] Stated differently, the references to "bets or wagers" in the second clause are best read as shorthand references to "bets or wagers on any sporting event or contest," as described in the first clause. According to the 2011 Opinion, the application of the Wire Act beyond sports betting was "counterintuitive," and limiting the entire subsection to "sports-related betting . . . makes functional sense of the statute."[40]

This interpretation was embraced by the industry and resulted in a significant expansion of the regulated Internet gaming industry, including interstate agreements and compacts negotiated among state governments. Most notably, in February 2014, Delaware and Nevada entered into a Multi-State Internet Gaming Agreement (MSIGA) that allowed the two states to share their online poker liquidity.[41] The MSIGA was subsequently expanded in October 2017 when New Jersey joined, making it a three-state pact.[42] Under the MSIGA, players from the three states would enter a single pool and compete against each other. The MSIGA is critical to the success of online poker in the three states, as their populations were too small individually to sustain a thriving online poker industry. As the Nevada governor at the time, Brian Sandoval, stated:

> New innovations and technological advancements are connecting more people and increasing the capabilities of Nevada's gaming industry. Gaming is one of our oldest industries and it's imperative that we continue to look for new opportunities to explore its full potential in a changing frontier.[43]

---

37. *See* 2011 Opinion, *supra* note 35, at 8.
38. *Id.*
39. *Id.* at 5.
40. *Id.* at 7.
41. *New Jersey Joins Multi-State Internet Gaming Agreement with Nevada and Delaware*, Nev. OFFICE OF THE GOVERNOR (Oct. 13, 2017), http://gov.nv.gov/layouts/Page_Style_1.aspx?id=228088.
42. *Id.*
43. *Id.*

iii. 2018 Opinion. The drama surrounding the proper interpretation of the Wire Act has continued. On January 14, 2019, the DOJ published an administrative opinion that had been originally issued on November 2, 2018. This 2018 Opinion reversed the 2011 Opinion on the applicability of the Wire Act and raised other issues.[44] Rather than the Wire Act being limited to sporting events and contests, the 2018 Opinion took the position that the 2011 Opinion described as "counterintuitive": namely, that the Wire Act applies to any form of interstate gambling, including Internet casino gambling and state lotteries.

The 2018 Opinion concluded that § 1084(a) consists of two general clauses, each of which prohibits two kinds of wire transmissions, thus producing four prohibitions in total. Specifically, the first clause bars anyone in a gambling business from knowingly using a wire communication facility to transmit either "bets or wagers" or "information assisting in the placing of bets or wagers on any sporting event or contest." The second clause bars any person from transmitting wire communications that entitle the recipient to "receive money or credit" either "as a result of bets or wagers" or "for information assisting in the placing of bets or wagers."

This interpretation of the Wire Act, if it is upheld or affirmed by the courts, could have enormous effects on the legal Internet gambling industry. For example, if the Wire Act applies to all forms of gambling, the current legal Internet poker industry, which is conducted via MSIGA, would violate the Wire Act. Additionally, the 2018 Opinion would also prohibit states from running interstate Internet lotteries.

But the 2018 Opinion was not content simply to reverse the 2011 Opinion's limitation of the Wire Act to sports betting. Another part of the 2018 Opinion threatens even the legality of what has previously been considered intrastate Internet gambling. This relates to the issue of intermediate routing, and it implicates yet another federal gambling statute.

In the past, the gaming industry and state regulators have relied on the Unlawful Internet Gambling Enforcement Act (UIGEA) to determine what constitutes an intrastate transaction for purposes of Internet gambling. Similar to the Wire Act, UIGEA excludes intrastate Internet betting or wagering from the definition of "unlawful Internet wagering."[45] Moreover, UIGEA provides that the "intermediate routing of electronic data shall not determine the location or locations in which a bet or wager is initiated, received or otherwise made."[46] Accordingly, even if communications constituting bets and wagers are electronically routed outside the state where the communications are initiated and received, they are still "intrastate communications." This intermediate routing is a function of the Internet's transmission of data using the most efficient electronic path available, even if it is one that directs the data out of state before reentering. Under UIGEA, the placing of bets and wagers

---

44. Office of Legal Counsel, *Reconsidering Whether the Wire Act Applies to Non-Sports Gambling*, Dep't of Justice (Nov. 2, 2018), https://www.justice.gov/olc/file/1121531/download [hereinafter 2018 Opinion].
45. 31 U.S.C. § 5362(10)(B) (2018).
46. 31 U.S.C. § 5362(10)(E) (2018).

initiated and received within a state where bets and wagers are authorized by, and placed in accordance with, that state's laws or regulations is *not* unlawful Internet wagering. State governments, tribal authorities, and commercial operators have relied on UIGEA's statement of what constitutes intrastate gambling in building Internet gambling markets.

According to the 2018 Opinion, however, these provisions in UIGEA do not apply to or influence the interpretation of the Wire Act. Specifically, the 2018 Opinion states:

> UIGEA's definition of "unlawful Internet gambling" simply does not affect what activities are lawful under the Wire Act. This definition applies only to the "subchapter" in which UIGEA is contained, 31 U.S.C. § 5362, and the Wire Act does not use the term "unlawful Internet gambling" in any event. Our conclusion follows from the plain meaning of the statutory definition, and Congress has confirmed it with a reservation clause stating that "[n]o provision of this subchapter shall be construed as altering, limiting, or extending any Federal or State law or Tribal-State compact prohibiting, permitting, or regulating gambling within the United States." *Id.* § 5361(b). UIGEA therefore in no way "alter[s], limit[s], or extend[s]" the existing prohibitions under the Wire Act.[47]

This view reinvigorates the prior DOJ position that a transmission is in "interstate or foreign commerce" for purposes of the Wire Act if the transmission *at any time* is routed across state or national boundaries, even though the transmission begins and ends in the same state. In 2006 testimony before Congress addressing proposed laws on Internet gambling, a DOJ representative noted:

> [The pending bills also permit] "intrastate" wagering over the Internet without examining the actual routing of the transmission to determine if the wagering is "intrastate" versus "interstate." Under current law, the actual routing of the transmission is of great importance in deciding if the transmission is in interstate commerce. The department is concerned that these two proposals would weaken existing law.[48]

This position was also expressed by the DOJ in a letter to the U.S. Virgin Islands Casino Control Commission, which was considering implementation of Internet gambling. In this 2004 communication, U.S. attorney David Nissman, writing for the

---

47. 2018 Opinion, *supra* note 44.
48. *Internet Gambling Prohibition Act of 2006: Hearing Before the Subcomm. On Crime, Terrorism, and Homeland Security of the H. Comm. On the Judiciary*, 109th Cong. 9–11 (2006) (statement of Bruce G. Ohr, Chief of Organized Crime and Racketeering Section, Department of Justice). Additionally, in a 2005 letter to the Illinois Lottery superintendent, the DOJ maintained the Wire Act prohibits intrastate Internet wagering if the transmission is routed outside the state. The letter was issued in response to the Illinois Lottery superintendent's inquiry about the possibility of selling state lottery tickets on the Internet. There, the DOJ stated:

> Although the activity might be considered to be lawful in the State of Illinois, we believe the acceptance of wagers through the use of a wire communication facility by a gambling business, including that operated by a component of the government of a state, from individuals located either outside a state or within the borders of the state (but where transmission is routed outside of the state) would violate federal law.

criminal division of the DOJ, asserted that it would violate federal law if the U.S. Virgin Islands were to make Internet casino gambling available to persons located on the island. In his letter to the chair of the U.S. Virgin Islands Casino Control Commission, he stated:

> As you know, the Department of Justice believes that federal law prohibits all forms of Internet gambling, including casino-style gambling, occurring within a state, commonwealth, territory, or possession of the United States and the Criminal Division [of the DOJ] has asked me to send you this letter. While several federal statutes are applicable to Internet gambling, the principal statutes are Sections 1084 and 1952, of Title 18, United States Code. . . . [W]e believe that the acceptance of wagers by gambling businesses located in the Virgin Islands from individuals located either outside of the Virgin Islands or within the Virgin Islands (but where the transmission is routed outside of the Virgin Islands) would itself violate federal law. . . .[49]

Therefore, the 2018 DOJ Opinion not only takes aim at interstate Internet gambling (which, as noted above, would prohibit states from compacting with one another to conduct regulated Internet gaming), but it may also strike at otherwise legal *intrastate* Internet gambling activities if a transmission happens to bounce outside of the state, even if it originates and ends in the state.

This position is contrary, however, to the very reason that Congress adopted the Wire Act: namely, to assist the states in enforcement of their own state policy toward gambling. This was even acknowledged by the DOJ. In testimony before Congress, a DOJ representative stated:

> That being said, 18 U.S.C. 1084—the Wire Communications Act—currently prohibits someone in the business of betting and wagering from using a wire communication facility for the transmission in interstate or foreign commerce of bets or wagers on any sporting event or contest. This law was originally enacted to assist the states and territories in enforcing their laws and to suppress organized crime involvement with gambling.[50]

The relationship between §§ 1084(a) and 1084(b) reflects Congress's intent to assist the states that restrict gambling by regulating interstate activities that are beyond the powers of the individual states to regulate and to suppress organized gambling activities.[51]

As noted, in the minds of many, UIGEA had laid to rest any application of federal law to intrastate Internet betting or wagering[52] and any conversion of intrastate

---

49. Letter dated January 2, 2004, from David M. Nissman, U.S. Attorney, District of the Virgin Islands, to Judge Eileen R. Petersen, Chair of the U.S. Virgin Islands Casino Control Commission, *Internet Casino Gambling* (2004).

50. *Hearing Before the Subcomm. On Crime Comm. On the Judiciary, U.S. House of Representatives, Concerning Gambling on the Internet*, 105th Cong. (1998) (statement of Kevin V. Di Gregory, Assistant Attorney General, Criminal Division).

51. *See* H.R. Rep. No. 967, 87th Cong., 1st Sess. at 2631 (1961).

52. 31 U.S.C. § 5362(10)(B) (2018).

communications into interstate ones through intermediate routing.[53] Accordingly, bets and wagers initiated and received in the same state, where bets and wagers are expressly authorized by and placed in accordance with that state's laws or regulations, would not constitute unlawful Internet betting or wagering. The 2018 Opinion's rejection of UIGEA's relevance to the Wire Act is of questionable legality, and it will be tested in the courts. Until this is resolved, states, gaming operators, payment processors, and others will be operating in a legal gray area.

iv. Initial reaction to the 2018 Opinion. Given the potential implications of the 2018 Opinion and its significant departure from the 2011 Opinion, numerous legal challenges are being and will continue to be brought. The first challenge, a complaint filed on February 15, 2019, by New Hampshire's attorney general on behalf of the New Hampshire Lottery Commission (Lottery Commission) requested declaratory and equitable relief.[54]

> Specifically, the complaint requested that the court:
>
> (1) declare that the federal Wire Act does not apply to state lotteries;
> (2) vacate the 2018 Opinion;
> (3) permanently enjoin the DOJ from enforcing the 2018 Opinion; and
> (4) grant further relief "as the court deems just and equitable."[55]

The complaint raised several arguments in support of the requested relief. First, the 2018 Opinion "is not faithful to the text, structure, purpose, or legislative history of the Wire Act." Moreover, the 2018 Opinion is unconstitutional because it violates the First Amendment, is void for vagueness, and violates the Tenth Amendment by intruding "upon the sovereign interests of the State of New Hampshire without unmistakably clear language demonstrating that Congress intended such a result."[56] The complaint was supported by amicus briefs from New Jersey and the Michigan Lottery that were joined by twelve other states.

On June 3, 2019, U.S. District Court judge Paul Barbadoro issued a sixty-page ruling rejecting the 2018 Opinion. The decision declared "that § 1084(a) of the Wire Act, 18 U.S.C. § 1084(a), applies only to transmissions related to bets or wagers on a sporting event or contest."[57] Judge Barbadoro came to this conclusion "based on the text, context, and structure of the Wire Act."[58]

Although the ruling is limited to the parties in the suit, Judge Barbadoro noted, "[I]t is clear, however, that the judgment binds the parties beyond the geographic boundaries of [the U.S. District Court for the District of New Hampshire]. And such an effect is necessary here."[59] Additionally, the ruling provided an opportunity

---

53. 31 U.S.C. § 5362(10)(E) (2018).
54. N.H. Lottery Comm'n v. Barr, No. 19-CV-163-PB, 2019 WL 2342674 (D.N.H. February 15, 2019).
55. *Id.*
56. *Id.* at *3.
57. *Id.* at *21.
58. *Id.* at *1.
59. *Id.* at *20.

for the Lottery Commission to pursue relief under a claim brought by Michigan that would allow the court to extend the declaratory judgment to nonparties on behalf of the Lottery Commission. The argument would be that New Hampshire, as a member of the Multi-State Lottery Association (MSLA), would suffer adverse financial effects if other MSLA members were shut down because the overall revenues of multistate lottery games would decline. Accordingly, nationwide equitable relief should be extended. A footnote in Judge Barbadoro's ruling provides, "Should the Lottery Commission wish to pursue such relief, however, I am willing to entertain its claim. Accordingly, I grant it 14 days from the issuance of this order to file an appropriate motion and supplement the record with adequate factual and legal support."[60]

As a result of this ruling, the DOJ is evaluating its options, and on June 12, 2019, it issued a memorandum extending the deadline for implementation of its reinterpretation of the Wire Act to "December 31 2019 or 60 days after entry of final judgment in the New Hampshire litigation, whichever is later."[61]

Although the 2018 Opinion creates uncertainty, it should be kept in perspective. It is an administrative opinion that has not been validated by a court. Moreover, the persuasive legislative history, the public policies involved, and the consensus of legal precedent do not support the 2018 Opinion. Nevertheless, as an appeal of the ruling is likely, the gaming industry may have to wait for this matter to be resolved by the U.S. Supreme Court.

B. The Wagering Paraphernalia Act

While the Wire Act is the preeminent federal law governing Internet gambling, several other laws need to be considered. One statute, the Interstate Transportation of Wagering Paraphernalia Act of 1961 (Wagering Paraphernalia Act) was enacted as part of the same federal legislation as the Wire Act and on the same day. This law criminalizes the interstate and foreign transportation "of any record, paraphernalia, ticket, certificate, bills, slip, token, paper, writing, or other device used, or to be used, adapted, devised or designed for use in" bookmaking, wagering pools with respect to a sporting event, or a numbers policy, bolita, or similar game.[62]

As one court stated, the Wagering Paraphernalia Act is intended to accomplish a very specific function: "It erects a substantial barrier to the distribution of certain materials used in the conduct of various forms of illegal gambling" by cutting off supplies used in illegal gaming.[63] Congress drafted the Wagering Paraphernalia Act with broad language to "permit law enforcement to keep pace with the latest developments."[64]

---

60. *Id.*
61. *See Updated Directive, supra* note 7.
62. 18 U.S.C. § 1953(a) (2018).
63. Erlenbaugh v. United States, 409 U.S. 239, 246 (1972).
64. United States v. Mendelsohn, 896 F.2d 1183, 1187 (9th Cir. 1990).

To help achieve this objective, many of the terms in the Wagering Paraphernalia Act are general, undefined, and unspecific. This includes *paraphernalia*, *paper*, *writing*, and *device*.[65] This gives the law flexibility and enables the DOJ and the courts to adapt the act's prohibitions as needed for the circumstances at hand.

For example, in *People v. World Gaming*, a New York state court ruled that an Internet gaming website located in Antigua violated the Wagering Paraphernalia Act by sending records of illegal gaming activity into the state of New York and transporting computers from the United States to Antigua that would ultimately be used for conducting illegal gaming operations.[66] Accordingly, the Wagering Paraphernalia Act encompasses practically any tangible devices intended to be used in illegal gaming activities, regardless of whether they have uses outside those activities.

Due to the potential breadth of its application, exceptions are included in the Wagering Paraphernalia Act to clarify which activities are legal. Otherwise, the transportation of any wagering paraphernalia across state lines would be illegal regardless of the legality of gaming or possession of this paraphernalia in either the state from which the paraphernalia originates or the state receiving the paraphernalia. The statutory exceptions include equipment, tickets, or materials to be used in a regulated state-run or foreign lottery; betting materials to be used to place bets or wagers on a sporting event into a state whose laws allow that betting; and any newspaper or similar publication.[67]

C. Travel Act

The Travel Act, 18 U.S.C. § 1952, was also adopted in 1961 as part of the package of laws championed by the U.S. Attorney General at the time, Robert Kennedy, to curb organized crime and racketeering. While, according to Kennedy, "the target [of the Travel Act] clearly is organized crime," the law elevates a wide variety of state crimes, including gambling offenses, to federal offenses if the criminal activity involves crossing state lines and satisfies other minimal requirements.[68]

The Travel Act prohibits any person from using any facility in interstate or foreign commerce with the intent to promote, manage, establish, carry on, or facilitate unlawful activity.[69] The term *any facility* is very broad and does not require persons or even physical items to be transported in interstate or foreign commerce. Likewise, the phrase *unlawful activity* is also defined broadly as "any business enterprise involving gambling . . . in violation of the laws of the State in which [it is] committed or of the United States." By its terms, a conviction under the Travel Act necessitates an independent violation of either state or federal law.[70]

---

65. *See* 18 U.S.C. § 1953(a).
66. People v. World Interactive Gaming Corp., 714 N.Y.S.2d 844, 852–53 (N.Y. Sup. Ct. 1999).
67. 18 U.S.C. § 1953(b) (2018).
68. S. Rep. No. 644, 87th Cong., 1st Sess., 2–3 (July 27, 1961).
69. 18 U.S.C. § 1952 (2018).
70. *See* 18 U.S.C. § 1952 (2018).

The Travel Act has broad application to a range of activities. Because of its breadth, federal prosecutors quickly favored use of the statute in a wide host of crimes going far beyond those perpetrated by organized crime.[71] With regard to Internet gambling, the Travel Act may be violated whenever the Internet (an interstate "facility") is used to place or receive a bet in a jurisdiction where gambling is prohibited.

D. Illegal Gambling Business Act

In 1970, Congress passed the Illegal Gambling Business Act.[72] Similar to the Wire Act, the Wagering Paraphernalia Act, and the Travel Act, the Illegal Gambling Business Act was aimed at syndicated gambling, which Congress felt had replaced liquor as the monetary foundation for organized crime.[73]

The Illegal Gambling Business Act prohibits any person from financing, owning, or operating an illegal gambling business.[74] An illegal gambling business is comprised of three elements. Specifically, it is defined as an operation that (1) violates state law, (2) involves five or more persons, and (3) either is in substantially continuous operation for over thirty days or has a gross revenue of more than $2,000 in any single day.[75]

Most courts have adopted a simple test to determine if a person "conducts" a gambling business. If he or she performs any function that is necessary or helpful in the illegal business,[76] they are conducting a business for purposes of the law. Under this analysis, virtually all, if not all, employees can be indicted.[77] Besides employees, the "necessary and helpful" standard can ensnare other participants if their activities go beyond that of a mere bettor.[78] As one court ruled, persons who regularly aid gambling enterprises are subject to prosecution, even though their conduct may not be strictly necessary to the success of the businesses.[79] Moreover, the government need not prove that the defendants themselves performed any act of gambling; it is participation in the gambling business that is a federal offense, and it is only the gambling business itself that must violate state law.[80]

---

71. Anthony Cabot, Federal Gambling Laws 125 (1998).
72. 18 U.S.C. § 1955 (2018).
73. *See* Organized Crime Control Act of 1970, Pub. L. No. 91–452, 84 Stat. 922, 923 (stating that organized crime derives power through money obtained from syndicated gambling and other forms of social exploitation and that the Act's purpose was "to seek the eradication of organized crime in the United States by strengthening the legal tools in the evidence-gathering process, by establishing new penal prohibitions, and by providing enhanced sanctions and new remedies to deal with the unlawful activities of those engaged in organized crime"). *See also* Cabot, *supra* note 69, at 151.
74. *See* 18 U.S.C. § 1955 (2018).
75. *Id.*
76. *See, e.g.*, United States v. Merrell, 701 F.2d 53, 55 (6th Cir. 1983).
77. *See id.* (finding a janitor that cleaned and straightened up a gambling room conducted the gambling operation); *see also* United States v. Bennett, 563 F.2d 879, 883–84 (8th Cir. 1977) (noting a cocktail waitress in an illegal casino could be deemed a participant).
78. *See, e.g.*, *Merrell*, 701 F.2d at 55.
79. *See id.*
80. *See* Sanabria v. United States, 437 U.S. 54, 57 (1978).

However, the scope of a state's criminal jurisdiction is generally restricted to its territorial limits.[81] In other words, at least part of an activity must take place within the physical territory of a state before its legislature can prohibit that activity. At a minimum, before a state can prohibit any "[a]cts done outside a jurisdiction," the actor must have "intended to produce and producing detrimental effects within [the state to] justify a state in punishing the cause of the harm."[82] This principle has been widely followed in state courts that have used the constructive presence doctrine to augment the state's authority to proscribe out-of-state conduct.[83] Ultimately, state law can reach out-of-state defendants only if their activities have in-state criminal effects.

E. The Unlawful Internet Gambling Enforcement Act

Discussed earlier in the context of the Wire Act, the UIGEA[84] has two objectives. The first was to provide new mechanisms to police Internet gambling that occurs across state or national borders by prohibiting transfers of funds through payment systems subject to U.S. regulation.[85] These regulations do not create criminal liability for those who provide payment systems, but they may create civil liability or result in other civil sanctions such as loss of licenses or injunctive relief.

The second objective of UIGEA was to create a new federal criminal offense imposed primarily against Internet gaming sites that accept financial payments in support of unlawful Internet gambling. This bolsters the federal authorities' ability to pursue off-shore Internet gambling operators. Accordingly, UIGEA significantly increases the risk to Internet casino and poker sites that have players from the United States, as it is unlawful for these sites to accept payment from players in states where the wagering is unlawful. UIGEA has two major sections.

1. Section 5364

As noted earlier, UIGEA created a new federal offense imposed primarily against Internet gambling websites that accept financial payments that support unlawful Internet gambling. The law directed the Department of the Treasury and the Federal Reserve Board to promulgate regulations that would require the payment systems used by credit card companies, banks, payment networks (including electronic fund transfers [EFTs]), stored value or money transmitting services, EFT terminal

---

81. *See* Lea Brilmayer, An Introduction to Jurisdiction in the American Federal System 321 (1986); *See also* B.J. George, Jr., *Extraterritorial Application of Penal Legislation*, 64 Mich. L. Rev. 609, 626 (1966).
82. Strassheim v. Daily, 221 U.S. 280, 285 (1911).
83. *See, e.g.*, People v. Blume, 505 N.W.2d 843, 845 (Mich. 1993) (citing *id.*) (asserting jurisdiction over out-of-state conspiracy to distribute cocaine); *see also* Pennington v. State, 521 A.2d 1216 (Md. 1987) (holding obstruction of justice perpetrated in Washington, D.C., was constructively present in Maryland); State v. McCurley, 627 So. 2d 339 (Miss. 1993) (finding Mississippi bank fraud defendants constructively present in Louisiana); State v. Sparks, 701 S.W.2d 731 (Mo. App. 1985) (holding out-of-state defendant constructively present when he received livestock stolen from Missouri).
84. 31 U.S.C. §§ 5361–5367 (2018).
85. *Id.*

operators, and money transfer businesses to identify and code restricted transactions and block the restricted transactions.[86] Specifically, the agencies had to:

1. identify the types of policies and procedures that would be reasonable to identify and block the acceptance of products and services with respect to each type of restricted transaction;
2. allow financial transaction providers[87] to choose alternative methods of blocking restricted transactions;
3. exempt certain restricted transactions of financial transaction providers from a regulation if the Department of Treasury and Federal Reserve Board determine it is not reasonably practical to identify and block that transaction; and
4. ensure that lawful Internet gambling is not blocked.[88]

The final regulations failed to carry out almost all of these congressional mandates.[89] First, the agencies did not attempt to spell out which activities are legal and which are illegal in the regulation, but rather continued using the UIGEA rule of construction that states legality is determined by applicable federal and state laws. Second, instead of establishing concrete policies and procedures, the agencies defined the designated payment systems and participants subject to the regulation and then required them to implement appropriate policies and procedures "reasonably designed" to identify and block or otherwise prevent or prohibit restricted transactions (policies and procedures).[90] While the regulations do

---

86. Restricted transactions are those transactions where a gambling business accepts funds directly or indirectly from a player in connection with unlawful Internet gambling. UIGEA defines "unlawful Internet gambling" as "to place, receive, or otherwise knowingly transmit a bet or wager by any means which involves the use, at least in part, of the Internet *where such bet or wager is unlawful under any applicable Federal or state law* in the state in which the bet or wager is initiated, received, or otherwise made." 31 U.S.C. § 5362(10)(A) (2018).

87. Financial transaction providers mean a creditor; credit card issuer; financial institution; operator of a terminal at which an EFT may be initiated; money transmitting business; or international, national, regional, or local payment network utilized to effect a credit transaction, EFT, stored value product transaction, or money transmitting service, or a participant in that network, or other participant in a designated payment system. 31 U.S.C. § 5362(4) (2018).

88. 12 C.F.R. § 233.5 (2018).

89. The regulations were promulgated jointly by the agencies, and identical sets of the regulations are published in the Code of Federal Regulations by the Board of Governors at title 12, Part 233 (12 CFR Part 233) and by the Department of the Treasury at title 31, Part 132 (31 CFR Part 132).

90. The regulation applies only to "designated payment systems" and "participants" therein, except that certain participants are exempted, as discussed below. Designated payment systems are generally automated clearing house (ACH) systems; systems for authorizing, clearing, and settling transactions involving purchases by credit cards, debit cards, prepaid cards, or stored value cards; systems for collecting, presenting, returning, and settling checks; and money transmitting businesses when transmitting funds (e.g., not when involved in check cashing, exchanging currencies, or issuing money orders or travelers' checks). 31 U.S.C. § 5362(3) (2018).

Participants in a designated payment system are operators of such a system, financial transaction providers that are members of or have contracted for services with such a system, and third-party processors. The term specifically does not include customers of a financial transaction provider, unless the customer is also a financial transaction provider participating in the designated payment system on its own behalf. Thus, individual gamblers are not participants and are not covered by the regulation. 31 U.S.C. §§ (1)(viii)–(ix) (2018).

not make clear exactly what these policies and procedures must contain, the regulations do provide some guidance and examples that, if followed, will be deemed compliant with the regulations.

The first example, to which all subsequent examples refer, suggests that nonexempt participants must adopt "know your customer" policies and procedures and use reasonable due diligence to ensure that the designated payment system is not involved in restricted transactions for its commercial customers.[91] The example provides that at the establishment of the commercial account or relationship, nonexempt participants must conduct due diligence about the potential commercial customer commensurate with the participant's judgment of the risk of restricted transactions presented by the customer's business. Based upon this due diligence, the nonexempt participant must determine the risk the commercial customer presents of engaging in an Internet gambling business.

For UIGEA, a commercial customer offering any games or contests over the Internet is engaged in an Internet gambling business. An Internet gambling business means "the business of placing, receiving or otherwise knowingly transmitting a bet or wager by any means which involves the use, at least in part, of the Internet, but does not include the performance of the customary activities of a financial transaction provider, or any interactive computer service or telecommunications service."[92] Accordingly, for a designated payment system to provide financial services to a commercial customer engaging in an Internet gambling business, the commercial customer must provide the financial transaction provider with either a copy of a government-issued or tribe-issued license authorizing that activity or, if the customer does not have such a license, a reasoned legal opinion that demonstrates the commercial customer's Internet gambling business does not involve restricted gambling transactions.[93]

To conclude, § 5364 of UIGEA mandates that financial transaction providers implement policies and procedures to block restricted transactions. Accordingly, it is imperative that financial transaction providers and Internet gambling operators engage gaming counsel to ensure the legality of the proposed operations.

2. Summary of § 5363

Section 5363 is the other major provision of UIGEA. It is a criminal statute with penalties that can include fines and imprisonment for up to five years.[94]

---

91. *Regulation GG: Prohibition on Funding of Unlawful Internet Gambling*, Fed. Reserve (last updated March 1, 2017), https://www.federalreserve.gov/supervisionreg/regggcg.htm.
92. 12 C.F.R. § 233.2(r) (2018).
93. *See* 12 C.F.R. § 233.2(x) (2018) of the regulations adopted pursuant to the enactment of UIGEA, 31 U.S.C. §§ 5361–5367 (2018). A reasoned legal opinion means "a written expression of professional judgment by a State-licensed attorney that addresses the facts of a particular client's business and the legality of the client's provision of its services to relevant customers in the relevant jurisdiction under federal and State law." 12 C.F.R. § 233.2(x).
94. 31 U.S.C. § 5366 (2018).

Section 5363 provides that no person engaged in the business of betting or wagering may knowingly accept most payments, including credit, the proceeds of credit, credit card payments, EFTs or the proceeds from EFTs, checks, drafts or similar instruments, or the proceeds from any other financial transaction from a player for unlawful Internet gambling.[95] In light of § 5363, therefore, a restricted transaction involves accepting these amounts by a person engaged in the business of betting or wagering from another person participating in unlawful Internet gambling.

Unlawful Internet gambling is defined as "to place, receive, or otherwise knowingly transmit a bet or wager by any means which involves the use, at least in part, of the Internet *where such bet or wager is unlawful under any applicable Federal or State law* in the state in which the bet or wager is initiated, received, or otherwise made."[96] The term *state* is defined as "any State of the United States, the District of Columbia, or any commonwealth, territory, or other possession of the United States."[97] The definitions of *bet* and *wager* include any game "subject to chance."[98]

The language of UIGEA is identical to that of the Travel Act and the Illegal Gambling Business Act[99] where federal prosecutors need to show a violation of state law in order to be a violation of these acts. UIGEA's language, however, is more favorable to the prosecution because UIGEA only requires the prosecution to prove that a *bet* on a game is illegal under state law, which is a much easier threshold to surmount than proving the Internet gaming operator violated a state or federal law.

For example, most states make it unlawful for persons to wager money on games of chance unless specifically exempted, as in the case of state lotteries or licensed casinos. These statutes would not directly assess liability on a gaming website because they are not players. The wagers, however, are unlawful under state law. Therefore, a gaming website may be charged under UIGEA for accepting the financial transfer, even if it did not violate the state law directly. UIGEA also removes other possible defenses that gaming websites may have previously offered, including that no federal law was specifically intended to apply to Internet gambling, and whether

---

95. *Id.* § 5363.
96. *Id.* § 5362(10) (emphasis added).
97. *Id.* § 5362(9).
98. *Id.* § 5362(1).
99. Neither the Travel Act nor the Illegal Gambling Business Act is violated unless another law is first violated. Both also can potentially apply to sports betting, on and off the Internet. The Travel Act prohibits any person from using "any facility in interstate or foreign commerce" (e.g., credit cards, bank teller machines, FedEx, telephone, etc.) with the intent to promote, manage, establish, carry on, or facilitate unlawful activity. Unlawful activity is defined as "any business enterprise involving gambling" in violation of state or federal laws. Therefore, a person using a facility in interstate or foreign commerce for an activity deemed to be in violation of state or federal gaming laws could be simultaneously deemed to violate the Travel Act. 18 U.S.C. § 1952 (2018).

The Illegal Gambling Business Act prohibits any person from financing, owning, or operating an illegal gambling business. An illegal gambling business is defined as an operation that violates state law, involves five or more persons, and either is in substantially continuous operation for more than thirty days or has a gross revenue of more than $2,000 in any single day. Under the Illegal Gambling Business Act, essentially anyone who participates in an illegal gambling business, other than a mere bettor, may be subject to criminal liability under federal law. 18 U.S.C. § 1955 (2018).

U.S. law could apply to a wager that is "consummated outside the United States"—that is, a bet that is placed by a person within the United States but accepted on servers located outside the United States.

Due to the many legal hazards presented by the law, after the passage of UIGEA, many gaming websites decided to cease offering their services to U.S. players.

F. Indian Gaming Regulatory Act

The Indian Gaming Regulatory Act (IGRA), 25 U.S.C. § 2701 et seq., recognized a statutory basis for the operation and regulation of gaming by federally recognized Indian tribes as a way to promote "tribal economic development, self-sufficiency and strong tribal governments." IGRA provides that tribes have the exclusive right to regulate gaming on their Indian lands if that gaming activity is not specifically prohibited by federal law and is conducted within a state that does not prohibit the activity.[100] IGRA divides gaming activities into three classes: Class I gaming covers traditional forms of Indian gaming and social games for prizes of minimal value;[101] Class II gaming covers the game of bingo and other games similar to bingo, pull-tabs, and card games that are explicitly authorized by the laws of the state or are not explicitly prohibited by the laws of the state and are played at any location in the state (excluding any banked-card games or electronic facsimiles of any game of chance or slot machines);[102] and Class III gaming covers all forms of gaming that are not Class I or Class II gaming.[103]

IGRA prohibits tribes from offering Class III gaming unless certain requirements are satisfied, which include a tribal–state compact entered into by the tribe and the state that sets forth what forms of gaming are authorized under the compact and other details of operation and regulation. Whether Internet tribal gaming is authorized pursuant to tribal–state compacts will depend on the particular compact and laws of the state. IGRA also limits Class III gaming to Indian lands, and circumstances may differ if a tribe decided to offer Internet gaming to persons not located on the reservation lands. A California tribe previously attempted to offer Internet gambling but its attempt was unsuccessful.

In November 2014, the Iipay Nation of Santa Ysabel (the Nation), located in San Diego County, California, operated a server-based bingo website, Desert Rose Bingo, for two weeks before a court order shut down the operation.[104] The Nation's Southern California casino was shuttered because of financial problems, and the Nation decided to offer gaming on the Internet. The servers for the online bingo games were located on tribal lands, and the players were located in California

---

100. 25 U.S.C. § 2701(5) (2018). See detailed discussion of IGRA in Chapter 9 on Tribal Gaming.
101. *Id.* § 2703(6).
102. *Id.* § 2703(7).
103. *Id.* § 2703(8).
104. Erik Gibbs, *Judge Nixes California Tribe's Shot at Opening Online Casino*, CALVINAYRE (Aug. 10, 2018), https://calvinayre.com/2018/08/10/business/california-tribes-shot-opening-online-casino-nixed-judge/.

off-reservation. After several years of litigation, the Ninth Circuit ruled in August 2018 that although IGRA protects gaming on Indian lands, players initiated bets while located in California outside of the Nation's Indian lands, so the Desert Rose Bingo violated UIGEA.[105] The court further held the Nation's decision to accept financial payments associated with bets or wagers placed over the Internet violated UIGEA because the players were located in a jurisdiction where those bets or wagers were illegal.[106]

III. CONCLUSION

Over the past two decades, the Internet has had a profound impact on commerce. It has provided merchants with the ability to disseminate their product worldwide without the expense of building brick-and-mortar stores, and it has provided consumers with the ability to receive the product at the click of a button. The gambling industry is no different. The Internet has become the most efficient medium for gambling operators to disseminate their casino games, sports wagering products, sweepstakes, and contests to participants worldwide.

Unfortunately, the Internet gambling industry in the United States has been shackled by a series of antiquated laws enacted decades before the invention of the World Wide Web in 1990. This has resulted in conflicting statutory interpretations and legal challenges as courts struggle to apply these laws to a technological infrastructure that the drafters could not have foreseen or intended to address. Until the contradictory and chaotic legal backdrop of Internet gambling in the United States is resolved, the growth of Internet gambling here will not be fully unleashed.

---

105. *Id.*
106. *Id.*

Chapter 10

State Lotteries

David M. Ranscht

Lotteries are ubiquitous today. They exist in almost every state. The North American Association of State and Provincial Lotteries (NASPL), an aggregate lottery organization, is comprised of fifty-two member lotteries from forty-four states, the District of Columbia, United States territories, and Canada.[1] Lotteries' wide reach can involve myriad legal issues with corresponding legal wrinkles. The focus of this chapter is to explore some of those legal wrinkles and examine issues involving lotteries that attorneys might encounter in their business practice.

Before getting there, however, some history is in order. "Much has been written about the history of lotteries."[2] Social and legal acceptance of lotteries has vacillated over time, including a period during which legal lotteries were completely absent from the United States for a generation. However, in the last fifty-five years, the pendulum has swung back, and lotteries are becoming more and more widespread.

I. HISTORY OF LOTTERIES—POPULAR, THEN OUTLAWED, THEN POPULAR AGAIN

Lotteries were both popular and controversial in early U.S. history.[3] "Some states used them as revenue opportunities, while others sought to outlaw them."[4] The revenue opportunities early lotteries provided helped to fund some prestigious universities and even helped to pay military expenses.[5]

---

1. *North American Lotteries*, N. Am. Ass'n of State & Provincial Lotteries, http://naspl.org/nasplmembers/.
2. Anthony N. Cabot & Keith C. Miller, The Law of Gambling & Regulated Gaming 678 n.1 (2d ed. 2016).
3. Kevin Washburn, Gaming & Gambling Law 172 (2011); *accord* Wenner v. Tex. Lottery Comm'n, 123 F.3d 321, 322 (5th Cir. 1997) ("Lotteries in various forms have been a part of the American life since colonial times.").
4. Washburn, *supra* note 3, at 172.
5. *See* Cabot & Miller, *supra* note 2, at 677; *see also* Wenner, 123 F.3d at 322 ("Among the beneficiaries of early colonial lotteries were such notable institutions as Harvard and Yale Universities.").

By the mid-1800s, however, controversies involving U.S. lotteries began to outweigh their popularity.[6] In 1850, the Supreme Court referred to the concept of a lottery as a "wide-spread pestilence" that "infests the whole community."[7] Thereafter, many states decided to prohibit lotteries, often by including a ban in their state constitutions.[8] "By 1878, lotteries were illegal in every state except Louisiana."[9] And even that lottery, known as the Serpent,[10] didn't last forever. Rather, "it became a national scandal."[11]

The scandal was national because although the Louisiana Lottery was legal within Louisiana, "ninety-three percent of the lottery's business came from outside of Louisiana."[12] Ticket sales occurred across state lines, through the mail.[13] In 1891, after the Louisiana Lottery had operated (and sold tickets across the country) for over a decade, one state supreme court went out of its way to express disapproval:

> This gigantic organization has become a national evil, intensified by state sanction, authority, and license. Octopus-like, it has laid its blighting hands upon every city and hamlet from ocean to ocean, corrupting the morals of the nation, and drawing money from the people by the million. National sentiment, which this great wrong outrages, will no doubt ultimately compel the withdrawal from it of state authority to carry on its nefarious business.[14]

Finally, in 1895, Congress effectively stamped out Louisiana's lottery by enacting a law "making it a felony to carry a lottery ticket from one state to another, through the mails, or otherwise."[15] That marked the end of legalized U.S. lotteries for a generation.

---

6. *See* CABOT & MILLER, *supra* note 2, at 677.
7. Phalen v. Virginia, 49 U.S. 163, 168 (1850).
8. WASHBURN, *supra* note 3, at 173; *accord* HERB DELEHANTY, THE LOTTERY INDUSTRY: CASES, PROBLEMS & PREVENTABLE INCIDENTS 107 (2005) ("[I]n the 1800s public pressure resulted in constitutional prohibitions against lotteries in most jurisdictions within the United States."); *see also, e.g.*, State *ex rel.* Six v. Kan. Lottery, 186 P.3d 183, 186 (Kan. 2008) (reciting Kansas's constitutional prohibition that was enacted in 1861); State *ex rel.* Sorensen v. Ak-Sar-Ben Exposition Co., 226 N.W. 705, 707 (Neb. 1929) (reciting Nebraska's constitutional prohibition against lotteries that was enacted to combat lotteries' "demoralizing influence"); Ecumenical Ministries of Or. v. Or. State Lottery Comm'n, 871 P.2d 106, 107–08 (Or. 1994) (reciting Oregon's constitutional prohibition that was enacted in 1857).
9. Michael Linton, Note, *A Nevada Lottery: Improving the Odds for Nevada's Public Education System*, 8 UNLV GAMING L.J. 253, 265 (2018).
10. *See* CABOT & MILLER, *supra* note 2, at 639.
11. Shawnee Milling Co. v. Temple, 179 F. 517, 523 (S.D. Iowa 1910); *see also* State v. Fleckinger, 93 So. 115, 116 (La. 1922) (referring colorfully to the "memorable fight to suppress the Louisiana Lottery"); DELEHANTY, *supra* note 8, at 107 (noting that after many states passed constitutional prohibitions against lotteries, "people all over the United States continued to purchase lottery tickets issued by the corrupt Louisiana Lottery Corporation").
12. Craig M. Bradley, *Racketeering and the Federalization of Crime*, 22 AM. CRIM. L. REV. 213, 216 (1984).
13. *See id.* at 217 (suggesting the Louisiana lottery "used the mails . . . with impunity").
14. State v. Burgdoerfer, 17 S.W. 646, 652 (Mo. 1891).
15. WASHBURN, *supra* note 3, at 173; *see Shawnee Milling*, 179 F. at 523 (noting the Louisiana Lottery "was struck at by denying it use of the mails"); DELEHANTY, *supra* note 8, at 107 (noting the federal law "effectively put the Louisiana Lottery Corporation, the last existing U.S. lottery, out of business").

Between the turn of the twentieth century and the 1960s, individuals commonly faced prosecution for operating illegal lotteries in various forms.[16] But then, "[l]egal lotteries returned with the passage of New Hampshire legislation in 1964,"[17] and it is fair to say that "since that time, lotteries have swept the nation."[18] Lotteries now exist in most states and sell a wide variety of products. In those states, lotteries are a state-sanctioned monopoly, and privately run lotteries remain illegal.[19]

II. LOTTERY PRODUCTS

"Lotteries typically offer several types of 'products.'"[20] The most prominent products are scratch tickets—the biggest seller in most lottery portfolios.[21] Scratch tickets are preprinted tickets with a protective coating that a player scratches or scrapes to uncover symbols or numbers indicating whether the ticket is a winner.[22] Traditionally, scratch tickets were available only in low denominations

---

16. *See, e.g.*, Maynard v. United States, 215 F.2d 336, 342 (D.C. Cir. 1954) ("That Mallette maintained a lottery establishment and also possessed lottery paraphernalia seems proved beyond peradventure."); Guthas v. State, 187 S.E. 847, 848 (Ga. Ct. App. 1936); Commonwealth v. Heffner, 24 N.E.2d 508, 508–09 (Mass. 1939); State v. Curry, 109 N.E.2d 298, 301 (Ohio Ct. App. 1952); State v. Wersebe, 181 A. 299, 302 (Vt. 1935).

17. Stephen J. Leacock, *Lotteries and Public Policy in American Law*, 46 J. Marshall L. Rev. 37, 71 (2012); *accord* Cabot & Miller, *supra* note 2, at 678.

18. Cabot & Miller, *supra* note 2, at 678; *see also* Wenner v. Tex. Lottery Comm'n, 123 F.3d 321, 322 (5th Cir. 1997) (noting even twenty years ago a "substantial majority of states" hosted "some form of state lottery").

19. *See, e.g.*, United States v. Edge Broad. Co., 509 U.S. 418, 423 (1993) ("Virginia . . . has chosen to legalize lotteries under a state monopoly and has entered the marketplace vigorously."); Washburn, *supra* note 3, at 21 n.3 ("While most states continue to prohibit private parties from engaging in for-profit lotteries, a majority of states have state-run lotteries. . . ."); *see also* Iowa Code §§ 725.12, 725.15 (2018) (prohibiting any person from making or establishing a lottery, but exempting activities conducted pursuant to the statutes authorizing a state-run lottery); Nat'l Gambling Impact Study Comm'n Report 2-3 (1999), http://govinfo.library.unt.edu/ngisc/reports/2.pdf [hereinafter NGISC Report] ("Lotteries are established and run exclusively by state governments. . . . Since the beginning of the wave of lotteries in the 1960s, state governments have seized on the lottery as a state-operated monopoly.").

20. Cabot & Miller, *supra* note 2, at 679 n.4.

21. *See, e.g.*, Iowa Lottery, Win!: 2018 Annual Report 4–5 (2018), https://ialottery.com/PDF/2018AnnualReport.pdf (showing scratch tickets accounted for approximately two-thirds of the Iowa Lottery's 2018 sales); Mo. Lottery, Comprehensive Annual Financial Report for Fiscal Years Ended June 30, 2018 and 2017, at 3 (2018), http://www.molottery.com/where_the_money_goes/documents/fy18_cafr.pdf ("For fiscal year 2018, Scratchers ticket sales were $906.8 million, which represents 64.8 percent of total ticket sales.").

22. *See, e.g.*, Iowa Code § 99G.3(6) (2018) (defining "instant ticket"); Ariz. Admin. Code § R19-3-701(3)–(4) (2018) (defining "instant game" and "instant scratch game"); 16 Tex. Admin. Code § 401.301(46) (2018) (defining "scratch ticket" but noting "[s]ometimes, scratch ticket games are called 'instant games'"); 11 Va. Admin. Code § 5-41-10 (2018) (defining "scratcher" and "scratch game"). Although the term *scratch ticket* has usually been interchangeable with *instant ticket*, some lotteries have recently begun offering "scratchless" instant tickets that are printed on demand from a lottery retailer terminal (rather than preprinted at a specialized printer and shipped in batches) and have no protective coating. *See* Iowa Admin. Code r. 531-18.2 (2018) ("'*Instaplay ticket*' means an instant ticket printed on lotto terminal paper with play symbols that are not concealed by a removable covering."). To account for these newer types of tickets, definitions for various lottery products will likely be changed or supplemented as lottery portfolios evolve.

such as $1, $2, or $5.[23] However, some lotteries have recently begun to offer higher denomination scratch tickets as well, including $10, $20, $30, and even $50—with correspondingly higher available jackpots.[24] Despite costing more, higher-denomination tickets are often popular, perhaps due to those higher jackpots.[25] When Iowa debuted a $20 ticket, the lottery "ordered two years' worth of tickets," which "sold out in four months."[26]

Although scratch tickets are popular, one recurring criticism of them, and of lotteries in general, is that they "exploit the most economically vulnerable members of society."[27] In 1999, the National Gambling Impact Study Commission collected data suggesting "lottery play is heaviest among economically disadvantaged populations and among some ethnic groups."[28] With specific respect to lottery players' *product preferences* (not just whether they play the lottery at all), a 2002 study focused on the Georgia Lottery found lower-income players were more likely to buy scratch tickets than higher-income players.[29] On the other hand, the NASPL organization considers it a myth that most lottery purchases come from low-income people, citing studies in multiple states finding a significant percentage of players have incomes above a certain level.[30] NASPL also questions the validity of conclusions drawn from examining sales data by zip code because people may not buy lottery tickets where they live and not all players within one zip code have the same income.[31] Regardless of whether lower-income people more often purchase scratch tickets, it is clear that scratch tickets are and will remain a major part of lotteries' product portfolios.

Lotto or draw games are another lottery staple. These types of games involve drawing or selecting winning numbers "on a daily, weekly or bi-weekly basis."[32] Lotto

---

23. CABOT & MILLER, *supra* note 2, at 679 n.5; *see also* Murphy v. NCAA, 138 S. Ct. 1461, 1482 (2018) ("State-run lotteries, which sold tickets costing only a few dollars, were thought more benign than other forms of gambling, and that is why they had been adopted in many States.").

24. *See* LA FLEUR'S, VOL. 26, NO. 2, at 44 (2018) (producing a table setting forth U.S. lotteries' scratch ticket sales by price point during the third quarter of 2018; all states that offer scratch tickets had sales in the $10/$15 category, and most had sales in the $20 and "$25+" category as well); *see also* Parsley v. State, 119 N.E.3d 131, 135 (Ind. Ct. App. 2019) ("The Lottery . . . creates and sells a variety of scratch-off ticket games. The games vary in price from $1 up to $25 per ticket, with prize values ranging from $1 to millions of dollars.").

25. *See* Lawrence Zelenak, *The Puzzling Case of the Revenue-Maximizing Lottery*, 79 N.C. L. REV. 1, 4 (2000) ("Between two bets with equal expected payoffs [i.e., jackpot amount multiplied by the odds of winning], players generally prefer the bet with the larger jackpot and longer odds.").

26. TERRY RICH, DARE TO DREAM, DARE TO ACT: UNLOCK YOUR IDEAS TO GREATER SUCCESS 82 (2015).

27. CABOT & MILLER, *supra* note 2, at 678 n.2; *see also* WASHBURN, *supra* note 3, at 97 ("[T]hose who play the lottery tend not only to be less educated, but also less wealthy.").

28. NGISC Report, *supra* note 19, at 3–4.

29. JOSEPH MCCRARY & THOMAS J. PAVLAK, WHO PLAYS THE GEORGIA LOTTERY? RESULTS OF A STATEWIDE SURVEY 13 (2002), https://athenaeum.libs.uga.edu/bitstream/handle/10724/19077/51.pdf?sequence=1 ("[A]lmost 41 percent of respondents who made less than $25,000 per year purchased instant game lottery tickets compared with only 24 percent of respondents making more than $75,000 annually."). When the study was published in 2002, "instant game" likely referred only to scratch tickets because "scratchless" instant tickets had not yet debuted. *See supra* note 22.

30. *Debunking Lottery Myths*, N. AM. ASS'N OF STATE & PROVINCIAL LOTTERIES, http://naspl.org/mythsandfaq/.

31. *See id.*

32. CABOT & MILLER, *supra* note 2, at 680 n.6.

games can be limited to players within a specific state or offered across state lines to enable greater player liquidity and therefore higher jackpots.[33] Players can either select their own numbers using a playslip—which is a form that is readable by a lottery terminal and resembles a multiple-choice answer sheet from a standardized test—or get a randomized quick pick ticket. Powerball and Mega Millions are two of the most well-known lotto games.

Because the game matrices for lotto games, especially Powerball and Mega Millions, allow for so many possible combinations of winning numbers, the odds of winning the jackpot are extraordinarily low—1 in over 290 million for Powerball and 1 in over 300 million for Mega Millions. Accordingly, advertised jackpots in lotto games can quickly skyrocket as multiple drawings in a row occur with no jackpot winner. When that happens, public fervor often spikes while the jackpot remains high. Recently, for example, a player won a $768.4 million Powerball jackpot in Wisconsin.[34] And in fall 2018, the Mega Millions jackpot increased "to an astonishing $1.6 billion, the highest in history"—so high that one writer described the prevailing public attitude as "cartoon dollar signs . . . popping into people's eyes."[35] When jackpots reach such high levels, newspapers and other media outlets frequently run or air stories or thought exercises examining what lavish, excessive, or massive items a person could buy if they won.[36]

Although scratch tickets and lotto games are the most popular lottery products, they aren't the only ones. Some lotteries also offer pull tabs, where play symbols and data are "hidden beneath a protective tab or seal that when opened reveals immediately whether the player has won."[37] Pull tabs are like scratch tickets in that players know instantly whether they have a winning ticket, but pull tabs have different play mechanics—peeling or opening rather than scratching. Typically, a winning pull tab features winning symbols "in a straight left to right matching situation or . . . in a criss-cross manner (like tic-tac-toe)."[38] Pull tabs are often comparatively low

---

33. *See* Keith C. Miller, *The Internet Gambling Genie and the Challenges States Face*, 17 J. Internet L. 1, 26 (2013) (discussing the Multi-State Lottery Association (MUSL), which administers some multijurisdictional lotto games and, by pooling money for jackpots, "allows states with smaller populations to participate in a lottery with a larger payout than the state could create on its own").

34. Tom Huddleston Jr., *The 24-Year-Old Winner of the $768 Million Powerball Had Under $1,000 In His Bank Account*, CNBC (Apr. 24, 2019), https://www.cnbc.com/2019/04/24/wisconsin-powerball-winner-franco-had-under-1000-in-his-bank-account.html.

35. Tanya Pai, *Is the "Curse" of the Lottery Real? And Other Questions About the Lottery, Answered*, Vox (Mar. 15, 2019), https://www.vox.com/the-goods/2019/3/15/18266238/lottery-explained-powerball-mega-millions.

36. *See, e.g.*, Emily Bohatch, *Here's What You Could Buy If You Won the $700 Million Powerball*, USA Today (Aug. 23, 2017), https://www.usatoday.com/story/news/2017/08/23/heres-what-you-could-buy-if-you-won-700-million-powerball/593752001/; Jordyn Noennig, *What in Wisconsin Can the Powerball Winner Buy? Maybe Fiserv Forum or 26.2 Million Cases of Beer*, Milwaukee J. Sentinel (Mar. 29, 2019), https://www.jsonline.com/story/news/local/milwaukee/2019/03/29/wisconsin-powerball-winner-could-buy-fiserv-forum/3312294002/; Marina Pitofsky, *Crazy Rich Lottery Winners: What Would You Buy With $1.2 Billion?*, USA Today (Oct. 17, 2018), https://www.usatoday.com/story/news/2018/10/17/mega-millions-powerball-winnings-what-would-you-buy/1669298002/.

37. Iowa Code § 99G.3(13) (2018).

38. *Pull Tabs*, Mass. Lottery, https://www.masslottery.com/games/pull-tabs.html.

stakes. Some tickets cost as little as $0.25 and few, if any, cost more than $5.[39] They are often sold at "nontraditional" lottery retailers—such as a tavern or restaurant—instead of, or in addition to, the local convenience store or grocery store.

Beyond scratch games, lotto games, and pull tabs, "[o]ther lottery products include raffles, keno, and video lottery terminals."[40] Newer products include ticket sales over the Internet or on mobile devices and, depending on the state, some aspects of legalized sports betting.[41] Lottery officials often "contend that it is essential to market their products in a digital format . . . to 'stay relevant.'"[42] And if relevance is measured in terms of sales, lotteries are certainly succeeding. In the third quarter of 2018, U.S. lotteries tallied over $18 billion in gross sales.[43]

III. LEGAL DISPUTES INVOLVING LOTTERIES
A. Generally

Despite their financial success, "the prevalence of lotteries in the United States has not reduced the controversy generated by having the state as a partner to this form of gambling."[44] Policymakers and academics frequently discuss whether governments should be in the gambling business, whether the lottery exploits the poor, and other policy issues. Considerable literature on those topics exists, but those interesting questions do not receive significant attention in this chapter. Rather, this chapter focuses more on the types of disputes lawyers might encounter in their role as legal counsel to an individual or organization.

Lottery disputes can take many forms.[45] Of course, one major issue is whether lotteries may legally operate at all. In early U.S. history, states often answered this question with a constitutional prohibition. However, now that those state constitutional prohibitions have largely been repealed or otherwise softened, a *federal*

---

39. *See, e.g.*, *IALottery Pull-Tabs*, Iowa Lottery, https://ialottery.com/Pages/Games-Pulltab/Pulltab GamesListing.aspx; *Pull Tab Games List*, Kan. Lottery, http://www.kslottery.com/Games/PullTabGamesList .aspx; *Tabs*, Idaho Lottery, https://www.idaholottery.com/games/tabs.

40. Cabot & Miller, *supra* note 2, at 680 n.6.

41. *See* Murphy v. NCAA, 138 S. Ct. 1461, 1484–85 (2018) (holding a federal law prohibiting states from authorizing sports betting is unconstitutional); *Sports Pick*, Del. Lottery, https://www.delottery .com/Sports-Lottery (explaining the types of sports wagers available through the Delaware Lottery); *see also Michigan's iLottery Program*, in La Fleur's, *supra* note 24, at 38 (discussing Michigan's Internet lottery program, which was "estimated to reach nearly $100 million in net revenues" for fiscal year 2018).

42. Cabot & Miller, *supra* note 2, at 681 n.7; *see also* Miller, *supra* note 33, at 20 ("[T]here continues to be a widely held feeling that Internet based gaming is inevitable—that it is not a matter of whether, but when, where, and how it will be implemented.").

43. La Fleur's, *supra* note 24, at 42.

44. Cabot & Miller, *supra* note 2, at 678; *accord* Delehanty, *supra* note 8, at 119 ("There are dozens of major policy issues that must be considered when establishing a lottery. Those considerations range from social issues to operational issues to profitability issues.").

45. One expert in the lottery industry has published a book that describes "cases, problems, and incidents . . . from more than forty lotteries on five continents." Delehanty, *supra* note 8, at intro. The disputes and incidents Delehanty describes provide additional helpful examples of scenarios in which lawyers might unexpectedly find themselves immersed. Delehanty's book purposely omits specific case-identifying details and is therefore a worthwhile contrast and supplement to this more specific chapter.

statutory question has recently arisen that calls into question fundamental aspects of the operation of lotteries.

The legal question at the heart of the dispute is whether a federal gambling law criminalizes all interstate transmission of bets or information related to bets. In 2011, the Illinois Lottery and New York Lottery asked the U.S. Department of Justice (DOJ) for an opinion analyzing this federal statute, known as the Wire Act, 18 U.S.C. § 1084(a). The Wire Act is a linguistically complicated statute[46] passed in 1961[47] that criminalizes some gambling activity. It does so with a multiclause sentence:

> Whoever being engaged in the business of betting or wagering knowingly uses a wire communication facility for the transmission in interstate or foreign commerce of bets or wagers or information assisting in the placing of bets or wagers on any sporting event or contest, or for the transmission of a wire communication which entitles the recipient to receive money or credit as a result of bets or wagers, or for information assisting in the placing of bets or wagers, shall be fined . . . or imprisoned not more than two years, or both.[48]

This lengthy sentence creates multiple prohibitions. The prohibitions criminalize knowingly using wire communication facilities in interstate commerce to place bets or wagers and to transmit information assisting in bets or wagers. One important modifier is the phrase "on any sporting event or contest." Much ink has been spilled analyzing just how much that phrase modifies.

In 2011, the two state lotteries asked the federal government whether the Wire Act prohibited them from selling lottery tickets on an intrastate basis over the Internet using out-of-state transaction processors.[49] The DOJ concluded that the Wire Act did not prohibit the transactions the lotteries proposed because the Wire Act applied only to bets and wagers on sporting events or contests.[50] In other words, the DOJ concluded the modifier "on any sporting event or contest" qualifies the *entire* Wire Act, not just one of its clauses. This conclusion was widely viewed as both a surprise and an opportunity. In response, many states launched online lottery ticket sales.

Recently, however, the DOJ changed course. In January 2019, it publicly released a new opinion abrogating what it said in 2011 and concluding that most of the Wire Act applies to *all* wagers.[51] The DOJ's current view is that the "sports modifier" only

---

46. *See* Anthony Cabot, *The Absence of a Comprehensive Federal Policy Toward Internet and Sports Wagering and a Proposal for Change*, 17 Vill. Sports & Ent'mt L.J. 271, 294 (2010) (calling the Wire Act an "abomination of the English language"); Elijah James Hayon Tredup, Note, *To the "Status-Quo" and Beyond: The Possible Unintended Consequences of the "Restoration of America's Wire Act,"* 6 UNLV Gaming L.J. 349, 349 (2016) (mentioning "the convoluted nature of the [Wire Act] and the headaches it has caused those who try to understand it").
47. Pub. L. No. 87-216, § 2, 75 Stat. 491 (codified at 18 U.S.C. § 1084[a]–[b] [2018]).
48. 18 U.S.C. § 1084(a) (2018).
49. *See* I. Nelson Rose, *The DOJ Gives States a Gift*, 4 UNLV Gaming L.J. 1, 3 (2012).
50. *See id.* at 1.
51. *See Reconsidering Whether the Wire Act Applies to Non-Sports Gambling*, 2018 WL 7080165, at *1 (Nov. 2, 2018) ("While the Wire Act is not a model of artful drafting, we conclude that the words of the statute are sufficiently clear and that all but one of its prohibitions sweep beyond sports gambling.").

qualifies the phrase "information assisting in the placing of bets or wagers," and the rest of the Wire Act therefore prohibits using wire communication facilities to transmit *all* bets or wagers of any kind.

Because the 2011 Opinion was sparked by an inquiry from state lotteries, the natural follow-up question to the DOJ's 2019 announcement was whether it now considered any state lottery that used out-of-state transaction processors, or that used transaction processors that incidentally cross state lines, to be violating federal law. Almost any data transmission that uses the Internet crosses state borders at least incidentally, as one commentator explains:

> If the traffic to a router or set of routers begins to slow down, the router sending a [data] packet to a next router will not send to the busy routers, it will send the packet to a less busy router. The selection of routers is not based on geographical location. Rather, it is based on electronic transmission performance and availability. Availability and transmission speed are higher between major network router installations that have larger capabilities than smaller local network router installations. Since most packets are transmitted in time measured in milliseconds, sending a packet 3,000 miles across the U.S. is, from a user['s] perspective, functionally equivalent to sending the packet 100 miles from one city to another.
>
> This dynamic method of routing packets has a consequence: for any specific packet, there is *no* guarantee that the packet will be transmitted through a specific router or set of routers, and there is *no* guarantee what actual physical links a particular packet may traverse. It all depends on traffic, router availability, and other considerations. In general, packet paths will vary and substantially all packetized data may include packets that crossed state lines at some point in their travels.[52]

As one example, the commentator tracked data packets used to access a Nevada government website from inside Nevada and found that one path traveled from Nevada to Arizona back to Nevada, while the other routed itself through California before returning to Nevada. The beginning and end points were always within the same state, but the data packets always crossed state lines.[53]

Fearing the possibility of prosecution under the DOJ's new opinion, the New Hampshire Lottery, which offers Internet lottery sales, filed a lawsuit asking the court to determine the authoritative meaning and correct interpretation of the Wire Act. In response, the DOJ stated it had not reached any conclusion about whether the Wire Act applied to state lotteries operating under their own state law but had begun to review that question. The DOJ further issued a memo explaining it would not commence any Wire Act prosecutions until it concluded its review of the lottery-specific question, announced its conclusion, and extended a ninety-day grace period for state lotteries to conform their operations to federal law.[54]

---

52. Russ Marsden, *Restore America's Wire Act: Cloud Killer?*, 21 Gaming L. Rev. 376, 382–83 (2017).
53. *See id.*
54. *See* Memo from the Deputy Attorney General to United States Attorneys (Apr. 8, 2019).

On June 3, 2019, the U.S. District Court for the District of New Hampshire issued a ruling that the Wire Act applied only to sporting events or contests.[55] The court found the 2018 Office of Legal Counsel (OLC) Opinion not to be consistent with the legislative history or language of the Wire Act. For the time being, lotteries can take comfort in the court's ruling. However, it is likely the government will appeal the decision. As of mid-2019, the issue is far from finally resolved.

While the Wire Act spawned an almost existential crisis for the New Hampshire Lottery (indeed, for much of the lottery industry), most lottery disputes are more isolated and do not go to the heart of whether the lottery can operate. For example, sometimes lottery players sue the lottery over a disputed jackpot, an unclaimed jackpot, allegations of fraud, or other legal requirements—such as a requirement that a winner forgo anonymity, a restriction on assignment of winnings, or a presentation requirement. Part III.B surveys these types of disputes.

While interactions with lottery players sometimes give rise to disputes, so do the back-end mechanisms and operations that make the lottery run. A dispute may arise with a lottery vendor, retailer, or contractor about whether their company can obtain or keep a license, whether their business can continue to operate, or whether their products or services have malfunctioned. Or, a *prospective* vendor who did not receive a contract award following a public competitive bidding process may take legal action to dispute the bid award. Part III.C surveys these kinds of disputes involving vendors, contractors, and other lottery-related companies.

But lottery-related disputes don't always involve the lottery as a party. Sometimes the dispute is solely between players. For example, people who play the lottery in a group or pool may find themselves disagreeing about who is entitled to share winnings on which tickets and in what proportions; a winning lottery ticket may be subject to disputed ownership, which can require analysis of property law principles; or lottery winnings may be subject to state debt offsets, which can lead to criminal charges for lottery players who seek to transfer winning tickets to avoid them. Part III.D surveys these situations where the dispute is about the lottery but not with the lottery.

The most important thing to remember in addressing lottery-related legal issues is that the vagaries of state law and administrative rules in whichever state the dispute arises can have a significant effect on the outcome. That common thread runs through every subpart below, and it is crucial for any lawyer to keep this in mind when wading into this potentially thorny and complicated area.

B. Disputes and Interactions between a Lottery and Players

Because lotteries so often advertise and pay large jackpots, the prospective damages in any litigation against a lottery are understandably attractive from a lawyer's

---

55. *See* Memorandum and Order, New Hampshire Lottery Commission v. Barr, Consolidated Case No. 19-cv-163-PB, Opinion No. 2019 DNH 091P (June 3, 2019). Chapter 9 on Internet gambling also considers the Wire Act issue.

standpoint. Perhaps that is one reason why players have often sued lotteries seeking prize money. Lottery players' complaints "take many forms."[56] The cases addressing entitlement to a prize at all—as opposed to the time for payment, the method of payment, or the assignability of payments—usually fall into one of several categories.

1. Players Who Do Not Meet the Prerequisites for Claiming a Prize

The first category involves players who appeared to have won a prize but did not satisfy a condition of collecting the money. For example, they may have submitted a prize claim after the game ended and the deadline to claim prizes from that game had passed.[57] Or, they may have possessed a winning ticket at one time but lost it or inadvertently destroyed it before presenting a prize claim and, therefore, could not collect a prize without physically presenting the ticket.[58]

2. Misprinted or Defective Tickets

The second category involves players who claim to have won a prize, but the lottery determines the player has a misprinted, defective, or illegible ticket that is not actually a winner.[59] One recent example occurred in South Carolina, where a programming error in the statewide computer system resulted in some lottery terminals at various retailers mostly dispensing, for two hours, tickets that appeared to have won the top prize amount. To make matters worse, the programming error occurred in late December 2017, leading one commentator to call it "the glitch that stole Christmas."[60] The South Carolina Education Lottery announced it would

---

56. CABOT & MILLER, *supra* note 2, at 702 n.2.
57. *See, e.g.*, DiGioia v. Div. of Special Revenue, No. CV930345340S, 1993 WL 526582, at *1 (Conn. Super. Ct. Dec. 8, 1993); Smith v. State Lottery Comm'n, 701 N.E.2d 926, 928 (Ind. Ct. App. 1998); Bailey v. Ky. Lottery Corp., 542 S.W.3d 305, 306–07 (Ky. Ct. App. 2018); Madara v. Commonwealth, 323 A.2d 401, 401–02 (Pa. Commw. Ct. 1974).
58. *See, e.g.*, Negrette v. Cal. State Lottery Comm'n, 26 Cal. Rptr. 2d 809, 809–10 (Ct. App. 1994) (player thought his winning ticket was not a winner and mailed it for entry in a second chance drawing instead of cashing it); Palese v. Del. State Lottery Office, No. 1546-N, 2006 WL 1875915, at *1 (Del. Ch. June 29, 2006) (ticket destroyed in laundry), *aff'd*, 2006 WL 3524054 (Del. Dec. 7, 2006); Miller v. State, 638 So. 2d 172, 172 (Fla. Dist. Ct. App. 1994) (lost ticket); Jackson v. Ind. State Lottery Comm'n, 585 N.E.2d 276, 277 (Ind. Ct. App. 1992) (ticket went through laundry, then lost in the mail); Fowles v. State, 867 P.2d 357, 358–59 (Kan. 1994) (lost ticket); Ramirez v. Bureau of State Lottery, 463 N.W.2d 245, 246 (Mich. Ct. App. 1990) (lost ticket); Karafa v. N.J. State Lottery Comm'n, 324 A.2d 97, 98–99 (N.J. Super. Ct. Ch. Div. 1974) (lost ticket); Bamberger v. Ohio State Lottery Comm'n, 685 N.E.2d 577, 578 (Ohio Ct. App. 1996) (lost ticket).
59. *See, e.g.*, Plourde v. Conn. Lottery Corp., No. X06CV980156557S, 2000 WL 1918014, at *2–3 (Conn. Super. Ct. Dec. 18, 2000); Curcio v. State, 164 So. 3d 750, 752–53 (Fla. Dist. Ct. App. 2015); Ga. Lottery Corp. v. Sumner, 529 S.E.2d 925, 928 (Ga. Ct. App. 2000); Ruggiero v. State Lottery Comm'n, 489 N.E.2d 1022, 1023 (Mass. App. Ct. 1986); Consola v. State, 922 N.Y.S.2d 638, 639–40 (App. Div. 2011); McLin v. State, No. 79AP-841, 1980 WL 353367, at *1 (Ohio Ct. App. Mar. 27, 1980); Valente v. R.I. Lottery Comm'n, 544 A.2d 586, 587 (R.I. 1988).
60. *See* Laurel Wamsley, *How the Glitch Stole Christmas: S.C. Lottery Says Error Caused Winning Tickets*, NPR (Dec. 28, 2017), https://www.npr.org/sections/thetwo-way/2017/12/28/574070736/how-the-glitch-stole-christmas-s-c-lottery-says-error-caused-winning-tickets.

refund players' ticket purchases but not pay the prize amounts on the defective or misprinted tickets caused by the programming error.[61] As of May 2018, two lawsuits were on file seeking full prize payments, not just refunds.[62]

3. Multiple Tickets Splitting a Jackpot Prize

The third category of player disputes involves players who purchased one of multiple jackpot winning tickets, collected a proportional share of the jackpot, and then later sought payment of an additional winning share when one of the other winning tickets went unclaimed.[63]

4. Players Who Did Not Double-Check Tickets

The fourth category involves players who believed they purchased or intended to purchase lottery tickets that were winners—but for whatever reason did not actually buy those tickets. This could be because they purchased tickets for a later drawing, believing they were valid for an earlier one,[64] or they purchased tickets on a subscription that wasn't effective when the player's numbers were selected.[65] Or it could be because the player's playslip was never converted into a valid ticket—due to transposed numbers, omitted numbers, other retail employee mistakes, equipment malfunctions, or even built-in security features.[66] Sometimes the player claims the retailer where he or she attempted to buy tickets, or the company that manufactures the equipment used, is liable rather than (or in addition to) the lottery itself.[67]

---

61. *See* Jacey Fortin, *Sorry, Lottery Winners. South Carolina Won't Pay, but Here's Your $1.*, N.Y. TIMES (May 31, 2018), https://www.nytimes.com/2018/05/31/us/south-carolina-lottery-glitch.html.

62. *See id.*

63. *See, e.g.*, Fullerton v. Dep't of Revenue Servs., 714 A.2d 1203, 1204–05 (Conn. 1998); Booker v. Rogers, 628 N.E.2d 1192, 1192–93 (Ill. App. Ct. 1994); Reifschneider v. State, 969 P.2d 875, 876 (Kan. 1998); Peters v. Ohio State Lottery Comm'n, 587 N.E.2d 290, 291 (Ohio 1992).

64. Driscoll v. State, 627 A.2d 1167, 1170 (N.J. Super. Ct. Law Div. 1993).

65. Paulsen v. Bureau of State Lottery, 421 N.W.2d 678, 680 (Mich. Ct. App. 1988) (subscription had ended); Estlow v. N.H. Sweepstakes Comm'n, 449 A.2d 1212, 1213 (N.H. 1982) (player's numbers selected between mailing subscription form and when the subscription was activated).

66. *See, e.g.*, Brown v. Cal. State Lottery Comm'n, 284 Cal. Rptr. 108, 110 (Ct. App. 1991) (terminal would not accept playslips and plaintiff arrived at another store too late to buy tickets that he asserted would have contained the winning numbers); Haynes v. Dep't of Lottery, 630 So. 2d 1177, 1178 (Fla. Dist. Ct. App. 1994) (player submitted ten different playslips but either the retail employee or computer system duplicated two of them, and the winning numbers were on one of the omitted slips); Dufrene v. La. Lottery Corp., 655 So. 2d 355, 356 (La. Ct. App. 1995) (machine would not accept playslip); Molina v. Games Mgmt. Servs., 449 N.E.2d 395, 396 (N.Y. 1983) (ticket was never properly processed by the contractor and sales agent); Stewart v. Tex. Lottery Comm'n, 975 S.W.2d 732, 734 (Tex. App. 1998); Kinnard v. Circle K Stores Inc., 966 S.W.2d 613, 615 (Tex. App. 1998) ("[O]ne of the playslips was processed twice."); Granton v. Wash. State Lottery Comm'n, 177 P.3d 745, 746–47, n.2 (Wash. Ct. App. 2008) (player attempted to buy tickets during the "draw break" between games); Thao v. Control Data Corp., 790 P.2d 1239, 1240 (Wash. Ct. App. 1990) (player submitted two different playslips seeking two different tickets but retail employee entered same playslip twice).

67. *See, e.g.*, *Brown*, 284 Cal. Rptr. at 111; *Haynes*, 630 So. 2d at 1179; *Driscoll*, 627 A.2d at 1169; *Molina*, 449 N.E.2d at 395–96; *Stewart*, 975 S.W.2d at 734; *Kinnard*, 966 S.W.2d at 615; *Thao*, 790 P.2d at 1240.

5. Prize Claims Involving Factors Beyond Relevant Law and Rules

The fifth category involves players who contended that something outside the face of the ticket, the relevant game rules, and state law made them a winner or increased their payout—promotional materials or the player's own ingenuity, for example.[68]

No matter the category, however, one result occurs repeatedly: when the player contends he or she won a prize but the lottery says otherwise, the player very rarely prevails. Of course, that is not to say players are never right or entitled to relief. But lawyers who are approached by a lottery player facing a possible prize dispute with a lottery must be aware that lotteries rarely lose these types of cases. Before taking on a case, the lawyer must identify and read the relevant statutes carefully. Administrative rules and game-specific rules often supplement the statutes. On the other hand, if a court concludes an administrative rule conflicts with a relevant statute, the statute controls the result no matter how strongly the rule may support the player's argument or legal theory.

In most instances, possession of a ticket is a fundamental—perhaps even the most important—requirement. That's why each of the cases in the first and fourth categories resulted in the player not receiving the prize they sought. Without a physical ticket, the lottery's security and validations processes either can't occur or become much more difficult to complete, the computerized barcode can't be scanned and compared with the lottery's electronic database, and other validation data contained on the ticket are unavailable.[69] Likewise, requiring a physical ticket prevents unsavory fraudsters from, for example, claiming prizes they did not actually win, while asserting they simply lost the ticket.

6. Players Suing the Lottery and Asserting Fraud

Some more recent lottery disputes have focused less on the existence of a ticket or the markings on the ticket and more on the lottery's operational workings. "One of the reasons historically given for lotteries periodically being banned is a concern about fraud."[70] And some players that become embroiled in disputes with lotteries have done so because they assert they have been defrauded.

For example, a lawsuit in Colorado contended "that the Lottery continues to sell scratch tickets for months after all the represented and advertised prizes have

---

68. *See, e.g.*, Collins v. Ky. Lottery Corp., 399 S.W.3d 449, 451 (Ky. Ct. App. 2012) (player claimed advertising established minimum prize was $25, when game rules established minimum prize was $20); Moody v. State Liquor & Lottery Comm'n, 843 A.2d 43, 45–46 (Me. 2004) ("the common definition of a wild card"); Jacobs v. State Lottery Comm'n, 801 N.E.2d 320, 320–21 (Mass. App. Ct. 2004) (promotional mats located at a retailer); Bretton v. State Lottery Comm'n, 673 N.E.2d 76, 77 (Mass. App. Ct. 1996) (advertisements); Triano v. Div. of State Lottery, 703 A.2d 333, 336 (N.J. Super. Ct. App. Div. 1997) (advertising brochure that did not distinguish between "*a* symbol" and "*the* symbol"); Keefe v. Ohio Lottery Comm'n, No. 06AP–14, 2006 WL 1990814, at *1 (Ohio Ct. App. July 18, 2006) (clerical error on lottery website).

69. *See* Delehanty, *supra* note 8, at 27 ("Most modern lotteries use a computer system to validate winning tickets. This is the most important line of defense against forgeries and frauds.").

70. Cabot & Miller, *supra* note 2, at 688 n.4.

already been awarded."[71] Specifically, the plaintiff purchased a scratch ticket "emblazoned with the words 'win up to $10,000,'" but "the Lottery had already awarded the last $10,000 grand prize seventy-two days earlier."[72] The lawsuit was unsuccessful because the court concluded the lottery was immune from the claim under the Colorado Governmental Immunity Act.[73] Nonetheless, this factual scenario—a lottery alleged to have sold scratch tickets after the last top prize was claimed—has occurred a few times over the last decade.[74] Some lotteries now automatically end sales of a particular ticket once a winner claims the last top prize.[75] And statutory changes have been proposed in at least one state to make such a practice a legal requirement rather than a voluntary decision on the lottery's part.[76]

Another recent dispute, couched in terms of fraud, occurred when a lottery player contended the zip codes of Powerball winners demonstrated the California Lottery and Multi-State Lottery Association were intentionally discriminating against him based on national origin and were fixing the result of Powerball drawings to prevent him from winning.[77] The case was thrown out in its entirety on a motion to dismiss.[78]

That lawsuit failed in part because "[l]otteries work diligently to maintain integrity and ensure their games are secure and fair"[79] and, as part of that effort, can never predict where a winner will hail from all the way down to the zip code. But there will always be people who try to compromise or cheat the system—sometimes from inside the lottery itself. Despite their best efforts, "lotteries periodically must deal with the actions and consequences of a rogue employee."[80] One early scheme involved "placing counterfeit balls in the machines used in the drawing."[81] Another involved a drawing director who entered, and selected, winning tickets under the alias of a friend.[82]

The most recent and most high-tech employee fraud, however, went on for several years before officials apprehended its perpetrator. The saga began when, "On December 23, 2010, someone purchased a Hot Lotto ticket from a Des Moines

---

71. Robinson v. Colo. State Lottery Div., 179 P.3d 998, 1001 (Colo. 2008).
72. *Id.* at 1002.
73. *Id.* at 1001.
74. *See generally* CABOT & MILLER, *supra* note 2, at 689 n.5.
75. *See He "Just Went With It" & Won $1 Million Prize*, IALOTTERYBLOG (Jan. 9, 2014), https://www.ialotteryblog.com/2014/01/he-just-went-with-it-won-1-million-prize.html ("Hernandez's prize claim triggered the $20 Lifetime Riches game to be removed from sale. As part of [our] standard procedures, we end sales in our scratch games . . . when the last top prize has been claimed.").
76. *See* Matthew Walberg, *Illinois Lottery Practice of Selling Tickets After Top Prizes Are Gone Could End Under Proposed Law Change*, CHI. TRIB. (June 6, 2018), https://www.chicagotribune.com/news/local/breaking/ct-met-lottery-top-prizes-illinois-law-20180605-story.html.
77. Hussein v. Multi-State Lottery Ass'n, No. 18-cv-01848-JSW, Order Granting Defendants' Motions to Dismiss at 2–3 (N.D. Cal. Aug. 13, 2018) ("Mr. Hussein's discrimination claim is based on his allegations that Defendants purposefully select winners in predominantly 'white' zip codes.").
78. *Id.* at 11.
79. DELEHANTY, *supra* note 8, at 1.
80. *Id.* at 93.
81. Commonwealth v. Katsafanas, 464 A.2d 1270, 1273 (Pa. Super. Ct. 1983).
82. United States v. Valavanis, 689 F.2d 626, 627 (6th Cir. 1982).

convenience store and won the jackpot of the Hot Lotto drawing on December 29. The Hot Lotto jackpot for that drawing was $16.5 million."[83] That significant prize went unclaimed for nearly a year, until lawyers representing a Belizean blind trust presented it "a little more than one hour before the lottery's one-year deadline."[84] Because Iowa law does not allow winners to claim prizes anonymously, the Iowa Lottery refused to pay the prize unless the trust disclosed the winning ticket's chain of ownership.[85] Unwilling to forgo anonymity, however, the trust's lawyers later unconditionally withdrew the prize claim.[86] The money was never paid.

Withdrawing the prize claim did not end the matter, however. Suspicious about the circumstances of the claim—the insistence on anonymity, the offshore location of the trust, a last-ditch effort to pay the entire prize to charity, and contact from a Canadian citizen who provided the ticket's security code but did not match known details of the ticket purchase—the Iowa Lottery asked state law enforcement officials to conduct an investigation.[87] The trail eventually led to Eddie Tipton, "a security expert employed by the Multi-State Lottery Association," who "wrote the [random number generator] program that produced the winning number combinations for a variety of lottery games."[88] Because he was involved in producing the software code used to generate winning numbers, "Tipton was ineligible to play the lottery."[89] The Iowa Supreme Court later recognized the Iowa Lottery's hesitance to pay the prize was prudent in light of the "very high" likelihood that "the undisclosed purchaser was not a qualified purchaser and the attempt to redeem the ticket was a fraudulent attempt to obtain an illegal payment."[90]

Tipton eventually confessed to buying the 2010 ticket. But the story went much deeper than that. Tipton bought that ticket because, when originally writing the random number generator software code years earlier, he had embedded several lines of code that were activated only on certain dates. On those dates, the added lines of code allowed him to duplicate the conditions of a drawing beforehand, then record results and buy tickets (or have friends and family buy tickets) for the upcoming drawing with all the combinations his "duplicate" drawing generated.

---

83. State v. Tipton, 897 N.W.2d 653, 662 (Iowa 2017).
84. *Id.* at 663.
85. *Id.* at 662 ("The lottery will not pay the prize on a winning ticket if the ticket was not validly purchased, legally presented, or legally possessed or acquired."); *see* Iowa Code § 99G.34(5) (2018) (subjecting "the names and addresses of prize winners" to Iowa's open records law); Cabot & Miller, *supra* note 2, at 688–89 ("Lottery officials refused to release the prize because the principals in the trust refused to give their identities, as required by Iowa law.").
86. *Tipton*, 897 N.W.2d at 663.
87. *See id.* at 662–63.
88. *Id.* at 663.
89. *Id.* at 663; *see* Iowa Code § 99G.31(2)(*h*) (2018); Cabot & Miller, *supra* note 2, at 689 ("An investigation revealed that the ticket had in fact been purchased by a man who worked as the director of information security for [the Multi-State Lottery Association]. Iowa law bars such employees from purchasing tickets or claiming prizes.").
90. *Tipton*, 897 N.W.2d at 687.

Tipton's "effort to unlawfully obtain millions of dollars in lottery winnings is a serious crime."[91] The discovery and publication of his criminal activity, however, has spawned at least three civil lawsuits seeking damages because of Tipton's fraud.

Larry Dawson, an Iowa resident who won a $9 million Hot Lotto jackpot in 2011—the next jackpot awarded in that game after December 29, 2010—brought the first civil lawsuit in 2016.[92] Dawson sued both the Iowa Lottery, which paid his initial prize in 2011, and the Multi-State Lottery Association, which employed Tipton until his participation in buying the 2010 ticket was revealed. "The lawsuit states that if Tipton hadn't rigged the game, the $16.5 million jackpot would have been added to the pool Dawson won."[93] Notably, Dawson won the pool over four months and thirty-six drawings later, after the jackpot had reset and built up again.

Dawson's lawsuit was not yet resolved at the time this chapter went to publication. The case is important because while it bears some resemblance to the other player disputes discussed in this chapter, it also has some distinguishing characteristics. All sides involved in the lawsuit have debated and briefed the extent to which previous lottery cases are relevant, material, and persuasive. Of course, they disagree firmly on the ultimate question: whether Dawson is entitled to the money Tipton unsuccessfully attempted to claim. As this chapter emphasizes, the language in and interplay among the relevant statutes and rules is crucial in answering that question.

Dale Culler, an Iowa resident who, unlike Dawson, did not win any previous lottery jackpots, brought a second civil lawsuit in 2017.[94] Culler's lawsuit sought certification as a class action; the class would consist of all those who bought tickets for games on dates in which Tipton's software was active.[95] The lawsuit seeks a court order allowing any person who bought a ticket for a lottery game on one of those dates, where the winning numbers were drawn with a computer using Tipton's software, to obtain a refund of their ticket purchase plus interest.[96] In other words, Culler's lawsuit does not seek affirmative payment of a prize, but only a refund. Although the lawsuit was filed in Iowa, the proposed class includes players from other states where Tipton's code may have affected drawings. Like the *Dawson* case, the *Culler* case was still pending at the time this chapter went to publication.

The third civil lawsuit is in Colorado and presents yet another factual wrinkle. Amir Massihzadeh, the plaintiff, won the in-state Colorado Lotto in 2005 on the same day as two associates of Tipton, splitting the jackpot three ways. His lawsuit asserts "that he's entitled to the other two-thirds of the prize because the other tickets

---

91. *Id.* at 688.
92. Disclosure: the author is counsel of record for the Iowa Lottery Authority in the *Dawson* case.
93. Michael Addady, *Lottery Winner Sues Saying Jackpot Should Have Been Bigger*, Fortune (Feb. 4, 2016), http://fortune.com/2016/02/04/lottery-winner-lawsuit/.
94. *Lawsuit Says Colorado Lottery Players Should Get Refund for Rigged Games*, Denver Post (Jan. 5, 2017), https://www.denverpost.com/2017/01/04/colorado-lottery-refund-rigged-games/.
95. *See id.*
96. *See id.* Notably, Culler sued only the Multi-State Lottery Association, not any individual state lottery.

were purchased through Tipton's conspiracy and should be invalid."[97] By contrast, Massihzadeh's ticket is valid because unlike the Tipton associates, he bought only quick-pick tickets.[98]

The Colorado district court granted a motion to dismiss the case, finding that the later discovery of Tipton's fraud did not renegotiate Massihzadeh's ticket or entitlement to a prize.[99] The court further found that the Colorado Lottery was discharged of liability under a Colorado statute.[100] It criticized Massihzadeh's assertion that he was entitled to more prize money because of fraud as "disingenuous and circular" because he, too, benefited (albeit inadvertently) from Tipton's criminal acts.[101] The court hypothesized that, had Tipton's criminal acts not occurred, the winning numbers for the drawing might have been different, and so Massihzadeh may have won nothing at all.[102] Massihzadeh appealed the ruling, and the Colorado Court of Appeals had not yet ruled on the case at the time this chapter went to publication.

Whatever the result of the appeal, the *Massihzadeh* case presents one important contrast with the *Dawson* case. Massihzadeh expressly asserted that, notwithstanding Tipton's software code, the drawing in which Massihzadeh won was valid and complied with all applicable laws and rules[103]—a necessary pleading step because if the drawing was invalidated by fraud, Massihzadeh himself would likely not be entitled to the winnings he had already collected.[104] By contrast, Dawson's case rests on the assertion that Tipton's fraud invalidated the Hot Lotto drawing on December 29, 2010—which he contends required the money to roll to the next drawing and eventually to him, rather than being removed from the prize pool. Tipton's software was the same in both states, so it remains an open question whether a "drawing," as defined in the relevant administrative rule or game rule, could occur in one state but not the other. It remains to be seen whether the Iowa court, where Dawson's case is pending, will find it necessary to resolve that legal question.

One important aspect common to "many of the cases where players sue the lottery" seeking prize money is a requirement to exhaust administrative remedies or a limitation on the available causes of action.[105] For example, some courts have clarified that challenges to lottery prize payments or refusals are only reviewable

---

97. Ryan J. Foley, *Winner Sues Colorado Lottery for Millions over Fixed Jackpot*, Associated Press (Oct. 5, 2017), https://www.apnews.com/ccc0b1bd8f3142f48e4c32ca37dfed22.
98. *See id.*
99. Order on Motion to Dismiss at 5, Massihzadeh v. Solano, No. 17CV33699 (Colo. Dist. Ct. Feb. 13, 2018).
100. *Id.* at 5–6.
101. *Id.* at 4 n.2.
102. *See id.*
103. Complaint and Jury Demand at 11, Massihzadeh, No. 17CV33699 (Colo. Dist. Ct. Oct. 4, 2017).
104. *See* Order on Motion to Dismiss at 3 n.1, Massihzadeh, No. 17CV33699 (Colo. Dist. Ct. Feb. 13, 2018) (questioning if the other winning tickets for the drawing were void and "whether [Massihzadeh's] own ticket could be voided" too).
105. Cabot & Miller, *supra* note 2, at 701–02 n.1.

under the relevant administrative procedure act and that freestanding causes of action (like breach of contract or negligence) are not cognizable.[106] A similar argument animates part of the defense to the claims in *Dawson*.

Even when freestanding claims are cognizable outside of administrative proceedings, courts sometimes hold that lotteries are immune or otherwise discharged of liability.[107] A relatively common provision across the country discharges the applicable lottery of liability upon making a prize payment.[108] The Colorado court dismissed the *Massihzadeh* case on that ground, and the Iowa Lottery raised it in the *Dawson* case as well. Any lawyer undertaking a prize dispute on a player's behalf should be cognizant of these potential obstacles.

7. Prizewinners Seeking Anonymity

Once a winner is in fact entitled to a prize, the level of anonymity available, if any, can complicate the prize-claim process. As one court recently quipped, a person who wins the lottery sometimes "becomes an instant celebrity."[109] Two recent examples illustrate contrasting approaches to anonymous prize claims.

The first is Iowa's statutory requirement that winner names and addresses are open records.[110] "The idea behind the law requiring disclosure of winners' information is to help ensure that the lottery is not being rigged."[111] That language was instrumental to uncovering the Tipton fraud discussed in this chapter because it foreclosed the possibility of an anonymous claimant or a Belizean trust claiming the

---

106. *See, e.g.*, Smith v. Jones, 497 N.E.2d 738, 741 (Ill. 1986); Fowles v. State, 867 P.2d 357, 362 (Kan. 1994) ("Plaintiff's sole action against the Lottery here is based on judicial review of an agency action . . . ; he may not maintain a separate action for breach of contract."); *Bretton*, 673 N.E.2d at 80 (rejecting common law counts and finding "no issue presented . . . that is appropriate for direct judicial determination" outside of judicial review); *Triano*, 703 A.2d at 340 ("[T]he interests of justice do not require by-passing the administrative remedies available to plaintiffs."). Some cases do not involve challenges to the available causes of action, but merely acknowledge through the discussion that administrative proceedings and appeals were the correct path. *See* Jacobs v. State Lottery Comm'n, 801 N.E.2d 320, 321–22 (Mass. App. Ct. 2004) (noting the player "pursued various administrative avenues"); *Granton*, 177 P.3d at 748 (reviewing "an administrative action" by applying "the Washington Administrative Procedure Act [APA] standards" [footnote omitted]).

107. *See, e.g.*, Rasche v. Lane, 150 F. Supp. 3d 934, 944–45 (N.D. Ill. 2015) (Eleventh Amendment immunity); *Brown*, 284 Cal. Rptr. at 112–13; Koehlinger v. State Lottery Comm'n, 933 N.E.2d 534, 542 (Ind. Ct. App. 2010) (applying essentially an economic loss rule to preclude tort claims against a lottery); *Molina*, 449 N.E.2d at 396 ("The State and the contractor are both exempt from liability. . . ."). Depending on the player's claim, immunity may also extend to contractors or vendors. *See* GTECH Corp. v. Steele, 549 S.W.3d 768, 804 (Tex. App. 2018) (extending the state lottery's sovereign immunity to some claims brought against a company that printed scratch tickets).

108. *See, e.g.*, Colo. Rev. Stat. § 44-40-113(4) (2018); Iowa Code § 99G.31(2)(f) (2018); Kan. Stat. § 74-8720(h) (2018); Ohio Rev. Code § 3770.07(G) (2018); Or. Admin. Code § 177-046-0160(1) (2018).

109. Geiger v. State, 174 A.3d 954, 961 (Md. Ct. Spec. App. 2017).

110. Iowa Code § 99G.34(5) (2018); *see also Can Prize Winners Be Anonymous?*, IALotteryBlog (Nov. 7, 2008), https://www.ialotteryblog.com/2008/11/can-prize-winne.html.

111. *What the Law Says about Lottery Winners' Info*, IALotteryBlog (Sept. 3, 2014), https://www.ialotteryblog.com/2014/09/what-the-law-says-about-lottery-winners-info.html.

prize without disclosing the identity of the ticket's purchaser, the ticket's chain of ownership, or the trust's beneficiaries.[112]

On the other hand, some subscribe to the notion—although others call it an urban legend[113]—that a "lottery curse" haunts winners of significant prizes. The purported curse occurs because publicizing the winner's identity and their newfound wealth causes them to become a target for fraudsters and swindlers.[114] To avoid saddling winners with such a curse—but more importantly (and more likely), to promote individual privacy—a minority of states allow anonymous prize claims. Those states that allow some level of anonymity usually do not allow *complete* anonymity. Generally, the relevant law requires the winner to provide all information to the lottery so that the lottery can conduct security and validations checks, but it then prevents the lottery from further disseminating names, contact information, and likenesses.[115] Further, the law may provide that only winners above a certain prize threshold can elect to remain anonymous.[116]

One anonymity provision recently came into play in New Hampshire. In January 2018, a Powerball drawing resulted in one New Hampshire winner, entitled to an annuity jackpot of $560 million. The winner contacted the New Hampshire Lottery and signed her own name on the ticket—allowing the lottery to perform its security and validation processes and check for any state debt offsets she might have—but wished to keep her name and hometown from being disclosed to the public. She filed a lawsuit seeking a court order that she could remain anonymous.[117] The court concluded that, based on a New Hampshire statute allowing exceptions to the general open records law for "files whose disclosure would constitute [an] invasion of privacy," she could remain anonymous, although the lottery could disclose her hometown.[118] The case serves as a contrast to states where winners' names must be public, and it demonstrates how state-specific laws and rules can control the outcome, depending on where the dispute occurs.

---

112. *See* State v. Tipton, 897 N.W.2d 653, 662–63 (Iowa 2017) (discussing the attempt to claim prize money through a Belizean blind trust); Kim St. Onge, *Why You Can't Remain Anonymous If You Win the Lottery*, KCCI (Jan. 15, 2016), https://www.kcci.com/article/why-you-can-t-remain-anonymous-if-you-win-the-lottery/6916850 ("Iowa lottery officials reference the Eddie Tipton Hot Lotto investigation as a prime example of why transparency is necessary.").

113. *See* CABOT & MILLER, *supra* note 2, at 727 n.5.

114. *See* Eduardo Montemayor, Comment, *Winner's Curse: The Necessity of Estate Planning for Texas Lottery Winners*, 7 ESTATE PLANNING & CMTY. PROP. L.J. 363, 374 (2014) ("The downfall of most lottery winners is the lack of anonymity that accompanies the collection of the prize. The publicity may present its own dangers. . . ." [footnote omitted]).

115. *See, e.g.*, OHIO REV. CODE § 3770.07(A)(1) (2018); TEX. GOV'T CODE § 466.411 (2018); W. VA. CODE § 29-22-15a (2018).

116. *See* TEX. GOV'T CODE § 466.411 (2018); W. VA. CODE § 29-22-15a (2018).

117. *See* Michelle Miller, *New Hampshire Powerball Winner Files Lawsuit to Remain Anonymous*, CBS NEWS (Feb. 6, 2018), https://www.cbsnews.com/news/new-hampshire-powerball-winner-files-lawsuit-to-remain-anonymous/.

118. *See* Order at 15, Doe v. N.H. Lottery Comm'n, No. 2018-CV-00036 (N.H. Super. Ct. Mar. 12, 2018); Camila Domonoske, *Call Her Jane Dough: New Hampshire Lottery Winner Can Stay Anonymous, Court Says*, NPR (Mar. 13, 2018), https://www.npr.org/sections/thetwo-way/2018/03/13/593141325/call-her-jane-dough-new-hampshire-lottery-winner-can-stay-anonymous-court-says.

8. Timing and Method of Payment

Once a lottery and a player agree on whether the player is a winner, in what amount, and what level of anonymity (if any) is available, the next possible area of dispute involves *how* they are paid. Lotteries pay most of the largest prizes either in yearly installments or in one present-value lump sum, at the player's option.[119] However, where there is no option, where the option results in vastly different prize amounts, or where the method and timing are unclear, litigation has sometimes resulted. For example, a Wisconsin winner asserted that a prize "paid in 25 installments" meant monthly rather than yearly installments.[120] Similarly, a New York winner asserted that the state's method of payment—a partial cash payment and the balance by way of annuity, which the player could not vary or opt out of—violated her due process rights.[121]

In both instances, the player was unsuccessful. Building on one of this subchapter's themes, the lottery often has significant (statutory) authority to dictate (by rule) the means of paying prizes, and when it does, courts often defer to the lottery's determinations. Along with limiting remedies against a lottery to an administrative process or judicial review, the method-of-payment question is another example of deference to the lottery's policy and fiscal choices.

A related category of cases involves "the prohibition that exists in many states against allowing a player to assign his winnings to another."[122] Usually this prohibition intends "to protect the Lottery from administrative hassles" inherent in collecting, monitoring, and verifying the intended (and possibly changing) payee of an annuity prize.[123] For these prohibitions to be effective, however, they must have been enacted *before* the winner first claims their prize.[124]

Numerous other cases have addressed anti-assignment provisions with mixed results.[125] Most importantly, however—and in keeping with the theme of this chapter—sometimes later-enacted statutes or rules can affect the outcome.[126]

Although this chapter focuses on disputes, not all interactions lawyers may have with a lottery are adversarial. Lawyers can be instrumental in advising

---

119. For example, in Iowa, the "lottery may offer cash prizes, annuitized installment prizes, and prizes with cash or annuity payment options available to the winners." Iowa Admin. Code r. 531-20.6 (2018).
120. Brown v. State, 602 N.W.2d 79, 81 (Wis. Ct. App. 1999).
121. Zapata v. Quinn, 707 F.2d 691, 692 (2d Cir. 1983) (per curiam).
122. Cabot & Miller, *supra* note 2, at 702 n.4.
123. Midland States Life Ins. Co. v. Cardillo, 797 N.E.2d 11, 16 (Mass. App. Ct. 2003).
124. *See* Peterson v. D.C. Lottery & Charitable Games Control Bd., 673 A.2d 664, 669 (D.C. 1996) (holding a regulation enacted in 1992 did not prevent a player from assigning his 1986 winnings).
125. *See, e.g.*, Singer Friedlander Corp. v. State Lottery Comm'n, 670 N.E.2d 144 (Mass. 1996); Singer Asset Fin. Co. v. State, 714 A.2d 317 (N.J. Super Ct. App. Div. 1998); Woodbridge Partners Grp., Inc. v. Ohio Lottery Comm'n, 650 N.E.2d 498 (Ohio Ct. App. 1994); State *ex rel.* Meyers v. Ohio State Lottery Comm'n, 517 N.E.2d 1029 (Ohio Ct. App. 1986); Tex. Lottery Comm'n v. First State Bank of DeQueen, 325 S.W.3d 628 (Tex. 2010); Lemieux v. Tri-State Lotto Comm'n, 666 A.2d 1170 (Vt. 1995); Converse v. State Lottery Comm'n, 783 P.2d 1116 (Wash. Ct. App. 1989).
126. *See* B P 7 v. Bureau of State Lottery, 586 N.W.2d 117, 118–19 (Mich. Ct. App. 1998) (finding two appeals were moot because the legislature "substantially amended" the relevant statute and, in doing so, answered the dispositive legal question).

prizewinners about how they should claim the prize, serving as a spokesperson for a winner who is not used to being in the public spotlight, and assisting in setting up an LLC, trust, or other organization to handle the money once the player receives it. They can also assist in addressing corollary tax issues or estate planning issues.[127]

C. Disputes Involving a Contractor, Vendor, or Other Business

Although lottery revenues ultimately flow to state treasuries or funds, operating the lottery is undoubtedly a collaborative enterprise. To enable ticket sales at more locations than just lottery offices, lotteries issue licenses to retailers across their respective states. Of course, should those licensed retailers act inappropriately—by not paying prizes correctly, selling tickets to underage players, or failing to satisfy financial obligations—the lottery can also suspend or revoke the license. Likewise, lotteries often collaborate with outside companies to obtain technology and equipment that helps the lottery run (such as software, network services, terminals, or monitors) and contract with outside companies to print scratch or pull tab tickets. Although many lotteries design their own game concepts, they may also contract with a marketing company or lottery consultant to do so.[128] These third-party relationships can generate disputes when a license is suspended, revoked, or denied; when the lottery selects one company and not another to contract with; or even when the state legislature passes a law that affects ongoing relationships a lottery might have.

One high-profile example occurred in Iowa in the early 2000s. "Following revenue shortfalls in 2000 and 2001, the Iowa General Assembly authorized" the Iowa Lottery to establish a game called TouchPlay.[129] A TouchPlay machine was essentially a glorified pull tab dispenser, which used "flashing lights and captivating sounds" as an elaborate way of revealing whether the lottery ticket the player received was a winner.[130]

The Iowa Lottery did not own any of the machines but simply contracted with a manufacturer to provide the machines and with licensed retailers to put the machines in their businesses, collect data from the machines, and administer the prize payouts.[131] The endeavor started small, beginning with 30 machines in the entire state

---

127. *See* Cabot & Miller, *supra* note 2, at 727 n.4 ("The lawyer whose client wins a substantial lottery prize has a number of issues to consider.").
128. One recent case involved a plaintiff's claim that "the Lottery stole his idea for a game that he invented." Leone v. Ohio Lottery Comm'n, No. 13AP-307, 2013 WL 5675367, at *1 (Ohio Ct. App. Oct. 17, 2013). The plaintiff's claim was unsuccessful because the plaintiff's game idea "had no rules, odds of winning, probabilities, or prize structure," and therefore "was so general and non-specific as to be of no value to the Lottery." *Id.* at *4.
129. Hawkeye Commodity Promotions, Inc. v. Vilsack, 486 F.3d 430, 435 (8th Cir. 2007).
130. *Id.*
131. *See id.*

in May 2003, but it rapidly expanded and featured 6,400 machines at over 3,800 businesses by April 2006.[132]

Some Iowans became concerned that the TouchPlay game constituted a rapid and unwarranted expansion of gambling in the state.[133] Their concerns occurred because these machines became ubiquitous across the state, yet they resembled slot machines[134] typically found only in casinos. Accordingly, the governor ordered a moratorium on new TouchPlay licenses, and eventually the legislature repealed the program, effective in May 2006.[135]

Many of the licensees who had invested in the program, including some companies that were organized solely as TouchPlay distributors or licensees, asserted the legislative repeal deprived them of the ability to realize their investment. In one federal case, the TouchPlay operators argued the legislative repeal violated the U.S. Constitution, specifically the Contracts Clause.[136] That federal case was one of many lawsuits that Iowa faced in 2006 and 2007.

The TouchPlay saga resulted in mixed success for the Iowa Lottery. The TouchPlay operators did not prevail in federal litigation, but in parallel cases in state court, "a series of settlements were reached between the state and various vendors."[137] The TouchPlay experience also had lasting effects. When a new Iowa Lottery CEO took over in 2009, the agency was "still reeling . . . from legislative action in 2006 that banned" TouchPlay, and the CEO later reflected upon the goal he adopted when starting his tenure: to "improve the lottery's image and grow existing lines of business."[138] The TouchPlay experience provides an important reminder that "public perceptions about the appropriate scope of gambling" are a key factor in continued legislative support for lotteries.[139] It also shows the significant issues and revenues at stake when the various participants who collaborate to run a lottery reach an impasse about some aspect of their collaboration.

Another place an impasse might occur is if the lottery denies an application for a lottery license or decides to suspend or revoke a license it has already issued. Denials can occur where an applicant does not pass a background check or where the lottery determines the applicant is otherwise unsuitable.[140] A finding of unsuitability might happen if the applicant or retailer appears to have trouble complying with the requirement that only people above the legal age may purchase tickets or

---

132. Id.
133. See id. at 436.
134. See id. at 435.
135. See id. at 436.
136. Id. ("Hawkeye's main argument is that [the repeal] 'completely destroyed' Hawkeye's contracts with the Lottery, and with over 200 Iowa businesses.").
137. CABOT & MILLER, supra note 2, at 710 n.1.
138. RICH, supra note 26, at 69.
139. Keith C. Miller, The Iowa Lottery's TouchPlay Debacle, 11 GAMING L. REV. 88, 88 (2007).
140. See Shree Swaminarayam Corp. v. Ohio Lottery Comm'n, 63 N.E.3d 768, 770 (Ohio Ct. App. 2016) ("When an applicant for a lottery sales agent license . . . is a director, officer, manager, or controlling shareholder of a corporation, that individual's character or general fitness can be considered as part of the application. . . .").

if the applicant or retailer has a history of not meeting financial obligations or of other lottery-related misconduct.[141] In general, lotteries possess wide discretion to approve or deny and suspend or revoke licenses, and they have broad authority to determine whether issuing a license or allowing a licensee to maintain their license would be in the public's best interest and convenience.[142] One court described the lottery's discretion as so wide that it essentially "gave the [lottery] commissioner the complete power and authority to determine whom the [lottery] will deal with or through."[143]

Of course, the ability to sell lottery tickets offers a clear benefit to almost any business. Especially when jackpots are high, demand for lottery tickets can drive traffic to a store and perhaps result in customers making some other incidental purchases.[144] But lotteries will not hesitate to decline licensure or suspend or revoke a license if a retail partner demonstrates that they "cannot be trusted."[145]

Apart from retailers, a lottery's relationship with a contractor or vendor can also generate a dispute. One way that can happen is at the very front end of creating the business relationship. Because they are state-run businesses, lotteries are usually subject to competitive bidding laws that govern the process by which a

---

141. *See, e.g.*, United States v. Patel, 370 F.3d 108, 113 (1st Cir. 2004) ("[T]he Massachusetts Lottery Commission had revoked Patel's lottery license because of his repeated failure to pay the Commission. . . . Patel owed the Commission over $40,000."); *In re* Gammo, Inc., 180 B.R. 485, 486 (Bankr. E.D. Mich. 1995) (noting the lottery suspended a license because the licensee missed a payment of several thousand dollars); Storcella v. State, 686 A.2d 789, 792 (N.J. Super. Ct. App. Div. 1997) (finding it reasonable for the lottery to deny a license application because "past criminal activity in conducting a bookmaking operation on the very premises for which the license is sought adversely reflects upon [an applicant's] moral character and will directly affect the public perception of the integrity of the Lottery"); *Shree Swaminarayam*, 63 N.E.3d at 771 (noting the lottery denied a license application because of the applicant's past conduct).

142. *See, e.g.*, Iowa Code §§ 99G.24(7)–(9) (setting forth guidelines for initial licensure), 99G.27 (listing multiple grounds for suspension, cancellation, revocation, or termination of a lottery license, including "conduct prejudicial to public confidence in the lottery" and conduct likely to result in injury to the lottery's reputation); N.Y. Tax Law § 1607 (2018); Ohio Rev. Code § 3770.05(C)–(D) (2018); N.J. Admin. Code § 17:20-5.1 (2018).

143. Bukhtia v. Bureau of State Lottery, 475 N.W.2d 475, 477 (Mich. Ct. App. 1991).

144. *See* Cabot & Miller, *supra* note 2, at 681 n.7 ("[Lottery retailers] derive substantial revenue from sales of lottery tickets, and sales of their other goods from ticket purchasers who shop there.").

145. *See, e.g.*, Hohmann v. GTECH Corp., 910 F. Supp. 2d 400, 404 (D. Conn. 2012) (noting a lottery revoked a retailer's license when the owner's wife presented a ticket for payment that was purchased from his store and had been altered after being scratched, to appear as though it was a winner); Parsley v. State, 119 N.E.3d 131, 133 (Ind. Ct. App. 2019) ("The Lottery had suspended [a store]'s license to sell tickets from May 24, 2014 to September 26, 2014, for paperwork issues. . . ."); *Bukhtia*, 475 N.W.2d at 476 (noting the lottery initiated revocation proceedings because a store clerk "was accused of cashing a winning lottery ticket at . . . less than its face value"); *Storcella*, 686 A.2d at 791 (concluding the Lottery properly considered "the nature of the activities underlying the crimes committed by [the applicant] and the impact that licensing someone who had conducted an illegal lottery" could have "on the public's perception of the integrity of the Lottery"); *Shree Swaminarayam*, 63 N.E.3d at 771–72 ("While Patel appeared remorseful over his part in the prior license revocations, the director could rationally find that Patel's inaction so violated the honesty and integrity of the lottery system that granting . . . a license would undermine the public trust in the lottery.").

government can obtain goods and services.[146] Competitive bidding is intended to prevent "favoritism in the awarding of government contracts," which can be lucrative.[147] Competitive bidding also aims "to maximize competition for government contracts in order to obtain the best work or product at the lowest practicable price."[148] Relatedly, because running a lottery today requires highly technical software programming and specialized equipment, not every state can develop its own independent expertise in these areas.[149] At the convergence of these two strands lies a category of bid disputes.

In general, when seeking specialized goods or services, lotteries issue public requests for proposals, and any interested and qualified bidder may submit a bid. The request for proposal describes what goods or services the lottery needs and what features the lottery wants those goods or services to have.[150] Typically, a reviewer or panel of reviewers evaluates all bids, scores them, and makes a recommendation to the person or people who make the final decision about which bid or bids should be awarded a contract.[151] Once a winning bid is selected, the lottery can then negotiate a final contract with the bidder or vendor.[152]

Multiple points in this competitive bidding process can generate a later dispute. The overarching categorization of most bid disputes is that an unsuccessful bidder believes the process was not fair.[153] But the details may vary. For example, unsuccessful bidders may contend that the process favored the bidder that

---

146. *See, e.g.*, Nat'l Harbor GP, LLC v. District of Columbia, 121 F. Supp. 3d 11, 14 (D.D.C. 2015) ("The District [of Columbia] uses procurement contracts for a range of government services performed by outside entities. . . . This includes operations for the District of Columbia Lottery Board."); State v. GTECH Corp., 816 So. 2d 648, 653 (Fla. Dist. Ct. App. 2001) (holding the lottery could not ignore the competitive bidding process set forth in state law); Datatrol, Inc. v. State Purchasing Agent, 400 N.E.2d 1218, 1225 (Mass. 1980) ("[T]he Lottery as a public agency has a duty to award contracts in accord with law."); Tex. Lottery Comm'n v. Scientific Games Int'l, Inc., 99 S.W.3d 376, 383 (Tex. App. 2003) ("The [Lottery] Commission is subject to a competitive-bidding statute.").
147. *Datatrol*, 400 N.E.2d at 1225; *see GTECH*, 816 So. 2d at 653 (noting the contract at issue was "a multi-million dollar contract for furnishing the gaming system that makes Florida's lottery work").
148. *Tex. Lottery Comm'n*, 99 S.W.3d at 382.
149. *See id.* at 379 ("The design and manufacture of instant-ticket [lottery] games is a highly specialized business. Worldwide, there are only three or four companies qualified to produce instant tickets to Texas's specifications.").
150. *See Datatrol*, 400 N.E.2d at 1220 ("[T]he Lottery issued an Invitation to Bid and Request for Proposals (RFP) for a lottery computer system. . . . The [RFP] sets out a description of the purposes of the system, the jobs it was supposed to do, and the support services to be furnished by the bidder.").
151. *See, e.g., GTECH*, 816 So. 2d at 650 ("[P]roposals were submitted to an evaluation committee for the purpose of ranking the contenders."); *In re* Protest of Award of On-Line Games Prod. & Operation Servs. Contract, 653 A.2d 1145, 1152 (N.J. Super. Ct. App. Div. 1995) (noting after three companies submitted bids, "an Evaluation Committee conducted a technical review of the bids"); Am. Totalisator Co. v. Seligman, 414 A.2d 1037, 1039 (Pa. 1980) (noting lottery vendors' bids for a computerized daily numbers game "were reviewed by an evaluation committee").
152. *See GTECH*, 816 So. 2d at 652 (noting the relevant request for proposals "envision[ed] finalizing an agreement by turning the winning proposal into a contract"); *Datatrol*, 400 N.E.2d at 1223 (noting the lottery and the vendor "proceeded to negotiate a contract" after the vendor's bid was selected).
153. *See* Nat'l Harbor GP, LLC v. District of Columbia, 121 F. Supp. 3d 11, 12 (D.D.C. 2015) ("[W]hen the District of Columbia issues a request for proposals from businesses to provide instant lottery tickets, prospective bidders expect they will each have a shot at winning the contract.").

ultimately received the award—perhaps because that bidder received an extension of time to submit their bid;[154] the lottery analyzed all bids using a factor that could only benefit one bidder;[155] or one bidder "purposely 'low balled' its proposal in order to attain superior ranking . . . and then negotiated a contract on much more favorable terms than it initially proposed."[156] Relatedly, a vendor may contend a lottery that awarded a contract without going through the competitive bidding process should have solicited new bids.[157] Or, a vendor may contend that the lottery should have awarded multiple non-exclusive bids instead of selecting one exclusive vendor.[158]

Once a lottery procurement contract is awarded and finalized, another source of possible dispute is what happens if the vendor does not perform as expected. For example, lotteries can be forced to discontinue sales of a game if a scratch ticket printer ships misprinted tickets.[159] Without adequate preimplementation testing, software or hardware updates can result in glitches or functionality gaps that enable chicanery by less-than-honest players or retail employees.[160] To anticipate a resolution to problems like this and prevent the need for lengthy and expensive litigation or other legal wrangling, many lottery vendor contracts contain liquidated damages provisions establishing the vendor is liable for liquidated damages in certain contingencies. Negotiating the proper amount of liquidated damages can also be its own dispute.

One final area in which a dispute can arise involves businesses that are not lottery licensees or lottery vendors but that nonetheless seek to participate in, or enable players to participate in, the lottery. These businesses can be generally categorized as "couriers," and they enable someone in one state to buy a ticket for another state's lottery, using a website or mobile app.

---

154. *See Datatrol*, 400 N.E.2d at 1224 (affirming a district court ruling finding that granting an extension to one bidder, which ultimately was the successful bidder, "was an act of favoritism").
155. *See* Tex. Lottery Comm'n v. Scientific Games Int'l, Inc., 99 S.W.3d 376, 380 (Tex. App. 2003).
156. *GTECH*, 816 So. 2d at 650.
157. *See* Control Data Corp. v. Controlling Bd. of Ohio, 474 N.E.2d 336, 339 (Ohio Ct. App. 1983) (noting the lottery "submitted a request to waive the competitive bidding requirements for the purchase of computer equipment," and a company that was not already in business with the lottery sought to enjoin the lottery from proceeding without soliciting bids); On-Point Tech. Sys., Inc. v. Commonwealth, 803 A.2d 1175, 1178–80 (Pa. 2002) (concluding the lottery could not "amend" an existing contract to add new goods and services without opening a new competitive bid process).
158. *See* KTSP-Taft Television & Radio Co. v. Ariz. State Lottery Comm'n, 646 F. Supp. 300, 305–06 (D. Ariz. 1986) (addressing a TV station's attempt to prevent the lottery from granting other stations, through a bid process, exclusive rights to broadcast lottery drawings).
159. *See* Steve Liewer, *Nebraska Lottery Officials Still Seeking Missing Tickets from Scratch-Off Snafu*, Omaha World-Herald (Nov. 23, 2018), https://www.omaha.com/news/nebraska/nebraska-lottery-officials-still-seeking-missing-tickets-from-scratch-off/article_c5c5fb27-1421-5b6e-9ab2-5e0a50d8d8cb.html (discussing a scratch game the Nebraska Lottery discontinued because of a misprint by the vendor).
160. *See* Ken Dixon, *Lottery Supplier Defends Role in Fraud Scandal*, CTPost (Nov. 1, 2016), https://www.ctpost.com/local/article/Lottery-supplier-defends-role-in-fraud-scandal-10427404.php ("[I]n June 2015 Scientific Games, without telling Lottery officials, implemented an equipment software change[] . . . [that] actually slowed down terminals and allowed crooked Lottery agents to review upcoming instant tickets, void losers and keep winning tickets for themselves. . . .").

Although today's lottery couriers use different technology, their precursors were involved in some litigation in the 1990s. One company, Pic-A-State Pa., Inc., was "a Pennsylvania corporation that was engaged in the business of taking orders for, and purchasing, out-of-state lottery tickets on behalf of customers."[161] Pic-A-State challenged a federal law that prohibited transmitting information used to procure a chance, share, or interest in a lottery conducted by another state, contending the law was unconstitutional under the Commerce Clause and Dormant Commerce Clause.[162] The U.S. Court of Appeals for the Third Circuit upheld the law, and Pic-A-State terminated its business.[163]

Lottery couriers today may face similar legal questions. Depending on the state or the lottery, officials may view couriers as unlicensed retailers or as businesses unlawfully reselling lottery tickets. If the lottery takes this position, it might refuse to honor tickets or pay prize claims from players who bought their tickets through a courier. And, to the extent the courier is utilizing interstate commerce or has users purchasing tickets in one state while present in another, the federal law discussed in *Pic-A-State* may apply to a courier's operations.[164]

Some states, however, have begun to allow lottery couriers, passing regulations about who can qualify as a courier and setting limits on what couriers may do. One state, Minnesota, even paid a major prize to a player who purchased the ticket through a courier.[165] Proponents of lottery couriers analogize their operations to a player simply giving money to a friend to buy lottery tickets for them. If those arrangements do not violate the law, the argument goes, then neither does making that relationship a little more electronic and a little more arm's-length.

It remains to be seen whether couriers will continue to proliferate. Again, however, their legality may vary from state to state. As with many other scenarios discussed in this chapter, lawyers working with lottery couriers must therefore be aware that a state-specific law or regulation can be dispositive.

D. Lottery-Related Disputes Where the Lottery Itself Is Not a Party

Sometimes a lawyer may be asked to assist with a dispute that is *about* the lottery but not *with* the lottery. For example, a person accused of a lottery-related crime may need the assistance of defense counsel when faced with criminal charges. The "dispute" in such a case is with a prosecutor, not with the lottery itself.

---

161. Pic-A-State Pa., Inc. v. Reno, 76 F.3d 1294, 1297 (3d Cir. 1996).
162. *Id.* at 1298.
163. *Id.* at 1298, 1304.
164. *See* 18 U.S.C. § 1301 (2018).
165. Greg Stanley, *St. Paul College Student Claims $1 Million Powerball Prize from Ticket Bought by App*, Star Trib. (July 12, 2018), http://www.startribune.com/concordia-student-used-mobile-app-to-buy-1-million-lottery-ticket/488065251/.

As one court put it, "there can be no question of the moral culpability of an offender attempting to swindle the lottery."[166] To defend against lottery-related criminal charges, an attorney may need to get up to speed quickly on intricacies of the lottery's process for claiming prizes,[167] validating tickets,[168] distributing tickets,[169] or even conducting a drawing to select winning numbers.[170]

In the civil arena, a lawyer can also find themselves immersed in a dispute that is about the lottery but not with the lottery. The most common scenario where this occurs is a disagreement among friends, family members, or coworkers about exactly who owns a winning ticket or whether there exists an enforceable agreement to share winnings.[171] One court addressing a case such as this described it bluntly as "the story of two friends who split the price of a [lottery] ticket only to have the ticket win and split their friendship."[172] Handling these kinds of cases may require analyzing contract law and property law principles, such as whether

---

166. State v. Tipton, 897 N.W.2d 653, 688 (Iowa 2017).
167. *See* Riddle v. State, 687 S.E.2d 165, 166 (Ga. Ct. App. 2009) (concluding a person could be charged with a lottery-related crime for "presenting a stolen lottery ticket for redemption of a prize").
168. *See* Parsley v. State, 119 N.E.3d 131, 135–36 (Ind. Ct. App. 2019) (describing one lottery's process for activating and deactivating tickets that are delivered to or returned by a specific store, which a store employee attempted to circumvent to claim a $2 million prize).
169. *See* Foreman v. State, 865 N.E.2d 652, 653–54 (Ind. Ct. App. 2007) (noting a lottery employee was charged with disseminating confidential lottery information when he determined where winning tickets were shipped, told his friends what store it was, and encouraged them to drive there and buy all the remaining tickets for a specific game).
170. *See Tipton*, 897 N.W.2d at 660 ("The State claimed Tipton engaged in a technologically sophisticated 21st Century crime, while the defense characterized the State's version of events as derived from *Mission: Impossible*.").
171. *See, e.g.*, Medrano Diaz v. Vazquez-Botet, 204 B.R. 842, 843–44 (D.P.R. 1996) (determining whether divorced spouses had equal 50 percent claims to a winning lottery ticket that they purchased while engaged); Dickerson v. Deno, 770 So. 2d 63, 63–64 (Ala. 2000) (concluding an agreement purportedly made in Alabama to share Florida lottery winnings was unenforceable); Sokaitis v. Bakaysa, 975 A.2d 51, 52–53 (Conn. 2009) (concluding two siblings' agreement to share winnings was enforceable); Talley v. Mathis, 453 S.E.2d 704, 706 (Ga. 1995) (concluding a contract made in Georgia, for the purpose of buying Kentucky Lottery tickets in Kentucky, was enforceable); Fitchie v. Yurko, 570 N.E.2d 892, 894 (Ill. App. Ct. 1991) (noting the plaintiffs sought "a declaration of their rights to a $100,000 prize claimed by [the] defendant"); Kaszuba v. Zientara, 506 N.E.2d 1, 2 (Ind. 1987) ("The issue presented is whether an Indiana agreement to purchase an Illinois Lotto ticket, in Illinois, is . . . unenforceable by Indiana courts."); Browning v. Poirier, 165 So. 3d 663, 663–64 (Fla. 2015); Welford v. Nobrega, 586 N.E.2d 970, 973 (Mass. 1992) ("The uncontroverted affidavits establish . . . that Gerald purchased the winning lottery ticket for himself and Welford as legitimate co-owners pursuant to their prior understanding."); Pando v. Fernandez, 499 N.Y.S.2d 950, 952–53 (App. Div. 1986) (finding a question as to whether the parties entered an enforceable oral contract); Cole v. Hughes, 442 S.E.2d 86, 87 (N.C. Ct. App. 1994) ("[P]laintiffs filed an action . . . seeking a declaratory judgment that they are the sole owners of a winning Virginia lottery ticket and its proceeds."); Meyer v. Hawkinson, 626 N.W.2d 262, 270 (N.D. 2001) (declining to enforce a contract to share lottery winnings because it contravened the state's public policy against gambling); Stepp v. Freeman, 694 N.E.2d 510, 514–15 (Ohio Ct. App. 1997) (determining whether coworkers who created a lottery pool established an implied contract entitling one participant to share in the winnings even though he did not contribute to the pool before the drawing); Parsons v. Dacy, 502 N.W.2d 108, 109 (S.D. 1993) (analyzing "an individual's claim to ownership" of a winning ticket); Domingo v. Mitchell, 257 S.W.3d 34, 37 (Tex. App. 2008); Hughes v. Cole, 465 S.E.2d 820, 823 (Va. 1996) (characterizing the issue the court was addressing as "the validity of an agreement among several residents of North Carolina to share the proceeds of winning tickets in the Virginia lottery").
172. Pearsall v. Alexander, 572 A.2d 113, 114 (D.C. 1990).

a contract or agreement was formed, whether a ticket was jointly owned or possessed, or whether one person made a valid gift to another.[173]

IV. CONCLUSION

Lotteries are complex business operations involving considerable interaction between the lottery and the player, the lottery and businesses, and between players. This chapter illustrates that these interactions can often lead to legal disputes and that lawyers with clients involved in such disputes must proceed with caution. As with other areas of regulated gambling, the legal principles that inform lottery cases can be subtle and peculiar to a particular state. Even more than in many areas of business law, fastidious attention to the details of statutes and regulations is essential. The business of operating a lottery requires ample collaboration and interaction between the lottery and other people or businesses. Players, contractors, vendors, and nearly anyone else who interacts with a lottery could find their interaction blossoming into a legal dispute.

The aim of this chapter has been to collect examples of disputes involving the lottery that can arise and to categorize and describe them. Along the way, some recommendations have been given. Hopefully, lawyers who find themselves unexpectedly handling a lottery-related case will benefit from this discussion and have a sense of the relevant legal principles at play.

---

173. *See* Remak v. Quinn, 17 V.I. 552, 555 (D.V.I. 1980) (concluding a lottery ticket was not gifted to a minor because it remained in the parents' continuous possession).

Chapter 11

Sports Betting in the United States

Tamara S. Malvin

I. INTRODUCTION

On May 14, 2018, the sports betting landscape in the United States changed dramatically with the Supreme Court holding in consolidated cases, *Murphy v. NCAA* and *New Jersey Thoroughbred Horsemen's Association, Inc. v. NCAA*,[1] that the Professional and Amateur Sports Protection Act of 1992 (PASPA)[2] was unconstitutional and therefore invalid.[3] The primary basis for the Court's ruling was that the federal law violated the anticommandeering principle of the Tenth Amendment of the U.S. Constitution,[4] which forbids Congress from requiring states to affirmatively execute PASPA's federal mandate.[5]

Murphy's repeal of PASPA did not automatically legalize full-scale sports betting across the United States. Instead, the decision simply removed the federal prohibition that for a quarter of a century had prevented states other than Nevada from authorizing sports betting.[6] With that federal ban erased, state legislatures now can decide

---

1. Murphy v. NCAA, 138 S. Ct. 1461, 200 L. Ed. 2d 854 (2018) (hereinafter *Murphy*). Notably, when the case began, Christopher Christie was the governor of New Jersey and the named party in the suit; however, by the time the Supreme Court handed down its opinion, Mr. Christie's term expired, and Phil Murphy had been elected governor. Thus, Mr. Murphy's name was substituted in Mr. Christie's place.
2. 28 U.S.C. §§ 3701 et seq (2018) *declared unconstitutional by id.*
3. *Murphy*, 138 S. Ct. at 1484–85.
4. *Id.* at 1476.
5. *Id.* at 1485.
6. Prior to the *Murphy* decision, Nevada was the only state with the power to authorize full-scale sports betting. This monopoly existed because Nevada was the only state conducting a full-range of sports betting at the time of PASPA's enactment. Because legislators were concerned that Nevada's economy would be damaged if sports betting was eliminated, the state was "grandfathered in" by PASPA. 28 U.S.C. § 3704. Other states came within the grandfather provision as well, but none of those states had full sports betting at the time of PASPA's enactment or thereafter. *See* Jonathan Holden et al., *Sports Gambling Regulation and Your Grandfather (Clause)*, 26 Stanford L. & Pol'y Rev. 1, 3–4 (2014).

whether and how they want to legalize, regulate, and tax sports betting within their borders. Indeed, in the one year since PASPA was struck down, the American Gaming Association (AGA) calculated that almost $8 billion was legally wagered on sports within the United States, with $3 billion of that figure representing wagers made outside the state of Nevada.[7] In addition, the AGA reported that more than thirty-five business partnerships have been formed between leagues, teams, and gaming companies in the year since the repeal of PASPA, and that number continues to grow.[8] With a multibillion-dollar backdrop for sports betting,[9] lawmakers in many states continue to be eager to consider the opportunities now available to them for the first time since 1993.

II. THE LIFE AND DEMISE OF PASPA

PASPA reflected Congress's desire to eliminate sports betting in the United States. However, PASPA did not forbid sports betting as a matter of federal law. Instead, PASPA forbade the states from authorizing or licensing sports betting operations.[10] Directing the prohibition at the states rather than acting directly to outlaw sports betting is ultimately what led to PASPA's demise. Indeed, most people assume Congress would have the authority to pass a law banning sports betting in the United States.[11]

PASPA had exceptions. It expressly excluded pari-mutuel sports betting (horse racing, dog racing, and jai alai) from its reach.[12] Additionally, there was a provision that effectively "grandfathered" states that had conducted sports betting operations in the past or were conducting that activity at the time the law was enacted. These states, most notably Nevada, were allowed to continue to authorize and regulate those preexisting operations.[13] Finally, in somewhat obscure language, PASPA gave the state of New Jersey one year from the effective date to authorize sports betting.[14] However, New Jersey failed to meet this time deadline.[15]

---

7. *One Year Post-PASPA, American Gaming Association Establishes Responsible Marketing Code for Sports Wagering: Industry Commits to Self-Regulation of Sports Betting Advertising*, Am. Gaming Ass'n (May 14, 2019), https://www.americangaming.org/new/one-year-post-paspa-american-gaming-association-establishes-responsible-marketing-code-for-sports-wagering/.

8. *Id.*

9. The AGA posited in 2017 that at least $150 billion is illegally wagered on sports betting in the United States each year. *See* Amicus Curiae Brief for American Gaming Association at pg. 1 and 13, *Murphy v. NCAA*, 138 S. Ct. 1461 (2018) (citing American Sports Betting Coalition, *Sports Betting FAQs*, Am. Sports Betting Coal., https://perma.cc/8RK7-KX2T).

10. 28 U.S.C. § 3702 (2018).

11. *Murphy*, 138 S. Ct. at 1484–85 ("Congress can regulate sports gambling directly, but if it elects not to do so, each State is free to act on its own.").

12. 28 U.S.C. § 3704 (2018).

13. *Id.* §§ 3704(a)(1) and (2). *See also* OFC Comm. Baseball v. Markell, 579 F.3d 293 (3d Cir. 2009) (holding Delaware was restricted to offering only the forms of sports betting it offered pre-PASPA and could not expand beyond that).

14. The language of 28 U.S.C. § 3704(a)(3) made no explicit mention of New Jersey or Atlantic City, but the statutory language defined the exception in terms that only that state and that municipality satisfied.

15. *See In re* Petition of Casino Licensees for Approval of a New Game, Rulemaking and Authorization of a Test, 633 A.2d 1050 (N.J. Super. Ct.), *aff'd* 647 A.2d 454 (N.J. 1993) (finding as a new form of gambling, sports betting needed explicit constitutional authorization and did not qualify as a "gambling game").

Many years passed with the landscape of sports betting frozen by PASPA as of January 1, 1993. This left Nevada as the only state permitted to offer full sports betting. It was not until 2011 that New Jersey voters passed a constitutional referendum allowing sports betting.[16] One year later, legislators enacted laws that established a regulatory structure for sports betting, motivated in part by the desire to spark an economic revival of Atlantic City and the ailing pari-mutuel facilities in the state.[17]

Before New Jersey could begin making sports betting available, however, the major sports leagues obtained an injunction claiming the New Jersey plan violated PASPA.[18] What followed was a years-long battle in the federal courts within the Third Circuit. New Jersey's initial legislative effort to establish sports betting was successfully challenged by the sports leagues and the Department of Justice, first by a decision of the District Court of New Jersey,[19] then by the Third Circuit.[20] New Jersey sought a writ of certiorari from the Supreme Court, but it was denied.[21] This case is often referred to as *Christie I.*

New Jersey was undeterred. Taking heed of the courts' language in the *Christie I* rulings, the New Jersey legislature passed, and Governor Chris Christie signed into law, New Jersey Senate Bill No. 2460 (216th Legislature).[22] This new law essentially deregulated the industry within New Jersey's borders—an option seemingly approved in *Christie I.* Indeed, the Third Circuit opinion in *Christie I* stated that PASPA gives states the choice to either expressly ban sports gambling or to completely deregulate the industry.[23] States were not required to take any particular action by PASPA; they were simply forbidden from taking the affirmative step of authorizing sports betting.[24] Based on that, New Jersey's new law partially repealed certain sports betting state prohibitions so as to deregulate the field rather than to expressly legalize and regulate it.[25]

What ensued was a second round of litigation and appeals, including a rehearing en banc before the Third Circuit that again yielded unfavorable rulings for New Jersey and its Thoroughbred industry.[26] However, a second request for a writ of

---

16. *See, e.g., New Jersey Voters Endorse Making Sports Betting Legal*, Chi. Trib., (Nov. 8, 2011), https://www.chicagotribune.com/sports/ct-xpm-2011-11-08-chi-new-jersey-voters-endorse-making-sports-betting-legal-20111108-story.html.
17. S. 3113, 214th Leg. (N.J. 2012); *see also* Matt Friedman, *Gov. Christie Signs Bill Allowing Gamblers to Place Bets on Pro, College Sports Teams*, NJ.com (Jan. 17, 2012), https://www.nj.com/news/index.ssf/2012/01/gov_christie_signs_bill_allowi_4.html.
18. NCAA v. Christie, 926 F. Supp. 2d 551 (D.N.J. 2013).
19. *Id.*
20. NCAA v. Governor of N.J., 730 F.3d 208 (3d Cir. 2013) [hereinafter Christie I].
21. Christie v. NCAA, 134 S. Ct. 2866 (2014).
22. NCAA v. Christie, 61 F. Supp. 3d 488, 494 (D.N.J. 2014); *see also* Friedman, *supra* note 18.
23. Christie I, 730 F.3d at 235–36.
24. *Id.* at 232.
25. S. 2460, 216th Leg. (N.J. 2014).
26. NCAA v. Christie, 61 F. Supp. 3d 488 (D.N.J. 2014); NCAA v. Governor of N.J., 799 F.3d 259 (3d Cir. 2015).

certiorari bore fruit, as the Supreme Court granted the petition seeking review of the case.[27]

The issue before the Supreme Court was whether PASPA violated the concept of anticommandeering that formed the basis of the Tenth Amendment. New Jersey argued that PASPA prevented the state from repealing its laws that prohibited sports betting, as it wanted to do. This amounted to Congress telling the state what action it could and could not take, and that was inconsistent with the limited powers granted to Congress and the rights reserved to the states by the Tenth Amendment. The leagues and the government continued to maintain that PASPA simply prevented the state from taking the affirmative action of authorizing sports betting in the state and thus did not commandeer.[28]

The Supreme Court came down squarely on the side of the state in a 7 to 2 vote. According to the Court, PASPA "unequivocally dictates what a state legislature may and may not do."[29] Any distinction between whether Congress is telling a state what it must do or what it is prohibited from doing is irrelevant and "empty."[30] As the Court put it, "Congress can regulate sports gambling directly, but if it elects not to do so, each State is free to act on its own."[31]

With the Supreme Court's holding in *Murphy*, the individual states found themselves no longer restricted by federal law from legislating and regulating sports betting within their individual borders. Indeed, several states quickly seized the opportunity and passed laws allowing sports betting in their state.[32] And with other states in various stages of implementing legislation providing for sports betting,[33] this phenomenon is likely to spread.

If the *Murphy* decision taught sports betting proponents anything, it is that the death of PASPA did not mean clear sailing for sports betting. While there is currently no federal regulatory framework in place for U.S. sports betting, several other federal statutes place limitations on the activity.

Further, several issues relating to the operation and details of legal sports betting have arisen and will need continuing attention from legislators. This includes the sports leagues' stated need for an integrity fee, who may control—and to what extent—player official data, whether to allow online and mobile sports betting, and

---

27. Christie v. NCAA, 137 S. Ct. 2327 (2017).
28. *Murphy*, 138 S. Ct. at 1478.
29. *Id.*
30. *Id.*
31. *Id.* at 1484–85.
32. Soon after the decision, Delaware passed its law allowing sports betting, followed by New Jersey. They were quickly joined by Rhode Island, Pennsylvania, West Virginia, and Mississippi. New Mexico rounded out the first wave of states joining Nevada in offering sports betting. *See, e.g.*, Ryan Rodenberg, *State-by-State Sports Betting Bill Tracker*, ESPN (Nov. 26, 2018), http://www.espn.com/chalk/story/_/id/19740480/gambling-sports-betting-bill-tracker-all-50-states.
33. As of June 25, 2019, ten additional states were in a "pending launch" mode. *See US Sports Betting News*, Legal Sports Rep. (last updated June 25, 2019), https://www.legalsportsreport.com/sports-betting/; *see also Sports Betting in the United States*, Am. Gaming Ass'n (Jan. 7, 2019), https://www.americangaming.org/state-gaming-map/.

if so, whether to anchor that betting to a brick-and-mortar gaming establishment. All of these matters have been a source of contention among industry participants with few signs of a truce.

Ultimately, the decision in *Murphy* did not legalize sports betting in the United States. It simply gave the individual states the authority, in the absence of federal regulation, to authorize sports betting. With that authority now established, many states have turned their focus to whether to allow sports betting. Once that is done, knotty problems of regulation remain.

III. THE UNITED STATES OF SPORTS BETTING: STATE OF THE STATES

As a result of the *Murphy* decision, sports betting is currently being legislated on a state-by-state basis. As noted, in a matter of months after the Supreme Court handed down its decision, seven states joined Nevada in opening state-approved sports books.[34] Additionally, New Mexico houses sports betting operations but on tribal land only. New Mexico is unique in that sports betting was not made legal by the state prior to the launch of sports betting within its borders; rather, sports betting is live on tribal land pursuant to the preexisting state compact authorized by the Indian Gaming Regulatory Act of 1988 (IGRA).[35]

The authorization, operation, and regulation of sports betting in each state varies. For example, in Delaware and West Virginia, sports betting is regulated and operated by the state lotteries, not private gaming entities. In New Jersey, Nevada, Pennsylvania, and West Virginia, sports betting is lawful not only in licensed, brick-and-mortar facilities but also on the Internet. Due to other federal laws that limit interstate sports betting, sports betting must be conducted on an *intrastate* basis, even where it is lawful to be offered through online and mobile avenues.[36] Additionally, how the term *intrastate* is defined in this context has been put at issue in a federal lawsuit initiated in New Hampshire.[37]

According to the American Gaming Association, in addition to the states already offering sports betting and those in some type of prelaunch phase, seven states have active sports betting bills as of June 2019, and nineteen states ended their 2019 legislative session with "dead" sports betting bills.[38] May and June of 2019 were hectic months for states. Notably, after months of political intrigue, Illinois passed its sports betting bill SB 690 in June 2019, and after some delay

---

34. *See* Rodenberg, *supra* note 32.
35. 25 U.S.C. §§ 2701 et seq. (2018). In contrast to New Mexico, Mississippi was the first state to introduce tribal sports betting in conjunction with state-sponsored legislation.
36. *See* Wire Act 18 U.S.C. § 1084 (2018), discussed *infra* in notes 69–81.
37. *See* N.H. Lottery Comm'n v. Barr, 2019 WL 2342674 (D. N.H. 2019).
38. *Sports Betting in the United States*, *supra* note 33.

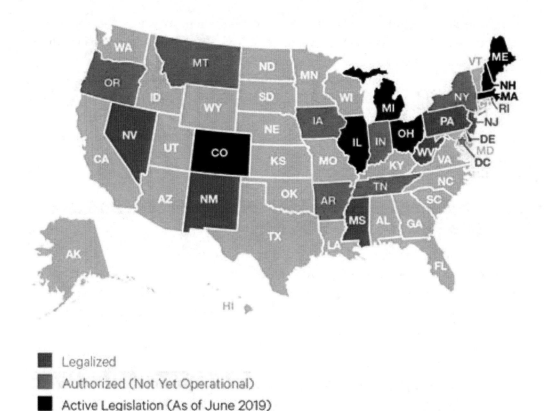

the governor signed the bill into law on June 28.[39] Similarly, as of June 2019, New Hampshire had passed House Bill 480, with the bill anticipated to be sent to and signed into law by the governor soon thereafter.[40] New Hampshire's law authorizes the state lottery to operate and regulate its sports betting industry, which will also be conducted online.[41]

Notably absent from the list of states that had active sports betting bills in their 2019 legislative sessions are California and Florida. With a combined population of 60 million, these states would inject massive liquidity into the sports betting industry. Rumors of movement in 2019 in Florida are tempered by reference to the state's mature tribal gaming interests and the IGRA compacts that would be implicated, a problem in California as well.[42] The image above depicts the ever-changing state of the states as of June 2019.

---

39. Jill R. Dorson, *It's Official: Pritzker Signs Illinois Sports Betting Into Law*, SportsHandle, June 28, 2019 https://sportshandle.com/pritzker-to-make-sports-betting-law-in-illinois-friday/.
40. *New Hampshire House Bill 480*, Legiscan (2019 Regular Session), https://legiscan.com/NH/bill/HB480/2019.
41. *Id.*
42. Matthew Kredell, *Senate President Says Florida Sports Betting Could Be Part of Tribal Negotiation*, Legal Sports Rep. (Mar. 14, 2019), https://www.legalsportsreport.com/30186/florida-sports-betting-tribal-compact/.

IV. STATE LEGISLATIVE AND REGULATORY CONSIDERATIONS

As the several states consider and shape their legal and regulatory structures for authorized sports betting, there are myriad variables for consideration in implementing the scheme that works best for each state, its existing and potential operators, and its residents. For example, the applicable tax rate, eligibility requirements and fees for licensure, the number of available licenses, compensation (if any) to the sports leagues, limitations as to the types of games on which consumers may bet, determining the types of bets available, and whether to allow online or mobile betting are all issues a state must consider and work out when enacting legislation and regulations. Many of these issues can be intensely political.

Before these issues are considered, however, it is important to understand the economics of operating a legal sports book and how this form of gambling differs from all others. Although hundreds of billions of dollars are estimated to be wagered on sports in the United States in a given year, sports books' margins are actually quite slim. Operators typically hold only between 4.5 percent and 5.5 percent of the handle, depending on the type of bet and the set lines and odds.[43] And anomalies still occur. For example, while $159 million was wagered on the Super Bowl in Nevada's sports books in 2018, the hold percentage was a mere 0.7 percent, or $1.1 million.[44] In other words, sports books cannot always be expected to be big profit centers, and they can even lose money. Unlike a slot machine, they have no computer chip that can be set to give the house a guaranteed return. Unlike a table game, they cannot count on a house statistical edge that, over the long run, leads to profitability and luxurious casinos. Legislators must be aware of this fact as they determine the details of sports betting laws.

A. Tax Rates, Licensing Fees, and Miscellaneous Costs

Perhaps the most fundamental issue that must be carefully considered by states is the tax rate for sports books. States looking to regulate sports books as a revenue stream and operators looking to profit from such an enterprise are being cautioned to view sports books as amenities, not cash cows, and to recognize that setting the tax rate too high can have the opposite intended effect of legalizing sports betting.[45] Indeed, even a conservative tax rate can be a barrier to entry

---

43. *The Economics of Sports Betting Research Brief April 2018*, GLOBAL MARKET ADVISERS (April 2018), http://globalmarketadvisors.com/wp-content/uploads/2018/04/GMA-The-Economics-of-Sports-Betting-Research-Brief-April-2018.pdf.
44. *Id.*
45. Devin O'Connor, *Third Pennsylvania Casino Submits Sports Betting Application, but State Tax Remains High*, CASINO.ORG (Sep. 25, 2018), https://www.casino.org/news/third-pennsylvania-casino-submits-sports-betting-application.

into the legal market. In the seven states that operated sports books in June 2019, the tax rates are as follows:[46]

Nevada	6.75 percent on gross gaming revenues
New Jersey	8.5 percent for land-based sports betting revenue
	13 percent for casino-based online sports betting revenue
	14.25 percent for racetrack-based online sports betting revenue
Delaware	50 percent revenue share with state
	10 percent revenue share with racetrack industry
Pennsylvania	36 percent
West Virginia	10 percent
Rhode Island	51 percent revenue share with state
Mississippi	12 percent

State legislators can perhaps be excused for wanting to tax sports betting at a high rate. After all, they have been told that sports betting has been a $150 billion industry in the United States alone.[47] But what that figure refers to is the betting handle, the total amount *wagered* by bettors. Handle is not revenue. Remember that historically 95 percent of the amount bet is returned to successful bettors. Even assuming a $150 billion handle, one could expect revenue of approximately $7.5 billion. And revenue is not profit. Profit takes into consideration the taxes, wages, and other costs associated with running a sports book. In short, from a pure profit perspective, a casino would do better to install more slot machines than to create a sports book. Viewed as an amenity that draws patrons to consume other products of a betting establishment, however, sports books can be very lucrative.

In addition to the state tax rate a sports book is subject to, there are one-time or renewable license fees established by each state for the issuance of a sports wagering license. Tax rates and license fees vary state by state and can also vary based on the applicants and their proposed method of operation. For example, in Pennsylvania, an initial sports wagering license costs $10 million with renewals of $250,000, while in New Jersey an initial sports wagering license costs $100,000 with unspecified annual renewals thereafter.[48] And an online sports book in New Jersey will also pay a $400,000 fee for an initial gaming permit and a responsible Internet gaming fee of $250,000, among other fees.[49]

In addition to licensing fees and state taxes, there is a 0.25 percent federal excise tax on the money wagered—the handle—that also affects a sports book's bottom line.[50] Moreover, a sports book, whether operated in a brick-and-mortar establishment or online, will incur costs associated with other taxes such as employment, income, and

---

46. *Sports Betting Revenue by State 2019*, THE LINES, https://www.thelines.com/betting/revenue/.
47. *See supra* note 9.
48. 4 PA CONS. STAT. § 13C61 (2018); 58 PA CODE § 1401.6 (2018); N.J. ADMIN. CODE §§ 13:69 A-9.4, 13:69 N-1.3 (2018).
49. N.J. ADMIN CODE § 13:69 A-9.4 (2018).
50. IRC § 4401(a)(1) (2018).

business taxes. Notably, now that the federal prohibition ended, new sports betting outlets will be subject to the Bank Secrecy Act (BSA) and will need to establish anti–money laundering (AML) compliance programs.[51] For those operations already in existence and already subject to strict regulation, they should review their current processes to determine where they may need to update or otherwise bolster their compliance program.

Under the BSA, also known as the Currency and Foreign Transactions Reporting Act, casinos are required to assist U.S. government agencies in detecting and preventing money laundering. In doing so, they must file Currency Transaction Reports (CTRs) of each transaction involving cash in or cash out of more than $10,000. The BSA also requires gaming operators to develop and maintain AML compliance programs, which involve know-your-customer standards of procedure. These are designed to ensure those betting have a legitimate source of funds, prevent "messenger betting," and track individual play to identify if suspicious betting patterns emerge involving suspected money laundering or fraud, and if so, to file Suspicious Activity Reports (SARs).[52] With sports betting will come increased regulatory oversight and the hope and potential for a stream of new customers. Attention to and investment of resources into compliance programs will be essential.[53]

B. The Integrity Fee Debate

A proposal of an additional type of tax on the operator that has created some controversy and criticism is what has been called an *integrity fee* that would be paid to the sports leagues.[54] Primarily lobbied for by the professional sports leagues, the concept of an integrity fee was inserted into the sports betting debate during the pendency of the *Murphy* case.[55] Initially, the National Basketball Association (NBA) led the charge, proposing a fee of 1 percent of the betting handle; other leagues eventually joined the NBA, and over time the more common suggestion by the leagues is a 0.25 percent fee computed on handle that sports books would

---

51. *See* 31 CFR §§ 1021.311–313.
52. *Id.*
53. Other costs of operation include the cost of a mistake or technology failures, such as when a glitch in the system creates an opportunity for a savvy bettor—or maybe just someone lucky—to make a wager at odds set in error. Colloquially, these situations are referred to as *palps* and have led to legal disputes and PR nightmares for the young industry. *See, e.g.*, *FanDuel Pays New Jersey Man in Full After Pricing Error in Raiders-Broncos*, ESPN (Sep. 21, 2018), https://www.espn.com/chalk/story/_/id/24744967/fanduel-pay-man-full-82000-disputed-bet. Similarly, a lawsuit ensued as a result of sports-betting-tournament participants having been disparately treated based on whether they were playing live or remotely, which cost certain mobile players waiting on overtime game results the opportunity to make bets on the next game, which live participants were able to do. *See* Adam Candee, *Inevitable Sports Betting National Championship Suit Drops, But From Where?*, Legal Sports Rep (Jan. 17, 2019), https://www.legalsportsreport.com/27778/sbnc-sports-betting-national-championship-lawsuit/.
54. *The Impact of an "Integrity Fee" on Sports Betting Handle*, Am. Gaming Ass'n (Mar. 30, 2018), https://www.americangaming.org/resources/league-fee-analysis/.
55. Adam Candee, *NBAs Adam Silver on Sports Betting: "The Integrity Fee Is Something That We Are Entitled To,"* Legal Sports Rep. (June 1, 2018), https://www.legalsportsreport.com/20904/nba-commissioner-adam-silver-talks-sports-betting/.

pay to them.[56] The leagues argue an integrity fee is necessary because their costs associated with regulating players, monitoring betting lines, and ensuring fairness will rise with the proliferation of legal sports betting. Gaming executives and those with experience operating sports books retort that the margins involved in sports betting make it essentially impossible for sports books to carve out a percentage of their handle for payment to the leagues if the sports books are to make a profit.[57] Thus far, efforts to incorporate an integrity fee into the regulatory structures have been fruitless. As of mid-2019, no state with live legal sports betting requires such an arrangement.[58]

Perhaps one reason for the legislators' lack of embrace of the integrity fee is the fact that the free market seems to be resolving the issue. The NBA, National Hockey League (NHL), and Major League Baseball (MLB) have entered into deals with MGM Resorts, whereby MGM will be their official gaming partner and receive rights previously unavailable to sports books, such as use of league highlights, logos, and a direct data feed.[59] Other similar agreements are being pursued by teams' ownerships as well, with individual National Football League (NFL) teams entering into sponsorship deals with casinos and sports book operators.[60] Those partnerships must all comply with NFL rules regarding gambling, namely that they operate as marketing deals and do not directly promote betting on NFL games.[61]

C. Online and Mobile Betting

Liquidity is a significant consideration for businesses operating sports books. In this context, liquidity means simply having betting markets that are of such a size that betting lines will attract roughly the same amount of money on both sides of a betting proposition. One of the best enhancers of liquidity would be to have online sports betting that crosses state lines and pools customers. However, federal laws apply when a transaction crosses state lines. As discussed later, the federal Wire Act is currently an impediment to interstate sports betting operations. Either a judicial

---

56. David Purdum, *One Year into Legal U.S. Sports Betting: What Have We Learned?* ESPN (May 14, 2019), https://www.espn.com/chalk/story/_/id/26740441/one-year-legal-us-sports-betting-learned.

57. Adam Kilgore, *With States Free to Legalize Sports Betting, Do the Pro Leagues Deserve a Cut?*, Wash. Post (May 17, 2018), https://www.washingtonpost.com/sports/with-states-free-to-legalize-sports-betting-do-the-pro-leagues-deserve-a-cut/2018/05/17/d6c9cc9e-59dd-11e8-858f-12becb4d6067_story.html?utm_term=.be0ae60b5eda.

58. Steve Ruddock, *How the MGM-NBA Deal All but Ends the Integrity Fee Debate*, Legal Sports Rep. (Aug. 9, 2018), https://www.legalsportsreport.com/22645/mgm-nba-integrity-fees/.

59. David Purdum & Darren Rovell, *NBA Signs Deal with MGM to Be Gaming Partner*, ESPN (Aug. 9, 2018), http://www.espn.com/chalk/story/_/id/24245142/nba-first-league-betting-sponsor-deal-mgm. *See also* Matt Rybaltowski, *MGM Resorts Hits Trifecta with MLB Gaming Partnership, Not Close on Potential NFL Betting Deal*, Forbes (Nov. 29, 2018), https://www.forbes.com/sites/mattrybaltowski/2018/11/29/mgm-resorts-hits-trifecta-with-mlb-gaming-partnership-not-close-on-potential-nfl-betting-deal/#767e0af13fda.

60. Darren Rovell, MGM Resorts, *Jets Forge Gaming Partnership, First Deal of Its Kind*, ESPN (Oct. 31, 2018), http://www.espn.com/chalk/story/_/id/25132999/mgm-resorts-signs-gaming-partnership-new-york-jets-first-kind.

61. *Id.*

repeal of the Wire Act or new federal legislation will be required in order to accomplish interstate pools. Unless and until this occurs, online sports betting will need to be on an intrastate basis. This is not as easy as it sounds.

The cornerstone of regulating online intrastate sports betting is that operators and vendors of online sports books are required to implement effective geolocating tools to verify that those wagering online are located within the jurisdiction in which they claim to be. Though it is legal to bet on sports in both Pennsylvania and New Jersey, it is not legal for an operator to allow someone physically located in Pennsylvania to make a bet online in New Jersey nor would it be lawful to allow someone who lives in New Jersey to make a bet while physically located in Florida.

This intrastate model thus proves burdensome for both compliance and liquidity. It requires extremely accurate geolocation technology. Moreover, the processing of online payments through credit cards and similar tools may also need to occur within the same state in which the bet is made, another challenging and expensive hurdle. Because sports betting already offers very thin margins for the operator, the additional costs associated with compliance in an online environment might cause an operator to conclude the additional benefits of online wagering aren't sufficient to make it a worthwhile venture. This is true in jurisdictions where private commercial entities operate sports books as well as in those where sports betting is operated by the state lottery.

Where sports betting has been legalized and operates in a regulated environment and an online component has been authorized by state law, the general trend has been to require online vendors to anchor to a land-based casino, racetrack, or lottery. This does not shut out companies that have historically operated online and on mobile platforms, nor does it mean that companies with no background in sports betting must navigate unchartered territory; rather, it requires that businesses interested in this new legal opportunity partner with one another. Under these rules, a sports book provider such as William Hill, PointsBet, or DraftKings may provide the infrastructure and framework for sports betting, but the point of access for consumers would be through a licensed casino or the state lottery. And regardless of the access point or overall branding of the sports book, whether online or physically located, all partners in a sports betting venture should be expected to satisfy licensure qualifications.

As more states roll out sports betting, one can expect a variety of models to be proposed, rendering some of the current models obsolete. For example, sports stadiums and arenas have been included in the New York sports betting bill as facilities that may take part in offering sports book opportunities to patrons, albeit as affiliates to established physical gaming locations such as existing casinos and racetracks.[62] In the Illinois legislation, there is the opportunity for in-stadium betting

---

62. S. 17D 2019–2020 Leg., (N.Y.), https://www.nysenate.gov/legislation/bills/2019/s17/amendment/d.

for a license fee of $10 million.[63] The "friendly confines" of Wrigley Field could host sports books as well as the Chicago Cubs. Innovation and creativity will test the boundaries of the regulation of sports betting.

Operators looking to implement multiple betting options across different media and in multiple jurisdictions must be mindful of the varying laws in each individual state to ensure they remain compliant in each market in which they operate. For example, New Jersey does not authorize wagering on a college sporting event being played in New Jersey nor on a game played by a team from a school located in New Jersey regardless of where that team is playing,[64] but this prohibition is not necessarily found in other states authorizing sports betting. Compliance is key in operating a sports book, as these individualized restrictions can lead to penalties and fines when wagers are allowed in jurisdictions where they are not lawful.[65]

Further, since PASPA's repeal, operators have been entering into agreements with vendors to provide the technology and the back-end infrastructure for this new offering. Each individually branded platform is referred to as a "skin," and the jurisdictions that have made sports betting, and specifically online sports betting, lawful within their borders do not all allow the same number of skins. For example, New Jersey allows a casino or racetrack with a sports wagering license to conduct an online sports pool and authorizes up to three third-party Internet sports pool operators to be licensed to operate online and mobile sports pools on any given casino's or racetrack's behalf; in other words, each sports wagering licensee may offer up to three skins.[66] On the other hand, Pennsylvania's Gaming Control Board has limited the number of online skins to one per operator.[67] Additionally, the types of bets legally offered will vary state by state.

Historically, the individual states determine whether, and to what extent, to authorize gambling within their individual borders, and in light of the *Murphy* decision, this certainly applies to sports betting.[68] However, while the states are free to determine what they deem to be the best framework in authorizing sports betting (or to authorize it at all), federal laws exist that impact the ability to wager on sports in the United States. Those laws do not appear to possess the fatal flaws of PASPA, and they add another layer of complexity to all participants in the sports betting industry.

---

63. Eric Ramsay, *Illinois Lawmakers Vote to Approve Sports Betting on Last Day Of Session*, LEGAL SPORTS REP. (June 4, 2019), https://www.legalsportsreport.com/33131/illinois-sports-betting-last-day-2019/.
64. N.J. CODE § 5:12 A-10 (2018).
65. Wayne Parry, *New Jersey Eyes Stiffer Penalties for Prohibited Sports Bets*, ASSOCIATED PRESS (Mar. 7, 2019), https://www.apnews.com/fcc10431db564528acda43f47843d951.
66. N.J. CODE § 5:12 A-11 2. A (2018).
67. *Pennsylvania Gaming Control Board Rules and Regulations Title 58, Part VII*, PENN. GAMING CONTROL BD. (March 9, 2019), https://gamingcontrolboard.pa.gov/files/regulations/EXGAMING_Temporary_Regulations_PUBLISHED.pdf.
68. *See* Gulfstream Park Racing Ass'n v. Tampa Bay Downs, 399 F.3d 1276, 1278 (11th Cir. 2005).

V. FEDERAL LAWS GOVERNING SPORTS BETTING

A. The Federal Wire Act

Enacted in 1961, the federal Wire Act[69] restricts the interstate transmission of bets and wagers by wire communication.[70] Specifically, the Wire Act in pertinent part states:

(a) Whoever being engaged in the business of betting or wagering knowingly uses a wire communication facility for the transmission in interstate or foreign commerce of bets or wagers or information assisting in the placing of bets or wagers on any sporting event or contest, or for the transmission of a wire communication which entitles the recipient to receive money or credit as a result of bets or wagers, or for information assisting in the placing of bets or wagers, shall be fined under this title or imprisoned not more than two years, or both.

(b) Nothing in this section shall be construed to prevent the transmission in interstate or foreign commerce of information for use in news reporting of sporting events or contests, or for the transmission of information assisting in the placing of bets or wagers on a sporting event or contest from a State or foreign country where betting on that sporting event or contest is legal into a State or foreign country in which such betting is legal.

As technology has evolved, the Wire Act has been interpreted as applying to Internet-based (online and mobile) wagers that cross state lines.[71] Notably, the Wire Act has consistently been held by courts to apply to sports betting specifically.[72] In 2011, the Office of Legal Counsel of the Department of Justice issued a memorandum concluding that the Wire Act applied *only* to sports betting. This opened the door for states to permit online gambling and allow operators to enter compacts with one another and establish interstate pools for Internet gambling and the operation of online lotteries.[73] However, because PASPA was still in force and the Wire Act has always been interpreted to apply to sports betting, no interstate sports betting compacts have been consummated.

After the *Murphy* decision, several states authorized online sports betting along with sports wagering on-site at a physical sports book. But even with the demise of PASPA, the Wire Act's application to sports betting is still intact, and that precludes interstate sports betting pools. Though interstate sports betting would increase

---

69. 18 U.S.C. § 1084 (2018).
70. *Id.*
71. *In re* MasterCard Int'l Inc., 313 F.3d 257 (5th Cir. 2002).
72. *Id.* at 263, n. 20 (citing *In re* MasterCard, 132 F. Supp. 2d 468 [E.D. La. 2001]) ("[A] plain reading of the statutory language [of the Wire Act] clearly requires that the object of the gambling be a sporting event or contest."); *see also* United States v. Lyons, 740 F.3d 702, 718 (1st Cir. 2014); *cf.* United States v. Lombardo, 639 F. Supp. 2d 1271 (D. Utah 2007) (holding the Wire Act applies not only to sports betting but also to all gambling online).
73. Office of Legal Counsel, *Whether Proposals by Illinois and New York to Use the Internet and Out-of-State Transaction Processors to Sell Lottery Tickets to In-State Adults Violate the Wire Act*, U.S. Dep't of Justice (Sep. 20, 2011), https://www.justice.gov/sites/default/files/olc/opinions/2011/09/31/state-lotteries-opinion.pdf [hereinafter 2011 Opinion].

liquidity, intrastate online sports betting has been successful and has broadened the market of persons who bet on sports.[74] This has led to a particularly high density of sports bets made along state borders, where the region's geographical layout allows for those in neighboring states to drive into the state in which sports betting online is legal. In populous states where bettors cross into a bordering state where betting online is legal, intrastate sports wagering has been an undeniable success. This is shown most remarkably by New Jersey. In its legislation authorizing sports betting, New Jersey included wagering online, and records show that roughly 80 percent of all sports bets in the state have been made via the Internet (including the use of mobile applications).[75] The impact of the availability of online sports betting in New Jersey is especially dramatic because sports betting has not been made available in neighboring states, including New York. The following image of New Jersey online border bettors shows the popularity of online betting generally.[76]

---

74. Andrew Coen, *Online Bets Drive New Jersey's Sports Gambling Tax Revenue Growth*, BOND BUYER (June 14, 2019), https://www.bondbuyer.com/news/online-betting-puts-new-jersey-in-sports-gambling-tax-revenue-lead.

75. *See id.*; *see also* Robert Dellafave, *Pay Attention: More than Four-Fifths of Sports Betting Handle in New Jersey Comes from Online*, NJ ONLINE GAMBLING (May 14, 2019), https://www.njonlinegambling.com/online-sports-betting-revenue-nj-april/.

76. Image of New Jersey border users courtesy of GeoComply. As of February 2019, GeoComply's technology is used by 100 percent of the New Jersey online market as part of their compliance programs to aid operators in ensuring they do not violate applicable federal and state laws, most notably the Wire Act and UIGEA.

This image signifies the central role online betting plays in the growth of the industry. The pins inside the shaded area signify a snapshot of all of New Jersey's online gaming traffic, representing geolocation checks for sports betting, casino, and poker traffic for all online sites in the state. Approximately 80 percent of the state's traffic falls within ten miles of the border and approximately 44 percent within two miles.

As noted earlier, an integral part of any online casino or sports book is the use of advanced geolocation technology that can accurately determine location. A New York resident using a mobile application to wager on sports at a New Jersey sports book must be in New Jersey to legally place this wager. For example, once he exits the Holland Tunnel back into New York (or somewhat before), the ability to wager must be blocked. Operators must be able to effectively prevent any out-of-state bettors, which includes proper detection of remote-location spoofing attempts. An effective solution will control digital fences, manage risk, eliminate location fraud, and provide valuable player behavior data.

While intrastate online sports betting has proven to be a valuable component to the overall sports betting market, a cloud has potentially been cast over its future. In January 2019, the Office of Legal Counsel published a Wire Act memorandum dated November 2, 2018,[77] reversing the previously issued 2011 Opinion. The new opinion declared that the Wire Act applies to *all* gambling online—not solely sports betting. The implications of the shift in position on sports betting may not appear obvious at first, considering sports betting has never been viewed as outside the purview of the Wire Act's restrictions. However, in adopting the view that the Wire Act implicates all forms of gaming online, the Department of Justice also opined that even transactions previously viewed as effectively intrastate in nature (or otherwise not unlawful) could be in violation of the Wire Act.[78]

Prior to the 2018 Opinion, the assumption was that if a person placing a sports bet on the Internet or through a mobile application was in the same state as the sports book, the transaction was intrastate in nature. However, the Internet sends packets of data using the most efficient path available, without respecting state lines. This 2018 Opinion's suggestion, discussed in more detail below, that the data's "intermediate routing" converted the transaction from a legal intrastate wager to an interstate wager prohibited by the Wire Act could destroy the market for *any* online sports betting.

Additionally, the memorandum acknowledged that online lotteries had been authorized in many states in reliance upon the 2011 Opinion that said their operations were outside the purview of the Wire Act. In reversing course, this acknowledged reliance did not stop the 2018 Opinion from pronouncing that the lotteries'

---

77. Office of Legal Counsel, *Reconsidering Whether the Wire Act Applies to Non-Sports Gambling*, Dep't of Justice (Nov. 2, 2018), https://www.justice.gov/sites/default/files/opinions/attachments/2018/12/20/2018-11-02-wire-act.pdf [hereinafter 2018 Opinion].

78. *Id.* at 18.

operations—and in particular their payment processing transactions—may be unlawful under federal law.[79]

If this interpretation stands, online operators should expect not only state inspection but also federal scrutiny of their intrastate affairs to ensure that they are not becoming interstate in any way. So, although the demise of PASPA had no effect on the meaning and application of the Wire Act and interstate sports betting remains unquestionably illegal, a new question has emerged regarding whether intrastate online sports betting must also cease. If so, the young industry will be negatively impacted, if not decimated.

The New Hampshire Lottery was the first to take steps to try to overturn the 2018 Opinion. It sued, seeking an injunction and declaratory relief against the Department of Justice.[80] The trial court ruled in favor of the original Wire Act interpretation, concluding that the Wire Act applies only to sports betting.[81] It is uncertain whether the Department will appeal this decision. Moreover, the narrow ruling does not provide the clarity needed for the sports betting industry to determine whether the intermediate routing of data or information constitutes an interstate or intrastate online betting transaction in the context of sports wagering.

B. The Unlawful Internet Gambling Enforcement Act

To understand fully the issues emanating from the 2018 Wire Act Opinion requires analysis of another federal statutory scheme. Enacted in 2006, the Unlawful Internet Gambling Enforcement Act (UIGEA)[82] addressed Internet gambling. For several years, there had been efforts in Congress to prohibit Internet gambling altogether. Those attempts had not achieved the stated goal, so instead, opponents of Internet gambling went after the lifeblood of Internet gambling—the funding of accounts through online financial transactions. UIGEA sought to stifle that process by prohibiting financial institutions and payment processors from facilitating transactions with companies engaged in "unlawful Internet gambling" and by making it unlawful for a person engaged in the business of betting to knowingly accept money in connection with unlawful Internet gambling.[83]

UIGEA did not make Internet gambling illegal. Rather, UIGEA made it more difficult for illegal gambling to occur online. But for states where online gambling is authorized and properly regulated, UIGEA provides definitions and a federal framework for lawful operations within that jurisdiction. In particular, UIGEA states, "[I]ntermediate routing of electronic data shall not determine the location or locations in which a bet or wager is initiated, received or otherwise made."[84] This is a

---

79. *Id.* at 22–23.
80. N.H. Lottery Comm'n v. Barr, 2019 WL 2342674 (D.N.H. 2019).
81. *Id.* Chapter 9 on Internet Gambling also addresses the Wire Act.
82. 31 U.S.C. §§ 5361–5366 (2018).
83. 31 U.S.C. §§ 5362–5364 (2018).
84. 31 U.S.C. §§ 5362(10)(E) (2018).

significant provision that has guided legislators, regulators, and operators alike in feeling confident that online and mobile gaming can be lawfully accomplished in an effectively intrastate environment.

While UIGEA carved out certain online transactions as expressly not prohibited, it did not impact the prevailing consensus that online interstate sports betting is unambiguously unlawful; however, after the *Murphy* decision, UIGEA's provisions regarding intermediate routing seemed to offer reassurance that *intrastate* online and mobile sports wagering could be lawfully offered without worrying about those data packets that crossed state lines before arriving back in the very state where they originated.

And herein lies the rub. In the 2011 Wire Act Opinion, the Department of Justice did not answer whether UIGEA affected the scope of the Wire Act; rather, it concluded that the Wire Act itself had no effect on bets or wagers not considered to be sports bets or wagers.[85] However, the 2018 Opinion noted that because UIGEA does not repeal or otherwise expressly state that it amends the Wire Act, that law had no effect on the meaning and application of the Wire Act.[86] Accordingly, UIGEA's carve-out for intermediate routing has no relevance to the Wire Act, the 2018 Opinion concluded.[87]

The intermediate routing issue's possible application to sports wagers previously thought to be intrastate has created significant confusion. The 2018 Opinion has left the gaming industry unsure of how to proceed and regulatory bodies equally unclear on what they can and cannot authorize. Additionally, even if a sports book goes forward with online sports wagering in the belief it is genuinely a lawful intrastate transaction, it may be hard-pressed to find partners in the payment processing industry who share that confidence. Any disruption of the payment processing stream throws online gambling of any type into disarray. As of mid-2019, the 2018 Department of Justice Opinion is a serious, if not existential, threat to the growth of online sports wagering, which is the form of sports betting that customers have indicated, with their wallets, that they prefer.

C. The Interstate Horseracing Act

The Interstate Horseracing Act (IHA),[88] a 1978 law subsequently amended in 2000,[89] permits cross-border pari-mutuel viewing and wagering. So long as pari-mutuel wagering is lawful under the relevant states' laws and those states also permit simulcasting and wagering on races conducted in other states, the IHA allows entities

---

85. 2011 Opinion, *supra* note 75.
86. 2018 Opinion, *supra* note 79.
87. *Id.*
88. 15 U.S.C. §§ 3001 et seq (2018).
89. Adding that a wager can be legal where transmitted "via telephone or other electronic media," the amendment made the IHA current and accounted for changes in technology, specifically the advent of the Internet. 15 U.S.C. § 3002(3) (2018).

to negotiate simulcasting agreements on an interstate level and allows pari-mutuel bets to be made in one state on an activity being conducted in another.[90]

Pari-mutuel wagering is a system of betting typically conducted on horse racing, dog racing, or jai alai, wherein a pool is created from the monies wagered to be distributed to the winning players, less the takeout. In a pari-mutuel system, the odds are not fixed and can fluctuate up until race or game time. While horse racing, dog racing, and jai alai themselves are sports and the recent Wire Act reinterpretation references horse racing in the context of sports betting,[91] pari-mutuel wagering is differentiated from sports betting under federal law[92] and has a history of unique treatment.[93]

The IHA has served as the source of authority for the pari-mutuel industry's continued success, first in allowing interstate simulcasting and wagering at brick-and-mortar facilities, thereby contributing to greater liquidity pools, and then by supporting the advent and developments. ADW sites allow users to essentially bank funds with them in order to make wagers on pari-mutuel activities via the Internet, regardless of the locations of the host, player, or server. Remarkably, in its ability to offer online and mobile betting across state lines, the pari-mutuel industry enjoys a unique and enviable status.

D. The Indian Gaming Regulatory Act

The Indian Gaming Regulatory Act (IGRA)[94] will play a significant role in shaping the future for sports betting in the United States. Several states are home to recognized Native American tribes, and many of those states have negotiated compacts with tribes whereby a tribe receives some form of exclusivity over certain gaming operations. In exchange for this valuable benefit, the tribe agrees to compensate the state from the tribe's gaming revenues.

IGRA organizes gaming into three categories,[95] with sports betting considered Class III gaming.[96] Under IGRA, for a tribe to engage in Class III gaming, it is required to enter into a compact with the state in which it is located, which must be approved by the Department of the Interior.[97] Thus, any addition of sports gambling by an

---

90. 15 U.S.C. § 3004 (2018).
91. 2018 Opinion, *supra* note 79.
92. 25 C.F.R. § 502.4(c).
93. For example, the recently repealed PASPA expressly carved out pari-mutuel betting from its reach. 28 U.S.C. § 3704 (a)(4) (2018).
94. 25 U.S.C. §§ 2701 et seq (2018).
95. Class I gaming is solely regulated by tribal governments and defined as traditional Indian gaming that may be ceremonial or celebratory in nature or social gaming for minimal prizes. 25 U.S.C. § 2703(6) (2018); 25 C.F.R. § 502.2. Class II gaming includes bingo and non-banked card games. 25 U.S.C. § 2703(7) (2018); 25 C.F.R. § 502.3. Finally, Class III gaming is all gaming that does not qualify as Class I or II gaming, including, but not limited to, house-banked games, such as blackjack and baccarat; casino games such as roulette, craps, and keno; slot machines; sports betting; pari-mutuel wagering on sports such as horse racing, dog racing, and jai alai; and lotteries. 25 U.S.C. § 2703(8) (2018); 25 C.F.R. § 502.4.
96. 25 C.F.R. § 502.4(c).
97. 25 U.S.C. § 2710(d) (2018). Chapter 8 on tribal gaming discusses the classes of gaming under IGRA.

Indian tribe may require a new gaming compact, review and revision of an existing gaming compact, potentially a great deal of renegotiation, a citizens' vote, and approvals by the appropriate state and federal branches of government.

New Mexico offers a variation on this situation. In that state, Native American tribes enjoy exclusivity over Class III gaming in return for multimillion-dollar revenue sharing; an expansion of sports betting statewide might constitute a breach of the compact and would relieve tribes of the duty to share those revenues. Nevertheless, despite a lack of express state legal authority, sports betting operations are currently conducted on tribal lands. The Pueblo of Santa Ana opened a sports book at its casino after the repeal of PASPA, citing language in its compact that generally allows the tribe to operate Class III games. Specifically, the compact provides, "The Tribe may conduct, only on Indian Lands, subject to all of the terms and conditions of this Compact, any or all forms of Class III Gaming."[98] It defines Class III Gaming as "all forms of gaming as defined in 25 U.S.C. § 2703(8), and 25 C.F.R. § 502.4."[99] Because sports betting is a Class III game under those federal authorities and neither the federal government nor the state of New Mexico expressly prohibit sports betting, the Pueblo of Santa Ana found themselves in a unique position to open a sports book.

That scenario is unlikely to play out similarly across the United States. For example, in Mississippi, state law was enacted to authorize commercial sports betting pools,[100] which in turn, by virtue of language in their preexisting compact,[101] presented the opportunity to the Mississippi Band of Choctaw tribe to enact its own gaming commission regulations. They did, thereby authorizing sports betting pools on tribal land in Mississippi as well.[102] Compacts are creatures of contract, and each one has been negotiated with involvement from several differing interests.

VI. PROPOSED FEDERAL LEGISLATION

On December 19, 2018, a bill entitled the Sports Wagering Market Integrity Act of 2018 (Sports Wagering Act) was introduced in the U.S. Senate by Senate minority leader Chuck Schumer (D-NY) and Senator Orrin Hatch (R-UT). The Sports Wagering Act would require, inter alia, that individual states' sports betting laws comply with certain federal standards and be affirmatively approved by the U.S. Attorney

---

98. New Mexico Compact § 3 A (2015).
99. *Id.* § 2 C.
100. Miss. Code § 75-76-89 (2018).
101. *Tribal-State Compact for Regulation of Class III Gaming on the Mississippi Band of Choctaw Indians Reservation in Mississippi*, § 4.7, http://www.choctaw.org/Government/tribal_code/Title%2015%20-%20Gaming.pdf.
102. Jill R. Dorson, *Choctaw Plan to Be First in Mississippi to Offer Sports Betting*, SportsHandle (June 13, 2018), https://sportshandle.com/choctaw-plan-to-be-first-in-mississippi-to-offer-sports-betting/.

General.[103] The proposed Sports Wagering Act initially predated the new Wire Act opinion. However, now that the new Wire Act opinion has been issued, Senator Hatch has circulated a new draft of the bill.

The Sports Wagering Act proposes to create a central and mandatory information-sharing repository and would require the filing of a "suspicious transaction report" if any unusual wagers or line movements are found.[104] The proposed law also attempts to curb the illegal market, providing the framework for federal prosecution and shutting down of offshore online sports books that serve the U.S. sports betting public.[105] Under the proposed law, the U.S. Attorney General is authorized to file a civil action against anyone allegedly in violation of the proposed law.[106]

Most notably, the proposed Sports Wagering Act would amend the Wire Act to include the same definition for intermediate routing as is included in UIGEA and to allow for interstate sports betting by permitting two or more states or tribes that have legalized sports betting to enter into compacts to allow the pooling of bettors.[107]

While currently working pursuant to and within the existing state-by-state model, several sports leagues have also been advocating for broader federal regulation of sports betting.[108] The benefits of a federal framework would undoubtedly include consistency that could lower compliance costs and create added liquidity. At a minimum, a federal act concerning sports betting should clarify the interplay between the Wire Act and UIGEA, and make the amendments necessary to bring the Wire Act into the twenty-first century and in harmony with UIGEA. A federal act could repeal the Wire Act altogether and open the door for nationwide betting pools. On the other hand, a federal act could greatly hamper the burgeoning industry if those who advocate against online sports betting successfully lobby their position. Moreover, the integrity fee lobbied for by the leagues on a state-by-state basis may find more favor at the federal level. It is also likely that a federal approach would address the issue of official data, such as who owns it and what information must be shared or made public. This is the most recent emerging dispute among the varying industry participants.

---

103. The AGA is not in favor of federal oversight and posits that, with regard to sports betting, market forces should guide the conversation. *See AGA Opposes Federal Government Overreach on Sports Betting*, Am. Gaming Ass'n (Dec. 19, 2018), https://www.americangaming.org/new/aga-opposes-federal-government-overreach-on-sports-betting/.

104. David Purdum & Ryan Rodenberg, *What You Need to Know About the New Federal Sports Betting Bill*, ESPN (Dec. 20, 2018), http://www.espn.com/chalk/story/_/id/25581529/what-need-know-sports-wagering-market-integrity-act-swmia-2018.

105. *Id.*

106. *Id.*

107. *Discussion Draft*, https://www.legalsportsreport.com/wp-content/uploads/2018/12/Sports-Betting-Discussion-Draft.pdf.

108. Rey Mashayekhi, *Inside the Battle for the Future of Sports Betting*, Fortune (Apr. 10, 2019), http://fortune.com/longform/sports-betting-battle/.

VII. CONCLUSION

Even assuming the passage of a federal law, sports betting will still be heavily regulated by the states allowing the activity. One can anticipate that more states will be added to the list of those that adopt sports betting, and that the variation in regulation will be increasingly vast. It is important to be aware of and to closely monitor the respective states' individual laws in order to remain compliant in the jurisdictions in which one operates.

Sports betting also presents professional opportunities for the business lawyer who does not have a practice predominately involving regulated gambling. For example, before the repeal of PASPA, sports betting was operated in a lottery format outside of Nevada, and that remains a viable option for jurisdictions. In such an environment, there are numerous opportunities for the private sector to participate. This could include providing back-end infrastructure, location monitoring, and payment processing, among others. It would be helpful for business attorneys representing entities providing services or technology in those spaces to be knowledgeable about the burgeoning gaming industry.

Similarly, in states where existing casinos or racetracks may obtain sports betting licenses, business attorneys will play a crucial role in representing those facilities as well as the third-party vendors with which they will likely contract to support their new sports books. Additionally, in a jurisdiction in which sports betting is authorized on tribal lands, it is imperative that counsel for a tribe understand the mechanics of the tribe's particular compact and know the federal laws with which the tribe must still comply, such as the BSA and UIGEA.

Sports betting is proliferating across the United States in a patchwork of varying rules, regulations, and policies. As laws authorizing the activity continue to develop and take shape, the well-informed business lawyer will recognize the opportunities presented to businesses in the varying sectors that converge to support this expanding industry.

Chapter 12

Data Privacy Issues and GDPR

Sean McGuinness and Katie Fillmore

I. INTRODUCTION

Nearly all casinos and gaming operations track player data in some fashion; doing so is essential for certain regulatory compliance and reporting purposes, and it also makes business sense for operators to know more about their customers. Due largely to technological advances, the amount of data collected by businesses in recent years has increased exponentially.

At the same time, however, laws regulating the collection, usage, and dissemination of this data have similarly increased in number and breadth. These legal requirements are not limited to federal and state law in the United States. European privacy law, most notably the General Data Protection Regulation (GDPR) of the European Union (EU), prescribes standards for data protection and privacy and is written so broadly that it applies to businesses in the United States. Taken together, these laws and regulations present a formidable burden on gaming operators. This chapter discusses the recent surge in data collected by casino and gaming tracking systems and the increasing duty of those in the gaming industry to protect the confidentiality and security of collected information. At the outset, it should be noted that this is a rapidly evolving area of law, and an attorney needs to be especially vigilant in researching the legal treatment of data issues by state, federal, and relevant international authorities.

II. DATA TRACKING BY CASINOS

Over the past twenty years, many casinos have implemented "loyalty" programs of some type, often called players' clubs, offering benefits such as discounted rooms, dinners, and shows.[1] For the patron, a club offers perks such as valuable discounts on rooms, dinners, and shows, and rewards like free play or cash. For the casino, the club is a powerful marketing tool that collects a wealth of information on its customers' preferences and spending habits, including how much a customer is wagering and in what way.

To join a club and obtain a playing card, customers typically must provide government-issued identification to confirm eligibility, supply contact information, and establish a password or pin to access the account. Some playing clubs also store financial information. Certain information collected and stored by casinos constitutes personal information (PI). PI is information that allows the identity of an individual to be reasonably inferred.[2] Unlike public information, PI must be collected, maintained, and disseminated in a protected fashion and in accordance with applicable laws.[3]

III. STATE LAW AND DATA PRIVACY

Currently, the United States does not have a comprehensive law at the federal level governing data protection, except in narrow specific instances such as health information under the Health Insurance Portability and Accountability Act (HIPAA).[4] Thus, in the United States, data protection is governed mostly by state law.

The majority of U.S. states have laws that govern the collection of customer data. These state laws can impose significant responsibilities as well as harsh financial

---

1. For example, some of the more popular players' clubs include MGM's M Life, Caesar's Total Rewards, and Wynn Resorts' Red Card Club. *See M Life Rewards*, MGM Resorts, https://www.mgmresorts.com/en/mlife-rewards-program.html; *Caesars' Rewards*, Caesar's, https://www.caesars.com/total-rewards; *Red Card Club*, Wynn Resorts, https://www.wynnredcard.com/en/benefits. With each program, users sign up and can use their membership to earn rewards on stays, purchases, and casino play within the resorts.

2. For example, the 2018 California Consumer Privacy Act, section 1798.140 (o)(1) defines PI as "information that identifies, relates to, describes, is capable of being associated with, or could reasonably be linked, directly or indirectly, with a particular consumer or household."

> The statute goes on to specify a number of data elements that constitute "personal information," such as (1) identifiers such as any unique personal identifier or IP address; (2) electronic network activity information, including, browser histories, search history, and any information regarding a consumer's interaction with a Web site, application or advertisement; (3) audio, electronic, visual, thermal, and olfactory information; and (4) geolocation data. In addition, the Act specifies that any "inferences drawn" from various data elements of PI "to create a profile about a consumer reflecting the consumer's preference, characteristics, psychological trends, preferences, predispositions, behavior, attitudes, intelligence, abilities and aptitudes" constitutes PI.

Chris Cwalina, Jeewon Kim Serrato, Steve Roosa, & Tristan Coughlin, *Data Protection Report*, Norton Rose Fulbright LLP (Aug. 27, 2018), https://www.dataprotectionreport.com/2018/08/california-consumer-privacy-act-gdpr-like-definition-of-personal-information/.

3. The majority of states in the United States have state-based laws addressing breaches of personal information. *See* Gina Stevens, *Data Security Breach Notification Laws*, Congressional Res. Serv. 4 (April 10, 2012), https://fas.org/sgp/crs/misc/R42475.pdf.

4. *See* Pub. L. 104-191, 110 Stat. 1936 (1996) [hereinafter HIPAA].

penalties for breach. What makes this especially challenging for an attorney is that each state's regulation of the issue will have differing scopes of applicability and requirements. For example, some state laws apply to collection of data regarding residents of that state only,[5] while others apply more broadly to data collected in the state.[6] Some states require notification of breach as soon as practical,[7] while others set out a specific time frame, such as seventy-two hours.[8] Who must be notified varies as well, with some states requiring a government entity to be notified,[9] while other states require that just the consumer be notified of a breach.[10]

Data protection and privacy are hot topics and a frequent area of interest to lawmakers. As a result, the law in this area is constantly changing. This makes it essential that businesses collecting data be aware of applicable laws and to have a process of regularly determining changes in the requirements and revising polices accordingly.

A. Nevada Law

For the purposes of this chapter, Nevada state law is highlighted, as it is similar to what other states have enacted. These laws also help to illustrate the interplay between Nevada's state law and gambling specific laws. Nevada's laws on data privacy are located at Nev. Rev. Stat. §§ 603 A.010–.100, 603 A.220, 603 A.900–.920.[11] While Chapter 603 A is not part of the Nevada Gaming Control Act, gaming licensees are nevertheless subject to the provisions. This is because Nevada Gaming Commission Regulation 5.011 deems noncompliance as an unsuitable method of operation and grounds for disciplinary action. In fact, failure to comply with or make provisions for compliance with any federal, state, or local laws and regulations pertaining to the operations of an establishment may be determined to be unsuitable methods of operation. Moreover, the Nevada Gaming Commission has the authority to determine, in the exercise of its sound discretion, whether a gaming licensee has failed to comply with any federal, state, or local laws or regulations.[12]

As is typical in many states, Nevada's data protection law applies to electronically stored PI that is owned, licensed, or maintained by a business. In Nevada, PI is defined as a person's first name or first initial and last name in combination with any one or more of the following data elements, when the name and data elements are not encrypted: (1) Social Security number; (2) driver's license number

---

5. *See, e.g.*, Neb. Rev. Stat. §§ 87-801–807 (2018); Mass. Gen. Laws 93 H § 2(a) (2018).
6. *See, e.g.*, Cal. Civ. Code § 1798.91.04 (2018).
7. *See, e.g.*, Miss. Code Ann. § 75-24-29 (2018).
8. *See, e.g.*, New York Cybersecurity Regulation of Financial Services, N.Y. Comp. R. & Regs. 23, § 500 (2018).
9. *See, e.g.*, Del. Code Ann. tit. 12B, § 100 (2018).
10. *See, e.g.*, Ark. Code Ann. § 4-110-101 (2018).
11. Under Nevada law, PI does not include the last four digits of a social security number or driver's license number. *Id.* § 603 A.040(2).
12. Nev. Gaming Comm. Reg. 5.011.8 (2018).

or identification card number; or (3) account number, credit card number, or debit card number, in combination with any required security code, access code, or password that would permit access to the person's financial account.[13] If any of this information is disclosed, the business entity must notify consumers of a breach at the most expedient time possible and without unreasonable delay, except when law enforcement determines that notice may impede a criminal investigation.[14] Nevada law does not require that a governmental entity be notified. A breach is defined as an unauthorized acquisition that materially compromises the security, confidentiality, or integrity of the covered information.[15] Potential penalties for violations include civil penalties, criminal penalties, or both. However, there is a safe harbor for encrypted electronic data.[16] Given the protection provided for encrypted electronic data, it is a best practice for businesses implicated by the Nevada law to encrypt personal information.

Additionally, the Nevada Gaming Control Board has taken an interest in the influx of players' club programs and the storage of information. The board has investigated data breaches of these databases and has repeatedly emphasized that casinos should conduct ongoing reviews of policies on data storage and protection, especially when the data includes financial information.[17]

IV. EUROPEAN UNION'S PRIVACY LAW: GDPR

A. Generally

On May 25, 2018, the European Union's GDPR took effect.[18] Although the EU's laws often do not have a worldwide impact, the GDPR will affect businesses across the globe, including those based in the United States. The GDPR has an extremely broad application, as it was adopted as an effort to hold businesses, including those outside the EU, accountable for the use and protection of data belonging to EU citizens. Because gaming is a worldwide industry, most U.S. gaming attorneys and law firms have clients (or individuals who are associated with a client entity) that have protected EU status under the GDPR. The regulation also would apply to casinos in the United States that have EU citizens as customers. Complicating matters is the issue of persons residing in the United States that have both U.S. and EU citizenship.

---

13. Nev. Rev. Stat. § 603 A.040 (2018).
14. *Id.* § 603 A.220.
15. *Id.* § 603 A.020.
16. *Id.* § 603 A.215.
17. *See Cyber Challenges in the Gaming Industry: For the House to Win, It Can't Gamble on Cybersecurity*, Nev. Bus. J. (Oct. 1, 2017), https://www.nevadabusiness.com/2017/10/cyber-challenges-gaming-industry/.
18. *See* Regulation (EU) 2016/679 of the European Parliament and of the Council of 27 April 2016 on the Protection of Natural Persons with Regard to the Processing of Personal Data and on the Free Movement of Such Data, and repealing Directive 95/46/EC (General Data Protection Regulation), http://data.europa.eu/eli/reg/2016/679/oj [hereinafter GDPR].

B. Applicability

The GDPR applies not only to European entities but also to entities located outside the EU that offer goods or services to people in the EU or that monitor the behavior of people in the EU.[19] Clearly, this would apply to U.S.-based law firms and attorneys, as any business with EU residents as customers or clients is required to comply. The GDPR applies to businesses offering goods or services to EU residents, regardless of whether payment for the good or service is required. As such, even a pro bono legal representation by U.S. counsel is implicated if it collects data from or monitors EU residents. The GDPR applies to both controllers (defined as an entity that determines why and how personal data is being collected)[20] and processors (defined as an entity that processes the data on behalf of the controller).[21] A law firm would fall into these categories, especially if it does gaming licensing work for EU citizens. Of course, a U.S. casino company with EU citizens as customers would clearly be subject to the GDPR.

C. Covered Data

The GDPR regulates "personal data," which is defined as any information related to a natural person or data subject that can be used directly or indirectly to identify that person. Personal data includes, for instance, a name, photo, email address, bank details, medical information, GPS location data, and IP address.[22] Clearly, gaming applicants that are EU citizens would need to share this type of personal data with U.S. gaming regulators as part of their licensing investigations. Accordingly, U.S.-based attorneys or law firms with such clients need to comply with the GDPR.

D. Enhanced Privacy Rights

The GDPR imposes significantly greater data privacy obligations than the U.S. obligations that were already in place when the GDPR was enacted. The GDPR also adds more penalties, including fines as high as the greater of 20 million euros or 4 percent of annual worldwide revenue.[23] One should anticipate that the GDPR is likely to cause an increase of enforcement activity as the EU member states continue to enact their companion GDPR statutes, although it is not yet clear exactly how this will be done. The significant enhancements referenced above include the following:

- *Consent*: Controllers and processors are required to be transparent with how information is used, and as a general rule, consent must be obtained from the individual. The request for consent must be in clear, plain

---

19. *Id.* art. 3(2).
20. *Id.* art. 4(7).
21. *Id.* art. 4(8).
22. *Id.* art. 4(1).
23. Laura Clark Fey et al., *What Is the GDPR?*, DRI vi (2018), http://www.dri.org/docs/default-source/webdocs/2018_gdpr_02-21-18-fnl.pdf?sfvrsn=2.

language. Simply asking an individual to accept a privacy policy that is not provided is insufficient.[24]

- *Rectification and Erasure of Data*: The GDPR confers rights on an individual to access his or her own data and rectify or erase inaccurate data.[25]
- *Assessments*: Controllers are required to conduct data protection impact assessments, involving routine evaluation of the potential impact of lost or diverted data.[26]
- *Breach Notification*: The GDPR mandates breach notification within seventy-two hours of awareness of the breach if the breach is likely to result in a risk for the rights and freedoms of individuals.[27]

Indeed, with the international nature of the gaming industry, it is not unusual to see gaming companies with EU citizens that need to be licensed in the United States. This can result in the sending of data privacy questionnaires to U.S. law firms and attorneys (in addition to requesting W-9 s and other typical, vendor-compliance diligence information). These questionnaires identify what sort of personal information the law firm/attorney may be receiving, what jurisdictions that law firm/attorney will be using the personal data, and what protocols would be in place for the EU citizen to receive notification concerning the date and where it is being transmitted to, as well as what security measures are in place to protect the personal data.

As mentioned above, the economic sanctions for noncompliance have the potential to be steep. The amount of the fine will vary depending on what provision is breached and the behavior of the organization, with the purpose being to impose an amount that is effective, proportionate, and dissuasive.[28] EU residents can enforce the GDPR's protections by lodging a complaint with the supervisory authority of the EU member state or by filing an action if the supervisory authority fails to address the complaint properly.[29] Additionally, an EU resident may take direct action through class action proceedings. Thus, increased litigation of privacy issues in the EU is likely.

E. Legal Ethics Considerations

One important implication of the GDPR's relevance to U.S. law firms and attorneys is the applicability of legal ethics requirements administered by the various state bars in the United States. A standard legal ethics canon requires a lawyer to preserve the confidences and secrets of a client. Certainly, the personal data of an EU-citizen client would fall under this canon. Similarly, rules 1.6 (Confidentiality of Information) and 1.15 (Safekeeping Property) of the ABA Model Rules of Professional Responsibility

---

24. GDPR, *supra* note 18, art. 7.
25. *Id.* arts. 16, 17.
26. Clark Fey, *supra* note 23, at 5.
27. *Id.* art. 33(1).
28. Clark Fey, *supra* note 23, at 8.
29. GDPR, *supra* note 18, art. 77(1).

would add the possibility of legal discipline from a state bar authority for noncompliance with the GDPR. An adverse GDPR action against a U.S. law firm or attorney would be problematic in a state bar disciplinary action concerning noncompliance with the GDPR. Also, any law firm/attorney should expect that if a legal action is made pursuant to the GDPR, a corresponding bar complaint would follow.

F. GDPR Application and Enforcement

GDPR is still a relatively new statute, and there are many unknowns with regard to how the GDPR will be enforced, especially against non-EU companies.

It is likely that the application and enforcement of the GDPR will be inconsistent across the member states. Each member state is required to enact enabling legislation to carry out the GDPR and designate its own supervisory authority. The member states have taken varying approaches both in the enabling legislation and the designated regulators. For instance, some member states have adopted stricter interpretations of the GDPR, while others failed to enact legislation until after the GDPR was already in effect. Additionally, Germany has designated multiple regulators, while other member states just have one. With the variances in the enacting legislation and regulators to enforce the law, it is possible there will be significant differences in the implementation and enforcement of the law.

G. Complaints and Suits Relating to the GDPR

EU residents can enforce the GDPR's protections by lodging a complaint with the supervisory authority of the EU member state or by filing an action if the supervisory authority fails to address the complaint properly.[30] Additionally, an EU resident may take direct action through class action proceedings.

As of October 2018, the newly formed European Data Protection Board had received more than 42,000 complaints since the GDPR went into effect on May 25, 2018. Many of these complaints focused on consent being improperly obtained or not obtained at all.

GDPR privacy complaints relating to practices of U.S. companies have already been filed. In fact, some of the very first complaints lodged pursuant to the GDPR were against U.S. companies. On May 25, 2018 (the day the law went into effect), a consumer group filed complaints against Google,[31] Facebook,[32] Instagram,[33] and WhatsApp[34] for "forced consent," arguing that the companies were offering users no

---

30. Clark Fey, *supra* note 23, at 8.
31. *Complaint Under Article 77(1) GDPR Against Google*, European Center for Digital Rights (May 25, 2018), https://noyb.eu/wp-content/uploads/2018/05/complaint-android.pdf.
32. *Complaint Under Article 77(1) GDPR Against Facebook*, European Center for Digital Rights (May 25, 2018), https://noyb.eu/wp-content/uploads/2018/05/complaint-facebook.pdf.
33. *Complaint Under Article 77(1) GDPR Against Instagram*, European Center for Digital Rights (May 25, 2018), https://noyb.eu/wp-content/uploads/2018/05/complaint-instagram.pdf.
34. *Complaint Under Article 77(1) GDPR Against WhatsApp*, European Center for Digital Rights (May 25, 2018), https://noyb.eu/wp-content/uploads/2018/05/complaint-whatsapp.pdf.

choice but to have their personal data processed to be able to use certain services and pointing out that the GDPR requires freely given consent. In November of 2018, a privacy complaint was filed by another consumer group challenging Google's location tracking on cellular devices, arguing the company uses manipulative tactics in order to maintain the tracking of Web users' locations for ad-targeting purposes.[35]

Additionally, one U.S. company has been targeted with a class action suit related to the GDPR. On August 22, 2018, a shareholder of Nielsen Holdings PLC sued the company, seeking class certification on behalf of shareholders for the company's alleged misleading statements regarding its preparedness for the GDPR and the impact the statute would have on the company's business.[36] This case is significant because the plaintiff's claims do not allege that the company violated the GDPR; rather, they are based on alleged violations of U.S. securities law relating to the defendant's alleged lack of preparation for the GDPR and for making misrepresentations about that preparation.[37] Nielsen provides comprehensive data regarding consumer television consumption and purchase decisions and how those choices intersect. The suit alleges that the company misled investors in describing how the GDPR's new privacy laws would impact its ability to continue providing this type of data. This case is an action brought under U.S. law seeking damages against a U.S. corporation for the company's alleged failure to adequately assess the impact of the GDPR on the company's revenue streams.[38]

These complaints and claims underscore the importance of U.S.-based companies reviewing their data privacy compliance with applicable data protection law, including the GDPR and domestic state law. Although the extent and manner of enforcement remains unclear with the GDPR, it is advisable for U.S. companies to take steps now to ensure compliance.

H. Compliance Tips

Given the expansive application of the GDPR and the practical difficulty of differentiating citizenship (situations with individuals with dual citizenship) among customers and clients, many companies and law firms with worldwide operations have opted to apply the GDPR principles to the management of all customer data or client data. In contrast to GDPR, the United States does not currently have an omnibus federal law regulating the collection, use, and disclosure of personally identifiable information. However, there are several sector-specific laws, such as HIPAA, that apply to the use and disclosure of personal health information.[39] As discussed

---

35. *Complaint to the Datatilsynet Under Article 77(1) of the European General Data Protection Regulation Against Google*, Norwegian Consumer Council (Nov. 2018), https://fil.forbrukerradet.no/wp-content/uploads/2018/11/complaint-google-27-november-2018-final.pdf.

36. Phil Muncaster, *Nielsen Shareholder Sues over GDPR Statements*, InfoSecurity (Sep. 6, 2018), https://www.infosecurity-magazine.com/news/nielsen-shareholder-sues-over-gdpr/.

37. *See id.*

38. *See id.*

39. *See* HIPAA, *supra* note 4.

above, however, all fifty states in the United States have enacted data protection laws, primarily governing cyber breaches. For a business with global operations, there is a patchwork of potentially applicable law and regulation. Defining a privacy policy that meets the most stringent requirements may likely be the best approach.

As an initial step, it is critical that companies and law firms conduct a comprehensive review of data collection and processing to ensure compliance with all applicable laws. This should include the following actions:

- Consider what information is collected, why, and whether collection is necessary.
- Evaluate what privacy laws are implicated, both domestically at the state and federal level and abroad. The international gaming company's data privacy questionnaire referenced above is helpful in this regard.
- Stay current with changes in the law, including interpretations in case law, agency guidance, and enforcement actions.
- Revise privacy statements and requests for consent. All customer-facing documentation will require revision to comply with the GDPR, which entails providing detailed information to data subjects regarding the processing of personal data in a concise, transparent, intelligible, and easily accessible form.
- Consider purchasing insurance that provides cyber coverage, including protection for data breaches. Many traditional, general liability insurers have added cyber liability exclusions to their policies. Companies should carefully read the terms of their insurance policies to fully understand what is covered and consider purchasing additional insurance.

V. CONCLUSION

With an assortment of state, federal, and international law affecting casinos and gaming entities, it is especially important for each business to conduct a thorough review of the data being collected and maintained and the implications of applicable law. The GDPR is arguably the most significant data privacy regulation that has been enacted to date, and the full breadth of the GDPR is far beyond the scope of this chapter. Many states in the United States have started to propose enhanced data protection law, mirroring the GDPR. The law in this area continues to change, and as new law comes into effect, the attentive lawyer must watch to see how the law is interpreted and enforced. It is essential that law firms and attorneys take the time to understand the various requirements and act to ensure compliance with all applicable data privacy laws.

About the Authors

Jason Bacigalupi is an attorney in Lewis Roca Rothgerber Christie's Gaming Practice Group. He assists clients with a variety of gaming and transactional issues, including corporate formation and governance, real estate and financing, and licensing and regulatory approvals for land-based operators, gaming manufacturers, and service providers. He also has experience in interactive gaming, contests, sweepstakes, and promotions.

Anthony Cabot joined the Boyd School of Law in March 2018 as a distinguished fellow in gaming law. Before that he practiced gaming law for thirty-seven years and was a former chair of the gaming law practice and executive committee member at Lewis Roca Rothgerber Christie LLP. While in private practice, Chambers Global as Leading Lawyers for Business, for Gaming Regulation selected Cabot as the highest tier (star) gaming attorney for ten consecutive years. Chambers USA, as Leading Lawyers for Business, for Gaming Regulation recognized Professor Cabot as one of only four top-tier gaming lawyers in the United States from 2004–2017.

Katie Fillmore is an attorney in the Austin office of Butler Snow LLP, where she focuses on representing businesses in a wide variety of civil litigation matters. Katie practices before state and federal courts at the trial and appellate level.

Jennifer J. Gaynor is a member in the Las Vegas office of Dickinson Wright PLLC. Her practice is a mix of gaming law, government relations, privileged licensing, and land use and zoning. She represents clients before the Nevada Legislature in Carson City, Nevada, as well as professional and licensing boards and state and local authorities. In addition, Jennifer represents clients on matters involving First Amendment law, public records, and open meeting law.

Gregory R. Gemignani is a member in the Las Vegas office of Dickinson Wright PLLC. His practice focuses primarily on intellectual property law, gaming law, technology law, Internet law, online gaming law, and online promotions law. Greg has represented many clients ranging from the largest casino companies to start-up

Internet ventures. He is an adjunct professor at the University of Nevada–Las Vegas William S. Boyd School of Law, teaching gaming law and gaming law policy.

Peter J. Kulick is a Member and Co-Chair of the Tax Practice Group at Dickinson Wright PLLC. Peter primarily practices in the area of federal tax law and also has an active administrative law practice, principally focused on gaming law. Prior to practicing law, Peter served on the staff of U.S. Senator Spencer Abraham and U.S. Congressman Dick Chrysler. Peter regularly speaks at North American and international conferences and is a prolific author on gaming and tax law matters.

Adam M. Langley is an attorney and certified public accountant at Butler Snow LLP in Memphis, Tennessee, and practices in the firm's Finance, Real Estate, and Restructuring Group. He is a double graduate of the University of Georgia, Tull School of Accounting in the Terry College of Business, and received his juris doctor degree from the University of Memphis, Cecil C. Humphreys School of Law, where he also serves as an adjunct professor. Mr. Langley clerked for the Hon. David S. Kennedy in the U.S. Bankruptcy Court for the Western District of Tennessee. He specializes in representing debtors, creditors, and trustees in corporate and governmental bankruptcies and regularly presents and authors materials on compelling bankruptcy questions and subjects.

Glenn Light is a partner in Lewis Roca Rothgerber Christie's Gaming Practice Group.

Steve Light is Professor of Political Science and past Dean of the College of Business & Public Administration at the University of North Dakota, where he co-directs, with Kathryn Rand, the Institute for the Study of Tribal Gaming Law & Policy, the first university research institute dedicated to advancing knowledge and understanding of Indian gaming. Light is the author or co-author of more than fifty publications, including the books *Indian Gaming Law: Cases and Materials* (2d ed. 2019), *Indian Gaming Law and Policy*, and *Indian Gaming and Tribal Sovereignty: The Casino Compromise*, which was featured on C-SPAN's BOOK TV. Light has testified before the U.S. Senate Committee on Indian Affairs, serves on the Editorial Board of the *Gaming Law Review*, is a member of the International Masters of Gaming Law and the American Bar Association Business Law Section's Gaming Law Committee, and has been a featured speaker at numerous university and gaming industry events throughout the world. His current focus highlights legal, regulatory, and practical opportunities and barriers for the exploding markets in eSports and sports betting.

Kate C. Lowenhar-Fisher is the chair of Dickinson Wright PLLC's Gaming & Hospitality Practice Group. A leading Nevada gaming attorney, Kate counsels many of the world's premier gaming companies on regulatory issues in connection with mergers and acquisitions, corporate restructuring, financings, and compliance. She has extensive experience advising clients on issues related to Internet gaming, sports betting, pari-mutuel wagering, social gaming, fantasy sports, liquor licensing, sweepstakes, contests, and promotions. Because of her knowledge and her cutting-edge gaming practice, she has been sought after by major media outlets, including Yahoo! Finance, ESPN, and Bloomberg to comment on current gaming issues.

Tammy Malvin is a Partner at Akerman LLP, a leading transactions and trial law firm with more than 700 lawyers and government affairs professionals and a network of twenty-five offices. She focuses her litigation practice on gaming and hospitality clients, representing resort, hotel, casino, and pari-mutuel owners and operators locally and abroad. Tammy was named to the Emerging Leaders of Gaming "40 Under 40" Class of 2018–2019 by *Global Gaming Business* magazine and The Innovation Group, has been listed as a Rising Star for Gaming Law and Business Litigation from *Super Lawyers Magazine*, and is an active member of the ABA Business Law Section's Gaming Committee. She has been quoted for her analysis of gaming law updates by publications such as ESPN and Gambling Compliance and often participates in live panels and webinars discussing the state of sports betting, online gaming, and the pari-mutuel industry in the United States.

Sean McGuinness is an attorney at Butler Snow LLP and practices gaming law in Colorado, Iowa, Mississippi, and Nevada. He is a member of the International Masters of Gaming Law and the International Association of Gaming Advisors. Sean served as a gaming regulator with the Iowa Racing & Gaming Commission and the Mississippi Gaming Commission. He received his doctor of jurisprudence from Drake University in Des Moines, Iowa.

Kathryn Rand is Floyd B. Sperry Professor and past Dean of the School of Law at the University of North Dakota, where she co-directs, with Steve Light, the Institute for the Study of Tribal Gaming Law & Policy, the first university research institute dedicated to advancing knowledge and understanding of Indian gaming. Rand is the author or co-author of more than fifty publications, including the books *Indian Gaming Law: Cases and Materials* (2d ed. 2019), *Indian Gaming Law and Policy*, and *Indian Gaming and Tribal Sovereignty: The Casino Compromise*, which was featured on C-SPAN's BOOK TV. Rand has testified before the U.S. Senate Committee on Indian Affairs and the Sycuan Band of Kumeyaay Nation, serves on the Editorial Board of *Gaming Law Review*, is Vice President of Educators of the International Masters of Gaming Law, is a member of the leadership of the American Bar Association Business Law Section's Gaming Law Committee, and has been a featured speaker at numerous university and gaming industry events throughout the world. Her current focus includes the application of the Indian Gaming Regulatory Act to sports betting, online gaming, and other new and emerging markets in tribal gaming.

David Ranscht is an Assistant Attorney General in the Iowa Department of Justice. He practices primarily in administrative law, with a focus on gaming law and regulation. He advises and represents Iowa's gaming regulators and agencies and since joining the Iowa Department of Justice in 2016, has handled most gaming-related litigation, in both state and federal courts, that involves the State of Iowa or its agencies. The views expressed here are personal to the author and do not represent the views of the State of Iowa, the Iowa Department of Justice, or any Iowa state agency.

Karl Rutledge is Chair of the Lewis Roca Rothgerber Christie Gaming Industry Group and provides counsel to clients and the business community about the nuances of gaming, particularly eSports, fantasy sports, sports betting, and promotional marketing. Karl is knowledgeable of the gaming regulatory framework and is an expert on skill gaming (e.g., fantasy sports, eSports, and casual skill games). He is the chair of the Gaming Law Committee of the American Bar Association Business Law Section and is currently a member of the Executive Committee of the Gaming Law Section of the Nevada State Bar. Karl has been listed in Best Lawyers in America in the category of Gaming Law since 2012, was featured in the April 2014 edition of *Global Gaming Business Magazine* as an emerging leader in the gaming industry, and was named to Vegas Inc.'s "40 Under 40" for the Las Vegas Valley in 2019.

Jeffrey A. Silver is of counsel in the Las Vegas office of Dickinson Wright PLLC. Jeff's practice focuses on every aspect of gaming, liquor licensing and regulatory law, as well as planning and zoning matters, contractor licensing, and transportation law. He has testified before the Nevada Legislature and U.S. Congressional subcommittees on gaming law issues and has consulted on gaming regulatory matters in several jurisdictions. Jeff served as a Clark County Chief Deputy District Attorney, heading the Consumer Affairs and White Collar Crimes Division and was the resident Las Vegas Member of the Nevada Gaming Control Board during the state's tumultuous period of developing regulatory oversight. Jeff has also held CEO and Board positions at Las Vegas resort hotels, the Landmark and Riviera, and was a former Senior Vice-President of Marketing at Caesars Palace.

Stacey A. Tovino serves as the Judge Jack and Lulu Lehman Professor of Law at UNLV William S. Boyd School of Law. An elected member of the American Law Institute, Professor Tovino is a leading expert in health law, bioethics, and the medical humanities, with particular expertise in the civil, regulatory, operational, and financial aspects of health law. Trained in both law and the medical humanities, Professor Tovino publishes her interdisciplinary work in textbooks, casebooks, encyclopedias, law reviews, medical and science journals, and ethics and humanities journals. Professor Tovino founded the UNLV Health Law Program, an academic partnership between the UNLV Boyd School of Law and the UNLV School of Public Health, and served as its Director from 2013 to 2018.

Mary Tran is an associate in the gaming practice group of Lewis Roca Rothgerber Christie LLP. She assists commercial and tribal gaming clients in various areas that include drafting gaming regulations, liquor and gaming licensing, assistance with sweepstakes and promotions, and drafting website privacy policies and terms of use.

About the Editor

Keith C. Miller is the Ellis and Nelle Levitt Distinguished Professor of Law at Drake University in Des Moines, Iowa. Professor Miller teaches the course on Gaming Law at Drake along with courses in the area of Torts. In addition to numerous law review articles, he is co-author (with Anthony Cabot) of two books on gaming law. *The Law of Gambling and Regulated Gaming* (2d ed.) is the leading casebook on gaming law. *Sports Wagering in America: Policies, Economics, and Regulation*, a comprehensive treatment of the issues informing regulated sports betting, was published in 2018.

Professor Miller is Vice-Chair of the Gaming Law Committee for the Business Law Section of the American Bar Association. He also served as the Vice-President of Educator Affiliates of the International Masters of Gaming Law (IMGL). Professor Miller is a member of the Editorial Board for *Gaming Law Review*, the leading peer-reviewed gaming law journal, and is a member of the *UNLV Gaming Law Journal* Advisory Board.

Professor Miller has spoken on and moderated panels for the IMGL and the ABA on gaming law issues and has conducted symposia and lectured at law schools in France and the United States, including being a Visiting Professor at the University of Nevada–Las Vegas Boyd School of Law. Professor Miller also consults on gaming law cases, has been an expert witness in gaming law litigation, and is a frequent resource for media on matters involving gaming law.

Professor Miller received his JD from the University of Missouri–Kansas City and after practicing law in Kansas City, Missouri, obtained his LLM degree from the University of Michigan Law School before beginning his career as an academic lawyer.

Index

Note: *f* indicates figure; n, note; and *t*, table.

1700s Pennsylvania and New Jersey outlaw gambling, 4n2
1869 Gambling first legalized in Nevada, 4
1877 Nevada bans gambling on Sunday, 4
1877 Nevada raises gaming age to twenty-one, 4
1878 Lotteries illegal in every state but Louisiana, 216
1895 Congress makes it felony to carry lottery ticket across state lines, 216
1905 Nevada licenses slot machines, 4
1908 *Fauntleroy v. Lum* Supreme Court decision, 120
1908 Kentucky Derby adopts pari-mutuel wagering, 16
1910 Nevada bans casino gambling, 4
1915 Nevada permits poker, 4
1931 Nevada Supreme Court confirms government can regulate gambling, 6
1931 Wide Open Gambling Law, 5, 117
1933 Securities Act, 66n35, 86n38
1934 Indian Reorganization Act (IRA), 174
1934 Securities Exchange Act, 86n38
1945 Nevada creates first casino gambling tax, 6
1945 Nevada legislature creates Nevada Tax Commission, 6
1947 Nevada Tax Commission has right to regulate gambling, 7
1949 Nevada requires state gambling license, 7
1949 Nevada Tax Commission requires fingerprinting of casino employees, 7
1951 Federal law proposed to tax Nevada gambling receipts, 8
1952 Travel Act, 13n58, 195, 207–208
1953 Wagering Paraphernalia Act, 13n58
1954 Supreme Court decision on consideration (*FCC v. American Broadcasting Co.*), 32–33
1955 Illegal Gambling Business Act, 13n58, 195
1955 Nevada Gaming Control Board created, 8
1958 Nevada Gaming Commission created, 9
1959 Modern Gaming Control Act, 12–13
1961 Federal Wire Act, 10
1961 Interstate Transportation of Wagering Paraphernalia Act, 195, 206–207
1961 Interstate Wire Act, 10n42, 23n1, 221
1961 Wagering Paraphernalia Act, 206–207
1961 Wire Act, 195, 255
1961 Federal Wire Act, 16
1964 Civil Rights Act, Title VII, 185
1964 New Hampshire authorizes first modern state lottery, 11, 19, 217
1970 Bank Secrecy Act, 86
1970 Illegal Gambling Business Act, 11, 208–209
1970 Organized Crime Control Act, 208n73
1973 Rehabilitation Act, 149

1975 Indian Self-Determination and Education Assistance Act, 185n87
1978 Interstate Horseracing Act (IHA or IHRA), 17, 259
1978 New Jersey introduces casino gambling to Atlantic City, 11
1986 Arizona Supreme Court decision on skill-based games, 25
1986 Money Laundering Control Act, 86
1987 Indian Gaming Regulatory Act, 11
1987 U.S. Supreme Court rules Indian tribes can conduct gambling on Indian lands if state allows, 11, 14–15
1988 Indian Gaming Regulatory Act (IGRA), 15, 169, 247
1990 Americans with Disabilities Act (ADA), 149
1990 World Wide Web invented, 214
1992 Professional and Amateur Sports Protection Act (PASPA), 12
1994 Casinos as financial institutions covered by BSA, 88
1994 Federally Recognized Indian Tribe List, 175n40
1994 Money Laundering Suppression Act, 88n46
1996 Mental Health Parity Act (MHPA), 139
1996 Nevada requires licensure of manufacturer of cashless wagering system, 64
2001 Nevada enacts Interactive Gaming Act, 18
2001 USA PATRIOT Act, 82, 86
2002 DOJ says online gaming violates Wire Act, 18
2002 Sarbanes-Oxley Act, 86n38
2004 Ninth Circuit says Native American tribes do not have sovereign immunity from Bankruptcy Code, 108
2005 Nevada approves mobile gaming, 18
2006 Internet Gambling Prohibition Act, 203n48
2006 Unlawful Internet Gambling Enforcement Act
2008 ADA Amendments Act (ADAAA), 149, 152
2008 Medicare Improvements for Patients and Providers Act, 138n4
2008 Mental Health Parity and Addiction Equity Act (MHPAEA), 141
2009 Illinois and New York offer online, intrastate lottery, 18
2010 Affordable Care Act (ACA), 142
2010 FinCEN reorganized BSA regulations, 86n25
2010 Health Care and Education Reconciliation Act (HCERA), 143
2010 Office of Legal Counsel (DOJ) says Wire Act applies only to sports betting, 255
2010 Patient Protection and Affordable Care Act, 143
2011 Nevada revises 2001 Interactive Gaming Act, 18
2011 New Jersey's constitutional referendum to allow sports betting, 245
2011 OLC says Wire Act only applies to sports wagering not intrastate wagering, 18
2011 Opinion, reversed by Office of Legal Counsel 2018 Opinion, 257
2011 Opinion, Wire Act does not apply to casinos, poker, or lottery, 200
2011 Opinion, Wire Act only applies to interstate transmission of sports betting, 200
2012 Nevada Gaming Commission licenses of online poker, 18
2013 *DSM-5* reclassifies gambling disorder under Substance-Related and Addictive Disorders, 146
2013 HHS Final Regulations on ACA's EHB requirements, 144
2014 New Jersey challenges constitutionality of PASPA, 12
2018 Bank Secrecy Act, 82
2018 California Consumer Privacy Act, 266n2
2018 European Data Protection Board formed, 271
2018 European Union's GDPR takes effect, 268
2018 Professional and Amateur Sports Protection Act, 23n1
2018 Sports Wagering Market Integrity Act (Sports Wagering Act), 261–262

2018 Supreme Court decision on *Murphy v. National Collegiate Athletic Association*, 15
2018 Supreme Court deems PASPA unconstitutional, 12, 193, 243
2018 Tribal Labor Sovereignty Act, 186
2018 DOJ Opinion on Wire Act, reverses the 2011 Opinion, 202
2018 HHS Final Regulations, 147
2018 Opinion, intrastate Internet gambling, 204
2018 Opinion, New Hampshire Lottery Commission and problems with the, 205
2018 Opinion, Office of Legal Counsel says Wire Act applies to all online gambling, 257
2018 Opinion, rejects UIGEA's relevance to the Wire Act, 205
2018 State of the States: the AGA Survey of the Commercial Casino Industry, 83n10
2019 OLC Opinion that Wire Act applies to all forms of wagering, 18–19
2019 Sixth Circuit says Native American tribes have sovereign immunity and exemption from Bankruptcy Code, 108
2019 U.S. District Court for New Hampshire rules Wire Act only applies to sporting events, 223
363 sale
   definition of, 105
   continued operation with reorganization of debtor during, 106
   factors considered by court during, 105
   similar to sale of assets in Chapter 11, 106

A

A Guide to Tribal Employment, 185n89
A Nevada Lottery: Improving the Odds for Nevada's Public Education System, 216n9
AA. *See* Alcoholics Anonymous
ABA, Model Rules of Professional Responsibility and GDPR, 270–271
abrogation of sovereign immunity, applies to tribes, 190
Absence of a Comprehensive Federal Policy Toward Internet and Sports Wagering and Proposal for Change, 221n46
absolute priority rule, definition of, 107
ACA. *See* Affordable Care Act
acceptance, definition of, 48, 112
access controls, as component of internal control system, 70
account, Nevada and New Jersey regulations for opening, for non-U.S. citizen, 123n66
accounting controls, government objective in setting, 69
accounting failures, examples of casino, 75
accounting regulatory powers, administrative agency's, 52–53
ACH. *See* automated clearing house
Acts
   ADA Amendments, 149
   Affordable Care, 142
   Americans with Disabilities, 149
   Bank Secrecy, 82, 86, 251
   California Fair Employment and Housing, 152
   Civil Rights, 185
   Consumer Protection, 42
   Employee Retirement Income Security, 144n46
   Federal Wire, 16
   Federally Recognized Indian Tribe List, 175n40
   Gun Lake Trust Land Reaffirmation, 176
   Health Care and Education Reconciliation, 143
   Health Insurance Portability and Accountability (HIPAA), 266, 272
   Illegal Gambling Business, 13n58, 108, 195, 208–209
   Indian Gaming Regulatory (IGRA), 14, 83n11, 108, 167n1, 169, 213–214, 247
   Indian Reorganization, 174
   Indian Self-Determination and Education Assistance, 185n87
   Internet Gambling Prohibition, 203n48
   Interstate Horseracing, 17, 259
   Interstate Transportation of Wagering Paraphernalia, 206–207
   Interstate Wire, 23n1

Acts *(continued)*
  Medicare Improvements for Patients and Providers, 138n4
  Mental Health Parity, 139
  Mental Health Parity and Addiction Equity, 141
  Money Laundering Control, 86
  Money Laundering Suppression, 88n46
  New Jersey Casino Control, 124–125
  Organized Crime Control, 208n73
  Professional and Amateur Sports Protection (PASPA), 23n1, 193, 243
  Public Health Service, 144n46
  Quiet Title, 176n43
  Recovery of Money Lost at Gambling, 42
  Rehabilitation, 149, 149n73
  Sarbanes-Oxley, 86n38
  Section 504 of Rehabilitation, 151
  Securities, 66n35, 86n38
  Securities Exchange, 86n38
  Sports Wagering Market Integrity, 261–262
  Title VII of the Civil Rights, 185
  Travel, 13n58, 195, 207–208
  Tribal Labor Sovereignty, 186
  Uniform Enforcement of Foreign Judgments, 120
  Unlawful Internet Gambling Enforcement, 13n58, 195, 209–213, 258
  USA PATRIOT, 82, 86, 95
  Wagering Paraphernalia, 206–207
  Washington Administrative Procedure, 231n106
  Wheeler-Howard (Indian Reorganization), 174n34
  Wire, 17–18, 195, 221, 223, 255, 257
ADA. *See* Americans with Disabilities Act
ADA Amendments Act (ADAAA)
  clarifies ADA definition of disability, 149
  definition of disability, 152
  list of major life activities from, 152
ADAAA. *See* ADA Amendments Act
Addady, Michael (author, *Lottery Winner Sues Saying Jackpot Should Have Been Bigger*), 229n93
addictive disorders, MHPA did not cover persons with, 140
adjudication of cases, regulators and, 50

administrative agency, casino gaming regulated by, 51–53
administrative functions, examples of, 51
administrative proceedings, for patron disputes, 132
admonition, example of type of sanction against an attorney, 154
Ad-Tab™ coupon cards, 39
advance-deposit wagering (ADW), pari-mutuel betting and, 260
Advantage Play and Commercial Casinos, 112n1
adversarial type, gaming license applicant who is, 56
ADW. *See* advance-deposit wagering
Affordable Care Act (ACA)
  could become irrelevant depending on U.S. Supreme Court decision, 143
  EHB provision of, for content of state's benchmark plan, 144–145
  has states define scope of EHBs, 147
  Individual Mandate unconstitutional and invalid, 143n39
  regulations (the 2015 Final Regulations), 146
  requires health plans provide mental health and substance use disorder benefits, 143–144
  requires Medicaid benchmark plans offer essential health benefits (EHBs), 144
  requires Medicaid benchmark plans offer mental health and substance use disorder benefits, 144
  requires some health plans to provide gambling disorder benefits, 146
  unrepealed portions of, 147
  provision for mental health parity, 143
after acquired lands, Indian tribe gaming on, 177
AGA. *See* American Gaming Association
age, twenty-one is gaming, in Nevada (1877), 4
age restrictions, government affects gambling contracts through, 49
Agency Development of Policy Through Rule-Making, 50n4
alcohol, gambler says gambling losses are due to, 127–128

alcohol laws, casino failure to comply with, 72
Alcoholics Anonymous (AA) meetings, 157, 158
Alex Rodriguez, a Monkey and the Game of Scrabble: The Hazard of Using Illogic to Define the Legality of Games of Mixed Skill and Chance, 24n6
allowance race, definition of horse racing, 16
alternative free method of entry, examples of, 39
alternative method of entry (AMOE)
  free, 36
  option of promotion and, 38
  sweepstakes and examples of, 35
Am. Totalisator Co. v. Seligman, 237n151
American Academy of Actuaries, 142
American Gaming Association (AGA)
  2018 State of the States Report, 167n2
  amount legally wagered on sports in U.S., 244
  not in favor of federal oversight of sports betting, 262n103
  number of state casinos that extend credit, 114n17
  number of states offering sports betting, 15, 247
  Survey of the Commercial Casino Industry, 114n17
  website for, 246n33
American gaming regulation, history of, 4–13
American Horse Council Foundation, website of, 16n75
American Horse Industry Council Foundation, 2017 study by, 16
American Indian tribal gaming industry. *See also* tribal gaming; tribal gaming industry
American Indian tribal governments, casinos operated by, 167n1
American Indian tribal sector, part of the casino gaming industry, 167
American Psychiatric Association's *Diagnostic and Statistical Manual of Mental Disorders* (DMS), 141
American Sports Betting Coalition, 244n9
American Stock Exchange, 66n34

Americans with Disabilities Act (ADA)
  Amendments Act of 2008 (ADAAA), 149
  definition of disability/impairment, 150
  reason why compulsive gambling excluded from disability, 150–151
AML. *See* anti-money laundering
AMOE. *See* alternative method of entry
Animal Protection Soc. v. State, 37
anonymity
  I-gaming offers player, 84
  player insistence on, complicates lottery prize-claim process, 231
  prizewinners seeking, 231–232
anonymous wagers, surveillance video of person making, 76
anticommandeering principle, PASPA violates Tenth Amendment of Constitution's, 243
antigambling laws, intent of, 31
antigaming forces, in Nevada (1931), 5
Antigua, Internet gambling in, violated Wagering Paraphernalia Act, 207
anti-money laundering (AML)
Anti-Money Laundering: A Comparative Review of Legislative Development, 85n16
anti-money laundering compliance program
  casino and, 251
  components of, 95
  FinCEN enforcement action for failure to have, 96
  helps financial institutions comply with BSA, 86n29
  obligations and casino operators, 81–97
  required of financial institutions by BSA, 86
  sports betting and, 251
  USA PATRIOT Act requires casino to have, 95
anti-money laundering laws
  penalties for noncompliance with, 82
  policy goal, purpose, and substance of, 85–87
anti-money laundering legal obligations, casinos and, 87–97
anti-money laundering standards, international Internet gaming industry and, 82n7

antiracketeering laws, IHRA and Wire Act are, 17–18
antitrust law, casino failure to comply with, 72
any chance test, description of, 27
APA. *See* Washington Administrative Procedures Act
applicability, of GDPR, 269
applicants, government's role in investigating and licensing casino, 49
Arizona Supreme Court (1986), decision on skill-based contests by, 25
Arnold, Gregory S. (author, *Employment Law in Indian Country: Finding the Private-Action Jurisdictional Hook Is Not Easy*), 185n89
Assembly Bill 98 (Wide Open Gambling Bill of 1931), 5
asset sales, regulatory hurdles for gaming debtor's, 105
"associated equipment," definition of casino, 64
Atlantic City
    casino gambling introduced (1978) to, 11
    New Jersey allowed sports betting to economically revive, 245
ATM. *See* automated teller machine
attachment of conditions to retain license, regulators' use of, 50
attorney
    advises clients to consider cyber coverage insurance, 273
    assists in securing credit for tribal casino, 190
    categorized as controller and processor by GDPR when does gaming licensing work, 269
    examples of sanctions against an, 154
    gambling with clients' money, case histories of, 155–162
    gambling with client's trust fund or personal injury settlement funds, 154–156, 158
    has fiduciary duty to safeguard client's trust funds, 153–154
    helps gaming applicant clients who are EU citizens and GDPR, 269
    helps gaming companies with EU citizens who want U.S. licensure, 270
    helps U.S. company review data privacy compliancy for state law and GDPR, 272
    knows applicability of GDPR if doing licensing work for EU citizen, 269
    knows Civil Rights Act and tribal exemption, 185
    knows client's gambling debt cannot be treated like other debts, 127
    knows IGRA and NIGC requirement for submission of management contracts, 184
    knows that tribal gaming law is complex, 192
    monitors states' laws about sports betting, 262
    own improper conduct not obviated by gambling addiction, 156
    recognizes increased data privacy obligations from GDPR, 269
    recognizes relevance of GDPR to state bar legal ethics canon, 270
    questions if tribe is eligible for bankruptcy protection, 191
    researches changing data privacy and GDPR, 265
    researches laws applicable to tribal labor and employment, 185
    understands tribe's tribal-state compact and BSA and UIGEA, 263
    See also lawyer
attorney disciplinary proceedings, trends in, 162–163
attorney license reinstatement, 162
audit gaming violations found by, 52
    government regulators and unannounced casino, 72
    objectives of casino, 72
audit regulatory powers, administrative agency's, 52–53
audit trail, documentation controls and, 70
auditing, government's role in casino, 49
auditing and accounting, 69–76
automated clearing house (ACH), 210n90

automated teller machine (ATM), in some states not allowed in casino gaming area, 114n16
"automatic stay," bankruptcy filing and an, 102, 102n31
auxiliary services, examples of, 51
"awards glass," 131

B

B2B. *See* business-to-business
B2C. *See* business-to-consumer
B2G. *See* business-to-government
baccarat
   gambling game favored by Chinese players, 123
   Indian Class III gaming, 260n95
   one of casino's biggest money games, 123
baccarat commission, failure of casino to collect, 74
background agent, reviews gaming license applicant's history and character, 59–60
ball drawing devices, 64
Balzar, Governor (Nevada, 1931), 5
Bamberger v. Ohio State Lottery Comm'n, 224n58
Bank Night and Similar Devices as Illegal Lotteries, 31n49
bank secrecy, criminals' use of business principle of, 85n22
Bank Secrecy Act (BSA)
   also known as Currency and Foreign Transactions Report Act, 251
   categories of reporting requirements under, 89–94
   Congress and Department of the Treasury expanded AML activities of, 86
   definition of financial institution by, 87
   detects and prevents money laundering, 251
   financial institutions and requirements of, 86
   goals of, 87
   of 2018, 82
   of 1970, 86
   penalties for noncompliance with requirements of, 95–97
   purpose of information reporting of, 85n23, 89n52
   recordkeeping requirements of, 94
   regulations, transferred to Code of Federal Regulations, 86n25
   says what must be included in AML compliance program, 95
   sports betting subject to, 251
   treats casinos and card clubs as financial institution, 88
bankruptcy, 99–109
   how financial restructuring of Native American casino is done in, 108–109
   Indian tribe pre-bankruptcy negotiation, 109
   petition, filed in U.S. Bankruptcy Court, 102
   restrictions imposed on the debtor, 103
   tribal sovereign immunity and, 190
Bankruptcy Code
   allows debtor to obtain financing, 104
   basic structure and purpose of (Chapters 7 and 11), 99–101
   Chapter 11, reorganization governed by, 100
   disagreement over applicability to Native American tribe gaming, 108
   not utilized by any Native American tribe, 108
   Section 363, sale of debtor's estate, 104
   Title 11 of the United States Code, 99
bankruptcy code, tribe not mentioned in definition of debtor in federal, 191
bankruptcy court, can order sale of all Chapter 11 debtor's assets, 100n10
bankruptcy estate, includes all legal and equitable interests of debtor, 102
bankruptcy petition
   consequences, protections, and safeguards after filing a, 102–104
   debtor's counsel files emergency motion for relief, 103
bankruptcy protection, reason gaming debtors seek, 101
bankruptcy sales, subject to bid procedures for a public auction, 105
Bar Counsel, proof of attendance at Gamblers Anonymous meetings required by, 157

Barbadoro, Paul (U.S. District Court judge), rejected 2018 Opinion, 205
Barry, Colleen L. (author, *The Political Evolution of Mental Health Parity*), 140n19
Beauregard, Steve (author, *States Where It Is Legal to Bet on Horse Racing Online*), 16n77
Beck v. Fox Kansas Theatre, consideration and, 30
Bellicini, Samuel, attorney who used client's trust funds to gamble, 158–159
Belmont Stakes, horse racing and the, 16
benchmark plan
　2013 HHS Final Regulations require states to select, 144–145, 147
　Illinois only state to select third, 147
　Nevada's First, 144
Berlizean blind trust, claiming winning ticket, 228
Bernhard, Bo J. (author, *Problem Gambling and Treatment in Nevada*), 145n55
Bernhard, Peter C. (Chairman, Nevada Gaming Commission), 18n85
"best interest" exception, tribe and, 178
bet, definition and components of, 13, 25n10
betting
　gambling and off-track, 3
　legal off-track, in U.S. (1800s to early 1900s), 4
　online and mobile, 252–254
　See also wagering
betting handle, definition of, in sports betting, 250
"beyond a reasonable doubt," used in court but not in licensing, 59
Beyond the SAR-C: Best Practices for Gaming Companies to "Know Their Customer" and Avoid Money Laundering, 82n2
Bible, Attorney General Alan (Nevada, 1947), 7
Bid and Request for Proposals (RFP), lottery services, 237n150
Big Lagoon Rancheria v. California, 176
bill acceptor, 64
Bill Proposed to Define and Allow eSports in Maryland, 20n100

bill validator, 64
bingo
　electronic cards for, 64
　gambling and high-stakes, 3
　Indian Class II gaming, 260n95
　inter-casino linked systems for, 64
Blackburn v. Ippolito, 30n34
Blackford v. Prairie Meadows Racetrack & Casino, Inc., 114n13
blackjack
　"counting cards" in, 112
　Indian Class III gaming, 260n95
blackjack table, written statement of wagering contract at, 113
Blanco, Kenneth A. (FinCEN Director), 89n52
Blizzard Games, creator of *Overwatch*, 20n98
Bohatch, Emily (author, *What You Could Buy If You Won the $700 Million Powerball*), 219n36
Bohrer v. City of Milwaukee, 38n85
bond
　issued by casino to evidence debt owed, 63
　taxable gaming revenue, 184
bond indenture, 184
bookmaking
　definition of, as form of gambling, 13
　Wire Act deals primarily with, 196
boxperson, regulatory requirements for, 69
Boyd v. Piggly Wiggly S., Inc., 32n50
Bradley, Craig M. (author, *Racketeering and the Federalization of Crime*), 216n12
breach notification, GDPR policy for PI, 270
breach of contract, between bettor and casino, 111
breach of insurance contract, if insurer refuses to pay for gambling-related treatment, 148
breach of personal information (PI)
　definition of, 267
　Nevada's definition of, 268
Breeders' Cup, horse racing and the, 16
Bretton v. State Lottery Comm'n, 226n68
Bridge the Gap program, State Bar of Nevada's, 157
"bright line," between state's concessions and tribe's economic benefit there is no, 181

Brody, Kathleen E. (author, *Show Me the Money: Casinos' Anti-Money-Laundering Obligations and Enforcement*), 96n98
Brown v. Cal. State Lottery Comm'n, 225n66
Brown v. State, 233n120
Browning v. Poirier, 240n171
brushperson, regulatory requirements for, 69
BSA. *See* Bank Secrecy Act
Buchler, Harold, Jr (author, "Louisiana" in *International Casino Law*), 67n41
Bukhtia v. Bureau of State Lottery, 236n143
burden of proof, on gaming license applicant, 58–59
Bush, George H. W. (President)
 Americans with Disabilities Act (1990) signed by, 149
Bush, George W. (President)
 ADA Amendments Act (2008) signed by, 149
 expansion of MHPA by, 141
 signed ADAAA, 152
business
 games and sweepstakes build brand name of a, 43
 must regularly revise data privacy policies, 267
business experience, applicant for gaming license must have, 53
business relationship failure, examples of casino, 74
business-to-business (B2B), I-gaming category of, 84
business-to-consumer (B2C), I-gaming category of, 84
business-to-government (B2G), I-gaming category of, 84

C

C-level officers, license required for casino, 68
C&L Enterprises, Inc. v. Citizen Band Potawatomi Indian Tribe of Oklahoma, 187n95
Cabol, Anthony N. (author)
 Absence of a Comprehensive Federal Policy Toward Internet and Sports Wagering and Proposal for Change, 221n46
Advantage Play and Commercial Casino, 112n1
Alex Rodriguez, a Monkey and the Game of Scrabble, 24n6
Casino Collection Lawsuits: The Basics, 122n56
Economic Value, Equal Dignity, and the Future of Sweepstakes, 29n32
Fantasy Sports: One Form of Mainstream Wagering in the United States, 27n17
"Nevada" in *International Casino Law*, 67n43
The Law of Gambling & Regulated Games, 215n2
Caesars Riverboat Casino LLC v. Kephart, 129n109
Caesars Tahoe, player stopped payment on markers at, 118
Caesars Total Reward, players' club, 266n1
cage and credit system, 64
cage manager, regulatory requirements for, 68
Cal. Gasoline Retailers v. Regal Petroleum Corp. of Fresno, 36n68
California
 rule against enforcing gambling debts, 118
 separate state divisions investigate and enforce gambling laws, 51
 sports betting versus IGRA compact, 248
 tribal gaming is large industry in, 167–168
California Consumer Privacy Act, definition of personal information in, 266n2
California Fair Employment and Housing Act, excludes compulsive gambling from definition of disability, 152
California Fair Housing and Employment Act, protection from housing discrimination, 149–150
California Gasoline Retailers v. Regal Petroleum Corp., 36
California Lottery, lawsuit that Powerball discriminated on player's national origin, 227

California Supreme Court
  free method of entry and consideration, 36
  postage is not a valuable consideration, 34n65
California v. Cabazon Band of Mission Indians, 11n47, 15, 15n67, 169n8
California v. Iipay Nation, 191n118
Call Her Jane Dough: New Hampshire Lottery Winner Can Stay Anonymous, 232n118
Campione v. Adamar of New Jersey, 112
Candee, Adam (author)
  Inevitable Sports Betting National Championship Suit Drops, But From Where?, 251n55
  The Integrity Fee is Something We Are Entitled To, 251n53
Carcieri v. Kempthorne, 174n35
Carcieri v. Salazar, Supreme Court's decision in, 174
card
  live-racing, 17
  work, 59
card clubs
  financial institution under BSA, 88
  subject to same BSA rules as casinos, 88n48
card counter, 113, 113n9
card counting, no court ever ruled, was cheating, 113n9
card rooms, gambling and, 3
card shuffle, as example of systemic chance, 28
casas de cambios
  FinCEN advisory on transactions with, 96n106
  Mexican money-exchange houses, 96
case law
  on both sides of whether Wire Act is limited to sports wagering or not, 200
  suggests the Wire Act applies only to sports betting, 198
cash and debtor in possession financing, 104–108
cash collateral, must be approved by bankruptcy court, 105
cash-in and cash-out transaction, when are subject to BSA reporting, 89–90
cash-in transaction, definition and examples of, 89
cashless wagering system, definition of and licensing requirement for, 64
cash-out transaction, definition and examples of, 89–90
Casiello, Nicholas, Jr (author "New Jersey" in *International Casino Law*), 67n44
casinos
  advertisements do not constitute an offer to play by, 112–113
  Aladdin Casino and Hotel, 101
  AML legal obligations of, 87–97
  ancillary financial services and potential money laundering activities in, 97
  Aria Resort and, 126n88
  as a cash business in financial services industry, 87n41
  Atlantic City, 3
  Atlantic Club Casino Hotel, 101
  Big Fish, 42
  Boardwalk Regency, 132n118
  Caesars Entertainment, 100
  Caesars Riverboat, 129n109
  Caesars Tahoe, 118
  can be location for online sports betting, 253
  cannot include loss on bad debt in its deductible operating expenses, 119
  credit department of, 116
  data tracking by a, 266
  does not allow player to place bets with credit or debit card, 114
  example of land-based gaming, 83
  financial institution under BSA, 88
  Fitzgeralds Reno, 100
  Flamingo Casino (Nevada, 1947), 7
  Foxwoods Resort Casino, 3, 191
  gambling contract favors the, 48
  gambling revenue from commercial, 14
  Grand Casino Biloxi, 135
  Grand Casino-Coushatta, 132n118
  Greate Bay Hotel and Casino, 101n24, 114n13
  Hard Rock Hotel Biloxi, 100
  Harrah's, 135
  Herbst Gaming, 100
  Klondike Sunset Casino, 100

Lake of Torches Resort Casino, 184
Las Vegas Sands, 93, 96
Lucky Dragon Hotel & Casino, 100
Maxim Hotel, 100
must file CTRs, 251
Nevada Gaming Partners, LLC, 100n2
no duty to prevent compulsive gambler from playing, 129n109
not liable when files SAR on a person, 93
numbers and revenues of U.S., 14
number of tribal owned and operated state, 192
Pauma Band of Mission Indians, 186
operating requirements for, 72–76
players' clubs and "loyalty" programs, 266
Prairie Meadows Racetrack and Casino, 114n13
Premier Interval Resorts, 100n2
process of granting credit to player, 115
provides financial services like depository institutions, 87
publicly traded business with shareholders, 86–87
reasons for patron disputes at, 129
regulated as a publicly traded business, 86
regulator's decision that, did not act improperly, 133
required to file CTR and SAR reports, 89
Resort at Summerlin, 101
Resorts Int'l Hotel, 129n109
Revel Casino Hotel Atlantic City, 101
riverboat gambling, 3, 11–12
Riviera, 100
San Manuel Indian Bingo & Casino, 186
Sands Hotel & Casino, 101
Soaring Eagle Casino & Resort, 186
Stateline Casino, 101
Station, 100
stores player's personal information (PI), 266
Stratosphere Casino and Hotel, 100
subject to BSA under definition of financial institution, 86
Tahoe Village, 7
Tinian Dynasty Hotel, 96
Trump Entertainment Resorts, 101
Trump Hotels & Casino Resorts, 101
ways to lose license of, 72–76
WinStar World Casino and Resort, 3
casino cage, surveillance camera in the, 76
Casino Collection Lawsuits: The Basics, 122n56
Casino Credit and Collections in New Jersey—An Overview, 125n76
casino gambling, command-type regulation of, 49
casino gambling tax, Nevada creates first (1945), 6
casino games, not considered gambling if prizeless, 24
casino gaming, regulated by administrative agencies, 51–53
Casino Gaming in New Jersey, 11n46
casino gaming industry, includes commercial sector and American Indian tribal sector, 167
casino manager, licensing requirement for, 68
casino transactions, categories that are exempt from CTR requirements, 90–91
Cassidy Amanda (author, *Essential Health Benefits…What's Next?*), 145n54
Caught in the Intersection between Public Policy and Practicality: Survey of Legal Treatment of Gambling Obligations, 123n62
CDRP. *See* Chemical Dependency Recovery Program
censure, example of type of sanction against an attorney, 154
Centers for Medicare and Medicaid Service, explanation of Medicare and Medicaid by, 142n31
"chasing one's losses," 137n2
chance
    as an element of a legal sweepstakes, 39
    State v. Lindsay analyzed term, 28
    types of, 28–29
    Webster's New International Dictionary's definition of, 28
chance games, tests to distinguish between skill games and, 25–27
chance-based gambling
    examples of, 23–24

Chapter 11
  bankruptcy plan and disclosure statement, 107
  benefits of filing bankruptcy in other districts, 102, 102n30
  prepackaged bankruptcy and Native American casino, 109
  sale of assets similar to 363 sale, 106
Chapter 11 plan
  designates classes of claimants and interest holders, 107
  liquidates gaming debtor's assets, 101
  process of, 106–108
Chapter 11 reorganization
  courts commonly used for, 102
  rights in, 102–109
Cheater's Justice: Judicial Recourse for Victims of Gaming Fraud, 112n1
checks, passing of bad, 122
checks and balances, as component of internal control system, 71
Chemical Dependency Recovery Program (CDRP), Kaiser Permanente's, 158
Cherokee Nation v. Georgia, 14n66
Chertoff, Michael (Assistant Attorney General), 18n85
chess
  contrasted to imperfect information of game rock, scissors, paper, 28
  legal game of pure skill, 25
Chevron U.S.A., Inc. v. Natural Resources Defense Council, Inc., 175n38
Cheyenne River Sioux Tribe v. South Dakota, 174n32
China's State Administration of Foreign Exchange (SAFE), 124n69
Chinese gamblers, baccarat is game of choice, 123
Chinese Gamblers—The Rewards and Challenges Facing Las Vegas Casinos, 123n68
Chinese law, controls amount of money transferred out of country, 123–124
"Chinese lottery," *State v. Cox* and, 33
chip fill, request of additional chips from the cage, 71
chip inventory, at gaming table, 71
chip runner, regulatory requirements for, 69
chips
  casino use of unapproved tokens or, 73
  wagering with denominated, 114
Choctaw Plan to Be First in Mississippi to Offer Sports Betting, 262n102
Christie, Chris (Governor of New Jersey), 245
Christie I case, New Jersey plan for sports betting, 245
Christie v. NCAA, 245n26, 246n27
Chronology of (Legal) Gaming in the U.S., 4n2
Cica, Dawn M. (co-author, *When Gaming Goes Heads Up with the Bankruptcy Code...*), 103n38
City of Milwaukee v. Burns, 27
City of Las Vegas, challenge to 1931 Nevada gambling law by, 6
City of Milwaukee v. Burns, 27n20
Civil Rights Act (Title VII), exempts tribes from federal labor and employment statutes, 185
claiming race, definition of horse racing, 16
Clark County (Nevada), unpaid casino markers cases referred to, 122
Clark, Laura (author, *What is the GDPR?*), 269n23
Class I Indian gaming
  definition and examples of, 170, 171t
  examples of, 213
  not under BSA rules, 88
  types of and control of, 260n95
Class II Indian gaming
  control of, 260n95
  examples of, 213
  definition and examples of, 170, 171t
  not regulated by state, 170
  only legal in states that already permit gambling, 170
  regulated by the tribe, IGRA, and NIGC oversight, 170
  tribe must adopt tribal gaming ordinance to govern, 170
Class II and III, casinos operated by American Indian tribes, 167n1
Class III gaming
  definition and examples of, 170, 171t, 213, 261

only legal in states that already permit gambling, 170
regulated by tribal ordinance and tribal-state compact, 170, 179
tribe and state to negotiate as governments, 171
tribe retains right to regulation of its own, 180
types of and control of, 260n95
class action lawsuit, against social gaming operators, 42
Classic Oldsmobile-Cadillac-GMC Truck, Inc. v. State, 37, 38n80
Clemens, Samuel. *See* Twain, Mark
client trust account, attorney as fiduciary duty to safeguard, 153–154
client trust fund
attorney prohibited from withdrawing money from, for personal use, 155–156
sanctions against attorney for failing to safeguard, 153–154
Clinton, Bill (U.S. President), signed Mental Health Parity Act, 139
Clinton's Little White Lies: The Materiality Requirement for Perjury in Civil Discovery, 55n12
"closed participation" gift enterprise schemes, 36
code, tilt, 133
Code of Federal Regulations, 86n25
Coen, Andrew (author, *Online Bets Drive New Jersey's Sports Gambling Tax Revenue Growth*), 256n74
Coghill v. Boardwalk Regency Corp., 121n55
cognitive behavioral therapy, benefits for gambling disorder include, 146
coin counter, 64
Cole v. Hughes, 240n171
collateral agreement
NIGC definition of, 183
tribal gaming and, 183–185
Collier Guide to Chapter 11, 83n10
Collins v. Ky. Lottery Corp., 226n68
colorable claim, 155
Colorado Governmental Immunity Act, 227
Colorado River Indian Tribes v. Nat'l Indian Gaming Comm'n, 181n69

Colorado, definition of gambling in, 24n5
Comanche-Oklahoma Compact Approval Letter, 181n72
"comity," principles of, 122–123
Commerce Clause and Dormant Commerce Clause, 239
commercial casino, AGA definition of, 14n64
common law "right to exclude," 113n9
Commonwealth v. Frate, 37
Commonwealth v. Heffner, 33n61, 217n16
Commonwealth v. Katsafanas, 227n81
Commonwealth v. Plissner, 23n2, 29, 29n28
Commonwealth v. Webb, 37n75
communism, McCarthy investigation of U.S. government and, 7–8
competitive bidding process, for state lottery contracts, 236–237
competitive integrity, eSports and, 21
complaints, regulatory agency investigation of patron, 77
comptroller, regulatory sensitivity and requirements for, 68
compulsive gambler
casino has no duty to stop, 129n109
See also gambling addiction/disorder
compulsive gambling
excluded from ADA definition of disability, 150
why ADA's definition of disability excludes, 151
See also gambling disorder; pathological gambling
conciliatory type, gaming license applicant who is, 56
Congress
constitutional power of, does not abrogate state sovereign immunity, 172
excludes compulsive gambling from definition of disability, 152
Indian tribes in Constitution as regulated by, 14
consideration
absent when chance to win is free, 37n73
any inconvenience to patron entering a promotion is, 31
definition and description of, 29, 33
element of a wager, 112
example of cases of, 30–31

consideration *(continued)*
   free method of entry negates, 36
   gambling and, element, 29–39
   how much consumer effort is required for, 34
   inconvenience to the patron and, 31
   methods of removing, 35–39
   nominal fee to enter sweepstakes is not, 33–34
   person pays, 23
   prohibited gambling becomes sweepstakes with removal of, 36
   promoter benefit test and, 31–32
   sweepstakes does not have element of, 35
   theories and tests for analyzing, 29–34
Consola v. State, 224n59
Constitution, Indian tribes regulated by Congress in, 14
constructive presence principle/doctrine, 209
Consumer Protection Act, 42
contest of chance
   Alabama definition of, 26
   New York definition of, 27n17
Contests and the Lottery Laws, 31n49
contracts
   adhesion, take-it-or-leave-it, 111
   formed through wagers not subject to negotiation, 112
   lottery procurement, 238
   lottery vendor, 238
   wagering, 112–114
   who is the offeror and offeree, 111
   See also wagering contract
contract law, gaming industry and special nature of, 111
Contracts Clause, of U.S. Constitution, 235
contractor, lottery disputes involving vendor or, 234
Control Data Corp v. Controlling Bd. of Ohio, 238n157
controller, GDPR definition of, 269
Converse v. State Lottery Comm'n, 233n125
corporation
   depth of licensing for, 66
   stock ownership and publicly traded, 67
corporate reorganization, 99–109

counseling, health benefits for gambling disorder include, 146
count room
   regulatory agent observes, 77
   surveillance camera in the, 76
counterchecks, casino draws on player's bank account using, 119
Counter-Strike, eSports game of, 20
counting cards, type of advantage play in blackjack, 112, 113n9
"cramdown," bankruptcy and, 107
"crane game," 29
craps, Indian Class III gaming, 260n95
craps table, example of understood rule at, 113
Crawford, Douglas, attorney used client's trust fund to gamble, 159–162
Crazy Rich Lottery Winners: What Would You Buy with $1.2 Billion?, 219n36
credit
   casino extends, when player signs marker, 111
   casino must determine creditworthiness of gambler seeking, 123
   granting of casino, 114–116
   information requested on casino application form for, 115
   not all states allow casinos to offer, 115
   pros and cons when casino extends, to player, 114–115
   requirements casino must follow when granting, 124
   rim, 126
   states that prohibit gambling on, 47
credit/collection failures, examples of casino, 76
credit and collection manager, regulatory requirements for, 69
credit application
   information requested on, 115
   website for example of (Caesars Palace), 115n21
credit play, percentage of total wagers is on, 114, 118, 127
Credit Scores Come to Debt-Leery Chinese—To Boost Consumption the Government Wants More Borrowers, 123n67

creditors
    priority and unsecured, 108
    types of regulated commercial, 63
crime. *See* organized crime
criminal elements, applicant for gaming license must have no connection to, 53
criminal penalty, lack of licensure or offering unapproved gambling games and, 24
Crouch, Michelle (author, *10 Things You Can't (Easily) Buy with Credit Cards*), 114n15
CTR. *See* Currency Transaction Report
CTR-C, failure to complete, 75
Cudd v. Aschenbrenner, 36n67
Culler, Dale, class action lawsuit, 229
Currency and Foreign Transactions Report Act, another name for BSA, 251
currency counter, 64
currency reporting, 81–97
Currency Transaction Report (CTR)
    for cash more than $10,000, 251
    when must be filed with FinCEN, 89
currency transaction reporting, money laundering includes avoiding, 86
currency transactions
    categories of CTR-exempt casino, 90–91
    FinCEN Form 112 for reportable, 90
Currency Transfer Report (CTR), 75
Current Battles and the Future of Off-Reservation Indian Gaming, 178n57
customer deposit accounts, BSA requirements for casino, 94
customer experience, vital to success of eSports, 19–20
Cwalina, Chris (co-author, *Data Protection Report*), 266n2
Cyber Challenges in the Gaming Industry: For the House to Win, It Can't Gamble on Cybersecurity, 268n17
cyber coverage, insurance policy for, 273
cyber coverage insurance, often excluded from general liability insurers' policies, 273
Czarnetzky, John M. (author, *When the Dealer Goes Bust: Issues in Casino Bankruptcies*), 106n50
Czyzewski v. Jevic Holding Corp., 102n31

D

D.C. Circuit, 186
D.C. federal court, NLRA applies to tribes, 186
data privacy issues, 265–273
data protection
    European Union (EU) standards for, 266
    governed mostly by state law, 266
    laws enacted for, in all states, 273
    Nevada law for, 267
    state law applies to business with electronically stored PI, 267
    U.S. does not have comprehensive federal law for, 266
    See also GDPR
Data Protection Board, European, 271
data protection impact assessments, required by GDPR, 270
Data Security Breach Notification Laws, 266n3
Datatrol, Inc. v. State Purchasing Agent, 237n146
Davis, Governor Gray (California), 181
Dawson, Larry, lawsuit based on random number generator fraud, 229
de novo appeal, 160
Deal or No Deal? Understanding Indian Country Transactions, 187n97
dealer, regulatory requirements for, 69
Dealing with Troubled Tribal Casinos, 184n83
debenture, definition of, 63
debt
    Chinese residents' collection of casino gambling, 123
    collection of casino, 116–124
    collection of, when bettor's bank account has insufficient funds, 122
    death of bettor and collection of casino, 117
    enforceability of gambling, 116–117
    rim, 126
    See also gambling debt
debtor in possession (DIP), 104
"debtor in possession," fiduciary acts as, 102n31
debtor in possession (DIP) financing, 104
Debunking Lottery Myths, 218n30
"deferential standard of review," 131

definition of
  363 sale, 105–106
  absolute priority rule, 107
  acceptance, 48
  administrative functions, 51
  allowance race (horse racing), 16
  auxiliary services, 51
  bankruptcy estate, 102
  bet, 13
  bet (Wisconsin), 25n10
  betting handle (sports betting), 250
  bookmaking, 13
  breach of PI, 267
  breach of PI (Nevada), 268
  breadth of licensing, 61–65
  business, 197
  cash-in transaction, 89
  cashless wagering system, 64
  cash-out transaction, 89–90
  casino "associated equipment," 64
  casino lender, 63
  chance (*Webster's*), 28
  claiming race (horse racing), 16
  Class I Indian gaming, 170
  Class II gaming, 260n95
  Class II Indian gaming, 170
  Class III gaming, 261
  Class III Indian gaming, 170, 261
  collateral agreement (NIGC), 183
  commercial casino (AGA), 14n64
  common law, gambling, 23, 25
  consideration, 29
  contest of chance (Alabama), 26
  contest of chance (New York), 27n17
  controller (GDPR), 269
  debenture, 63
  designated payment system, 210n90
  disability (ADA), 150
  disability (ADAAA clarification of ADA), 149, 152
  dual-sovereign system, 23
  facility (Travel Act), 207, 212n99
  financial institution, 86n30
  financial transaction provider (UIGEA), 210n87
  financial institution (BSA), 87
  gambling, 13
  gambling (Colorado), 24n5
  gambling (states' gambling statutes), 39–40
  gambling (Tennessee), 27n17
  gaming day, 90, 90n60
  gaming devices, 63
  gaming licensure fixed criteria, 53–54
  gaming licensure of discretionary criteria, 53–54
  "golden whale," 96
  "government unit," 190n112
  "handle" (horse race betting), 17
  honesty, 55
  illegal gambling (Minnesota Gambling Control Board), 13n56
  Indians, 175n36
  Indian gaming (IGRA), 169
  Indian land, 174
  information assisting, 197
  instant scratch game (Iowa), 217n22
  instaplay ticket, 217n22
  integration (money laundering), 85
  integrity, 55
  intermittent explosive disorder (*DSM-III*), 151n95
  internal controls, 70
  Internet gambling business (UIGEA), 211
  interstate or foreign commerce (DOJ), 203
  intrastate (New Hampshire), 247
  intrastate wagering, 18
  junket, 94n86
  kleptomania (*DSM-III*), 151n93
  large employer, 140
  large employer (MHPAEA), 141–142
  layering (money laundering), 85
  licensing, 53
  liquidity, 252
  lottery courier, 238, 239
  management contract (NIGC), 183
  marker, 115
  mental health benefits, 140n22
  money laundering, 84–86
  off-reservation, 178
  offer, 48
  palps (sports betting), 251n53
  pari-mutuel system, 17
  pari-mutuel wagering, 260
  pay line, 48
  person, 191n119
  person who gambles (New York), 26n15

personal data (GDPR), 269
personal information (California Consumer Privacy Act), 266n2
personal information (Nevada), 267–268
physical or mental impairment (ADA), 150
placement (money laundering), 85
playslip (lotto game), 218
processor (GDPR), 269
public offering, 66n37
publicly traded company, 66
pyromania (*DSM-III*), 151n94
revenue sharing, 181
sagacity, 27
"scratcher," 216n22
"scratchless," 217n22
skill (Alabama Supreme Court), 27
skimming, 52–53
skin (sports betting), 254
small employer, 140n16
something of value (Missouri), 39–40
stakes race (horse racing), 16
state (UIGEA), 213
thing of value (Washington statute), 42
tribal sovereign immunity, 186
trichotillomania (*DSM-III*), 151n96
truthfulness, 54
turnover (horse race betting), 17
unlawful activity (Travel Act), 207
unlawful Internet gambling (UIGEA), 202–203, 210n86, 212
unsuitable association, 57
wager, 13
Delaware
  first state since Nevada to offer sports betting, 246n32
  offers (2011) intrastate, online gaming, 19
  reason for exemption from PASPA, 12
  signed MSIGA with Nevada and New Jersey for internet poker, 201
  sports betting regulated and operated by state lottery, 247
Delehanty, Herb (author, *The Lottery Industry: Cases, Problems & Preventable Incidents*), 216n8
Dellafave, Robert (author, *Pay Attention: More than Four-Fifths of Sports Betting Handle in New Jersey Comes from Online*), 256n75

demoralizing influence, early lottery said to have, 216n8
Department of Health and Human Services (HHS). *See* HHS
Department of Justice (DOJ)
  2019 opinion that Wire Act applies to all types of betting, 221
  definition of "interstate or foreign commerce," 203
  new interpretation of the Wire Act, 10n43
  Office of Legal Counsel and new interpretation of Wire Act by, 18
  Office of the Legal Counsel (OLC) is under, 194
  online gaming violates federal Wire Act, 18
  updated interpretation of Wire Act by, 12
  Wire Act applies only to bets on sporting events, 221
Department of the Treasury
  can designate person as a financial institution, 87–88
  UIGEA directed, to make regulations to block restricted transactions, 209–210
"dependent domestic sovereigns," Supreme Court says Indian tribes are, 14
depression, mental state as defense against gambling debts, 128
derogation, statute on gambling debts was in, of common law, 118
DeRosa, Ed (author, *What Does Pari-Mutuel Betting Mean in Horse Racing?*), 15n78
Desert Palace, Inc. v. Michael, 126n95
Desert Rose Bingo, server-based bingo website violated UIGEA, 213
designated payment system, definition and examples of, 210n90
desk clerk, regulatory requirements of, 69
"device," not defined by Wagering Paraphernalia Act, 206
Di Gregory, Kevin V. (Assistant Attorney General, Criminal Division), 204n50
Diagnostic and Statistical Manual of Mental Disorders (DSM), 141
  gambling disorder included since 1980 in, 148

Diagnostic and Statistical Manual of Mental Disorders (DSM-5)
    diagnostic criteria for and symptoms of gambling disorder, 137n2
    reclassified gambling disorder as Substance-Related and Addictive Disorders, 146
    renames pathological gambling as gambling disorder, 152

Diagnostic and Statistical Manual of Mental Disorders (DSM-IV-TR)
    APA classified gambling as impulse-control disorder, 151
    classified pathological gambling as impulse control disorder, 144

dice throw, example of systemic chance, 28

Dickerson v. Deno, 240n1171

diminished capacity, gambler tries to avoid paying gambling loss by claiming, 127–129

DIP. *See* debtor in possession

directives, regulators' use of, 50

disability
    ADA's definition of, excludes gambling disorder, 150
    ADAAA's definition of, 152
    gambling disorder not entitled to protection as, 149
    lawyer must read state's statute defining, to see if gambling client is eligible, 150

disability nondiscrimination laws, protection under, 149–153

disbarment, type of sanction against an attorney, 154, 160

disclosure statement, Chapter 11 bankruptcy plan and, 107

discretionary criteria, definition and examples of gaming licensure, 53–54

discrimination, health care plans, against persons with gambling disorder, 143

disorder
    addictive, 140
    drug use, 162
    gambling. *See* gambling disorder
    impulse control, 144, 145n57
    intermittent explosive, 151n95
    substance use, 140, 141, 141n29, 143–144

Disorder, Diagnostic and Statistical Manual of Mental (DMS), 141

Disorder, Substance-Related and Addictive, 146

disparity, gambling disorder health plan benefit, mostly eliminated now, 139

disputed jackpot, reason for patron complaint, 129–133

distribution at point-of-purchase, 35

District Court of New Jersey, 245

District of Delaware, court commonly used for Chapter 11 reorganization, 102

District of Nevada, court commonly used for Chapter 11 litigation, 102

diversion, example of type of sanction against an attorney, 154

Dixon, Ken (author, *Lottery Supplier Defends Role in Fraud Scandal*), 238n160

documentation controls, as component of internal control system, 70

Doe v. N.H. Lottery Comm'n, 232n118

dog racing, pari-mutuel wagering on, 260

DOJ. *See* Department of Justice

The DOJ Gives States a Gift, 221n49

Domenici, Pete, MHPAEA and, 141

dominant factor test, also known as predominance test, 25

Domingo v. Mitchell, 240n171

Domonoske, Camila (author, *Call Her Jane Dough: New Hampshire Lottery Winner Can Stay Anonymous*), 232n118

Dorman v. Publix-Saenger-Sparks Theatres, 30n33

Dorson, Jill R. (author)
    Choctaw Plan to Be First in Mississippi to Offer Sports Betting, 262n102
    It's Official: Pritzker Signs Illinois Betting Into Law, 248n39

Dota 2, eSports game of, 20

DraftKings, sports book provider, 253

dram shop liability, New Jersey, 127

"draw break," between games, 225n66

"drawing," defined in administrative rule or game rule, 230

Driscoll v. State, 225n64

"drop," money in a casino's, 90n61

"drop box," table games and a, 71

drug trafficking, AML laws combat, 84

DSM. *See Diagnostic and Statistical Manual of Mental Disorders*
dual-sovereign system, definition of, 23
Dubai World Cup, horse racing and international, 16
Duff v. Harrah South Shore Corp., 129n109
Dufrene v. La. Lottery Corp., 225n66
Dunbar, Marc W. (author, *The History of Internet Cafes and the Current Approach to Their Regulation*), 83n23
Duncan, Robert (author, "Colorado" in *International Casino Law*), 67n40

E

Eadington, William R. (gambling studies scholar), 182
Eash v. Imperial Palace of Mississippi, LLC, 130–131
Eastern District of New York, Wire Act only applies to sports betting, 199
Eastern District of Pennsylvania, considered DSM's inclusion of pathological gambling, 151
economic growth, gambling regulations to stimulate, 47
Economic Impact of the U.S. Gaming Industry, 3n1
Economic Impact of the United States Horse Industry, 16n75
The Economic Impact of Tribal Gaming: A State-by-State Analysis, 83n11
The Economics of Sports Betting Research Brief, 249n43
economic value test, 32–34, 36
Economic Value, Equal Dignity, and the Future of Sweepstakes, 29n32
Ecumenical Ministries of Oregon v. Oregon State Lottery Comm'n, 216n8
education, state lotteries provide funding for, 19
EFT. *See* electronic fund transfers
EHBs. *See* essential health benefits
Eighth Circuit, tribal sovereign immunity and, 191
Einhorn, Bruce (author, *Credit Scores Come to Debt-Leery Chinese—To Boost Consumption the Government Wants More Borrowers*), 123n67

electronic associated equipment, common forms of, 64
electronic fund transfers (EFT), UIGEA and, 209
electronic gaming machine, description of, 48
electronic shoe, 64
Eleventh Amendment immunity, state invokes, 172
embezzlement, accounting controls to prevent, 69
Embry-Riddle Aeronautical University, student health insurance excludes gambling disorder, 139
emergency motions, also known as "first day motions," 103
employee
  examples of failure of casino, 75–76
  licensing and regulatory requirements for casino, 68
  tribal sovereignty applies to tribal gaming operators and, 187
Employee Retirement Income Security Act (ERISA), governed multiemployer welfare arrangements and EBHs, 144n46
employer
  MHPAEA definition of large, 141–142
  MHPAEA regulated only insured and self-insured group health plans of large, 141–142
Employment Law in Indian Country: Finding the Private-Action Jurisdictional Hook Is Not Easy, 185n89
encryption, business best practice is, of personal information, 268
enforceability, of gambling debts in foreign countries, 122–124
enforcement, methods of detection of violations, 52
enforcement actions, types of FinCEN, on casinos, 96
enforcement agencies, functions performed by, 76–77
enforcement regulatory powers, administrative agency's, 52
English law, Statute of Anne, 117–118
Epic Games, creator of *Fortnite*, 20n98

equal dignity
    example that precluded a finding of, 37
    Illinois interpretation of rule of, 37n73
    material disparity and, 38
    no-purchase must be clearly disclosed, 38
    principle and examples of, 36–38
Erickson v. Desert Palace Inc., 129
ERISA. *See* Employee Retirement Income Security Act
Erlenbaugh v. United States, 206n63
ESIC. *See* eSports Integrity Coalition
ESIC (eSports Integrity Coalition), 20
eSports
    accessed via PlayStation or Xbox, 20
    customer experience and, 19–20
    global audience and revenues for, 20
    Internet contests and, 24
    issues for gambling component of, 21
    Nevada permits wagering on professional contest of, 20
eSports Integrity Coalition (ESIC), 20
essential health benefits (EHBs)
    HHS regulations implementing ACA's, requirements of, 144
    mental health and substance use disorder categories included in, 144
    requirements of, do not apply to grandfathered health plans or self-insured health plans, 146
    Eidelman, Michael (co-author, *Dealing with Troubled Tribal Casinos*), 184n83
Essential Health Benefits Provisions of the Affordable Care Act: Implications for People with Disabilities, 144n46
Essential Health Benefits: States Have Determined the Minimum Set of Benefits to be Included in Individual and Small-Group Insurance Plans. What's Next?, 145n54
Estlow v. N.H. Sweepstakes Comm'n, 225n65
estopped, 126
EU. *See* European Union
European Data Protection Board, 271
European Union (EU), GDPR privacy laws of, apply to U.S., 265, 268–273

European Union citizens
    attorney and gaming applicant clients who are, 269
    GDPR and gaming companies with, 270
European Union member states, differences in enforcement of GDPR, 271
Even Moe Dalitz Would Blush: Why the District Attorney Has No Business Collecting Unpaid Casino Markers, 122n58
ex ante, 132
Exclusions and Countermeasures: Do Card Counters Have a Right to Play?, 113n9
exclusivity period, Chapter 11 debtor's plan, 106
exemplary conduct, of attorney with gambling disorder, 158
expedited hearing, bankruptcy court first day motions and, 104
extended play
    constitutes a prize, 42
    extended play, some states forbid, 42
extension of a service, something of value and, 41

F

F.A.C.E. Trading, Inc. v. Dep't of Consumer & Indus. Serv., 33n56
F.A.C.E. Trading, Inc. v. Todd, 39
F.C.C. v. Am. Broad. Co., 23n2
Facebook, GDPR complaints about "forced consent" filed against, 271
facility, definition of (Travel Act), 207, 212n99
fair and equitable, bankruptcy plan that is, 107
Faiss, Robert D. (author)
    Nevada Gaming Industry Credit Practices and Procedures, 114n17
    Nevada Gaming Statutes: Their Evolution and History, 6n16
fantasy sports
    some states require licensing for daily, 24n3
    unregulated gaming of, 83n12
Fantasy Sports: One Form of Mainstream Wagering in the United States, 27n17
fast-food restaurants, AMOE and promotions at, 35

"*Fauntleroy* Doctrine," provisions of the, 120
FBI. *See* Federal Bureau of Investigation
FCC Attacks Radio Give-Away Programs, 28n22
FCC v. American Broadcasting Co., 32–33
Featherstone v. Indep. Serv. Station Ass'n of Texas, 32n50
federal bankruptcy laws, 190–192
Federal Bureau of Investigation (FBI)
　gambling employee terminated by, 151
　investigates Nevada casinos with Gaming Control Board (1961), 10
federal government
　does not have major role in gaming regulation, 23
　regulation of Indian commerce under exclusive control of, 172
federal law
　assists in enforcing state gambling prohibitions, 13
　Illegal Gambling Business Act is a, 13n58
　Internet gambling and, 195
　prohibits forms of gambling that violate existing state law, 195
　Travel Act (1952) is a, 13n58
　Unlawful Internet Gambling Enforcement Act (2012), 13n58
　Wagering Paraphernalia Act (1953) is a, 13n58
federal legislation, needed to harmonize Wire Act and UIGEA, 262
Federal Reserve Board, IUGEA directed, to make regulations to block restricted transactions, 209–210
Federal Wire Act
　federal government's changing interpretation of, 16
　provisions, prohibitions, and exemptions of, 10
　to combat interstate revenue-generating of organized crime, 10
　See also Wire Act
Federally Recognized Indian Tribe List Act (1994), 175n40
fee-to-trust process, Interior Department and revisions to, 178n60
felony, materiality of noncompliance and a, 56

felony conviction, disqualifies applicant for gaming license, 55
Fenich, George G. (author, *Chronology of (Legal) Gaming in the U.S.*), 4n2
fiduciary, acts as "debtor in possession," 102n31
field observation, gaming violations found by, 52
Fifth Circuit
　decisions about tribal gaming, 173
　interpretation of Wire Act, 198
financial agent, reviews gaming license applicant's finances, 59–60
financial capability, gaming license applicant's, 58
financial information, gaming application and types of required, 60
financial institution
　casinos and card clubs are a, 88
　BSA definition of, 87
　definition of, 86n30
financial requirements, description of types of MHPAEA, 141
financial services system, AML laws limit criminals' access to, 85
financial transaction provider, definition and examples of (UIGEA), 210n87
financing, debtor in possession (DIP) and post-petition bankruptcy, 104
FinCEN. *See* Financial Crimes Enforcement Network
FinCEN Frequently Asked Questions: Casino Recordkeeping, Reporting, and Compliance, 94n81
Financial Crimes Enforcement Network (FinCEN)
　advisory on transactions with *casas de cambios*, 96n106
　advisory on unlawful structuring transactions, 91–93
　BSA regulations transferred to Code of Federal Regulations by, 86n25
　Form 111, file SAR electronically on, 93
　Form 112, for reportable currency transaction, 90
　enforcement action for failure to file SAR, 96

Financial Crimes Enforcement Network *(continued)*
   enforcement action for failure to have AML, 96
   examples of casino fines by, 96
   guidelines for identifying suspicious behavior, 91–92
   list of gaming institutions subject to BSA casino regulations, 88n48
   when CTR must be filed with, 89
"finder's fees," 61
fine
   regulators' use of, 50
   tool to motivate and ensure compliance, not punishment, 51
fingerprinting, Nevada Tax Commission requires (1949) casino employees have, 7
First Benchmark Plan, Nevada's, 145
First Circuit, *United States v. Lyons* and, 198
"first day motion," bankruptcy and examples of, 103
First Mortgage Co. v. Fed. Leasing Corp., 29n31
First Move Advantage in Chess, 25n9
Fitchie v. Yurko, 240n171
fixed criteria, definition and examples for gaming licensure, 53–54
Flamingo casino (Nevada, 1947), 7
"flexible participation" scheme, 36
Florida, sports betting versus tribal gaming and IGRA compact, 248
Florida Council on Compulsive Gambling, Inc., 115 n18
Florida House of Representative v. Crist, 179n63
Foley, Ryan (author, *Winner Sues Colorado Lottery for Millions over Fixed Jackpot*), 230n97
"forced consent," complaints filed with GDPR about U.S. companies, 271
Forcing the Tribe to Bet on the House: Limited Options and Risks to the Tribe When Indian Gaming Operations Seek Debtor Relief, 191n116
foreign country, enforcing gaming debts in a, 122–124

foreign gaming report, casino failure to file, 72
Foreign Gaming Reporting Requirements Policy Statement, 50n5
Foreman v. State, 240n169
formal rulemaking, 50
Fortin, Jacey (author, *Sorry, Lottery Winners, South Carolina Won't Pay*), 225n61
Fortnite, eSports game of, 20
Fowles v. State, 224n58
Foxwoods Is Fighting for Its Life, 191n116
Foxwoods Resort Casino, Mashantucket Pequot Tribal Nation and, 191
fraud
   AML laws combat, 84
   Hot Lotto ticket and high-tech, 227
free, participants enter sweepstakes for, 35
"free" tickets, for a chance at a prize, 32
free alternative method of entry (AMOE), sweepstakes examples of, 35
free entry blank, must be regarded as chimerical, 37n73
free entry form, not dispositive, 37n73
free market competition, gambling regulations and, 47
free method of entry
   consideration negated by, 36
   does not meet economic value test, 36
free to participate, consideration removed by, 36
freemium online casino games, class action lawsuits against, 42–43
From the Archives: Here's How Nevada Banned Gambling, Reintroduced It, 5n8
Fuchs, Ralph F. (author, *Agency Development of Policy Through Rule-Making*), 50n4
Full Faith and Credit Clause
   foreign jurisdictions may refuse to enforce U.S. gambling debt, 123
   no public policy exception to, 120–121, 120n51
   of the U.S. Constitution, 120–121, 120n51
Fullerton v. Dep't of Revenue Servs., 225n63
Functions of a Tribal Gaming Commission, 49n2

G

GA. *See* Gamblers Anonymous
G.A. Carney, Ltd. V. Brzeczek, 37n73
Galanda, Gabriel (author)
   Deal or No Deal? Understanding Indian Country Transactions, 187n97
   Getting Commercial in Indian Country, 187n97
gambler. *See also* patron
Gamblers Anonymous (GA) meetings, 150–151, 157
gambling
   1931 Nevada law (1931) taxed but did not regulate, 6
   as a pastime and business, 3
   common law definition and elements of, 23–25
   definition and types of, 13
   effect of Great Depression on acceptance of, 5
   examples of money changing hands during, 48
   first legalized in Nevada (1869), 4
   illegal in China, 124
   illegal in most U.S. states (1800s to early 1900s), 4
   Internet, 193–214
   is a consensual agreement, 48
   is privilege not a right (Nevada Governor Sawyer, 1958), 9
   Nevada casino (prior to World War II), 6
   Nevada Supreme Court confirmed government can regulate, 6
   public perception is key factor in legislative support for, 235
   recent U.S. history of, 12–13
   rule breaches and allowing underage, 52
   states' statutes definition of, 39–40
   types of, 3
   United States and regulated, 3–21
   what is, 23–43
   See also gambling industry
gambling addiction
   is it defense in a collection case, 128
   when casino knows person has this, 129, 129n109
   See also compulsive gambler; gambling disorder
Gambling and the Law: The Role of Credit in the Third Wave of Legal Gambling, 115n19
Gambling and the Law: The Third Wave of Legal Gambling, 83n13
gambling contract
   consensual nature of, 49
   favors casino over time, 48
gambling debt
   enforcing and nonenforcing state, 118
   how to collect Chinese, 123
   See also debt
gambling disorder
   ACA requires some health plans to provide benefits for, 146
   ADA excludes diagnosis of, 150
   ADAAA's definition of, 152
   attorney dealing with, 158
   attorney reinstatement after violations due to, 163
   being fired for, is violation of Rehabilitation Act, 149, 151
   Bellicini, Samuel, practicing attorney with, 158–159
   biologically based mental illness does not include, 138–139
   business lawyer and issues related to, 137–163
   California Fair Employment and Housing Act does not include, 152
   classified as impulse-control disorder by APA, 144
   classified as non-substance-related (APA), 152
   cognitive behavioral therapy and counseling for, 146
   considered EHB (Nevada, 2017–2019), 146
   Crawford, Douglas, practicing attorney with, 159–162
   discrimination by health care plans against, 143
   DSM-5 diagnostic criteria for, 137n2
   DSM-5 renames pathological gambling as, 152
   excluded from ADA's definition of disability, 150

gambling disorder *(continued)*
　federal and state disability nondiscrimination laws do not protect persons with, 164
　federal and state disability nondiscrimination laws not helpful for, 149
　health insurance coverage issues, 137–148
　health plan benefit disparities for, mostly eliminated now, 139
　initially classified as impulse-control disorder, 151
　included in *DSM* since 1980, 148
　issues with health insurance coverage, 137–148
　issues for lawyers representing client with, 153–164
　insurance benefits include counseling and cognitive behavioral therapy for, 146
　MHPAEA does not guarantee health care coverage for, 140
　MHPAEA does not require health plans to treat, 142
　Nebraska Benchmark Plan excludes coverage for, 144–145, 147
　not a defense in casino debt collection cases, 128
　not entitled to protection under disability nondiscrimination laws, 149
　pathological gambling renamed in *DSM-5* as, 152
　parity laws may exclude, 139
　professional discipline for attorney with, 153–163
　reasons why health insurance plan will not cover, 138
　Reilly, Michael, practicing attorney with, 155–156
　statutes about (Nevada), 128
　reclassified under Substance-Related and Addictive Disorders in 2013, 146
　state guidelines not specific for attorney reinstatement after, 163
　symptoms of, 137
　trends in attorney disciplinary proceedings for, 162–163
　unclear if considered as essential health benefit (EHB), 144
　Winder, Danny, practicing attorney with, 156–157
　See also pathological gambling
　Gambling Disorder, Vulnerability, and the Law: Mapping the Field, 137n3
gambling industry
　after World War II factors that fueled Nevada's, 6
　examples of segments of U.S., 14–20
　history of American regulation of, 4–13
　introduction to, 83–84
　organized crime and Nevada's, 6
　U.S. economy and creation of jobs by, 3
　See also gaming industry
gambling instinct test, description of, 27
gambling machine
　casino must have proof of malfunction of, 135
　error code and, 134
　malfunction of, 133–135
　programming error difficult to categorize as malfunction of, 134
Gambling on Credit: Exploring the Link between Compulsive Gambling and Access to Credit, 115n18
gambling operations, consist of land-based casinos and Internet gaming, 82
gambling prohibitions, states, tribes and federal government have concurrent jurisdiction for, 13
gambling regulations
　in the European Union (EU) privacy and, 268–273
　in the United States, 13–20
　policy goals of, 47–48
　See also laws
gambling winnings, reported on IRS tax form W-2G, 75
Gambling with Bankruptcy: Navigating a Casino Through Chapter 11 Bankruptcy Proceedings, 106n50
gambling-related behavior. *See* gambling disorder
gambling-related treatment
　health insurance may have exclusion for, 138

game
    may be more expensive than treatment for physical conditions, 138
game
    house-banked, 13
    lawsuit over rules of lottery, 226
    of skill versus game of chance, 24–29
    player-backed, 13
    See also gambling; gaming
gaming
    federal and state laws regulate Indian nation, 13
    history of regulation of American, 4–13
    mobile online, 18
    Native American, 108–109
    off-reservation, 178
    on Indian land. *See* tribal gaming
    tribal, 167–192
    worldwide industry under GDPR, 268
    See also gaming industry; social gaming
gaming age, Nevada (1877), 4
Gaming and Gambling Law, 215n3
gaming assets, bankruptcy and buyer of, 106
gaming business, Bankruptcy Code applies to, 99
Gaming Commission, role of Nevada, 51, 52f
gaming companies, business partnerships between leagues and teams and, 244
gaming contract, gaming regulation and the, 48–53, 111–136
Gaming Control Board
    administered gambling regulations in Nevada (1958), 9
    creation of Nevada's (1955), 8
    disputed jackpot reviewed by, 130
    investigates Nevada casinos with FBI (1961), 10
    role of Nevada, 51, 52f
gaming day, definition of duration of a, 90, 90n60
gaming debt, represented by a marker versus unpaid slot machine jackpot, 130
gaming device
    casino use of unapproved, 72
    definition and examples of, 63
gaming device holds, difference between actual and theoretical, 78

gaming device manufacturer
    full licensing required for, 63–64
    responsibilities of, 63
gaming dispute, casino fails to report $500 or more, 73
gaming equipment, government's role in approving, 49
gaming floor, Iowa Racing and Gaming Commission defined area of, 114n16
gaming industry
    AML laws and, 86–87
    groups involved in, 61
    special nature of contract law in, 111
    See also gambling industry
gaming law, subtleties of, 136
Gaming Law & Practice, 13n55
gaming license
    363 sale and gaming regulators investigate, 106
    county sheriffs issue (Nevada, 1869), 4
    publicly traded corporations must apply for casino, 67
gaming licensee, Nevada Gaming Commission determines noncompliance of, 267
gaming machine malfunction, examples of, 135
gaming pit, 71
gaming properties, anti-money laundering requirements for, 81–97
gaming regulation
    basics of, 47–79
    done by state and local jurisdictions, 23
    govern the gaming contract, 48–53
    government's tax revenue protected by, 81n1
gaming regulatory functions, description of critical, 49–51, 50f
gaming tax revenues, Nevada (1907) law for, 4
gaming tracking systems, data gathered by casino, 265
gaming violation, prosecution for, 52
gaming websites, UIGEA violations for, 212
GDPR. *See* General Data Protection Regulation
Geiger v. State, 231n109

General Data Protection Regulation (GDPR), 265–273
  ABA's Model Rules of Professional Responsibility and, 270–271
  affects United States-based businesses, 268
  application and enforcement of, 271
  applies to any business that offers goods or services or monitors people in EU, 269
  attorney has increased litigation of privacy issues from, 270
  attorney research changes in data privacy and, 265
  complaints and lawsuits relating to, 271–272
  compliance tips for, 272–273
  controllers must do data protection impact assessments, 270
  definition of "personal data," 269
  definition of a controller, 269
  definition of a processor, 269
  differences in EU member states enforcement of, 271
  European Union's privacy law, 268–273
  "forced consent" complaints filed against U.S. companies, 271
  gaming companies with EU citizens who want licensed in U.S., 270
  greater data privacy controls than U.S., 269
  PI breach notification policy of, 270
  policy for breach of PI and notification, 270
  right of person to change or erase inaccurate PI, 270
  U.S. pro bono legal representation may be subject to, 269
  worldwide gaming industry is under, 268
geolocating tools, to verify jurisdiction of online sports wagering, 253, 257
Getting Commercial in Indian County, 187n97
GNOC Corp. v. Aboud, 127n99
golden "whale," definition of, 96
good faith, when state fails to negotiate with tribe in, 172
Google, GDPR complaints about "forced consent" filed against, 271
government, gambling contract and interference from, 49
government regulations, objectives of accounting controls in, 69
"government unit," definition of, 190n112
Grand Canyon Skyway, 191
Grand Casino Biloxi v. Hallman, 135
grandfathered health plans, ACA's EHB requirements do not apply to, 146
Granton v. Wash. State Lottery Comm'n, 225n66
gray list (denied applicants), casino, 74
Great Depression, Nevada favorable to gambling after, 5–7
Griggs v. Harrah's Casino, 135
Grimes v. Board of Commissioners of City of Las Vegas, 6n13
Grogan v. Garner, 101n28
Gromer, Don (author, "South Dakota" in *International Casino Law*), 67n45
"gross gambling revenue," definition of, 14n61
Guidiville Band of Pomo Indians v. NGV Gaming, Ltd, 177n48
"guilt by association," 57
Gulf Collateral, Inc. v. Morgan, 119n44
Gulfstream Park Racing Ass'n v. Tampa Bay Downs, 254n68
Gun Lake Trust Land Reaffirmation Act, 176
Guthas v. State, 217n16

H

Hakimoglu v. Trump Taj Mahal Associates, 127
handle
  federal excise tax on, 250
  horse race betting and definition of, 17
  sports betting operators and, 249
hand pays, gambling using, 42
harness racing, wagering on horse, 16
Harrah's Atlantic City Operating Co. v. Dangelico, 128n106
Harrah's Club v. Van Blitter, 128n104
Haskell v. Time, Inc., 34n65
Hatch, Orrin, (U.S. Senator), 261
Hawaii
  forbids regulated gambling, 13n53
  no legalized state Internet gambling in, 195

Hawkeye Commodity Promotions, Inc v. Vilsack, 234n129
Haynes v. Dep't of Lottery, 225n66
HCERA. *See* Health Care and Education Reconciliation
Health and Human Services (HHS)
   HHS Final Regulations (2013), say states must select benchmark plan, 144
   HHS Final Regulations (2018), states have option to select third benchmark plan, 147
   HHS Final Resolutions (2015), states required to select new benchmark plan, 146
   HHS Notice of Benefit and Payment Parameters for ACA (2016), 146n58
   regulations implementing ACA's EHB requirements, 144
Health Care and Education Reconciliation (HCERA), 143
health information, HIPAA and disclosure of personal, 272
health insurance, may have exclusion for gambling-related treatment, 138
health insurance coverage, gambling disorder and issues with, 137–148
health insurance plans, may only cover biologically-based mental illnesses, 138
Health Insurance Portability and Accountability Act (HIPAA), disclosure of personal health information, 266, 272
Health Plan of Nevada Point of Service Group 1, Nevada's First Benchmark Plan, 144
Health Plan of Nevada Solutions Health Maintenance Organization Platinum Plan, 146
Heinrich, Alan (author, *Clinton's Little White Lies: The Materiality Requirement for Perjury in Civil Discovery*), 55n12
Here's How the Real High-Rolling VIPs Gamble, 127n97
HHS. *See* Health and Human Services
Hicks, Alvin J. (author, *No Longer the Only Game in Town: A Comparison of Nevada and New Jersey Regulatory Systems of Gaming Control*), 114n17
Hilton of San Juan, Inc. v. Lateano, 119n44
HIPAA. *See* Health Insurance Portability and Accountability Act
history
   Great Depression and effect on gambling, 5–7
   growth of regulated gambling (1960s through 1990s), 10–12
   Nevada gambling (prior to and after World War II), 6
   of American gaming regulation (1800s to early 1900s), 4–5
   of legal gambling (1950s to 1960s), 7–10
   of organized crime in casinos, in *The Limits of Gaming Control*, 87n39
   recent U.S., 12–13
   See also specific dates
Hohmann v. GTECH Corp., 236n145
"hold harmless," gaming applicant must sign, release, 60
Holden, Jonathan (author, *Sports Gambling Regulation and Your Grandfather (Clause)*), 243n6
Holodny, Elena (author, *Here's How the Real High-Rolling VIPs Gamble*), 127n97
Holz and *Agresta* cases, comparison of, 121
Home Planners Depository v. Hughes, 31n49
honest, materiality standard and, 55
honesty
   applicant for gaming license must have, 54–55
   definition of, 55
   in business conduct is needed for gaming license, 55
honor, difference between a prize and an, 40
Hoover, J. Edgar, (chairman, Nevada Gaming Control Board, 1958), 9
Hoover, Stephen A. (author, *Forcing the Tribe to Bet on the House*), 191n116
horse races, most authorized type of state online wagering, 193
horse racing, 16–18
   employment numbers and revenue from, 16
   gambling and, 3

horse racing *(continued)*
  names and types of, 16
  pari-mutuel wagering on, 260
horse racing track, not considered casino and exempt from BSA, 88–89
Hot Lotto, suspicious circumstances of winning ticket, 227–228
house advantage, casino can modify the, 48
House Edge: On Gambling and Professional Discipline, 137n3
house-banked games, as form of gambling, 13
How Much Do Leagues Stand to Gain from Legal Sports Betting?, 15n72
How the Glitch Stole Christmas: S.C. Lottery Says Error Caused Winning Tickets, 22460
How the MGM-NBA Deal All but Ends Integrity Fee Debate, 252n58
Hughes v. Cole, 240n171
Hunter v. Fox Beatrice Theatre Corp., 31n49
Hurley, Lawrence (author, *U.S. High Court Paves Way for States to Legalize Sports Betting*), 15n72
Hussein v. Multi-State Lottery, 227n77

I

ICD. *See* International Classification of Diseases
ICS. *See* internal control system
Idea Research & Dev. Corp. v. Hultman & Cent. Broad. Co., 32n50
I-gaming
  also known as Internet gaming or Internet-based gaming, 82n6
  categories of providers operating, 84
  See also Internet gaming
I-gaming business model, characteristics of, 83–84
I-gaming operator, player's money in account in name of, 84
IGRA. *See* Indian Gaming Regulatory Act
IGT. *See* International Game Technology
IHA. *See* Interstate Horseracing Act
Iipay Nation of Santa Ysabel (California), 191, 213

illegal gambling business
  Illegal Gambling Business Act definition of, 212n99
  three elements of, 208
Illegal Gambling Business Act
  aimed at organized crime, 208
  one of four federal Acts that help states enforce gambling laws, 13n58
  originally passed in 1955 to combat organized crime, 195
  revised in, 208–209
  provisions of, 11
illegal sports betting market, extent of, before *Murphy* decision, 15
Illinois
  considering license for in-stadium betting, 254–255
  interpretation of equal dignity rule, 37n73
  offers (2009) online, intrastate lottery, 18
  only state to select third benchmark plan, 147
Illinois Lottery, asked DOJ to clarify wording of Wire Act, 220
Illinois Lottery Practice of Selling Tickets After Top Prices Gone, 227n76
iLottery products, states that offer online, 19
Impact of an "Integrity Fee" on Sports Betting Handle, 251n54
impaired or unimpaired classes, of claimants and interest holders in Chapter 11, 107
imperfect information, game of rock, scissors, paper and, 28
imperfect knowledge/information, type of chance, 28
impulse control disorder
  DSM-IV-TR had pathological gambling as, 144
  Nevada's First Benchmark Plan excluded coverage for, 144
  Iowa EHB Benchmark Plan excludes, 145n57
in personam judgment, 121
incompetence, gaming license applicant's, 58
indenture, trust, 184
Indian. *See also* Native American

Indian ceremonial or celebratory gaming, Class I, 260n95
Indian country, older term used in federal law, 174n32
Indian gaming
   conducted by Indian tribes as part of land-based gambling, 83
   IGRA defines classes of, 15
   IGRA definition of, 169
Indian Gaming and Beyond: Tribal Economic Development and Diversification, 83n11
Indian Gaming and Tribal Sovereignty: The Casino Compromise, 167n5
Indian gaming law, complex and challenging, 168
Indian Gaming Regulatory Act (IGRA)
   authorizes Class II and Class III gaming only on Indian lands, 174
   authorizes three federal causes of action for enforcement, 172n21
   casinos operated by American Indian tribal governments are regulated by, 167n1, 169
   categorizes classes of gaming, 170, 171*t*, 260–261
   Class I gaming not subject to provisions of, 170
   classes of gaming activities, 213–214
   comprehensive overview of, 213–214
   contains severability clause, 172n26
   created National Indian Gaming Commission (NIGC), 169
   defines gaming on Indian land, 15
   definition of Indian gaming by, 169
   divides regulatory responsibility between state and federal, 15
   does not apply to tribal ceremonies, 171*t*
   does not authorize tribes to shift tort jurisdiction to states, 188
   does not guarantee tribe right to do Class III gaming, 173
   enacted in 1988, 15, 247
   established framework for Native American gaming, 108
   federal causes of action for enforcement of tribal-state compact, 172n21
   framework for tribes to enter into tribal-state compacts, 108
   gaming classes and regulatory framework of, 171*t*
   introduced the term *Indian lands*, 174n32
   legal and regulatory framework of, 83n11
   limits Class III gaming to Indian lands, 213
   promotes tribal economic development, 213
   requirements before tribes can offer Class III gambling, 213
   sports gaming considered Class III gaming by, 260
   state can negotiate tribal reimbursement for state regulatory costs, 180
   state cannot be sued in court by a tribe under IGRA, 172
   states now regulate some forms of Indian gambling, 15
   Supreme Court says tribes can conduct gaming without state regulation if state already has that type of gaming, 11
   tribe has sole proprietary interest and responsibility for its gaming, 183
   tribes can make payments to states for extra benefits beyond Class III, 181
   tribes have right to regulate gaming on their Indian lands, 213
   will shape future of sports betting, 260
Indian land
   definition of and scope of, 174–179
   NIGC's Office of General Counsel determines what qualifies as, 174
   not always same as Indian country, 174n32
   question if non-reservation lands qualify as, 174n32
   term introduced by IGRA, 174n32
Indian nation, sovereignty of, 14
Indian nation gaming, federal and state laws regulate, 13
Indian Reorganization Act (IRA), 174
Indian Self-Determination and Education Assistance Act (1975), 185n87
Indian tribal gaming, revenue from, 83n11
Indian tribe
   Congress's authority over, 14
   Constitution says, are regulated by Congress, 14

Indian tribe *(continued)*
   high-stakes bingo and card room gambling (1980s), 11
   Indian tribe casino, example of land-based gaming, 83
Indians, definition of, 175n36
industrial espionage law, casino failure to comply with, 72
industry notice, 50n5
informal rulemaking, 50
information assisting
   courts' definition and examples of, 197
   placing bets or wagers and, 197–198
information gathering, regulatory agency and, 78–79
infrastructure, government commits community funds and, to casino, 58
Inside the Battle for the Future of Sports Betting, 262n108
insolvency risks, gaming business and, 99
insolvent business
   options of liquidation or reorganization, 99
   rights of debtors and creditors, 101
Instagram, GDPR complaints about "forced consent" filed against, 271
instant scratch game, Iowa state definition of, 217n22
"instaplay ticket," definition of, 217n22
Intangible reward, Supreme Court of Arkansas decision on, 40
integration, money laundering and definition of, 85
integrity, definition of, 55
integrity fee, tax on sports betting to be paid to sports leagues, 251
Integrity Fee is Something We Are Entitled To, 251n53
intelligence gathering, regulatory agency and, 78–79
inter alia, 261
Interactive Gaming Act
   description of, 18
   Nevada revises (2011), 18
interim suspension, example of type of sanction against an attorney, 154
Interior Department's Office of the Solicitor, meaning of "under federal jurisdiction," 175

Interior Secretary, can approve or disapprove tribal-state compacts, 179
intermediate routing
   electronic data and, 202
   OLC 2018 Opinion on, 194
   online sports betting and issue of, 259
intermittent explosive disorder, *DSM-III* definition of, 151n95
internal control standards, governments' role in accounting for revenue with, 49
internal control system (ICS)
   components of, 70–71
   functions of, 95
   part of AML compliance program, 95
   pronounced as "icks," 95n91
internal controls, definition and types of, 70–71
Internal Revenue Service (IRS)
   investigates Nevada casino skimming operations (1961), 10
   IRS tax form W-2G, gambling winnings and, 75
International Casino Law, 67n40
International Classification of Disease (ICD), 141
International Game Technology (IGT), 131
international wagering, based on where the bettor resides and location of betting service, 14
Internet
   best way to offer gambling worldwide, 214
   eSports skill games and, 24
   sends packets of data by most efficient route (sometimes intrastate), 257
   sweepstakes and third-party advertisers on, 34
   See also online
Internet-based gaming. *See* Internet gaming
Internet cafe, unregulated gaming in, 83n12
Internet fantasy sports, 193
Internet gambling, 193–214
   as violation of the Travel Act, 208
   conflicting statutory interpretations and legal challenges for, 214
   federal legal and regulatory framework of, 195–214

regulated at state level, 193
types of, 193, 195
UIGEA allows federal authorities to go after off-shore, 209
See also online wagering
Internet Gambling Genie and the Challenges States Face, 219n33
Internet gambling industry, limited by antiquated laws, 214
Internet Gambling Prohibition Act (2006), 203n48
Internet gambling sites, UIGEA federal offense for accepting money that supports illegal gambling, 209
Internet gaming, activities encompassed by, 84. *See also* I-gaming
Internet lottery ticket sales (third quarter, 2018), 220
Internet poker industry, conducted via MSIGA could violate Wire Act, 202
interstate commerce, Illegal Gambling Business Act and, 11
Interstate Horseracing Act (1978), 259–260
allowed interstate simulcasting and wagering at locations, 260
permits cross-border pari-mutuel wagering, 259–160
regulates interstate off-track wagers, 17
Wire Act and, give authority to online race wagering, 17
interstate revenue-generating activities, Wire Act aimed at organized crime and, 10
Interstate Transportation of Wagering Paraphernalia Act (1961), 195, 206–207
interstate wagering, based on where the bettor resides and location of betting service, 14
Interstate Wire Act of 1961, new interpretation of, 10n43. *See also* Wire Act
intoxicated player, casino does not have to permit gambling by person who is, 73
intoxication, gambler says losses due to, 127–128

intrastate model
compliance and liquidity problems for sports betting and, 253
intrastate, definition subject to New Hampshire lawsuit, 247
wagering, definition of, 18
Introduction: Problem Gambling and the Law, 137n3
investigation
applicant's conduct during, 57
methods for detecting casino regulatory violations, 77–78
types of regulatory agency, 77–78
investigative regulatory powers, administrative agency's, 51–52
Iowa
does not allow lottery winner to claim prize anonymously, 228
EHB Benchmark Plan excludes impulse control disorders, 145n57
statute that lottery must have winner's name and address, 231
Iowa Lottery's TouchPlay Debacle, 235n139
Iowa Racing and Gaming Commission, 132
Iowa Rules of Professional Conduct, 155
Iowa Supreme Court, 132
Iowa Supreme Court Attorney Disciplinary Board v. Reilly, 155n128
IRA. *See* Indian Reorganization Act
IRS. *See* Internal Revenue Service
Is the "Curse of the Lottery Real?, 219n35
Is "Contract" the Name of the Game? Promotional Games as Test Cases for Contract Theory, 30n34
Isle of Man, eSports in the, 20

J

jackpot
court awards gambler larger, than casino, 132
lawsuit over disputed, 223
Jackson v. Indiana State Lottery Comm'n, 224n58
Jacobs v. State Lottery Comm'n, 231n106, 226n68
Jahng, David (author, *Bill Proposed to Define and Allow eSports in Maryland*), 20n100

jai alai, pari-mutuel wagering on, 260
jai alai frontons, 14n64
Jets Forge Gaming Partnership, First Deal of Its Kind, 252n60
Johnson v. M'Intosh, 14n66
Julian, Tom (author, *Exclusions and Countermeasures: Do Card Counters Have a Right to Play?*), 113n9
junket, definition of, 94n86
junket account, front-money account and, 94n86
junket representative, unlicensed, 74

K

Kaiser Permanente's 2012 Small Group Colorado Health Benefit Plan, 138–139
Kaszuba v. Zientara, 240n171
Kater, Cheryl, class action suit against Big Fish Casino, 42
Kater v. Churchill Downs, Inc., 42
Keefe v. Ohio Lottery Comm'n, 226n68
Kefauver Committee, Nevada not screening gambling license applicants (1949), 8
Kefauver, Estes (Senator, 1950), investigation of organized crime by, 7–8
Keith, Norm (author, *Anti-Money Laundering: A Comparative Review of Legislative Development*), 85n16
Kelly, Joseph (author)
    Caught in the Intersection between Public Policy and Practicality: Survey of Legal Treatment of Gambling Obligations…, 123n62
    U.S. Land-Based and Internet Gaming: Would You Bet on a Rosy Future?, 83n13
Kennedy, John F. (U.S. President), 9–10
Kennedy, Robert (U.S. Attorney General)
    goal to eliminate organized crime, 9–10
    introduced the Wire Act, 196
    Travel Act and, 207
keno
    Indian Class III gaming, 260n95
    type of lottery product, 220
keno manager, regulatory requirements for, 69
keno runners, regulatory requirements for, 69
keno system, computerized, 64

Kentucky attorney general, equal dignity concept and, 36
Kentucky Derby, horse racing and the, 16
Kentucky Off-Track Betting, Inc. v. McBurney and KRS, 122n56
Kickapoo Traditional Tribe of Texas, negotiating Class II gaming compact with state, 173
Kilgore, Adam (author, *With States Free to Legalize Sports Betting, Do the Pro Leagues Deserve a Cut?*), 252n57
Kim, Ji Hun (author, *Rolling the Dice on Debtor Eligibility: Native American Tribes and the Bankruptcy Code*), 191n116
Kinnard v. Circle K Stores Inc., 225n66
Kiowa Tribe v. Manufacturing Technologies, 187n95
kleptomania, *DSM-III* definition of, 151n93
know your customer
    casino standards, 251
    examples of types of information, 90, 94
    policies and procedures, 211
Koehlinger v. State Lottery Comm'n, 231n107
Koerner, Brendan (author, *Russians Engineer a Brilliant Slot Machine Cheat…*), 48n1
Kredell, Matthew (author, *Senate President Says Florida Sports Betting Could Be Part of Tribal Negotiation*), 248n42
Krystal Energy Co. v. Navajo Nation, 108n72, 190n113
KTSP-Taft Television & Radio Co. v. Ariz. State Lottery Comm'n, 238n158
Kulick, Peter (author)
    Regulating Internet Gaming, 81n1
    Regulating Land-Based Casinos, 87n40

L

Labit v. Akzo-Nobel Salt, Inc., 150n81
labor unions, need for licensing of casino-related, 65–66
Lac Courte Oreilles Band of Lake Superior Chippewa Indians (Wisconsin), 178n57
Lac du Flambeau Band of Lake Superior Chippewa Indians (Wisconsin), 184

land-based gaming, physical locations, characteristics, and regulatory environment of, 83
land-in-trust process, requirements of, 178–179
landlords, full licensing sometimes required for casino, 62
large employer, definition of, 140
Las Vegas Sands Corp.
   FinCEN fine against, 96
   fines and obligations from Zhenli Ye Gon incident, 97
   payment for AML compliance failures by, 82
law
   English common, 117
   IHRA and Wire Act as antiracketeering, 17–18
   past compliance is indicator of future compliance with, 56
   wide-open gambling, 117–118
   See also Act; federal law; legislation; state law
Law of Gambling & Regulated Games, 215n2
lawsuit
   discrimination against lottery player based on national origin, 227
   over multiple tickets split for jackpot prize, 225
   random number generator fraud, 229
   types of vendor, patron, tickets, or jackpot, 223–224
lawyer
   advise employer whether gambling employee can be terminated, 149
   advise gambling client who has professional license revoked, 153
   advise lottery winner client about corollary tax issues and estate planning, 234
   advise lottery winner client how to claim the prize and set up an LLC trust, 234
   advise operator clients how to build brand with games and sweepstakes, 43
   advise policy questions and legal problems for client with gambling debt, 114
   apply GDPR principles to all customer or client data, 272–273
   be aware of illegal health insurer behavior and gambling disorder, 138
   complain to state or issuer of health insurance policy if benchmark plan requires gambling disorder coverage but does not comply, 148
   consider vagaries of state lottery law, 223
   consult benchmark plan requires coverage of gambling-related treatment, 148
   consult client's health plan's coverage of gambling-related treatment, 148
   defend person accused of lottery-related crime, 239
   determine if client with gambling disorder is protected under disability nondiscrimination law, 149
   have lottery courier as client of, 239
   know state rules and legal issues in representing clients with gambling disorder, 163–164
   know that gaming contract issues not always straightforward, 136
   know that player lawsuit against lottery rarely wins, 226
   mediate dispute among group as to who has winning ticket, 240–241
   mediate legal disputes involving lottery clients, 220
   problem with personal gambling and the business, 137–164
   question if gambling employee can be terminated, 149
   read state's statute defining disability re gambling client's eligibility, 150
   review administrative and game-specific rules before accepting lottery lawsuit, 226
   study examples of lawsuits involving the lottery, 223–224
   understand difference between two sectors of casino industry, 168
   understand federal Indian law and tribal law, 169
   See also attorney

Lawyers Concerned for Lawyers (LCL), meetings of, 157
layering, money laundering and definition of, 85
LCL. *See* Lawyers Concerned for Lawyers
Leacock, Stephen J. (author, *Lotteries and Public Policy in American Law*), 217n17
League of Legends, eSports game of, 20
Ledoux v. Grand Casino-Coushatta, 132, 135
legal problems, how an operator can avoid, 43
Legalize and Regulate Sports Betting, 15n72
Legislating and Regulating Casino Gaming: A View from State Regulators, 70n49
legislation, Nevada gaming and gambling (1800s), 4. *See also* Act
legislative support, public perception is key for gambling to have, 235
Lemieux v. Tri-State Lott Comm'n, 233n125
lender, definition and types of casino, 63
lenders/creditors, exempt from licensing, 63
Leone v. Ohio Lottery Comm'n, 234n128
Lestok, Jake (author, *Tackling Daily Fantasy Sports in the States*), 83n12
level of review, gaming license investigation and, 53
Levenson, Lloyd D. (author, *Casino Credit and Collections in New Jersey—An Overview*), 125n76
Lewis v. Clarke, Mohegan Tribal Gaming Authority and, 189
license
 attachment of conditions to, 50
 conditions to be fulfilled before reinstatement of attorney's, 161
 fixed or discretionary criteria needed to obtain gaming, 53
 how states determine who to give a, 53
 investigative review of applicant for gaming, 51–52
 lawsuit because of denial, suspension, or revoking of lottery, 235
 lower-level gaming employees and limited, 61
 Nevada regulates (1949) who can apply for gambling, 7
 Nevada requires state gambling (1949), 7
 privileged, versus professional, 54n9
 reasons by state could revoke lottery, 234–236
 reinstatement of attorney's, 153, 154
 revocation as sanction against attorney's, 50, 155
 suspension of, 50
 types of occupations that require a state, 53
 See also licensing; licensure
licensing
 definition of breadth and depth of, 61–69
 definition of, 53
 extent of investigation for full or partial gaming, 59–61
 fundamentals of, 53–69
 government affects gambling contracts through, 49
 Nevada casino, not required (1931), 6
 of casino employees, 68
 of casino suppliers and vendors, 63–65
 state administrative agency and casino, 51
 See also licensure
licensing application, personal and financial information needed for, 59–60
Licensing by Jurisdiction, 68n47
licensing exemption, states and different levels of, 67
licensing investigation, description of, 59–61
licensing review, tiers and levels of, 59–61
licensure
 not needed for sweepstakes and skill-based contests, 24
 requirements for gaming, 53
 See also licensing
lien on unencumbered property, Bankruptcy Code and, 104
Liewer, Steve (author, *Nebraska Lottery Officials Still Seeking Missing Tickets from Scratch-Off Snafu*), 238n159
Light, Steven Andrew (author)
 Indian Gaming and Tribal Sovereignty: The Casino Compromise, 167n5
 Spreading the Wealth: Indian Gaming and Revenue Sharing Agreements, 181n71
Limits of Gaming Control, 87n39

Linton, Michael (author, *A Nevada Lottery: Improving the Odds for Nevada's Public Education System*), 216n9
liquidating plan, example of casinos that went through, 101
liquidation, process governed by Chapter 7 of the Bankruptcy Code, 99
liquidity, definition of, 252
liquidity management, Internet gaming and, 84
litigation, courts commonly used for Chapter 11, 102
Little River Band of Ottawa Indians v. NLRB, 186
live-racing card, 17
Local Loan Co. v. Hunt, 101n28
Logan v. Ameristar Casino Council Bluffs, 129n109
loopholes, in Nevada's 1955 gambling laws and regulations, 9
Lost in the Shuffle: How Health and Disability Laws Hurt Disordered Gamblers, 137n3
Lotteries and Public Policy in American Law, 217n17
Lotteries, Revenues and Social Costs: A Historical Examination, 117n28
lottery
   as form of gambling, 13
   can be location for online sports betting, 253
   criticism that it exploits economically vulnerable people, 218
   early use of, to fund universities and the military, 215
   employee fraud and, 227–228
   federal statutory questions about operation of a, 220–221
   gambling and state, 3
   history of, 215–217
   illegal to have privately run, 217
   legal disputes involving, 220–241
   lottery employee ineligible to play, 228
   New Hampshire had first modern state (1961), 11
   no longer have state constitutional prohibitions to, 220
   nontraditional sites for, 220
   overview of, 19
   period of time in U.S. when no legal, 215
   promotion constitutes an illegal, 30
   reasons for lawsuits against, 223–232
   social and legal acceptance of, 215
   state may design their own game concept or hire someone to, 234
   state-run business subject to competitive bidding laws, 236–237
   state-sanctioned monopoly, 217
   states that do not have a, 19n92
   Supreme Court (1850) says is "wide-spread pestilence," 216
   thinly veiled, 38–39
   timing and method of payment to winner of, 233–234
   use of computer to validate winning ticket and avoid fraud, 226n69
   See also state lottery
lottery courier, definition of, 238, 239
lottery curse, as lottery winners are target for fraud, 232
lottery games, types of, 19
Lottery Industry: Cases, Problems & Preventable Incidents, 216n8
lottery procurement contract, 238
lottery products, examples and types of, 217–220
Lottery Supplier Defends Role in Fraud Scandal, 238n150
lottery ticket
   claim by divorced spouses to winning, 240n171
   crime for person to present stolen, 240n167
   lawsuit because continue to sell, after prize money awarded, 226–227
   misprinted, 238
   not possible to win lawsuit without actual, 226
   unlawful to resell, 239
lottery winner, New Hampshire open records law and invasion of privacy, 232
Lottery Winner Sues Saying Jackpot Should Have Been Bigger, 229n93
lotto games
   description of, 218–219
   odds of winning very low, 219

lotto games *(continued)*
  Louisiana
    lottery known as the Serpent was national scandal, 216
    Serpent lottery (1878) of, 216
Louisiana Supreme Court Rules, for attorney reinstatement after alcohol or drug use, 163
Lowenhar-Fisher, Kate (author, *Gaming Law & Practice*), 13n55
"loyalty" program," benefits offered by casino, 266
Lucky Calendar Co. v. Cohen, 30n33
Lucky Shamrock, emergency phone card sweepstakes entry as thinly veiled lottery, 38–39

M

M & R Investments, Co., v. Hacker, 121n55
Macey, Jonathan R. (author, *Regulation 13D and the Regulatory Process*), 67n39
machine programming, errors in, 131–132
Madara v. Commonwealth, 224n57
main-cage consolidation, 65n31
Major League Baseball (MLB), 252
major life activities, ADAAA's definition of, 152
Malasky, Hunter (author, *Tribal Sovereign Immunity and Need for Congressional Action*), 187n97
malfeasance, gaming license applicant's, 58
Malone, Howard (Nevada assemblyman, 1931), 5
Malta, eSports in, 20
management contract
  NIGC definition of, 183
  tribal gaming and, 183–185
  managerial competency, gaming license applicant's, 57–58
Marcangelo v. Boardwalk Regency, 132n118
marker
  as a credit instrument when signed by bettor, 121
  casino can collect when gambler refuses to sign, 126
  definition of, 115
  dishonored, 122
  executed, is a negotiable instrument, 115–116
  negotiable instrument between casino and player receiving credit, 111
marketing/advertising failures, examples of casino, 75
Marsden, Ross (author, *Restore America's Wire Act: Cloud Killer?*), 222n52
"Marshall Trilogy," Supreme Court cases known as, 14
Maryland, may remove eSports from their gaming statutes, 20
Mashantucket Pequot Tribal Nation, Foxwoods Resort Casino of, 191
Mashayekhi, Rey (author, *Inside the Battle for the Future of Sports Betting*), 262n108
Mason v. Mach. Zone, Inc., 41n96
Massachusetts Gaming Commission, fine imposed on Wynn Resorts by, 55
Massihzadeh v. Solano, 230n99
Massihzadeh, Amir, lawsuit for splitting of jackpot, 229–230
Match-E-Be-Nash-She-Wish-Band of Pottawatomi Indians v. Engler, 177n48
Match-E-Be-Nash-She-Wish-Band of Pottawatomi Indians v. Patchak, 176–177
material disparity, between paying and nonpaying entrants can make sweepstakes illegal, 38
material element test, description of, 26–27
materiality, relationship of lying and concept of, 55n12
materiality of noncompliance, components of, 56
Maynard v. United States, 217n16
McCarran, Pat (Nevada Senator; chairman, Senate Judiciary Committee), 8
McCarthy, Joseph (Senator, 1950), investigation of communism by, 7
McCoy, Padraic I. (author, *Sovereign Immunity and Tribal Commercial Activity*), 185n88
McCrary, Joseph (author, *Who Plays the Georgia Lottery?*), 218n29
McGee, Richard G. (author, *A Guide to Tribal Employment*), 185n89

McGinness, Brett (author, *From the Archives: Here's How Nevada Banned Gambling, Reintroduced It*), 5n8
McKee v. Isle of Capri Casinos, Inc., 132
McKittrick v. Globe-Democrat Pub Co., 31n49
McLin v. State, 224n59
Mechanics of Indian Gaming Management Contract Approval, 183n78
Medicaid
   MHPA did not apply to, 140
   MHPAEA did not apply to, 142
Medicaid benchmark plans, required by ACA to offer mental health benefits, 142–144
Medicare
   MHPA did not apply to, 140
   MHPAEA did not apply to, 142
Medicare Improvements for Patients and Providers Act (2008), 138n4
Medicare Part B, imposed 50% beneficiary coinsurance for mental health services, 138
Medrano Diaz v. Vazquez-Botet, 240n171
Mega Millions, lotto game with highest jackpot in history (2018), 219
Meister, Alan P. (author)
   Indian Gaming and Beyond: Tribal Economic Development and Diversification, 83n11
   The Economic Impact of Tribal Gaming: A State-by-State Analysis, 83n11
mental disability, California Fair Employment and Housing Act does not include compulsive gambling or substance abuse disorders as, 152
mental disorders, inferior insurance benefits for, 138. *See also* disorders
mental health benefits
   definition of, 140n22
   large group health plans and, 139
   MHPAEA requires health plan's, be consistent with DSM or ICD, 141n29
Mental Health Parity Act of 1996 (MHPA)
   lack of coverage for Medicare, Medicaid, or substance use disorder, 140
   expansion of, by President George W. Bush, 141
   "increased cost" exemption of, 140
   not a mandated offer or mandated benefit law, 140
   only applied to group health plans of large employers, 139
Mental Health Parity and Addiction Equity Act (MHPAEA)
   built on benefits provided by MHPA, 141
   comprehensive parity requirements on large group health plans, 141
   determination of exemption-qualifying cost increases of health plan required by, 142
   did not apply to small group health plans, Medicare, or Medicaid, 142
   does not require health plans to treat gambling disorder, 142
   financial requirements and treatment limitations, 141
   not a mandated offer nor mandated benefit law, 142
   protected persons with substance-related and addictive disorders, 141
   regulated only insured and self-insured group health plans of large employers, 141–142
   requires health plan's definition of mental health benefit be consistent with DSM or ICD, 141n29
   way in which a health plan could be eligible for exemption from, 142
mental illness, biologically-based does not include gambling disorder, 138–139
Merrill v. Trump Indiana, Inc., 129n109
method of entry, equal dignity concept and, 36
Metropolitan Creditors Service v. Soheil Sadri, 118n37
Mexican money-exchange houses, *casas de cambios*, 96
Meyer v. Hawkinson, 240n171
Meyers v. Ohio State Lottery Comm'n, 233n125
Meyers v. Oneida Tribe of Indians of Wisconsin, 108n71
MGM Desert Inn, Inc. v. Holz, 120n46
MGM Resorts Hit Trifecta with MLB Gaming Partnership, 252n59

MGM Resorts, deal with NBA, NHL, and MLB, 252
MGM's M Life, players' club, 266n1
MHPA. *See* Mental Health Parity Act (1996)
MHPAEA. *See* Mental Health Parity and Addiction Equity Act
Miccosukee Tribe of Indians (Florida), 178n58
Michigan v. Bay Mills Indian Community, 187–189
MICS (minimum internal control standards), 181n69
Mid-Atlantic Coca-Cola v. Chen, 39
Midland States Life Ins. Co. v. Cardillo, 233n123
Midwestern Enterprises, Inc. v. Stenehjem, 38n86
Miller v. Zoby, 125n85
Miller, Keith C. (author)
    The Internet Gambling Genie and the Challenges States Face, 219n33
    The Iowa Lottery's TouchPlay Debacle, 235n139
Miller, Michelle (author, *New Hampshire Powerball Winner Files Lawsuit to Remain Anonymous*), 232n117
minimum internal control standards (MICS), 181n69
Minnesota Gambling Control Board, definition of elements of illegal gambling, 13n56
minors, casino not to permit gambling by, 73. *See also* underage
misdemeanor, materiality of noncompliance and a, 56
Mississippi
    authorized commercial sports betting pools, 261
    first state to have tribal sports betting, 247n35
    separate state divisions investigate and enforce gambling laws, 51
Mississippi Band of Choctaw tribe, authorized sports betting pools on tribal land, 261
Mississippi Gaming Commission, patron dispute and, 132
Mississippi Supreme Court, 131–132

Missouri, something of value as defined by, 40
mitigating and aggravating circumstances, Douglas Crawford case and, 160–161
MLB. *See* Major League Baseball
mob influence, casino and, 87
Mobil Oil Corp. v. Att'y Gen., 33n61
mobile gaming, form of online gaming, 18
mobile sports wagering, Internet and, 194. *See also* Internet gambling
Model Tribal Gaming Ordinance (NIGC), 170n16
Modern Gaming Control Act, blueprint for state gaming regulation, 12–13
Mohegan Tribal Gaming Authority (MTGA), 189
Molina v. Games Mgmt. Servs., 225n66
money laundering
    accounting failures and, 75
    definition and activities of, 86
    definition of layering and integration in, 85
    definition of, 84–85
    gaming industry susceptible to, 81–82
    history of, 84–87
    I-gaming risks of, 84
    no hard and fast rules for detecting, 91n71
    stages of, 85
Money Laundering Control Act (1986), established crime of money laundering, 86
Money Laundering Suppression Act (1994), 88n46
monopoly, gaming environment of a, 58
Montana, reason for exemption from PASPA, 12
Montana Supreme Court, customer has pecuniary loss if purchase needed to enter contest, 33
Montemayor, Eduardo (author, *Winner's Curse: The Necessity of Estate Planning for Texas Lottery Winners*), 232n114
Moody v. State Liquor & Lottery Comm'n, 226n68
Mootz, Francis J. (co-author, *Even Moe Dalitz Would Blush: Why the District Attorney Has No Business Collecting Unpaid Casino Markers*), 122n58

moral character, applicant for gaming license must have good, 53
Morales v. Aria Resort and Casino, 126n88
More than Four-Fifths of Sports Betting Handle in New Jersey Comes from Online, 256n75
MSIGA. *See* Multi-State Internet Gaming Agreement
MSLA. *See* Multi-State Lottery Association
MTGA. *See* Mohegan Tribal Gaming Authority
Multi-State Internet Gaming Agreement (MSIGA), 201
Multi-State Lottery Association (MSLA), 206, 227, 228
Multistate Professional Responsibility Examination, 156, 161, 162
Muncaster, Phil (author, *Nielsen Shareholder Sues over GDPR Statements*), 273n36
Murphy v. National Collegiate Athletic Association
  states to authorize and regulate sports betting, 15
  struck down by PASPA, 15
Murphy v. NCAA, 243, 247
Murphy v. NCAA, did not legalize sports betting in U.S., 247

N
NA. *See* Narcotics Anonymous
Narcotics Anonymous (NA) meetings, 157
Narragansett Tribe, federally acknowledged tribe (1983), 174
NASDAQ. *See* National Association of Securities Dealers Automated Quotations
NASPL. *See* North American Association of State and Provincial Lotteries
Nat'l Harbor GP, LLC v. District of Columbia, 237n146
National Association of Securities Dealers Automated Quotations (NASDAQ), 66n33
National Basketball Association (NBA), 251
National Center for Responsible Gaming, 137n1
National Football League (NFL), 252

National Gambling Impact Study Commission (NGISC) Report, 217n19
National Gambling Impact Study Commission, lottery play highest among economically disadvantaged, 218
National Hockey League (NHL), 252
National Indian Gaming Commission (NIGC)
  created by Indian Gaming Regulatory Act, 169
  declination letter from, 185
  definition of a management contract and collateral agreement by, 183
  determines what qualifies as Indian land, 174
  federal regulatory agency authorized by IGRA, 170n16
  expedited versus formal review of management contract of collateral agreement, 184
  independent federal regulatory agency in Dept of the Interior, 169
  must approve tribe's gaming ordinance, 170n26
  must approve tribe's management contracts, 183
National Labor Relations Act (NLRA), 186
National Labor Relations Board (NLRB), ruling about NLRA, 186
Native American. *See also* Indian
Native American casino
  Chapter 11 prepackaged bankruptcy and, 109
  financial restructuring of, 108–109
Native American ceremonies, type of Class I gaming, 170
Native American gaming, 108–109
Native American Indian tribes, Class II gaming in New Mexico, 261
Native American tribe gaming, disagreement over applicability of Bankruptcy Code to, 108
Navajo Nation, tribal-state compact with New Mexico, 188
Navajo Nation, tribal-state compact with New Mexico, 188
Navajo Nation v Dalley, 188n103
NBA. *See* National Basketball Association

NBA Signs Deal with MGM to Be Gaming Partner, 252n59
NCAA v. Christie, 245n18
NCAA v. Governor of N.J., 245n20
Nebraska, Second Benchmark plan excludes coverage of gambling disorders, 146–147
Nebraska Lottery Officials Still Seeking Missing Tickets from Scratch-Off Snafu, 238n159
Needing a Fix: Congress Should Amend the Americans with Disabilities Act of 1990..., 150n77
negotiable instrument, when bettor signs casino marker, 122
Negotiating Enforceable Tribal Gaming Management Agreements, 183n78
negotiation, contract formed through wagers not subject to, 112
Negrette v. California State Lottery Comm'n, 224n58
Neilsen Holdings PLC, class action suit against, for misleading investors about GDPR preparedness, 272
Nevada
    antigaming forces (1931) in, 5
    approves (2005) mobile/online gaming, 18
    casino gambling banned (1910) in, 4
    checklist for minimum internal control standards, 70n48
    county sheriffs issue gaming license (1869) in, 4
    data privacy laws for, 267
    definition of PI, 267
    favorable to gambling after Great Depression, 5
    first legislation for online gambling, 18
    first state to authorize gaming in U.S., 83n10
    first state to legalize gambling (1869), 4
    first state to permit wide-open gambling, 5
    gaming regulatory policies model for other states, 11–12
    grandfathered in by PASPA, 244
    laws (1907) for collecting gaming taxes, 4
    licenses (1905) slot machines, 4
    no state licensing of casinos required (1931) by, 6
    one of largest gaming jurisdictions, 124
    only state before 2018 with power to authorize sports betting, 243n6
    only state with legal and regulated casino gambling (1961), 10
    operates under Statute of Anne in spite of 1931 Wide Open Gambling Law, 118
    public supported gambling as economic tool (1931), 5
    reason for exemption from PASPA, 12
    requirements for granting credit to a player, 124
    role of state Gaming Control Board and Gaming Commission in, 51, 52*f*
    signed MSIGA with Delaware and New Jersey for Internet poker, 201
    sports betting lawful in casinos and on Internet, 247
    state with most casinos, 14
    statutes about gambling disorder, 128
    where to find state law on data privacy, 267
Nevada Casino Commission, fine imposed on Steve Wynn by, 55
Nevada gambling, Kefauver investigation of organized crime and, 7–8
Nevada Gaming Commission
    creation of (1958), 9
    noncompliance with data privacy laws, 267
    Regulation 5.011, 267
    role in authorizing online gambling, 18
Nevada Gaming Control Board, 134
    comment on cash-out transactions, 90n61
    creates regulations for online poker, 18
    storage of PI in players' club programs, 268
Nevada Gaming Industry Credit Practices and Procedures, 114n17
Nevada Gaming Partners, LLC, 100n2
Nevada Gaming Regulations, 123
Nevada Gaming Statutes: Their Evolution and History, 6n16
"Nevada is not for sale," campaign slogan of Governor Sawyer, 9
Nevada regulatory system, 52*f*
Nevada Rules of Professional Conduct, 160
Nevada State Bar Examination, 161

Nevada Supreme Court, 130, 160
   confirmed government can regulate gambling, 6
   "intent to defraud," 122
   public opinion liberal on wide-open gambling, 118
Nevada Tax Commission
   creation of (1955), 8
   has right to regulate gambling (1947), 7
   state regulatory agency for gambling industry, 6
Nevada's First Benchmark Plan, excluded coverage for gambling disorders, 144–145
New Hampshire
   first modern state lottery (1964) in, 11
   first new state to offer lottery (1964), 217
   first state lottery (1964) in, 19
   lottery winner and anonymity, 232
   member of the MSLA, 206
New Hampshire litigation, U.S. District Court and, 194
New Hampshire Lottery
   offers Internet lottery sales, 222
   tried to overturn 2018 Opinion of DOJ, 258
New Hampshire Lottery Commission v. Barr, 223n55
New Hampshire Lottery Commission, complaint against 2018 Opinion, 205
New Hampshire Powerball Winner Files Lawsuit to Remain Anonymous, 232n117
New Jersey
   cap on percentage of credit gambling that is uncollectable, 119
   casino gambling introduced (1978) to Atlantic City, 11
   challenges constitutionality of PASPA (2014), 12
   dram shop liability, 127
   gambling outlawed (1700s) in, 4n2
   gaming regulatory policies model for other states, 11–12
   no authorization for wagering on college sports, 255
   offers (2011) intrastate, online gaming, 19
   one of largest gaming jurisdictions, 124
   online gaming traffic and border betters, 256
   passed constitutional referendum (2011) to allow sports betting, 245
   regulation of labor union and its casino employees, 65n32
   requirements for granting credit to a player, 124
   separate state divisions investigate and enforce gambling laws, 51
   signed MSIGA with Delaware and Nevada for Internet poker, 201
   sports betting lawful in casinos and on Internet, 247
   sports leagues claim, sports betting plan violates PASPA, 245
New Jersey Casino Control Act, 124–125
New Jersey Casino Control Commission, association with unsuitable person, 56
New Jersey Supreme Court, unknowing association with unsuitable persons not basis for gaming license applicant's unsuitability, 56
New Jersey Thoroughbred Horsemen's Association, Inc. v. NCAA, 243
New Mexico
   Indian tribes and Class III gaming, 261
   prohibits sports betting, 261
   Pueblo of Pojoaque lawsuit against state of, 173
   sports betting conducted on tribal lands, 247, 261
   New Mexico group health plans, mental health benefits exclude gambling addiction, 139
New Mexico v. U.S. Dep't of Interior, 174n31
New York
   a person gambles when he does this, 26n15
   offers (2009) online, intrastate lottery, 18
   question of state lottery but transaction processors cross state line, 200
New York Lottery, asked DOJ for clarification of wording of Wire Act, 220
New York Stock Exchange, 66n34
newly acquired lands, Indian tribe gaming on, 177–179

Newzoo, eSports data site, 20
Newzoo *Global 2018 Esports Market Report*, 20n96
NFL. *See* National Football League
NGISC. *See* National Gambling Impact Study Commission
N.H. Lottery Comm'n v. Barr, 194n6
NHL. *See* National Hockey League
Nielsen Shareholder Sues over GDPR Statements, 273n36
NIGC. *See* National Indian Gaming Commission
Ninth Circuit court (Washington)
   decision in *Big Lagoon Ranchiera v. California*, 176
   In re Indian Gaming Related Cases, 181
   Kater appeal and, 43
   Native American tribes do not have sovereign immunity from Bankruptcy Code (2004), 108
   NLRA applies to tribes, 186
   signed markers let casino collect debt from any player's bank accounts, 126
   tribe cannot stop distribution of union leaflets, 186
   tribes are "domestic dependent nations," 190
Nissman, David (U.S. attorney), 203
Nixon, Richard (President), signed Section 504 of the Rehabilitation Act (1973), 149
NLRB. *See* National Labor Relations Board
N.L.R.B. v. Bildisco and Bildisco, 100n8
No Longer the Only Game in Town: A Comparison of Nevada and New Jersey Regulatory Systems of Gaming Control, 114n17
"no purchase necessary," sweepstakes statement of, 35, 36
Noennig, Jordyn (author, *What in Wisconsin Can the Powerball Winner Buy?*), 219n36
noncompliance
   components of materiality of, 56
   penalties and enforcement actions from AML laws, 82
non-substance-related disorder, APA reclassifies gambling disorder as, 152

North American Association of State and Provincial Lotteries (NASPL)
   members and countries in, 215
   says myth that most lottery purchases by low-income people, 218
North American Association of State and Provincial Lotteries, website of, 218n30
North Carolina, contracts to repay gambling debts void, 120
North Dakota, providers who are licensed to treat gambling addition in, 147n64
North Dakota's Second Benchmark Plan, requires coverage for gambling disorder, 147–148
North Dakota Supreme Court Rules, for attorney reinstatement after alcohol or drug use, 163
notification of breach, customer data and, notorious person, gaming license applicant's association with, 56

O

O'Reiley, Tim (author, *Legal Battle Surrounding Grand Canyon Skywalk Still Flares*), 191n119
Obama, Barack (U.S. President), signed Affordable Care Act and HCERA, 142–143
occupational certification, for lower level casino employees, 58
occupational licensure, 54n9
OFC Comm. Baseball v. Markell, 244n13
offer
   definition of, 48
   element of a wager, 112
offeree
   in a contract, who is the, 111
   in a wager the casino is, 112
offerer
   casino player as, 49
   in a contract, who is the, 111
   in a wager the player is, 112
Office of Legal Counsel (OLC)
   2011/2019 Opinion of, Wire Act applies to all forms of betting, 194
   2018 Opinion of, 2011 OLC Opinion wrong, 198

2108 Opinion of, not consistent with history and language of Wire Act, 223
2018 Opinion of, Wire Act applies to all types of online gambling, 198
2019 Opinion of, Wire Act applies to all forms of wagering, 18–19
new interpretation of Wire Act, 10n43
Reconsidering Whether Wire Act Applies to Non-Sports Gambling, 202n44
within Department of Justice (DOJ), 18, 194
off-reservation gaming, definition of, 178
Off-Reservation Native American Gaming: An Examination of Legal and Political Hurdles, 178n57
off-track betting (OTB)
gambling and, 3
uncertainty of legal status of, 17–18
legal in U.S. (1800s to early 1900s), 4
Ohr, Bruce G. (Chief of Organized Crime and Racketeering Section, DOJ), 203n48
Oklahoma, tribal gaming is large industry in, 167–168
OLC. *See* Office of Legal Counsel
oligopoly, gaming environment of an, 58
One Year into Legal U.S. Sports Betting: What Have We Learned?, 252n56
online. *See also* Internet
Online Bets Drive New Jersey's Sports Gambling Tax Revenue Growth, 256n74
online gambling
global growth of, 18–19
Nevada enacts first legislation to enable, 18
online. *See also* Internet
online poker, Nevada begins (2012), 18
online race wagering, IHRA and Wire Act give authority to, 17
online slot metering system, 64
online wagering
horse races are most authorized state type of, 193
state control of horse racing, 17
See also Internet gambling
online world, something of value has questionable meaning in an, 40

On-Point Tech. Sys., Inc. v. Commonwealth, 238n157
on-track horse race wagering, only gambling outside of Nevada (1961), 10
operating failure, examples of casino, 72–73
operating requirements, examples of casino failure to comply with, 72–73
operator
full licensing required for casino, 62
must comply with federal and state gambling laws, 43
opportunity to win, equal dignity concept and, 36
Oregon, reason for exemption from PASPA, 12
organized crime
Federal Wire Act to combat revenue-generating of, 10
Kefauver investigation of Nevada gambling and, 7–8
no longer part of gambling, 81–82
U.S. Attorney General Robert Kennedy's goal to eliminate, 9–10
Wire Act passed to combat, 195
Organized Crime Control Act, 208n73
OTB. *See* off-track betting
owner, licensing and responsibilities for casino, 62
ownership
casino fails to report transfer of, 74
disguised as vendor participatory interest in casino, 62
examples of casino failure of, 74

P

Pacific Stock Exchange, 66n34
Pai, Tanya (author, *Is the "Curse" of the Lottery Real?*), 219n35
Palese v. Del. State Lottery Office, 224n58
palps, definition of, 251n53
Pandeli, Corina (author, *When the Chips Are Down: Do Indian Tribes with Insolvent Gaming Operations…File for Bankruptcy*), 191n116
Pando v. Fernandez, 240n171
Panzer v. Doyle, 179n63
"paraphernalia," not defined by Wagering Paraphernalia Act, 207

pari-mutuel industry, offers online and mobile betting across state lines, 260
pari-mutuel sports betting, exception to PASPA, 244
pari-mutuel system, description of, 17
pari-mutuel wagering
   adopted by Kentucky Derby (1908), 16
   as form of gambling, 13
   definition and examples of, 260
   federal law differentiates sports betting from, 260
   idea came from French race tracks, 16
   Indian Class III gaming, 260n95
   popularized by totalizator machine, 16
parity, federal government legislates mental health, 139
parity laws
   some exclude gambling disorder, 139
   to provide equal coverage for physical and mental health coverage by state, 139
Parry, Wayne (author, *New Jersey Eyes Stiffer Penalties for Prohibited Sports Bets*), 254n65
Parsley v. State, 218n24
Parsons v. Dacy, 240n171
"Part 291," 173
partnerships, limited partners and lower-level review required for, 68
PASPA. *See* Professional and Amateur Sports Protection Act
past-posting, wagers placed after a horse race begins, 17
pathological gambling
   APA's *DSM-5* renames, as gambling disorder, 152
   diagnosis included in *DSM* since third edition (1980), 148
   DSM-IV-TR classified, as impulse control disorder, 144
   originally classified by APA as impulse-control disorder, 151
   See also compulsive gambling; gambling disorder
Patient Protection and Affordable Care Act, 143
patron
   golden "whale," 96
   high-roller, 93
   money-laundering risk when casino tries to accommodate profitable, 93
   See also gambler
patron disputes
   casino and reasons for, 129–135
   government's role in resolving, 49
   state administrative agency and casino, 51
Paulsen v. Bureau of State Lottery, 225n65
Pauma Band of Mission Indians, unfair labor practices of, 186
Pauma v. National Labor Relations Board, 186n93
pay line, definition of, 48
payoff progression, casino changing rate of, 73
payout odds, horse racing and, 17
Pearsall v Alexander, 240n172
pecuniary detriment, customer suffers, if purchase required to enter contest, 33
penalty, reasons why casino given criminal or civil, 49
Pennington v. State, 209n83
Pennsylvania
   gambling outlawed (1700s) in, 4n2
   high tax rate on casinos, 47
   sports betting lawful in casinos and on Internet, 247
Pennsylvania Gaming Control Board, 59n22, 254, 254n67
penny slot machine, 132
People v. Blume, 209n83
People v. Carpenter, 36n70
People v. Mason, 29n27
People v. World Interactive Gaming Corp., 207
person, definition of, 191n119
"personal data," GDPR definition of, 269
personal health information, disclosure of and HIPAA, 272
personal information (PI)
   examples of, 267
   California Consumer Privacy Act's definition of, 266n2
   must be collected, maintained, and disseminated in protected way, Nevada's definition and elements of, 267–268
personnel controls, as component of internal control system, 70–71

persons doing business in casino, examples of, 65
persons of integrity, company seeking gaming license must be controlled by, 54–55
Petersen, Eileen R. (Chair, U.S. Virgin Islands Casino Control Commission), 204n49
Peterson v. D.C. Lottery & Charitable Games Control Board, 233n124
Phalen v. Virginia, 216n7
PHS. *See* Public Health Service Act
physical disability, California Fair Employment and Housing Act does not include compulsive gambling, 152
PI. *See* personal information
Pick-A-State, Pa., Inc., bought out-of-state lottery tickets for customers, 239
Pickett, Charles (author, *Contests and the Lottery Laws*), 31n49
Pickett, Larry (New Hampshire State Representative), 19
Picket v. IGT, 134
pinball machines, Milwaukee court says are gambling devices, 27
Pioneer Inv. Services Co. v. Brunswick Associates Ltd. Partnership, 100n7
pit boss, regulatory requirements for pit clerk and, 69
Pitofsky, Marina (author, *Crazy Rich Lottery Winners: What Would You Buy with $1.2 Billion?*), 219n36
Pitoniak, Edward (CEO, VICI Properties, Inc.), 19
Pittman, Vail (Governor, Nevada, 1947), 7
placement, money laundering and definition of, 85
plan of reorganization, examples of gaming debtors that used, 100
player
 can self-exclude themselves from casinos, 47
 does who not meet prerequisite for claiming lottery prize, 224
 lawsuit because intended to purchase ticket but didn't, 225
 lawsuit that zip codes were discriminating against, 227
 problem gambling and vulnerable, 47

player-as-offeror principle, 112
player-banked games, as form of gambling, 13
player data, casino gaming operations tracking of, 265
player rating records, 92, 94
players' clubs
 Nevada Gaming Control Board and storage of PI in, 268
 type of "loyalty" program, 266
playing card, join a players' club and get a, 266
playslip
 definition of, from lotto games, 218
 reasons why, not converted to valid ticket, 225
PlayStation, eSports accessed via, 20
PlayWithAl.com (PWA), Internet sports book from Netherland Antilles
Plourde v. Conn. Lottery, 224n59
point-of-purchase, distribution at, 35
PointsBet, sports book provider, 253
poker
 example of chance-based gambling, 23–24
 Nevada permits (1915), 4
 systemic chance in card shuffle and deal of, 28
poker industry, online helped by MSIGA of three states, 201
poker machine, accumulated credits in a bar, 41
poker manager, regulatory requirements for, 68
poker supervisor, regulatory requirements for, 69
political corruption, AML laws combat, 84
Political Evolution of Mental Health Parity, 140n19
Portland International Jetport, 38
postage, California Supreme Court says, is not valuable consideration, 34n65
Preakness, horse racing and the, 16
pre-bankruptcy plan, 101
predominance test
 also known as dominant factor test, 25
 "player skill" or "uncontrollable chance" factors in, 25–26
Premier Entertainment Biloxi, LLC, 100n16
prepackaged plan, bankruptcy and, 101

"preponderance of evidence," used in court but not in licensing, 59
priming lien, Bankruptcy Code and, 104
priority creditors, 108
prize
   as an element of a legal sweepstakes, 39
   difference between an honor and a, 40
   equal dignity concept and a, 36–37
   examples of nontraditional and noncash, 39–40
   prize element, awarding a, 39–43
prize money, *Fortnite*, *Dota 2*, *League of Legends*, *Overwatch* amount of, 20n98
prizeless gaming model, 41
pro bono legal representation by U.S. attorney, may be subject to GDPR, 269
probation, example of type of sanction against an attorney, 154
problem gambling
   the business lawyer and, 137–164
   See gambling disorder
Problem Gambling and Treatment in Nevada, 145n55
problem gambling information, casino fails to post, 74
processor, GDPR definition of, 269
Professional and Amateur Sports Protection Act (PASPA) (1992, 2018)
   activities that are unlawful under, 194n3
   deemed unconstitutional by Supreme Court (2018), 12
   demise of, had no effect on meaning of Wire Act, 258
   enacted in 1992, 12
   exceptions to, 244
   forbade states to license sports betting organizations, 243–244
   grandfathered in for Nevada, 244
   life and demise of, 244–247
   New Jersey (2014) challenges constitutionality of, 12
   prohibited states and tribes from doing sports wagering, 12
   prohibited states from legalizing or expanding sports betting, 193
   reflected Congress's desire to eliminate sports betting, 244
   state exceptions to, 12
   states have right to ban sports betting or deregulate it under, 245
   strikes down *Murphy v. National Collegiate Athletic Association*, 15
   Supreme Court rules, unconstitutional (2018), 243
professional discipline, gambling disorder and, 153–163
profits, persons entitled to casino, 62
progressive controllers, 64
progressive sign controller, 64
promoter
   cellular carrier sharing customer fees with sweepstakes, 34
   economic benefit received by, 32
promoter benefit test, consideration element and, 31–32
promotion
   constitutes an illegal lottery, 30
   examples of, 34
   instant-win, 35
promotion game, increased business patronage and, 32
promotional device, casino use of unapproved, 73
promotional materials, lawsuit over lottery, 226
protections and safeguards, examples of bankruptcy petition, 102
psychotherapy services, covered by Tufts Health Plan, 148
Public Health Service Act (PHS), 144n46
Public Morals Committee (Nevada, 1931), 5
public offering
   definition of, 66n37
   sale of company stock and, 66, 66n35, 66n37
public policy, gaming regulation driven by, 47–48
publicly traded company
   definition of, 66
   Sarbanes-Oxley Act established financial reporting obligations for, 86n38
   Securities Exchange Act established mandatory disclosure for, 86n38

Pueblo Indians of Santa Ana, 261
Pueblo of Pojoaque, tribal lawsuit against New Mexico, 173
Pueblo of Santa Ana v. Nash, 189n106
Pueblo of Santa Ana, sports book and, 261
pull tabs, type of lottery game, 219
purchase will not increase chance of winning, sweepstakes statement of, 36
Purdum, David (author)
    NBA Signs Deal with MGM to Be Gaming Partner, 252n59
    One Year into Legal U.S. Sports Betting: What Have We Learned?, 252n56
    What You Need to Know About the New Federal Sports Betting Bill, 262n104
Puzzling Case of the Revenue-Maximizing Lottery, 218n25
PWA. *See* PlayWithAl.com
pyromania, *DSM-III* definition of, 151n94

Q

Quarter Horse racing, wagering on, 16
question of fact, games of skill verses games of chance, 29
Quiet Title Act, Indian lands exception to, 176n43

R

race track
    can become a racino, 17
    can be location for online sports betting, 253
race track promoter, 16
racial discrimination, regulators look at applicant's history for, 55
racino
    description of and types of gambling at, 17
    gambling and a, 3
Racketeering and the Federalization of Crime, 216n21
raffle, type of lottery product, 220
Rahmani v. Resorts Int'l Hotel, Inc., 129n109
Ramirez v. Bureau of State Lottery, 224n58
Ramsay, Eric (author, *Illinois Lawmakers Vote to Approve Sports Betting on Last Day of Session*), 254n63
random event, outcome of gambling contracts determined by, 48

random number generator (RNG), 48, 64, 134
    description of, 48n1
    example of systemic chance, 28
Reader's Digest, mail-in sweepstakes is illegal lottery, 31
real estate investment trust (REIT), 19
Reception of English Common Law in the American Colonies, 117n32
Reconsidering Whether the Wire Act Applies to Non-Sports Gambling, 10n43, 18n83, 202n44
record
    casino compliance program, 94
    casino player rating, 92, 94
    casino know-your-customer information, 94
recordkeeping
    BSA requirements for, 94
    requirements for casino, 71
Recovery of Money Lost at Gambling Act (RMLGA), 42
redemption kiosk, 64
reel, gambling machine, spins for entertainment not for win or loss, 134
reel-type machine, 48
Reforming State Mental Health, 142n36
regulated gambling
    growth of national (1960s through 1990s), 10–12
    means wagering contract controlled by state regulations, 113
    See also gambling
Regulating Internet Gaming, 81n1
Regulating Land-Based Casinos, 85n23
Regulating Land-Based Casinos, 87n40
regulation
    basics of gaming, 47–79
    casino gambling and command-type, 49
    history of American gaming (1800s to early 1900s), 4–5
    See also gambling regulation; gaming regulation
Regulation 13D and the Regulatory Process, 67n39
Regulation of Legalized Gambling: An Inside View, 61n24

regulator
  failure of casino, 74
  powers of the, 49
  regulatory compliance and tools used by, 50
  rulemaking procedures and adjudication of cases by, 50
  send out industry notices, 50n5
  set minimum internal control standards, 70
regulatory agency
  government delegates to a, 49
  types of investigations of, 77–78
regulatory agents, visible throughout casino, 77
regulatory compliance
  tools used by regulators for, 50
  tracking of player data essential for, 265
regulatory powers, types of, 51–53
regulatory requirements
  casino employee positions and, 68
  of groups involved in gaming industry, 61
regulatory structure, administrative and auxiliary functions of, 51
regulatory violations, ways to detect, 76–77
Rehabilitation Act (Section 504), being fired for gambling disorder is violation of, 149, 151
Reilly, Michael, Grievance Commission of Iowa Supreme Court ruling on, 155–156
REIT. *See* real estate investment trust
reorganization, classes of, 100
reorganization
  goal, purpose, and examples of, 100, 100n8
  governed by Chapter 11 of the Bankruptcy Code, 100–101
request for proposal, lottery issues, 237
reservation, tribes that have acquired trust lands but not, 177–178
"reservation exemptions," 178
reservation lands, Indian lands are, 174
Resorts International Hotel, Inc. v. Salamone, 125
Resorts International Hotel, Inc. v. Agresta, 118
restitution, example of type of sanction against an attorney, 154

Restore America's Wire Act: Cloud Killer?, 222n52
restructuring, 99–109
Revel AC, LLC, 101n21
revenue sharing, definition of, 181–182
revenue-sharing agreement, 181
revenue-sharing provisions, of tribal-state compact, 182
revocation, regulators' use of license, 50–51
Rezza v. United States Department of Justice, 150–151
Rhode Island v. Narragansett Indian Tribe, 174n32
Riddle v. State, 240n167
"right to exclude," common law or, 113n9
RIH Acquisitions NJ, LLC, 101n25
Rillotta, Joseph (author, *Beyond the SAR-C: Best Practices for Gaming Companies to "Know Their Customer"*…), 82n2
rim credit, rim debt and, 126
Rincon Band of Luiseno Mission Indians, suit about revenue-sharing negotiations, 182
riverboat casino, gambling on, 3
riverboat gambling
  casinos and states do away with requirement for a boat, 11–12
  subject to BSA rules, 88n48
RMLGA. *See* Recovery of Money Lost at Gambling Act
RNG. *See* random number generator
Robinson v. Colo. State Lottery Div., 227n71
Rodenberg, Ryan (author), *State-by-State Sports Betting Bill Tracker*, 246n32
Rolling the Dice on Debtor Eligibility: Native American Tribes and the Bankruptcy Code, 191n116
Rolling the Dice on Precedent and Wagering on Legislation: The Law of Gambling Debt Enforceability in Kentucky, 122n56
Rose, I. Nelson (author)
  Gambling and the Law: The Role of Credit in the Third Wave of Legal Gambling, 115n19
  Gambling and the Law: The Third Wave of Legal Gambling, 83n13
  The DOJ Gives States a Gift, 221n49
  What China Means to Las Vegas, 123n63

Rosenbaum, Sara (author, *The Essential Health Benefits Provisions of the Affordable Care Act...*), 144n46
roulette
 illegal game of pure chance, 25
 Indian Class III gaming, 260n95
routing packets, crossing state lines with Internet bets and, 222
Rovell, Darren (author, *Jets Forge Gaming Partnership, First Deal of Its Kind*), 252n60
Ruddock, Steve (author, *How the MGM-NBA Deal All but Ends Integrity Fee Debate*), 252n58
Ruggiero v. State Lottery Comm'n, 224n59
rule, absolute priority, 107
rulemaking procedures, regulators and, 49–50
Russians Engineer a Brilliant Slot Machine Cheat—And Casinos Have No Fix, 48n1
Rybaltowski, Matt (author, *MGM Resorts Hit Trifecta with MLB Gaming Partnership*), 252n59
Rychlack, Ronald J. (author, *Lotteries, Revenues and Social Costs: A Historical Examination*), 117n28

S

Sa'Nyu Wa, tribally chartered corporation, 191
SAFE. *See* China's State Administration of Foreign Exchange
"safe harbor" provision of the Wire Act, 196
sagacity, definition of, 27
Saginaw Chippewa Indian Tribe (Michigan), 186
San Manuel Indian Bingo & Casino v. NLRB, 186
Sanabria v. United States, 208n80
sanctions, regulatory and state disciplinary board examples of, 154
Sandoval, Brian (Nevada governor), 201
SAR. *See* Suspicious Activity Report
Saratoga County Chamber of Commerce v. Pataki, 179n63
Sarbanes-Oxley Act (2002), 86n38
Sawyer, Grant (Nevada's Governor, 1958), 9

Schechtman, Joel (co-author, *Vegas Casino's Attempt to Collect Debt Exposes World of Chinese High-Rollers*), 123n64
Schillberg v. Safeway Store, Inc., 31n48
Schumer, Chuck (U.S. Senator), 261
Schwartz, David G. (co-author, *Nevada Gaming Win 2018*), 123n65
Schwarzenegger, Arnold (Governor of California), 182
Scrabble, systemic chance in, 28
scratch ticket, description of, 217–218
"scratcher," definition of, 216n22
"scratchless" instant ticket, description of, 217n22
Seattle Times Co. v. Tielsch, 30
SEC. *See* Securities Exchange Commission
Second Benchmark Plan, HHS required states to select, 146
secondary market, liability if operator attempts to stop, 41
Secretarial Determination for the Shawnee (Loyal) Tribe, 178n59
Secretary of Interior
 can allow tribe to do Class III gaming without tribal-state compact, 173
 holds land in trust for recognized tribes, 174
 can approve or disapprove tribal state compacts, 181
 regulations "Part 291," 173
Section 363 sale, examples of casinos doing this reorganization, 101
Section 364(a), authorizes debtor to obtain unsecured credit and incur unsecured debts, 104
Section 5363, UIGEA, 211
Securities Act (1933), 86n38
Securities Exchange Act (1934), 86n38
Securities Exchange Commission (SEC), role of, 67
security guards, regulatory requirements for, 69
Seigel, Benjamin "Bugsy," Nevada gambling and shooting death of, 6
self-certification/self-reporting model, in contrast to mandatory government audits, 96n96

self-insured health plans, ACA's EHB requirements do not apply to, 146
self-reporting, gaming violations found by, 52
Seminole Tribe v. Florida, 172
Senate Bill No. 2460, deregulated sports betting in New Jersey, 245
Senegl v. IGT, 133
Setness, Jeffrey B. (author, *Chinese Gamblers—The Rewards and Challenges Facing Las Vegas Casinos*), 123n68
Seventh Circuit, invalidated tribal bond indenture, 184
severability clause, IGRA and, 172n26
sexual harassment, regulators look at applicant's history for, 55
shareholders, license required for some casino, 67–68
Sharp Image Gaming, Inc. v. Single Springs Band of Miwok Indians, 184n83
Shawnee Milling Co. v. Temple, 216n11
Shepard, Thomas (author, "Mississippi" in *International Casino Law*), 67n42
Sherwood, Harry (owner, Tahoe Village Casino), shooting death of, 7
shills, regulatory requirements for, 69
Show Me the Money: Casinos' Anti-Money-Laundering Obligations and Enforcement, 96n98
Shree Swaminarayam Corp. v. Ohio Lottery Comm'n, 235n140
shuffler, automatic, 64
signage, Malfunction Voids All Pays and Plays on gaming machine, 131–132
Silver, Adam (National Basketball Association Commissioner), 15n72
simple contract consideration test, for analyzing consideration, 30
simulcasting of horse races, 17
Singer Asset Fin. Co. v. State, 233n125
Singer Friedlander Corp. v. State Lottery Comm'n, 233n125
sitting en banc, 176
Six v. Kansas Lottery, 216n8
Sixth Circuit
decision extending NLRA to tribal casinos, 186
Native American tribes have sovereign immunity, are exempt from Bankruptcy Code, 108
skill, Alabama Supreme Court definition of, 27
skill games
have social merit and not considered gambling, 24–25
tests to distinguish between chance games and, 25–27
skill vs. chance, must be decided on case-by-case basis, 29
skill-based contests, not considered gambling, 24
skimming, 52–53, 61, 69
skin, sports betting and definition of a, 254
Skolnick, Jerome H. (co-author, *The Limits of Gaming Control*), 87n39
slot booth cashier, regulatory requirements for, 69
slot fills, regulatory agent observes, 77
slot machine
casino exempt from CTR obligations for jackpot from, 91n69
Indian Class III gaming, 260n95
Nevada licenses (1905), 4
"stand alone progressive," 131
use of slot key to put machine in "stand by mode," 73
slot machine attendant, regulatory requirements for, 69
slot manager, regulatory requirements for, 68
slot monitoring systems, 64
slot player tracking system, 64
slot routes, gambling and, 3
small employer, definition of, 140n16
small group health plans, MHPAEA does not apply to, 142
Smith v. Jones, 231n106
Smith v. State Lottery Comm'n, 224n57
Smith, Jordan T. (author, *Cheater's Justice: Judicial Recourse for Victims of Gaming Fraud*), 112n1
Snyder, Lester B. (author, *Regulation of Legalized Gambling: An Inside View*), 61n24
Soaring Eagle Casino & Resort v. NLRB, 186

social gaming application, provided "freemium" online casino games, 42
soft count systems, 64
soft count team, soft count room and, 71
Sokaitis v. Bakaysa, 240n171
Sokolove, Michael (author, *Foxwoods Is Fighting for Its Life*), 191n116
something of value, definition of, 39–40
Sorry, Lottery Winners, South Carolina Won't Pay, 225n61
SOS. *See* Sports Off Shore
Soukup, Jeffrey B. (author, *Rolling the Dice on Precedent and Wagering on Legislation: The Law of Gambling Debt Enforceability in Kentucky*), 122n56
South Carolina Education Lottery, 224
South Carolina Supreme Court Rules, for attorney reinstatement after alcohol or drug use, 163
Southern District of New York, court commonly used for Chapter 11 reorganization, 102
Southern Nevada Disciplinary Board, 160–161
sovereign immunity, 108, 174
Sovereign Immunity and Tribal Commercial Activity, 185n88
sovereignty, Indian nations on Indian land have, 14
spending habits, casino data collection on player's, 266
spoofing, online sports betting and geolocation technology to stop remote-location, 257
sports, Internet fantasy, 193
sports betting
    AGA estimate of potential annual revenue from, 15
    amount wagered in U.S. annually according to AGA, 244
    federal laws governing, 255–261
    federal statutes that limit sports betting, 246
    geolocation technology and online, 257
    how differs from other forms of gambling, 249
    integrity fee to be paid to sports leagues by, 251
    is IGRA Class III gaming, 260–261
    legislated on a state-by-state basis, 247
    located along state borders to facilitate, 256
    Murphy v. National Collegiate Athletic Association let states authorize and regulate, 15
    must be conducted on intrastate basis, 247
    must have AML compliance program, 251
    no federal regulatory framework in U.S. for, 246
    Office of Legal Counsel (DOJ) says Wire Act applies only to, 255
    online must be located in a land-based casino, racetrack, or lottery, 253
    operated by private commercial business and by state lottery, 253
    palps and, 251n53
    PASPA and, 193–194
    state legislative and regulatory considerations for, 249–254
    state of the states, 247–248, *248*
    subject to Bank Secrecy Act (BSA), 251
    tax rates and licensing fees for, 249–251
    Wire Act is impediment to interstate, 252
    See also sports wagering
Sports Betting in the United States, AGA, 246n33
sports betting pools, Wire Act precludes interstate, 255
Sports Betting Revenue by State, 250n46
sports book, fees, license, taxes for online, 249–250, 253
sports book provider, names of companies, 253
Sports Gambling Regulation and Your Grandfather (Clause), 243n6
sports leagues, 245
sports betting
    violates PASPA, 245
    integrity fee to be paid to sports leagues by, 245, 251
"sports modifier," DOJ interpretation of phrase in Wire Act, 221
Sports Off Shore (SOS), 198
Sports Wagering Act, 261–262
sports wagering license, cost of state and number of skins, 250, 254

Sports Wagering Market Integrity Act.
　　See Sports Wagering Act
sports wagering
　　federal criminal law applies to multistate and international, 23
　　New Jersey did not regulate (1978), 11
　　PASPA prohibits states and tribes from doing, 12
　　See also eSport; sports betting
Spreading the Wealth: Indian Gaming and Revenue Sharing Agreements, 181n71
St. Croix Chippewa Indians (Wisconsin), 178n58
St. Onge, Kim (author, *Why You Can't Remain Anonymous If You Win the Lottery*), 232n112
St. Paul College Student Claims $1 Million Powerball Prize from Ticket Bought by App, 239n165
stakes race, definition of horse racing, 16
standard of proof, information in gaming license application and, 53, 59
Standardbred horse racing, wagering on, 16
state
　　ambiguity of Internet gambling laws in, 195
　　casino gambling on tribal lands in, 108
　　competitive bidding process for lottery contracts, 236–237
　　data protection laws for cyber breaches enacted in every U.S., 273
　　definition of (UIGEA), 213
　　differ in how each distinguishes skill games from chance games, 25
　　do not allow player to assign lottery winnings to another person, 233
　　does not regulate Class II Indian gaming, 170
　　gambling regulation primarily by, 13
　　prohibited from charging any fee prior to signing tribal-state compact, 181
　　prohibited lotteries by a ban in state constitution, 216
　　reasons why lottery license could be revoked by the, 234–236
　　regulates gambling by prohibiting certain forms of it, 195
　　regulates Internet gambling, 193
　　status of sports betting in U.S. by, 248
　　tax rate for, that has sports betting, 250*t*
　　tribal economic benefit versus concessions, 181
　　variation in collection of PI and notification of breach laws,
　　wagering contract affected by statutes and regulations of, 113
　　when does not negotiate tribal-state compact in good faith, 172–173
　　See also individual state names
State Bar of California, Hearing Department of, 158–159
State Bar of Nevada, 159
　　Bridge the Gap program offered by, 157
　　Client Security Fund, 162
state gambling. *See* individual state names
state guidelines, for attorney reinstatement, 162–163
state law
　　data privacy and, 265–273
　　gambling regulations are under domain of, 13, 23
state lines, Internet bets and routing packets that cross, 222
state lottery, number of states participating in and revenue from, 19
State of the States 2018 (American Gaming Association), 15n69
state regulator, 43
State v. Am. Holiday Ass'n, 24n4
State v. Becker, 31n49
State v. Burgdoerfer, 216n14
State v. Cox, Montana Supreme Court case (1960) of, 33
State v. Curry, 216n16
State v. Eckerd's Suburban, Inc., 30n33
State v. Fleckinger, 216n11
State v. GTECH Corp., 237n146
State v. Lindsay, 28
State v. McCurley, 209n83
State v. Razorback Room, Inc., 32n55
State v. Reader's Digest Assoc., Inc., 31n44
State v. Schubert Theatre Players Co., 32n52
State v. Schwemler, 31n49
State v. Sparks, 209n83
State v. Tipton, 232n112
State v. Tipton, 228n83
State v. Tipton, 240n166

State v. Wersebe, 216n16
state-authorized commercial gaming, a part of land-based gambling, 83
state-conducted lottery, a part of land-based gambling, 83
Statement Regarding Access to Free Online Poker Sites, 42n105
States Where It Is Legal to Bet on Horse Racing Online, 16n77
Statute of Anne, made gambling debts unenforceable, 117–118
Staudenmaier, Heidi (author)
    Current Battles and the Future of Off-Reservation Indian Gaming, 178n57
    Negotiating Enforceable Tribal Gaming Management Agreement, 183n78
    Off-Reservation Native American Gaming: Examination of Legal and Political Hurdles, 178n57
    Theseus, the Labyrinth, and the Ball of String: Navigating the Regulatory Maze...Tribal Gaming Contracts, 187n97
Stephens Indus., Inc. v. McClung, 100n10
Stephens Indus., Inc. v. McClung, 100n8
Stepnes v. Ritschel, 13n56
Stepp v. Freeman, 240n171
Stevens v. MTR Gaming Grp., Inc., 129n109
Stevens, Gina (author, *Data Security Breach Notification Laws*), 266n3
Stewart v. Tex. Lottery Comm'n, 225n66
Stocker, Robert W. (author)
    Collier Guide to Chapter 11, 83n10
    Gambling with Bankruptcy: Navigating a Casino Through Chapter 11 Bankruptcy Proceedings, 106n50
Stoebuck, William B. (author, *Reception of English Common Law in the American Colonies*), 117n32
Storcella v. State, 236n141
structuring transactions, FinCEN advisory on unlawful, 91–93
substance abuse, MHPAEA protected persons with, 141
substance use disorder
    included as essential health benefit (EHB), 144
    MHPA did not cover persons with, 140

Substance-Related and Addictive Disorders, gambling disorder in DSM-5 under, 146
suitability, applicant for gaming license must prove, 53, 58–59
Sunday, Nevada bans gambling on (1877), 4
super-priority administrative expense status, Bankruptcy Code and, 104
supplier, licensing for gaming devices, 64–65
Supreme Court of Washington
    newspaper football forecasting contest and consideration, 30
    Reader's Digest mail-in sweepstakes is illegal lottery, 31
Supreme Court, U.S.
    (1850), lotteries are "wide-spread pestilence," 216
    Carcieri v. Salazar, 174
    Congress, not states, has authority over Indian tribes, 14
    decision (1987) on tribal gaming within a state, 11, 14–15
    decision (2018) about regulated sports betting, 15
    decision (2018) on *Murphy v. National Collegiate Athletic Association*, 15
    deemed PASPA unconstitutional (2018), 12, 15, 243
    differentiated contracts from consideration related to gambling, 32–33
    Indian tribes under Congress not under states, 14
    might strike down entire ACA, 148
    sides with state of New Jersey re PASPA, 245
    state refused to negotiate compact to allow tribe to offer Class III games, 172
surveillance, types of casino, 76–79
surveillance operator, regulatory requirements for casino, 69, 76
suspension, sanction against an attorney, 50, 154
Suspicious Activity Report (SAR), 75, 85, 89, 251
    casino not liable when files, on a person, 93
    casino or employee not to reveal existence of a, 93n79

Suspicious Activity Report *(continued)*
   FinCEN enforcement action for failure to file, 96
   FinCEN Form 111 to electronically file, 93
   when casino must file, 91
suspicious behavior
   FinCEN examples of filing SAR due to, 93
   FinCEN guidelines for identifying, 91–92
suspicious transaction reports, Sports Wagering Act creates repository for, 262
sweepstakes
   does not have element of consideration, 35
   examples of free alternative method of entry (AMOE), 35
   material disparity can make, illegal, 38
   must treat paying and nonpaying participants equally, 36
   not considered gambling, 24
   participants enter for free, 35
   prize and chance elements needed for legal, 39
   require disclosure of no-purchase entry, 36
   Supreme Court of Washington says *Reader's Digest* mail-in, is illegal lottery, 31
systemic chance, description and examples of, 28

T

table game manager, regulatory requirements for, 68
table game supervisor, cannot handle chips or money, 71
table games, surveillance camera on the, 76
Talley v. Mathis, 240n171
tax, Nevada creates first casino gambling (1945), 6
Tax Commission, control of gambling taken away from Nevada (1958), 9
Tax Commission and Gaming Control Board, Nevada's two-agency model for gambling regulation (1958), 9
tax disputes, state administrative agency and casino, 51
tax evasion, money laundering includes, 86
tax rates, for sports books, 249
tax revenue, gaming regulations protect government's, 81n1
taxes
   gambling regulations to maximize, 47
   government affects gambling contracts through payment of, 49
   See also gaming taxes
(Ten)10 Things You Can't (Easily) Buy with Credit Cards, 114n15
Tennessee, definition of gambling, 27n17
Tenth Amendment, forbids Congress from requiring states to execute PASPA mandate, 243
Tenth Circuit
   analysis of *Bay Mills* case, 188–189
   decisions about tribal gaming, 173
TERO. *See* Tribal Employment Rights Ordinance
terrorism financing, AML laws combat, 84
test
   any chance, 27
   distinguish between skill games and chance games, 25–27
   dominant factor, 25
   economic value, 32–34
   for analyzing consideration, 30–34
   for distinguishing skill versus chance games, 27–29
   gambling instinct, 27
   material element, 26–27
   predominance, 25–26
   promotor benefit, 31–32
   simple contract consideration, 30
Tex. Lottery Comm'n v. Frist State Bank of DeQueen, 233n125
Tex. Lottery Comm'n v. Scientific Games Int'l, 238n155
Texas v. United States, 143n39
Thao v. Control Data Corp., 225n66
Theseus, the Labyrinth, and the Ball of String: Navigating the Regulatory Maze…Tribal Gaming Contracts, 187n97
thieving, prohibited by Nevada gambling law (1931), 6
"thing of value," definition of (Washington state), 41n97, 42

Third Circuit
    collection of gambling debt after casino served alcohol to intoxicated gambler, 127
    rehearing en banc of New Jersey sports betting, 245
Thoroughbred horse racing, wagering on, 16
ticket
    misprinted or defective lottery, 224
    quick pick lottery, 219
ticket in, ticket out (TITO), 64
"tilt code," 133
Tinian Dynasty Hotel & Casino, FinCEN fine against, 96
Tipton, Eddie (lottery employee), guilty of lottery fraud, 228–230
Title VII, permits certain employers to give preference to hiring Indians, 185n87
TITO. *See* ticket in, ticket out
tobacco use and sale laws, casino failure to comply with, 72
Tobin, Phil M. (Nevada lawmaker), introduced Wide Open Gambling Bill, 5
Tose v. Greate Bay Hotel & Casino Inc., 114n13
totalizator machine, automated posting of odds on race track tote board by, 16
tote board, race track, 16
"Touch Game Rules" button, 133
TouchPlay, Iowa Lottery and dispute with manufacturer of, 234–235
tournaments, based on eSports games, 20
Tovino, Stacey A. (author, *Reforming State Mental Health*), 142n36
Trammel v. Raytheon Missile Systems, 150n81
Travel Act (1952)
    originally passed to combat organized crime across state lines, 195, 207
    provisions of, 207–208
treatment limitations, description of types of MHPAEA, 141
Triano v. Div. of State Lottery, 226b68
tribal casino
    characteristics of, 168
    governed by federal and tribal law, 169
    methods of financing for, 190
    subject to tribal authority and federal laws and regulations, 168
    subject to tribal-state gaming compacts, 168
    under federal Indian Gaming Regulatory Act, 169
tribal ceremonies, gaming Class I, 171*t*
tribal economy, tribal gaming is tool to promote, 169, 170
Tribal Employment Rights Ordinance (TERO), 185n87
tribal gaming, 14–15, 167–192
    conducted by tribal governments, 169
    cuts in federal funding gave rise to, 11
    example of tribal sovereignty, 168–169
    included high-stakes bingo and card games (1980s), 11
    Indian Gaming Regulatory Act and, 11
    largest segment of U.S. casino industry, 167
    like state lotteries, 169
    management contracts and collateral agreements, 183–185
    numbers of tribes and revenue from, 15
    regulated by both federal and state laws, 13
    states' rights versus, 11
    Supreme Court decision (1987) on, 11
    tool to promote tribal economy and self-sufficiency, 169, 170
    tribe's own regulatory commission, 180–181
    See also Indian gaming
tribal gaming facilities, range of revenue for, 168*t*
tribal gaming industry, number of states and revenue of, 167
tribal gaming regulation, overview of, 169–174
tribal gaming revenue, top ten states', 167–168
tribal labor and employment, 185–186*t*
Tribal Labor Sovereignty Act, 186
tribal land
    most are held in trust by federal government, 190n110
    New Mexico allowed sports betting only on, 247
    states where there is casino gaming on, 108
    tribes are unable to encumber, 190

tribal ordinance, Class III Indian gaming
regulated by tribal-state compact
and, 170
tribal sovereignty
complexities and uncertainties of, 168–169
legal foundation of tribal gaming and, 14
tribal sovereign immunity
definition of, 186–191
includes tribe's commercial and gaming
activities, 187
Lewis v. Clarke and individual capacity
versus, 189–190
under bankruptcy laws, 190
*Tribal Sovereign Immunity and the Need for
Congressional Action*, 187n97
Tribal Troubles—Without Bankruptcy Relief,
190n111
tribal-state compact, 179–182
Class III Indian gaming regulated by
tribal ordinance and, 170
must be approved by U.S. Secretary of
the Interior, 172
necessary for tribe to do Class III
gaming, 179
provisions of, 180–181
reasons why Interior Secretary may
disapprove it, 179
Secretary of Interior can allow tribe to
do Class III gaming without, 173
tribal casinos subject to, 168
tribe cannot conduct Class III gaming
without, 170
website for Department of the Interior
list of, 179n65
*Tribal-State Compact for Regulation of Class
III Gaming on the Mississippi Band of
Choctaw Indian Reservation*, 262n101
tribal-state gaming compact, tribal casinos
subject to, 168
tribe
courts say NLRA applies to, 186
newly acknowledged Indian, 174–177
Ninth Circuit says are "domestic
dependent nations," 190
not mentioned in definition of a debtor
in federal bankruptcy code, 191
person or state cannot sue federally
recognized, 186–187

state's concessions versus economic
benefit to, 181
unable to encumber tribal lands, 190
without a reservation but have acquired
trust lands, 177–178
See also Indian tribe
trichotillomania, *DSM-III* definition of,
151n96
Triple Crown, three horse races that
comprise, 16
trivia contests, stress academics, 25
Trump, incremental health care reforms
signed by President, 147
trust indenture, 184
trust lands, cannot be encumbered or sold
by tribe without federal approval,
190n110
truthfulness, definition of, 54
Tufts Health Plan Coverage Guidelines,
cover outpatient psychotherapy
services, 148
"turnover," horse race betting and
definition of, 17
Twain, Mark (author, *Roughing It*),
comment about gamblers, 4
"two-part determination," tribe and, 178

U

U.S. Bankruptcy Court, bankruptcy
petitions filed in, 102
U.S. Bankruptcy Court Northern District
of Texas, *General Order Regarding
Procedures for Complex Chapter 11
Cases*, 104n40
U.S. Constitution, Congress cannot require
states to do PASPA mandate, 243
U.S. Court of Appeals for the Fifth Circuit,
ACA and, 143, 148
U.S. Court of Appeals for the Third Circuit,
Pic-A-State business and, 239
U.S. Department of Justice (DOJ). *See* DOJ
U.S. Department of the Treasury,
regulations of, 86n25
U.S. Department of the Treasury Financial
Crimes Enforcement Network
(FinCEN). *See* FinCEN
U.S. District Court, Wire Act applies only to
sports betting, 194

U.S. District Court for District of Utah,
    United States v. Lombardo in, 199
U.S. District Court for Northern District
    of Texas, strikes down entire ACA,
    143, 148
U.S. District Court for Seattle and Tacoma,
    lawsuits against social gaming
    operators in, 43
U.S. District Court for District of New
    Hampshire, 205
*U.S. High Court Paves Way for States to
    Legalize Sports Betting*, 15n72
U.S. Internet Gambling Regulatory Tracker,
    193n1, 194n4
*U.S. Land-Based and Internet Gaming: Would
    You Bet on a Rosy Future?*, 83n13
U.S. Secretary of the Interior, must approve
    all tribal-state compacts, 172
U.S. Senate Committee on Indian Affairs,
    181n71
U.S. Supreme Court
    Carcieri v. Salazar, 174
    might strike down entire ACA, 148
    state refused to negotiate compact
        to allow tribe to offer Class III
        games, 172
U.S. Virgin Islands, violation of federal law to
    make Internet casino there, 203–204
U.S. Virgin Islands Casino Control
    Commission, 203–204
UIGEA. *See* Unlawful Internet Gambling
    Enforcement Act
underage gambling, rule breaches
    allowing, 52
underage wagering, eSports and, 21
underaged gambler, jackpot win by, 129–130
"under federal jurisdiction," meaning is
    ambiguous, 175
Uniform Enforcement of Foreign Judgments
    Act, 120
union, tribe cannot stop distribution of
    leaflets from a, 186
United States
    adopted common law of England, 117
    does not have omnibus federal law
        regulating PI, 272
    gambling regulations in the, 13–20
    regulated gambling in, 3–21

segments of gambling industry in, 14–20
United States v. Barborian, 197n15
United States v. Bennett, 208n77
United States v. Cohen, 14n60
United States v. Corrar, 197n19
United States v. DiChristina, 199n21
United States v. Edge Broad. Co., 217n19
United States v. Kaczowski, 199
United States v. Lombardo, 199, 255n72
United States v. Lyons, 198, 255n72
United States v. Mendelsohn, 206n64
United States v. Merrell, 208n76
United States v. Patel, 236n141
United States v. Reeder, 197n20
United States v. Valavanis, 227n82
UnitedHealthcare, covered biologically-
    based mental illness but not
    gambling disorder, 138–139
United States of America, USA PATRIOT Act
    (2001), requires casino to have AML
    program, 82, 86, 95
University of Pittsburgh Medical Center,
    health plan excludes treatment for
    gambling disorder, 139
"unlawful activity," definition of (Travel
    Act), 207
unlawful Internet gambling/wagering
    definition of, 212
    UIGEA definition of, 202, 210n86
Unlawful Internet Gambling Enforcement
    Act (UIGEA)
    assists states in enforcing their gambling
        laws, 13n58
    definition of a financial transaction
        provider, 210n87
    definition of a state, 213
    definition of an Internet gambling
        business, 211
    definition of intrastate transaction and
        Internet betting, 202–203
    definition of "unlawful Internet
        gambling," 202, 210n86, 212
    did not make Internet gambling illegal
        but more difficult, 258
    does not repeal or amend Wire Act, 259
    intrastate online sports betting not a
        problem with data crossing state
        lines, 258

Unlawful Internet Gambling Enforcement Act *(continued)*
   language identical to Travel Act and Illegal Gambling Business Act, 212
   objectives and sections of, 209–213
   policy on Internet gambling across state lines, 209
   position on federal law and intrastate Internet betting, 204–205
   provides carve-out for intermediate routing, 259
   provides definitions and federal framework for online gambling, 258
   relevance to the Wire Act, 205
   rule of construction, 210
   Section 5363 to block restricted transactions, 209–211
   violations for gaming websites, 212
   Wire Act and unlawful Internet gambling versus, 203
unsecured credit, Section 364(a) authorizes unsecured debts and, 104
unsuitable association, regulators' definition and factors in, 57
unsuitable person, association with an, 56–57
Updated Directory Regarding Applicability of the Wire Act to Non-Sports Gambling, 194n7
USA. *See* United States of America
Utah, forbids regulated gambling or Internet gambling, 13n53, 195

V

Valente v. R.I. Lottery Comm'n, 224n59
Vegas Casino's Attempt to Collect Debt Exposes World of Chinese High-Rollers, 123n64
vendor
   lottery disputes involving a contractor or, 234
   licensing of casino, 63
Venetian Resort in Las Vegas, 82n5
video lottery terminal, 220
   casino exempt from CTR obligation for jackpot from, 91n69
   example of land-based gaming, 83
video poker, gambling and, 3
Viejas Band of Kumeyaay Indians-California Compact No Action Letter, 181n71
violation, prosecution for gaming, 52
Virginia Supreme Court, no enforcement of gambling debt and, 119
virtual chips, constitute a thing of value, 40, 42
virtual items
   bound to player with no transfer or exchange, 41
   have value subject to state law, 40
   not equivalent to money, 41n96
Volk, JoAnn (author, *States Need to Select Essential Health Benefit Benchmark Plans for 2017 Soon!*), 146n59
Volkswagen Group, diesel emissions scandal of, 82n2
vulnerable players, protecting, from problem gambling, 47

W

W-2G (IRS tax form for gambling winnings), 75
wager
   contract between player and casino, 112
   definition and components of, 13
   includes express and implied terms, 129
   not subject to negotiation in a casino, 112
   occurs where the bettor resides and at location of betting service, 14
   surveillance video of person making anonymous, 76
wagering
   casino data collection on player's, 266
   definition of intrastate, 18
   eSports and underage, 21
   "intrastate" versus "interstate," 203
   with denominated chips, 114
   See also betting; pari-mutuel wagering; sports wagering
wagering contract
   express and implied terms of, 114
   state statutes and regulations affect, 112–113
wagering excise tax bill, exemptions for Nevada's (1951), 8
wagering information, Wire Act does not define, 197
wagering integrity, accounting controls for maintaining, 69

Wagering Paraphernalia Act (1961), details of and statutory exceptions to, 13n58, 206–207
Walberg, Matthew (author, *Illinois Lottery Practice of Selling Tickets After Top Prices Gone*), 27n76
Wamsley, Laura (author, *How the Glitch Stole Christmas: S.C. Lottery Error…*), 224n60
Ward, Timothy P. (author, *Needing a Fix: Congress Should Amend the Americans with Disabilities Act of 1990…*), 150n77
Warren, Earl (Chief Justice), lottery laws' consideration element, 33
Washburn, Kevin (author, *Gaming and Gambling Law*), 215n3
Washburn, Kevin (author, *The Mechanics of Indian Gaming Management Contract Approval*), 183n78
Washington Administrative Procedures Act (APA)
  renames pathological gambling as gambling disorder, 151–152
  standards of, 231n106
Washington State Gambling Commission (WSGC), 42–43
Waterman, Steven (author, *Tribal Troubles—Without Bankruptcy Relief*), 190n111
website
  American Gaming Association (AGA), 246n33
  American Horse Council Foundation, 16n75
  credit application example (Caesars Palace), 115n21
  Department of the Interior list of tribal-state compact, 179n65
  North American Association of State and Provincial Lotteries, 218n30
  Pennsylvania Gaming Control Board, multijurisdictional application, 59n22
Weir, Rob (author, *First Move Advantage in Chess*), 25n9
Welford v. Nobrega, 240n171
Wellmark South Dakota's Blue Priority HSA Plan, specifically excludes pathological gambling, 139

Wells Fargo v. Lake of the Torches Economic Development Corporation, 184
Wellstone, MHPAEA and Paul, 141
Wenner v. Tex. Lottery Comm'n, 215n3
Wenner v. Tex. Lottery Comm'n, 217n18
Wessman, Mark B. (author, *Is "Contract" the Name of the Game? Promotional Games as Test Cases for Contract Theory*), 30n34
West Indies, Inc. v. First National Bank of Nevada, 118
West Virginia, sports betting lawful in casinos and on Internet, 247
Western District of New York, Wire Act prohibits sports betting, 199
What China Means to Las Vegas, 123n63
What Does Pari-Mutuel Betting Mean in Horse Racing?, 15n78
What in Wisconsin Can the Powerball Winner Buy?, 219n36
What is Problem Gambling or Gambling Disorder?, 137n1
What is the GDPR?, 269n23
What You Could Buy If You Won the $7 Million Powerball, 219n36
What You Need to Know About the New Federal Sports Betting Bill, 262n104
WhatsApp, GDPR complaints about "forced consent" filed against, 271
Wheeler-Howard (Indian Reorganization) Act, 174n34
When Gaming Goes Heads Up with the Bankruptcy Code: Unique Restructuring Issues for the Gaming Business in Difficult Economic Times, 103n38
When the Chips Are Down: Do Indian Tribes with Insolvent Gaming Operations Have the Ability to File for Bankruptcy Under Federal Bankruptcy Code?, 191n116
When the Dealer Goes Bust: Issues in Casino Bankruptcies, 106n50
Whitaker v. Dakota Finance, 191n114
Whitley v. McConnell, 32n59
Who Plays the Georgia Lottery?, 218n29
Why You Can't Remain Anonymous If You Win the Lottery, 232n112

wide-open gambling, not supported by public in Nevada (1931), 5
Wide Open Gambling Bill (1931), provided taxation but no state regulation of gambling, 5–6
Wide Open Gambling Law (1931)
    no reference to enforcing gambling debts, 117–118
    Nevada continued to operate under Statute of Anne in spite of, 118
Wiggins v. Texas, 55n11
William Hill, sports book provider, 253
Winder, Danny, gambling with client's personal injury settlement funds, 156–157
Winn-Dixie Stores, Inc. v. Boatright, 32n50
Winner Sues Colorado Lottery for Millions over Fixed Jackpot, 230n97
Winner's Curse: The Necessity of Estate Planning for Texas Lottery Winners, 232n114
Wire Act (1961), 195–206
    assists states in enforcing their own state gambling policy, 204
    convoluted nature is abomination of the English language, 221n46
    could be repealed in future, 262
    deals primarily with "bookmaking" in a state, 196
    DOJ (2002) says online gaming violates, 18
    DOJ (2019) says, applies to all types of bets, not just sporting events, 221
    DOJ says prohibitions apply only to sports gambling in interstate and foreign commerce, 201
    DOJ updated interpretation of, 12
    exemption of two activities from, 10
    fails to define a "business," 197
    federal law applicable to Internet gambling, 195
    has been interpreted to apply to Internet-based wagers that cross state lines, 255
    has been upheld to apply to sports betting, 255
    inconsistent interpretations of language of, 196
    "information assisting" not defined by, 197
    Internet gambling and the, 194
    is an antiracketeering law, 17–18
    is impediment to interstate sports betting, 252
    legislative history and language, review by DOJ of, 223
    linguistically complicated statute makes some gambling activities criminal, 220
    main federal law governing Internet gambling, 206
    new interpretation by DOJ of, 18
    new interpretation of by U.S. Department of Justice, 10n43
    not directed at the casual bettor, 197
    OLC says it applies to all forms of betting not just sports betting, 194
    originally passed to combat organized crime, 195–196
    precludes interstate sports betting pools, 255
    prohibits Internet wagering if transmission routed outside the state, 203n48
    restricts interstate transmission of bets by wire communication, 255
    See also Federal Wire Act; Interstate Wire Act
wire communication facilities, crime to use, for interstate bets, 220
With States Free to Legalize Sports Betting, Do the Pro Leagues Deserve a Cut?, 252n57
Wolff, Leonard, 117
Woodbridge Partners Grp., Inc. v. Ohio Lottery Comm'n, 233n125
Worcester v. Georgia, 14n66
work card, 59, 61
work permit, 61
World Health Organization's *International Classification of Diseases* (ICD), 141
writ of certiorari, New Jersey sought, from Supreme Court, 245–246
WSGC. *See* Washington State Gambling Commission
Wynn Resorts, fine imposed on, 55
Wynn Resorts' Red Card Club, players' club, 266n1
Wynn, Steve, sexual harassment allegations against, 55

X
Xbox, eSports accessed via, 20

Y
Yantis, Brittany (author, *Money Laundering*), 84n15
Ye Gon
    casas de cambios and, 96
    drug cartels and money laundering by, 96n104
    golden "whale" at Las Vegas Sands casino, 96–97

Z
Zahavi v. State of Nevada, 122n59
Zapata v. Quinn, 233n121
Zelenak, Lawrence (author, *The Puzzling Case of the Revenue-Maximizing Lottery*), 218n25
Ziglin v. Players MH, 113n8
Zoggolis v. Wynn Las Vegas, 127n96